AUTHORITARIAN LEGALITY IN ASIA

A cluster of Asian states are well known for their authoritarian legality while having been able to achieve remarkable economic growth. Why would an authoritarian regime seek or tolerate a significant degree of legality and how has such type of legality been made possible in Asia? Would a transition toward a liberal-democratic system eventually take place? And, if so, what kind of post-transition struggles would likely be experienced? This book compares the past and current experiences of China, Hong Kong, South Korea, Japan, Taiwan, Singapore, and Vietnam and offers a comparative framework for readers to conduct a theoretical dialogue with the orthodox conception of liberal democracy and the rule of law.

WEITSENG CHEN is Associate Professor at the National University of Singapore (NUS) Faculty of Law and Deputy Director at the NUS Center for Asian Legal Studies. He specializes in comparative Chinese law within greater China as well as law and development in East Asia. Before joining NUS Faculty of Law, he was Hewlett Fellow of the Center on Democracy, Development and the Rule of Law at Stanford University and also practiced as a corporate lawyer at Davis Polk & Wardwell.

HUALING FU is Professor and holds the Warren Chan Professorship in Human Rights and Responsibilities at the University of Hong Kong, Faculty of Law and Interim Dean of the University of Hong Kong Faculty of Law. He specializes in constitutional law and human rights with a particular focus on the Chinese criminal justice system, Chinese media law, and land law. Other areas of research include the constitutional status of Hong Kong and its legal relations with China. He has previously taught at the City University of Hong Kong, University of Washington, New York University, and University of Pennsylvania.

AUTHORITARIAN LEGALITY IN ASIA

Formation, Development, and Transition

Edited by

WEITSENG CHEN
National University of Singapore

HUALING FU
The University of Hong Kong

CAMBRIDGE
UNIVERSITY PRESS

CAMBRIDGE
UNIVERSITY PRESS

University Printing House, Cambridge CB2 8BS, United Kingdom

One Liberty Plaza, 20th Floor, New York, NY 10006, USA

477 Williamstown Road, Port Melbourne, VIC 3207, Australia

314-321, 3rd Floor, Plot 3, Splendor Forum, Jasola District Centre, New Delhi - 110025, India

103 Penang Road, #05-06/07, Visioncrest Commercial, Singapore 238467

Cambridge University Press is part of the University of Cambridge.

It furthers the University's mission by disseminating knowledge in the pursuit of
education, learning and research at the highest international levels of excellence.

www.cambridge.org
Information on this title: www.cambridge.org/9781009256513
DOI: 10.1017/9781108634816

© Cambridge University Press 2020

First published 2020
First paperback edition 2022

A catalogue record for this publication is available from the British Library

Library of Congress Cataloging in Publication data
Names: Chen, Weizeng, 1972– editor. | Fu, Hualing, editor.
Title: Authoritarian legality in Asia : formation, development and transition / edited by
Weitseng Chen, National University of Singapore [and] Hualing Fu, The University
of Hong Kong
Description: Cambridge, United Kingdom ; New York, NY, USA Cambridge University
Press, 2019. | Includes bibliographical references and index.
Identifiers: LCCN 2019028648 | ISBN 9781108496681 (hardback)
Subjects: LCSH: Rule of law – East Asia. | Authoritarianism – East Asia.
Classification: LCC KNC514 .A98 2019 | DDC 340/.11–dc23
LC record available at https://lccn.loc.gov/2019028648

ISBN 978-1-108-49668-1 Hardback
ISBN 978-1-009-25651-3 Paperback

CONTENTS

TABLES

NOTES ON CONTRIBUTORS

DAVID CAMPBELL is Professor of Law at Lancaster University Law School and he worked on this book when he held a Visiting Professorship at the Auckland University of Technology Law School, NZ.

JIANLIN CHEN is Associate Professor of Law at Melbourne Law School.

WEITSENG CHEN is Associate Professor and Deputy Director of the Center for Asian Legal Studies at National University of Singapore Faculty of Law.

RICHARD CULLEN is Visiting Professor of Law at the University of Hong Kong and Adjunct Professor at the University of Western Australia.

MICHAEL C. DAVIS is a Senior Research Scholar at the Weatherhead East Asia Institute at Columbia University, a Global Fellow at the Woodrow Wilson International Center for Scholars in Washington DC and Professor of Law and International Affairs at the Jindal Global University in India.

JACQUES DELISLE is the Stephen A. Cozen Professor of Law and Director of the Center for East Asian Studies at University of Pennsylvania.

MICHAEL DOWDLE is Associate Professor at National University of Singapore Faculty of Law.

HUALING FU is Professor of Law at the University of Hong Kong and holds the Warren Chan Professorship in Human Rights and Responsibilities.

TOM GINSBURG is the Leo Spitz Professor of International Law at the University of Chicago.

DO HAI HA is Research Fellow at the Asian Law Centre of Melbourne Law School.

THOMAS E. KELLOGG is Executive Director of the Asian Law Center at Georgetown Law School.

KOICHI NAKANO is Professor of Political Science and Dean of Faculty of Liberal Arts at Sophia University.

ERIK MOBRAND is Associate Professor of International Studies at Seoul National University.

PIP NICHOLSON is the William Hearn Professor of Law and Dean of Melbourne Law School.

EVA PILS is Professor of Law at the Dickson Poon School of Law at King's College London.

YEN-TU SU is Associate Research Professor at Institutum Iurisprudentiae, Academia Sinica (Taiwan).

KEVIN Y. L. TAN is Adjunct Professor, Faculty of Law, National University of Singapore; and Professor, S. Rajaratnam School of International Studies, Nanyang Technological University.

ACKNOWLEDGMENTS

The project would not have been possible without the financial support of the Center for Asian Legal Studies at National University of Singapore and the Centre for Chinese Law at the University of Hong Kong, or without the excellent research and administrative support from Lance Ang, Chong Siew Men, Delphine Goh, Benjamin Heng, Amy Kellam, Audrey Kwok, Nadene Law, Leong Lijie, Jonathan Lim, Jisheng Liu, Shazny Ramlan, Saranya Maran, Ayesha Wijayalath, Michael West, Damian Wong, and Han Zhu.

ABBREVIATIONS

AIDS	acquired immune deficiency syndrome
ASEAN	Association of Southeast Asian Nations
BORO	Hong Kong Bill of Rights Ordinance
CCP	Communist Party of China
CDP	China Democracy Party
CDPF	China Disabled Persons' Federation
CEC	Central Election Commission
CEMC	Central Election Management Commission
CEO	chief executive officer
CFA	Court of Final Appeal
CHRLCG	China Human Rights Lawyers Concern Group
CPC	Criminal Procedure Code
CPV	Communist Party of Vietnam
CSSTA	Cross-Strait Service Trade Agreement
DC	District of Columbia
DG	deputy governor
DPC	Democratic Party of China
DPJ	Democratic Party of Japan
DPP	Democratic Progressive Party
DRVN	Democratic Republic of Vietnam
EMB	Election Management Body
GAO	Government Accountability Office
GDP	gross domestic product
GRC	Group Representation Constituency
HIV	Human Immunodeficiency Virus
HKSAR	Hong Kong Special Administrative Region
HKU	University of Hong Kong
ICAC	Independent Commission Against Corruption
ICCPR	International Covenant on Civil and Political Rights
ICESCR	International Covenant on Economic, Social and Cultural Rights
ID	identity
IDEA	Institute for Democracy and Electoral Assistance
IPE	Institute for Public and Environmental Affairs

ISA	Internal Security Act
JCP	Japan Communist Party
KMT	Kuomintang
LDP	Liberal Democratic Party
LGBT	lesbian, gay, bisexual, transgender
LOOPC	Law on the Organization of People's Courts
LSG	leading small group
MITI	Ministry of International Trade and Industry
MP	Member of Parliament
NA	National Assembly
NCMP	Non-Constituency Member of the Parliament
NGO	nongovernmental organization
NMP	Nominated Member of Parliament
NPC	National People's Congress
NPCSC	Standing Committee of the National People's Congress
NPO	nonprofit organization
NTU	National Taiwan University
OCI	Open Constitution Initiative
OCM	Occupy Central Movement
PAP	People's Action Party
PD	pan-democrat
PRC	People's Republic of China
PSU	Professional Supervisory Unit
ROC	Republic of China
ROK	Republic of Korea
RSDL	residential surveillance in a designated location
RTL	Reeducation through Labor
RVN	Republic of Vietnam
SAR	Special Administrative Region
SARS	severe acute respiratory syndrome
SASPL	Students Against Secret Protection Law
SCAP	Supreme Commander of the Allied Powers
SEALDs	Students Emergency Action for Liberal Democracy
SNTV	single-non-transferable vote
SOE	state-owned enterprise
SRVN	Socialist Republic of Vietnam
SSC	State Supervision Commission
SSL	State Supervision Law
TI	Transition Institute
TSCS	Taiwan Social Change Survey
UK	United Kingdom
UPP	United Progressive Party

US	United States
USA	United States of America
USSR	Union of Soviet Socialist Republics
VBF	Vietnam Bar Federation
VM	vice-minister
WTO	World Trade Organization

Introduction

Authoritarian Legality, the Rule of Law, and Democracy

WEITSENG CHEN AND HUALING FU

One great fallacy in the study of law in authoritarian countries is to treat legality as the rule of law, and to then assume a linear development from the rule of law to democracy.[1] In reality, we have seen jurisdictions with a high level of the rule of law but without democracy, as well as authoritarian regimes that resort to legality for strategic purposes but treat legality as a mere tool to strengthen authoritarian rule. In other words, legality without the rule of law, and the rule of law without democracy, are common. This is particularly true in Asia, where authoritarian regimes embracing the idea of the rule of law usually enjoy sufficient levels of legitimacy in that the majority of the population in the respective countries view the political system as appropriate or that it should not be opposed.[2] As such, "authoritarian legality" constitutes a conceptual space where legality, authoritarianism, democracy, and legitimacy are intertwined and cause a great deal of ambiguity, coupled with divided views and competing evaluations of its operation.

Against this backdrop, this book aims to unveil how legality functions in authoritarian contexts. We focus on three questions: (1) How has authoritarian legality been made possible and stable? (2) Whether and under what conditions can a transition from authoritarian legality toward genuine rule of law and, eventually, democracy happen? and (3) If a transition happens, what would be the post-transition struggles caused by authoritarian continuity? The three questions seem to be framed as a life circle of authoritarian legality: formation, development,

---

[1] For a critical review of the literature in the context of the Taiwanese transition, see Weitseng Chen, "Twins of Opposites – Why China Will Not Follow Taiwan's Model of Rule of Law Transition toward Democracy," *American Journal of Comparative Law* 66 (2018): 481.

[2] See Eva Pils, Chapter 3 in this volume.

1

transition, and post-transition periods. However, we do not want to imply any linear trajectory of authoritarian legality toward the rule of law and democracy whatsoever. To the contrary, we stress that it is theoretically problematic and empirically wrong to hold such a linear view of the relationship between legality, the rule of law, and democracy. One only has to think of the contrasts within Chinese-majority jurisdictions to confront clear evidence against this linear view. Taiwan is a liberal democracy dependent on the rule of law, whereas China is not. While Hong Kong has been struggling to transform its rule of law into full democracy, the government and a majority of the people in Singapore are proud of their internationally recognized rule of law and prosperity and do not seem to feel the need to move toward liberal democracy.

To proceed, the first task is to define authoritarian legality in a way that serves the research goal for this book, which aims to compare authoritarian legality in China, Hong Kong, Japan, South Korea, Singapore, Taiwan, and Vietnam. We do not intend to articulate, defend, or apply a particular definition of authoritarian legality, either positively or normatively, but rather consider the core traits that bring these East Asian cases together or set them apart.[3] Neither do we want to develop a regime-type-centric typology, as useful as such a typology may be, which would limit our understanding as to how the law and legal institutions work in different societies.[4] As such, in this volume we define authoritarian legality broadly, based on the shared features of some of the post and existing authoritarian regimes in Asia. *Authoritarian legality* refers to legality and the rule of law as promoted by strong authoritarian states, where a merely instrumental commitment to law could nonetheless develop and even solidify without radical democratic and/or political reform.

This operational definition grants us sufficient conceptual space to focus on Asia's strong state-led rule-of-law development, in contrast to the experience of European countries where the rule of law took root when nation states were weak compared to the Catholic Church. Beginning in the twelfth century, the Catholic Church in West Europe played an essential role in creating a certain degree of autonomy of law from the state to the extent that law could inhibit the state's discretion.[5]

---

[3] Jacques deLisle, Chapter 1 in this volume.
[4] Kevin Y. L. Tan, Chapter 7 in this volume.
[5] Francis Fukuyama, *The Origins of Political Order* (London: Profile Books, 2011), 262–75; Harold J. Berman, *Law and Revolution: The Formation of the Western Legal Tradition* (Cambridge, MA: Harvard University Press, 1983), 199–224, 273–94.

In comparison, the Asian cases suggest a dilemma: legal system development is both dependent on and constrained by strong authoritarian states. This greatly complicates the function of legality and the trajectory of the rule-of-law development in Asia.

Authoritarian legality is not apolitical. It distinguishes, for example, between friends and enemies in China's political discourse,[6] between political parties and rebels under rigid party regulations in South Korea,[7] and between sedition and freedom of speech in Taiwan under martial law.[8] Such distinctions could be a line drawn between life and death under authoritarian regimes. As such, legality is highly political and cannot be separated from political ideologies that prevail in different part of the region. In liberal democracies, legality requires substantive, moral principles such as equality and human dignity as its backbone. In authoritarian regimes, however, rulers are tempted to utilize the political function of legality for the purpose of regime survival and political consolidation. Therefore, legality could differ significantly from the rule of law, both conceptually and functionally. Human rights abuses might be legalized, and such legalized abuse is definitely not the rule of law. In fact, it is arguably even worse than outright abuses, which would at least arouse awareness and an untamed sense of justice.

I The Possibility and Survival of Authoritarian Legality in Asia

The bottom line is that the law and institutional frameworks created by authoritarians has to be self-enforcing so that the majority of citizens feel better off with rather than without it. Likewise, political competitions, even in a very limited sense, also matter to institutional designs under authoritarian legality. For example, the Meiji's authoritarian constitution successfully stabilized Japan's political system for forty years by offering a checks-and-balances structure within the oligarchs, thereby contributing to political stability and economic prosperity during the period.[9] Similarly, rigid political party regulations created during the authoritarian era of South Korea reached an institutional equilibrium that persisted, even after the country's democratization, in that incumbent political elites from both the conservative and progressive camps benefited from limited political competition from new parties.[10]

---

[6] Pils, Chapter 3.
[7] Erik Mobrand, Chapter 14 in this volume.
[8] Weitseng Chen, Chapter 12 in this volume.
[9] Tom Ginsburg, Chapter 8 in this volume.
[10] Mobrand, Chapter 14.

Other examples can be found in Taiwan and postwar Japan. In Taiwan, the Nationalist Party (the Kuomintang, or KMT) was aware of the necessity to preserve a fair perception of its electoral system, which had served a vital political function in its authoritarian rule, because it contained political competition within the party's comfort zone while also granting dissidents a crucial space to participate in politics. As a result, a fair and transparent ballot supervision system was created to ensure the legitimacy of elections in which dissidents widely participated. This has continued to operate well for decades, even during the turbulent democratic transition period.[11] In postwar Japan, authoritarian legality persisted through strong bureaucratic control over the political system, despite the US-imposed democracy. Later, when elected politicians became the center of constitutional politics, both conservatives and liberals reached a consensus that they had to diminish this bureaucratic dominance by concentrating power in the democratically elected prime minster – an approach modeled upon a corporate structure under which the prime minister is considered the CEO of Japan Inc. As a result, however, due to the continuity of personnel and institutional culture, a new equilibrium labeled "corporatist authoritarian legality" has emerged based on the consensus among elected politicians and reformists in the face of their mutual enemy.[12]

More specifically, the function of legal institutions would usually be reconfigured under authoritarian regimes. For example, the Vietnamese procuracy functions not only as a prosecutor but also as the supervisor of the police and the judiciary.[13] Similarly, the Chinese courts are tasked to become part of the overall executive branch to identify, preempt, and solve social issues and tensions. In both cases, the difference between courts, procuracies, investigation bodies, and the police is mainly a matter of allocation of jobs and is also subject to various institutional experimentations.

Authoritarian legality is made possible through the reconfiguration of governmental structure, institutional design, and personnel composition. For example, while Chinese law provides legal rights and allows individuals to take legal action, it also aims to disaggregate disputes and restrict collective action. Chinese courts may break down collective cases into multiple individual cases, thereby isolating grievances and individualizing

[11] Yen-Tu Su, Chapter 11.
[12] Koichi Nakano, Chapter 13.
[13] Do Hai Ha and Pip Nicholson, Chapter 9 in this volume.

disputes.[14] In this way, as in China and elsewhere, legality aims to stabilize society rather than facilitate civil activism. Nonetheless, the reconfigured function of legal institutions continues to change over time due to their ambiguous nature in the first place. Some changes may substantially impede authoritarian legality from delivering on its rhetorical promises, but, even so, the overall structure of authoritarian legality could remain self-enforcing in that ambiguities are also a strategic asset for reformers and activists to exploit where possible.[15]

In the end, authoritarian legality is about "legalized authoritarianism,"[16] which is aimed at making the regime more stable and prosperous while remaining authoritarian. It demonstrates the maximum flexibility and pragmatism of authoritarian rulers, who might even at some point like the ideas of elections and democracy as long as they have all the tools to win and stay in power, as was the case in Taiwan and South Korea during their authoritarian years.

II The Possibility of an Authoritarian Transition

The circuit breaker of authoritarian legality is the authoritarians' revocation of their commitment to legality whenever they feel insecure. Hence, South Korean President Park Chung-hee revised the election rules after his rival Kim Dae Jung came too close to victory in the 1971 election. When rulers feel secure, rules may be relaxed again. Following the death of President Park and after orchestrating the 1979 coup, President Chun Doo Hwan introduced a military rule that was so iron-clad that some election rules were actually liberalized, such as allowing independent candidates to run for office.[17] If, however, constant switches in position appear politically costly and troublesome for authoritarian rulers, a "dual state" (in Ernest Fraenkel's terms) may be created to draw a clear line between matters subject to law and those that are not, as many observers of China's authoritarian legality have suggested. If so, the operation of law in such a dual state changes accordingly. For example, while normal criminal prosecution is based on acts, political prosecution in reliance on the same criminal law and determined by the same court can switch to an actor-centric basis, under which a prosecution is determined according to the political positioning of a person and the assessment of the person's

[14] Hualing Fu and Michael Dowdle, Chapter 2 in this volume.
[15] Ha and Nicholson, Chapter 9; Thomas E. Kellogg, Chapter 4 in this volume.
[16] deLisle, Chapter 1.
[17] Mobrand, Chapter 14.

political risks instead of the merit of his acts.[18] In contrast, whether the person at issue should be determined to be guilty and how severe the punishment should be are all negotiable during the proceedings, as long as the risks caused by the actors have been contained and minimalized.[19]

Nonetheless, authoritarian equilibrium proves to be unstable and transitions have happened in several authoritarian Asian countries in which the model of authoritarian legality did not appear as resilient as authoritarians had initially imagined. Studies have pointed out many factors contributing to democratic transitions, such as an increase in per-capita income,[20] unequal wealth distribution,[21] the rise of the middle class,[22] media proliferation,[23] the cultural and religious composition of the populace,[24] the size of a country,[25] and the electoral system,[26] all able to lead to a democratic tip. In terms of authoritarian legality, the transition can happen when the institutional equilibrium, which has successfully institutionalized authoritarian politics and power struggles, is unsettled.

For instance, Japan's Meiji Constitution failed to accommodate the rising military power, on the one hand, and the growing middle class after decades of economic growth, on the other.[27] The most recent case is unfolding in Hong Kong. As Richard Cullen and David Campbell argue

[18] Fu and Dowdle, Chapter 2.
[19] Ibid.
[20] See, e.g., Seymour Martin Lipset, "On the General Conditions for Democracy," in Stein Ugelvik Larsen (ed.), *The Challenges of Theories on Democracy* (New York: Columbia University Press, 2000), 11; Adam Przeworski and Fernando Limongi, "Modernization: Theories and Facts," *World Politics* 49 (1997): 155.
[21] See, e.g., Carles Boix, *Democracy and Redistribution* (Cambridge, UK: Cambridge University Press, 2003).
[22] Lipset, "On the General Conditions for Democracy"; cf. Andrew J. Nathan, "The Puzzle of the Chinese Middle Class," *Journal of Democracy* 27 (2016): 5; Jie Chen and Chunlong Lu, "Democratization and the Middle Class in China," *Political Research Quarterly* 64 (2011): 705.
[23] Jan Teorell, *Determinants of Democratization: Explaining Regime Change in the World 1972–2006* (Cambridge, UK: Cambridge University Press, 2010), 5–6.
[24] Steven Fish, "Islam and Authoritarianism," *World Politics* 55 (2002): 4; Seymour Martin Lipset, "The Social Requisites of Democracy Revisited," *American Sociological Review* 59 (1994): 1, 5.
[25] Teorell, *Determinants of Democratization*, 50–2; Boix, *Democracy and Redistribution*, 41–4; Robert Dahl and Edward Tufte, *Size and Democracy* (Stanford, CA: Stanford University Press, 1973).
[26] Ellen Lust, "Competitive Clientelism in the Middle East," *Journal of Democracy* 20 (2009): 122; Shelley Rigger, *Politics in Taiwan: Voting for Democracy* (Abingdon, UK: Routledge, 1999), 15.
[27] Ginsburg, Chapter 8.

in their chapter, the model of rule of law without democracy, based on A. V. Dicey's executive branch-centric jurisprudence, has served as a good match to Hong Kong's familialism as well as the agenda of stability and prosperity over more than a hundred years, until recent challenges by social movements such as the Occupy Central Movement.[28] The institutional equilibrium has been broken as activists resorted to civil disobedience to ignite the Hong Kong people's concerns about Beijing's interpretations of the Basic Law, which are considered to have diminished the rule of law that Hong Kong had worked hard to establish.[29]

Institutional changes usually fall behind social changes for various reasons, thereby triggering the failure of the existing institutional equilibrium. Rulers often have a bias toward the status quo and thus become slow, reluctant, or unable to change. In Taiwan, to mobilize support from young voters, the KMT in its early years encouraged college students' social participation by setting up student organizations committed to social services, solidarity buildup, and extracurricular studies of Sun Yat-Sen's theories. In this way, it successfully monitored and organized the social life of university campuses, until decades later when the KMT failed to realize that these organizations eventually became a vital window for students to learn about social reality and injustice during rapid industrialization. As a result, these organizations became the main bases of strong student movements that required the KMT to live up to the rule of law and the constitutionalism it had promised but only paid lip service to.[30]

Nonetheless, inherent risks associated with political openings and the failure to deliver rhetorical promises always exist, and may trigger a transition. Legal institutions, originally designed to strengthen authoritarian rule, may develop a life of their own and serve a role in undermining the credibility of the regime.[31] In Taiwan, the student activist associations that organized student movements against the KMT prior to the country's democratization were exactly those once created and used by the KMT to monitor and recruit elite students and opinion leaders.[32] Similarly, the KMT established an effective ballot-counting and poll worker system in order to preserve the legitimacy of its elections. Election rigging was an issue but not as serious an issue as the KMT's rivals suggested, partly because of the huge cost to the party for repressing

---

[28] Richard Cullen and David Campbell, Chapter 5 in this volume.
[29] Michael C. Davis, Chapter 6 in this volume.
[30] Weitseng Chen, Chapter 12.
[31] Fu and Dowdle, Chapter 2.
[32] Weitseng Chen, Chapter 12.

post-election protests against vote rigging, and partly because of the many other options available for the KMT to manipulate its electoral authoritarianism.[33] However, election rigging nonetheless turned out to be one of the most effective tools for its opponents to mobilize dissenting citizens to carry out the democratic transition.

That being said, a liberal and democratic transition is by no means an inevitable trajectory that authoritarian legal development will travel. A big dilemma for authoritarian legality in Asia lies in the core of the Asian model itself – a rule-of-law project promoted by a strong authoritarian state. How can a strong state that uses law to strengthen itself be at the same time constrained by its own rules? This state-led model was understandable and in fact desirable in war-torn postwar Asia where the non-state sector was weak and poor.[34] The presence of the rule of law is contingent not only on whether the knaves are likely to be deterred or punished, but also on whether there are sufficiently effective, ethical, and autonomous bureaucrats and professionals who can be counted on to do the right thing. For example, elections in authoritarian regimes are often run by non-voluntary poll workers from the public sector. This was the case in Taiwan, where the voting process was tightly controlled and operated by the KMT government, with little help from civil society which was too weak to deliver enough volunteers of good standing to handle large-scale elections.[35] In short, these developmental authoritarian regimes, led by a group of elites and technocrats, designed and delivered policy outcomes responsive to social demand through a top-down approach that focuses on substantive accountability, rather than a bottom-up approach that emphasizes procedural accountability. Such variation in the ideas of accountability and legality may also affect the trajectory of political reforms in that it has proven to be untenable for the autocrats to tie their own hands and carry out a transition that would cost their political career.[36]

For example, in China's context, authoritarianism and authoritarian legality appear to reinforce each other, and legality ultimately serves the overriding function of regime survival and entrenchment, instead of weakening authoritarian rule.[37] In Vietnam, like in China, legality simply reflects the allocation of jobs between the state and the party – the party

---

[33] Su, Chapter 11.
[34] Tan, Chapter 7.
[35] Su, Chapter 11.
[36] deLisle, Chapter 1.
[37] Fu and Dowdle, Chapter 2.

focuses on policy formulation while the main function of the state is translating party policy into law. A high level of uncertainty remains as legality simply reflects political arrangements and no clear mechanisms have been offered to realize the party's conceptual development from socialist legality.[38]

In the context of Singapore, a country that has achieved a high level of the rule of law, Jianlin Chen suggests that it is unrealistic to expect the government to cede its powers to courts entirely, even though a normative commitment to constitutionalism has taken root. The second-best approach, therefore, could be one that carves out politically sensitive cases from the courts' jurisdiction, thereby letting the judiciary focus on everyday justice and pursue professionalization without the disturbance of politics.[39] In Hong Kong, however, it appears that this alternative approach does not guarantee a more liberal or democratic regime. Under British rule, Hong Kong adopted a similar approach and thus achieved its solid status of rule of law in the absence of democracy.[40] For Davis, Hong Kong's recent struggle for universal suffrage demonstrates that authoritarian rulers are able to revoke the preexisting commitment to the rule of law when necessary,[41] highlighting the fundamental dilemma about the state-led project of authoritarian legality – what the king gives, the queen can take back.

Furthermore, authoritarian rulers can learn from each other's experiences and become more resilient. Studies of the collapse of authoritarian regimes in Taiwan, South Korea and other Eastern European countries could improve the survival kits of latecomers such as China and Vietnam. Since progressive lawyers have proven to be a force that drove the political transitions in peer countries (with many of them having even served as elected presidents in post-transition societies, such as Taiwan and South Korea), authoritarian rulers may rationally take preemptive measures against progressive lawyers in their own countries. In China, impact litigation has probably been the most effective tool developed by advocacy groups, often led by or with active participation of lawyers, for social mobilization since the mid-2000s. These NGOs, including women's rights and LGBT rights groups, realized that litigation was a potent tool to mobilize constituent groups, attract media attention, win allies in academia and the legal community, and highlight the need

[38] Ha and Nicholson, Chapter 9.
[39] Jianlin Chen, Chapter 10.
[40] Cullen and Campbell, Chapter 5.
[41] Davis, Chapter 6.

for policy change. However, these came to an end when President Xi decided to impose a tighter rein on this legal activist approach.[42]

That being said, these preemptive political moves do not necessarily endanger legal reforms in other less politicized areas of law. Legal reforms under the Xi administration have progressed at a much faster pace than the previous Hu-Wen administration, such as the effort to rein in the once heavily politicized police force.[43] Meanwhile, however, the Xi administration has also been legally empowered to suppress dissent and collective action, with authoritarian practices infecting various areas of law that are not particularly politically sensitive, such as civil procedure and family law.[44] Vietnam, mimicking China's model for decades, also restricts speech and tightens internet control while continuing to pursue legal reforms in an effort to create a "socialist law-based state."[45] The bottom line is that authoritarian rulers are fully aware of the possibility that law, when put in use by civil society forces in an organized manner, may evolve into a social movement creating a cascading effect that would eventually spin out of control.[46] They may, therefore, constantly engage with legitimacy engineering by all possible means.[47]

At the end of the day, authoritarian legality represents an approach of gradualism toward managed political and socioeconomic reforms provided that a systematic transition does not take place. However, in conventional understanding of "transition" as defined by political scientists, a drastic political and democratic change is often attached to the meaning of "transition."[48] This definition, however, restricts our understanding of transition, in that it does not tell us exactly at what point a constitutional authoritarian state tips and turns to a liberal democracy or descends into an absolutist constitutional state. Singapore has always been regarded as an interesting case in point, as scholars stick to a regime-type taxonomy to categorize Singapore's political system despite dramatic changes in its legal system over the past decades. Ranked as one of the top five countries in the world when it comes to the strength of the rule of law, Tan suggests that it remains unclear when Singapore can get rid of the label "authoritarian constitutionalism" and

---

[42] Kellogg, Chapter 4.
[43] Fu and Dowdle, Chapter 2.
[44] Pils, Chapter 3; Kellogg, Chapter 4.
[45] Ha and Nicholson, Chapter 9.
[46] Fu and Dowdle, Chapter 2.
[47] Weitseng Chen, Chapter 12.
[48] Tan, Chapter 7.

its negative connotation.[49] In a similar vein, Hong Kong is another jurisdiction that always triggers the debate about what the most suitable strategy toward a transition should be, as evidenced by the contrasting views expressed by the authors of two Hong Kong chapters in this volume.[50]

All in all, authoritarian legality should not be assumed as merely transitional. Political scientists have empirically suggested multiple determinants for democratic transition. Legality indeed could be a potential factor. However, the current literature has understudied legality in the authoritarian context and its contribution to democratic transition. Our studies show that the dynamics are too complex to tease out a single correlation or causation. While legality may create a further demand for greater political accountability, authoritarians may simultaneously become more adaptive and resilient by resorting to legality. Various structural factors, agency factors and the overall political economy all collectively constitute the equation that adds up to stable authoritarian legality, and any change may disturb the institutional equilibrium. The fall of authoritarian legality does not necessarily bring about a more liberal or democratic regime. The aftermath of the Meiji era in Japan is a case in point as it ended up with moves toward militarism and war. It is naive to hold a linear theory that predicts a transition from authoritarian legality to the genuine rule of law, and, eventually, democracy.

III Post-transition Contention

Certainly, transition does not always move easily toward a utopia; rather, it is usually the beginning of a new chapter of a continuous political struggle. In this book we have demonstrated a mixed picture of post-transitional societies where transition has taken place. Authoritarian legacy continues through personnel, persisting culture, legacy law and policies, and such influence has been reflected in institutional design, creating a path-dependence impact. Prolonged battles between authoritarians and reformists usually impede the capacity and performance of the new state and its institutions. Unsatisfying performance by the new regime can in turn generate a legitimacy crisis and provide room for the nostalgia for, and revival of, authoritarianism.

---

[49] Ibid.
[50] Cullen and Campbell, Chapter 5; Davis, Chapter 6.

For example, in Taiwan, student activism calling for liberal legality has transformed authoritarian legality but also paradoxically politicized the discourse of legality. Both reformists and conservatives have utilized legality to fight their prolonged political battles while weaponizing positive laws and normative jurisprudential values, such as the idea of civil disobedience. Consequently, divided politics has slowly weakened the state capacity to mediate socioeconomic conflicts, which are inevitable in post-transitional societies.[51] Erik Mobrand, in his chapter titled "Authoritarian Legality after Authoritarianism," also discusses South Korea's post-transition struggles in the context of electoral system reforms and demonstrates how authoritarian continuity has become the major obstacle of the post-transitional reforms.[52]

In the context of Japan, Koichi Nakano describes the unintended outcomes of the neoliberal trend of political reforms after the Liberal Democratic Party (LDP) lost its dominant status in the 1990s. The neoliberal reformers were skeptical of the conventional view of constitutionalism that aims to introduce check-and-balance mechanisms among various governmental agencies given LDP's dominance over every branch of the government. They instead focused on strengthening the democratic control over the bureaucratic system through democratically elected representatives. Decades later, however, the concentration of power among top elected politicians, especially the prime minister, has led to an emerging new form of authoritarian legality associated with an illiberal, right-wing political agenda.[53] This has triggered unprecedented civil protests organized by students and scholars (especially constitutional law scholars) since 2015.

Current literature on authoritarian legality often stops its exploration at the point where a transition has taken place, as if the transition disqualifies the country in transition as authoritarian. However, a young democracy is by no means immune from the continuing authoritarian impact. Authoritarian continuity and legacy operate like a virus incubated in the body of its healthy carrier, ready to exploit the body's vulnerability. Moreover, increasingly strong societies also breed populism that calls for fast and radical changes, which a weakened post-transition state might not be able to deliver. Law and legal institutions may well disappoint such political forces, given that they are in some

[51] Weitseng Chen, Chapter 12.
[52] Mobrand, Chapter 14.
[53] Nakano, Chapter 13.

respects conservative since radical change is not the norm.[54] As a result, the post-transitional society is likely to remain unstable and continues to transit in many regards.

IV Conclusion

Authoritarian legality is instrumental, ambiguous, and strategic. It could be used to improve transparency, accountability, and rights protection as long as it does not endanger the regime's survival. Authoritarian legality becomes stable if it is self-enforcing and thus can reach an institutional equilibrium. However, legality does not guarantee a transition toward genuine rule of law and democracy. Furthermore, authoritarian legality should not be assumed as merely transitional. At most, it opens up a new arena for contention between authoritarians and reformists using the newly introduced legal vocabularies. Even if a transition happens, authoritarianism continues to linger for decades, and can impede the capacity of subsequent liberal and democratic governments.

This book aims to unveil the formation, transition, and post-transitional development of authoritarian legality by comparing seven Asian jurisdictions where authoritarian legality seems to be a viable model for economic growth and, in some cases, the promotion of the rule of law. However, it does not depict a rosy picture in many other regards, as the selective enforcement of laws, human rights violations, and the cruel suppression of activists are the norms of authoritarian legality. That being said, authoritarian legality often challenges conventional wisdom and raises fundamental questions about the politics of law and law's ability to discipline power. Relevant discussions and debates could turn heated and politicized, with labels such as "hypocrite," "apologist," and "hawkish" being attached to people with different strategies and/or personal experiences. The authors of this volume do not intend to defend or criticize authoritarian legality per se in contrast to liberal/democratic rule of law. Rather, we hope to offer an alternative, and arguably more objective, matrix to evaluate the performance of authoritarian legality through an intra-Asia comparison among seven countries with diverse historical backgrounds; instead of lowering the bar by comparing one country with its own past, or raising the bar by comparing an Asian country with a Western liberal democracy.

---

[54] deLisle, Chapter 1.

PART I

Framework

1

Authoritarian Legality in East Asia

What, Why, and Whither?

JACQUES DELISLE

1.1 What?

It seems easy to brush aside "authoritarian legality" as an oxymoron. But the experiences of many polities in East Asia (including Southeast Asia) and a substantial scholarly literature suggest otherwise. Although authoritarian legality is a complex, contested, and elusive concept, there are several points of relative consensus about its parameters.

Authoritarian legality falls between liberal rule of law (wherein: individuals and institutions wielding state or political power are subject to relatively fixed laws; laws meaningfully protect liberal and, perhaps, welfarist individual rights; and law has significant "market share" in regulating economic, social and political behavior), and lawless autocracy (wherein: political or governmental power is unconstrained by legal rules or institutions which – although sometimes exhibiting formal trappings of liberal legality – are hollow facades more than functioning organs; and law has little role in structuring behavior). At least in the contemporary context, authoritarian legality entails "legal modernity": laws and legal institutions are relatively elaborate, comprehensive, and distinct from customary norms and non-state organizations.

Authoritarian legality is defined here principally as legality within an "authoritarian" political order.[1] Although the dividing line between authoritarian and democratic political orders is controversial, some distinctions seem relatively clear. Authoritarian political regimes sometimes

---

[1] Elements of authoritarian legality can persist after a democratic transition, as several contributors to this volume address. As recent experiences in Western liberal democracies show, legal systems in nonauthoritarian polities can adopt illiberal elements that resemble features of authoritarian regimes.

partly resemble democratic ones: they have elections in which regime-favored candidates sometimes lose (albeit not in contests for positions wielding decisive, or meaningful, power), multiple political parties, and tolerance for some expression of heterodox political ideas. But they differ from democracies in that they lack one or more definitive features: key positions exercising governmental or political power are subject to election (or appointment by those who are themselves elected); elections are held fairly frequently, according to rules set in advance, and are not subject to easy, discretionary suspension; elections are – in the now-somewhat-hackneyed phrase – "free and fair"; candidates can campaign on platforms that challenge the policies and performance of the ruling group (although perhaps not fundamental constitutional or institutional structures); and candidates compete on level, or at least not heavily skewed, playing fields, and do not face retribution as members of the political opposition (nor do their supporters). Alternation of political parties in power is not required, but it is powerful evidence of a democratic system (and arguably indispensable for a consolidated one). At least in the contemporary context, democratic governance requires universal suffrage.

The cases addressed in this book lie on the authoritarian side of the dividing line. Many unquestionably belong in the authoritarian camp. Others are closer calls. Is Singapore's system of partially competitive and law-governed elections, under conditions that limit political contestation and result in long-standing, one-party dominance, authoritarian? In their chapters, Kevin Tan and Jianlin Chen conclude that it is, but with caveats and cautions. Was Japan – by most reckonings democratic from the beginning of its postwar constitutional era – at the fringe of nondemocratic, vestigially authoritarian governance during the long era of Liberal Democratic Party hegemony? Although regularly classed as authoritarian, pre-1980s Taiwan and Korea, and contemporary Hong Kong include elements of democratic governance – relatively open and contested elections for posts with real, if limited, power (which Yen-Tu Su, in his chapter, sees as a law-governed feature of authoritarian rule in Taiwan, and which Michael Davis, in his chapter, considers a too-limited, and endangered, foundation for the rule of law in post-reversion Hong Kong) – that are absent in contemporary China or post-Taisho Japan.

Macro-comparative indexes' ratings of regimes considered as examples of authoritarian legality in this volume generally align with the conclusions that almost all fall on the authoritarian side of a plausible line of demarcation and that there is considerable variation in their degrees of authoritarianism. In Polity's rating of "regime characteristics," Vietnam and China are "autocracies," while Singapore is a "closed anocracy" (two levels below "democracy" in a five-category taxonomy).[2] According to the Economist Intelligence Unit's Democracy Index, Singapore and Hong Kong are "flawed democracies" (above global medians, at 6.38 and 6.42 on a 10-point scale), while China and Vietnam are "authoritarian" (at 3.14 and 3.38).[3] On Freedom House's Freedom in the World Index – which focuses on civil and political liberties but characterizes its 2017 findings in terms of "threats to global democracy," China scores 15, Vietnam 20, Singapore 51, and Hong Kong 61 on a 100-point scale, placing China and Vietnam among the quarter of polities that are "not free" and Singapore and Hong Kong among the nearly one-third that are "partly free."[4] Wherever a reasonable boundary between authoritarian and democratic rule may lie, authoritarian regimes show much variety in "hardness" of authoritarian rule, tolerance for democratic elements, and so on.

With the possible exception of strongly negative assessments of China and Vietnam, all contemporary cases – as well as almost all historical cases – considered in this book exhibit significant levels of legality. Singapore and Hong Kong maintain legality or a rule of law system – including courts with formal powers, occasionally used, of constitutional or quasi-constitutional review – that are high by global standards, notwithstanding significant shortcomings in law concerning political matters. They surpass other authoritarian polities in East Asia and fare well in global measures, ranking in the top five percent in the World Bank's rule of law index, and ninth (Singapore) and sixteenth (Hong Kong) among 113 polities in the World Justice Project's rule of law index.[5]

Whether reform-era China has achieved a level of legality worthy of the name – and what level it has achieved – are subjects of disagreement.[6]

[2] Polity IV Project, www.systemicpeace.org/polity/polity4.htm
[3] Economist Intelligent Unit's Democracy Index, infographics.economist.com/2017/DemocracyIndex
[4] Freedom House, *Freedom in the World 2017*, freedomhouse.org/report/freedom-world/free dom-world-2017
[5] World Bank, *World Governance Indicators 2015*, info.worldbank.org/governance/wgi/#reports; World Justice Project, *Rule of Law Index 2016*, data.worldjusticeproject.org
[6] Compare, for example, Randall Peerenboom, *China's Long March toward the Rule of Law* (Cambridge, UK: Cambridge University Press, 2002); Carl F. Minzner, "China's Turn against Law," *American Journal of Comparative Law* 59(4) (2011): 935; Stanley B. Lubman "Looking for Law in China," *Columbia Journal of Asia Law* 20(1) (2006): 1; Albert

In this book, Eva Pils, Thomas Kellogg, Michael Davis, and Hualing Fu and Michael Dowdle represent a significant swath of this spectrum of views. The extent to which Vietnam tracks, or surpasses, China is a salient inquiry, which Do Hai Ha and Pip Nicholson's chapter addresses in part. In macro-comparative rule-of-law ratings, China and Vietnam receive middling scores, a little below the international median in the World Bank's metric (46th percentile for Vietnam and 44th percentile for China) and somewhat lower (around the 40th percentile for Vietnam and 30th percentile for China) in the World Justice Project's rankings. Although cross-time-period comparisons are problematic, it is plausible to assert that somewhere between these two pairs of cases would lie Meiji Japan, and Taiwan and Korea during periods leading up to their transformations into liberal, rule-of-law-governed democracies.

The cases of authoritarian legality examined in this book (and in East Asia generally) – range from regimes that came to power through communist revolutions and remain in place today to polities that have transitioned from authoritarian rule to consolidated liberal democracy. Some of the cases considered in this volume adapted legal regimes inherited from a departing – and from the perspective of the colonized – authoritarian colonial ruler. Other examples had no colonial legacy or broke sharply with it. The colonial (or occupying) powers have been diverse: Japan, the United Kingdom, France, and the United States. So, too, have been external models and sources of legal influence. Authoritarian legal regimes in the region include civil and common law systems.

Legality in East Asian authoritarian regimes varies not only across polities but also across dimensions of legality. China's overall middling scores in comparative rule of law measures, for example, are composites of dismal ratings on "political" aspects of legality and higher ones on "economic" dimensions. In Davis's assessment, Hong Kong may be headed toward a similar pattern. In an analysis that contributes to the growing literature considering China as a possible example of Fraenkel's "dual state," Fu and Dowdle find a large gap – and a fuzzy and wavering boundary – between a regime of legality for many nonpolitical matters, and an area of state prerogative or zone of exception where the party-state perceives threats to its power (including from official corruption,

H. Y. Chen, "China's Long March towards Rule of Law or China's Turn against Law?," *Chinese Journal of Comparative Law* 4 (2016): 1; Jacques deLisle, "China's Legal System," in William A. Joseph (ed.), *Politics in China* (2nd ed., New York: Oxford University Press, 2014), 224–53.

civil society activists, social media, rights protection lawyers, ethnic "separatists," and unapproved religious groups).

Within the East Asian Model of development – broadly market-consistent and internationally engaged in its economics and, at least for the period of rapid development, authoritarian in its politics – the roles and importance of law for economic development vary across the major cases, ranging from Japan and Korea (relatively low) to Singapore and Hong Kong (very high).[7] The debate over the rule, and roles, of law in China includes contrasting views about law's contribution to China's economic development and whether low legality and rapid development can continue to coincide.[8]

China's project of constructing limited legality has reinvigorated distinctions between "thin," largely proceduralist or positivist versions of the rule of law, and "thick" ones that include substantive commitments to specific, generally broadly liberal, rights and values.[9] East Asia's remaining communist regimes raise questions of whether relatively positive evaluations of their levels of legality or optimistic projections concerning legal development without political transformation suggest that we need to take seriously non-liberal-democratic versions of the rule of law. Herein lies an authoritarian legality analogy – resonant with discourse about the *rechstaat* in hard-authoritarian polities and relevant across a diverse range of East Asian cases – to the much-discussed (and perhaps globally resurgent) phenomenon of illiberal democracy: although liberalism, democracy, and legality sometimes coincide, and some analysts make empirical claims about their causal relationships or normative claims about their collective desirability, it might – or might not – be possible to unbundle the trinity, at least for a long time, achieving authoritarian legality that could be colorably characterized as "authoritarian rule of law."

Characteristics that differentiate low and high levels of legality (or liberal rule of law) or authoritarian and non-authoritarian (or democratic)

---

[7] Jacques deLisle, "Development without Democratization? China, Law and the East Asian Model," in Jose V. Ciprut (ed.), *Democratizations* (Cambridge, MA: MIT Press, 2008), ch. 9.

[8] Jacques deLisle, "Law and the China Development Model," in S. Philip Hsu, Suisheng Zhao, and Yu-Shan Wu (eds.), *In Search of China's Development Model: Beyond the Beijing Consensus* (Abingdon, UK: Routledge, 2011), 147–63; Donald C. Clarke, "Economic Development and the Rights Hypothesis: The China Problem," *American Journal of Comparative Law* 51(1) (2003): 89; Frank Upham, "From Demsetz to Deng," *NYU Journal of International Law and Politics* 41 (2009): 551.

[9] See, for example, Peerenboom, *China's Long March*, 65–75; Fu and Dowdle, Chapter 2 in this volume.

regimes exist on continua, not as "yes/no" alternatives. Real-world cases are messy and ambiguous. An analytical framework of two variables – legality and authoritarian politics – suggests a scatterplot ranging across four quadrants. With an X-axis running from more authoritarian to more democratic politics, and a Y-axis from lower to higher levels of legality, cases of authoritarian legality fall in the northwest quadrant, lying more or less close the axes that define its boundaries. Contemporary Singapore and Hong Kong would be in the quadrant's north-northeastern reaches (high legality and not strongly authoritarian politics). Pre-democratic-transition Taiwan and Korea would be farther to the west (more strongly authoritarian politics) and south (lower legality). Contemporary China and Vietnam would be still farther toward the south and west.

This book's focus on East Asian cases makes analytical sense, for two seemingly conflicting reasons. First, the diversity among the cases – in time period, political ideology, wealth, scale, culture, history, legal family, level of legality, degree of authoritarianism, extent of international engagement, and much else – means that the examples considered here can provide general insights about authoritarian legality.

To return to the Cartesian quadrants, East Asia includes not only diverse cases of authoritarian legality (scattered about the northwest quadrant and the principal focus here). These cases are nested among regional experiences (addressed at various points in this volume) that also include democratic rule-of-law regimes (the northeast, including contemporary Taiwan, Korea, and Japan), authoritarian rule with very little legality (the southwest, including contemporary North Korea and late-Mao-era China). East Asia has not seen many polities that fall in the quadrant of relatively high (if illiberal) democracy and low legality (the southeast) although that pattern is relatively common in Latin America and may be emerging under Rodrigo Duterte in the Philippines (arguably the most "Latin America-like" state in East Asia).

Second, distinctive regional features make a focus on East Asian authoritarian legality coherent and potentially illuminating about regional politics and law more broadly. East Asian authoritarian regimes typically emphasize economic development. Authoritarian polities in East Asia generally have (adjusted for other factors, such as level of economic development) relatively strong and capable states. Authoritarian regimes in contemporary East Asia score high *among authoritarian states* on worldwide rule-of-law rubrics. Despite disparate overall rule-of-law rankings, East Asian authoritarian regimes generally do better on economic rule of law, order and security, criminal justice, civil justice, absence of corruption, and regulatory enforcement, than on open government, constraints on government powers, and protection for fundamental rights.[10]

Legal transplants, borrowings, and transnational contagion effects that affect legality in states generally also do so for authoritarian regimes. In authoritarian East Asia, such phenomena are partly intraregional, or reflect common external sources, and thus bring some commonality to authoritarian legal orders in the region (despite the presence of both common law and civil law systems and influences). Much the same is true of contextual factors – including culture – that shape law.

A restriction on analytical scope also contributes to the collection's coherence. Assessments of authoritarian legality can focus on "systemic" or "incremental" issues (with various cases or comparisons better suited for either type of inquiry). At the "systemic" level, the question of legality and the authoritarian state presents a "chicken and egg" problem. The state both creates and is a creature of law. For the authoritarian state, the paradox (and difficulty) of pursuing legality is most fundamental (and seemingly intractable) if one imagines (contrary to most real-world cases) a shift from virtually no law to seeking robust legality (or rapid replacement of a prior legal order).

The inquiry here is more circumscribed. It does not analyze cases of full-fledged revolution (such as China in the 1940s), or decolonization (such as Singapore from the late 1950s to the early 1960s), or foreign imposition of a new constitutional order (as in Japan after World War II). Even in those contexts, there is often much legal continuity, but there is much more continuity in the cases considered here. Moves to build legality under authoritarian rule, or less planned rises or declines in legality, that are the subjects of this chapter and this volume occur more at the margins – albeit sometimes very wide margins. The focus is on programs or trends that refashion, strengthen or expand laws and legal institutions (sometimes transformatively) or that preserve, and adapt, inherited laws and institutions, within the context of an already-existing state that was not previously devoid of laws and legal institutions. The cases examined here involve ongoing authoritarian legality, or transformation of legality in states transitioning from

[10] See World Justice Project's Rule of Law Index (2016). The World Bank's Global Governance Indicators (2015) tell much the same story when its "rule of law" indicator is disaggregated into component metrics. Vietnam is a partial outlier, scoring near its overall rank on fundamental rights and corruption, and below its overall median on regulatory enforcement and civil justice in the World Justice Project assessment.

authoritarianism. In such contexts, choices about legality may pose less evidently profound dilemmas, but they are often more complex in process and effects than in cases of sudden regime replacement.

How to define and compare cases of authoritarian legality in East Asia, and how to assess the persistence of aspects of authoritarian legality after a transition to democracy, entail close analysis and scholarly judgment, which authors in this volume undertake. Such an exercise is largely a positive, analytical project. Analysts in this book and in the study of authoritarian legality more broadly, hold diverse normative positions. Some see liberal-democratic politics and liberal legality as clearly superior. Others hold different views or eschew judgment. But the assessments of authoritarian legality in East Asia in this collection do not depend on how much one celebrates or condemns the political systems and legal orders examined.

In this chapter, questions that cut across cases – one about aims and imperatives, and others about features and trajectory – are the principal foci. The first inquiry, which has been addressed in this section, concerns characteristics of authoritarian legality in East Asia. The project has not been to articulate, defend, or apply a particular definition of authoritarian legality, but to consider traits that place the cases within the boundaries of plausible meanings of authoritarian legality, while also addressing what makes these cases different from one another and more or less easily included within the category.

The second inquiry is why an authoritarian regime would seek, welcome, or tolerate significant legality. The question is hardly novel,[11] but

---

[11] There is a large literature on the issue, and many traits and functions discussed therein are similar to categories used in Section 1.2. Examples include: Tom Ginsburg and Tamir Moustafa (eds.), *Rule by Law: The Politics of Courts in Authoritarian Regimes* (Cambridge, UK: Cambridge University Press, 2008) (esp. ch. 1, identifying functions of courts in authoritarian regimes: establishing social control and sidelining political opponents; bolstering a regime's claim to "legal" legitimacy strengthening administrative compliance within the state and coordinating among competing factions; facilitating trade and investment; and implementing controversial policies in ways that allow political distance from the regime's leadership); Mark Tushnet, "Authoritarian Constitutionalism," *Cornell Law Review* 100 (2014): 391–461 ("authoritarian constitutionalism" appeals to authoritarian rulers because of rulers' "modest normative commitment" to constitutionalism, and instrumental benefits of constitutionalism); Tom Ginsburg and Antonio Simpser, "Introduction: Constitutions in Authoritarian Regimes," in Ginsburg and Simpser (eds.), *Constitutions in Authoritarian Regimes* (Cambridge, UK: Cambridge University Press, 2013), 1–20 (constitutions in authoritarian systems facilitate coordination within the ruling elite, signal foreign and domestic observers, and give guidance to officials and subjects concerning permissible and required actions); Peter H. Solomon, "Authoritarian Legality and Informal Practices: Judges,

an examination of motivations, functions, and causes – focusing on East Asia – is still apposite.

The evident paradox of an authoritarian regime creating or accepting legal rules, institutions, and expectations that can constrain its own power (or generate pressure for such constraints) extends to East Asian polities which present regionally distinctive, as well as diverse, experiences of authoritarian legality.

A third undertaking is to consider, in light of East Asian experiences, the prospective durability and possible trajectories of authoritarian legality, whether in polities that remain authoritarian or ones that transform into liberal democracies.

1.2   Why?

Why would an authoritarian regime (in East Asia) incur the risks and costs associated with substantial legality, or significant increases in legality? Empirically supported and generally plausible explanations can be grouped into five, largely "functionalist" or "instrumentalist" categories: managing threats to order and security; fostering economic development; enhancing state capacity; preserving or bolstering regime legitimacy; and responding to demands from segments of society or from within the regime. In some of the most strongly authoritarian regimes, instrumentalism in turning to law is so pervasive (and limiting of legality) that "legalized authoritarianism" may be a more appropriate descriptor than "authoritarian legality."[12]

Lawyers and the State in Russia and China," *Communist and Post-Communist Studies* 43 (4) (2010): 351–62 (authoritarian states adopt formal legal institutions to meet foreign actors' demands while relying on informal practices to control administration of justice and avoid threats to regime's control of public life); Jacques deLisle, "Chasing the God of Wealth While Evading the Goddess of Democracy: Development, Democracy, and Law in Reform-Era China," in Sunder Ramaswamy and Jeffrey W. Casson (eds.), *Development and Democracy* (Lebanon, NH: University Press of New England, 2003), 252–93 (China turned to law to support economic development, limit state predation, and avoid pressures for democratic change); Jothie Rajah, *Authoritarian Rule of Law: Legislation, Discourse, and Legitimacy in Singapore* (Cambridge, UK: Cambridge University Press, 2012) (authoritarian regime's use of liberal rule-of-law forms to embody illiberal content, limit dissent, increase state's power and discretion, and secure domestic and international legitimacy); Chien-Chih Lin, "Constitutions and Courts in Chinese Authoritarian Regimes: China and Pre-Democratic Taiwan in Comparison," *International Journal of Constitutional Law* 41(2) (2016): 351–77 (Taiwan's authoritarian regime preserved unaltered constitution and allowed limited constitutional judicial review to legitimize claim to be sole government of China).

[12] I am indebted to Hualing Fu for the insightful phrase "legalized authoritarianism." On the highly instrumental approach to law in contemporary China, see, Jacques deLisle, "Traps,

Before undertaking a more detailed examination of these "whys" of authoritarian legality, a few points about context are in order. First, seeking to fulfill these "functions" is hardly unique to authoritarian regimes. In general form, these are concerns for any political regime that wishes to succeed, or even survive. These needs and challenges, however, manifest differently in authoritarian polities, including in East Asia. Other things being equal, authoritarian politics makes turning to law to perform these functions – and adopting and implementing laws that perform them effectively – more difficult. In part, this is due to the absence or weakness of the checks on the state's (or political leaders') transgressions of state- (or party-) limiting laws that come from democratic politics, independent judiciaries, vigorous and free media, and robust civil society organizations.

Second, there is a complicated relationship between description (the topic of Section 1.1) and functionalist analysis (the focus of this section) of authoritarian legality in East Asia. Concrete phenomena can serve multiple functions or purposes. Choices made for functionalist reasons may fall short or backfire. Authoritarian regimes' moves to create or change law and legal institutions that may seem instrumentally useful may fail on their own terms or evolve into threats to authoritarian rule.

Third, the discussion that follows draws extensively on Chinese examples. This partly reflects the author's relative expertise and the several China-focused chapters in this volume. It also reflects other considerations: China is an especially tough case (and, indeed, a fundamentally unique one, Fu and Dowdle argue), in part due to its strongly authoritarian political regime, comparatively weak and rapidly changing legal order, and thoroughgoingly instrumentalist approach to law; China is especially clearly grappling with – and ambivalent about – creating law and legal institutions that perform key functions that legality can serve for authoritarian regimes; contemporary China poses, in especially pointed form, questions about the trajectory of authoritarian legality; and China's sheer scale makes it singularly important.

Gaps and Law: Prospects and Challenges for China's Reforms," in Randall Peerenboom (ed.), *Is China Trapped in Transition? Implications for Future Reforms* (Oxford: Oxford Foundation for Law, Justice and Society, 2007); Jacques deLisle, "The Rule of Law with Xi-Era Characteristics," *Asia Policy* 20 (2015): 23.

1.2.1 Managing Threats to Order and Security

For an authoritarian regime, legality can offer promising means to fulfill the most indispensable function: regime survival – the most basic need in Maslow's hierarchy and the most elemental aim of state behavior in realist theories of international relations. Legality can address several types of threats to social and political order and the security of the regime and its leaders.

First, criminal law and related legal institutions – including courts, prosecutors, and police – provide mechanisms for punishing, preventing, or deterring behavior that can undermine social and political order or the rulers' grip on power. This includes disruptive activities in society that reflect or reveal state failure to fulfill vital functions of providing safety and security to its people, as well as acts by political opponents challenging the authority of powerholders or the state itself. Often, this task can be accomplished more effectively or efficiently through legality. Security forces in an authoritarian regime that operate through ad hoc commands or political campaigns may prove less disciplined, or create greater collateral costs, in maintaining order and control than would reliance on more law-based means. Totalitarian techniques – which are "low legality" – can be costly in material resources and political legitimacy. An approach that uses "lawless" methods to terrorize critics or denies citizens space secure from state intervention is hard to manage and sustain. A regime that uses such means can prove brittle. Mao-era China provides an abject lesson in some of these possibilities, one seemingly not lost on China's reform-era leaders.[13]

Second, and relatedly, legality – especially positivist legality in criminal law – can help quash the regime's political opponents by legitimating suppression to relevant audiences at home and abroad. During the post-Mao era, China's authoritarian regime has strived to portray persecution of political dissidents as prosecution for violating ordinary laws (such as those against disruption of public order or evasion of taxes) or politically neutral laws regarding state security (such as those against subversion or divulging state secrets). In Fu and Dowdle's assessment of Xi-era China, this is a tricky business, with the formal legal mechanisms of the ordinary

---

[13] See, generally, Sarah Biddulph, *The Stability Imperative: Human Rights and Law in China* (Oakland, CA: University of California Press, 2015); Susan Trevaskes et al. (eds.), *The Politics of Law and Stability in China* (Cheltenham, UK: Edward Elgar, 2014); Ronald C. Keith and Zhiqiu Lin, "The '*Falun Gong* Problem': Politics and the Struggle for the Rule of Law in China," *China Quarterly* 175 (2003): 623.

criminal process interacting uneasily and unstably with informal modes of political prosecution and informal, extralegal repression.

Other East Asian authoritarian regimes seem to have appreciated positivist legality's potential to legitimate uses of state power to support existing political orders and suppress dissent. During the postwar, pre-democratization periods in Taiwan and Korea, authoritarian governments used the positive public law of the Cold War national security state (influenced by the United States, as Erik Mobrand points out in his chapter's analysis of Korea) and adopted emergency measures to formally suspend constitutional limits to prosecute and suppress dissenters and prohibit opposition parties. As Davis addresses with foreboding, the National People's Congress Standing Committee has used – or abused – its power to interpret Hong Kong's constitution-like Basic Law, and the Hong Kong Special Administrative Region government has reacted negatively to the Occupy Central Movement – including prosecuting its leaders – in ways that have relied on proper forms of legality to rebuff or suppress social pressure for democratization. In Singapore, as Jianlin Chen explain, the government used libel laws against the regime's critics and pursued a procedurally punctilious parliamentary override of a court decision imposing modest limits on state powers under the Internal Security Act.

Third, legality can curb threats to social order and social peace by helping provide ordinary citizens with some security in their persons, property, and expectations. Laws and legal institutions that provide rights and protect material interests from infringement by private actors, the state, or hybrid entities, can reduce reasons for the people to turn against, and can give them reasons to support, the authoritarian status quo.

Here, again, reform-era China provides striking examples, largely because the regime had so thoroughly foregone this aspect of legality during much of the Mao era. Providing greater security and rights for much of the populace was central to a legal reform agenda that repudiated the then-recent Cultural Revolution, which had been characterized by twin evils of lawlessness: tyranny (by the party-state) and chaos (within society).[14] In many East Asian authoritarian states (including

---

[14] On "aversive" constitutionalism responding to past horrors, see Kim Lane Scheppele, "Aspirational and Aversive Constitutionalism," *International Journal of Constitutional Law* 1(2) (2003): 296–324. On the turn against recent anti-legalist experiences toward constitutional discourse from earlier eras (a pattern in Eastern European post-socialist states and East Asian reformist socialist states), see Bui Ngoc Son, "Restoration

Singapore, Hong Kong, and Japan), legality in the form of protecting economic rights and some civil liberties, but not rights to participate in politics or publicly and collectively criticize the regime, indicate the promise this type of legality holds for authoritarian rulers.

Fourth, legality – specifically, litigation and other formal means for addressing disputes and complaints – can steer potentially explosive political challenges into arenas that are safer for the regime. Lawsuits funnel conflicts that might be taken to the streets into courts and other organs that, even in authoritarian regimes, can be perceived as relatively apolitical and autonomous from ruling authorities, with their decisions thus more likely legitimate in the eyes of losing parties. This pattern is particularly prominent in suits against the state – the domain of administrative tribunals found in many East Asian authoritarian states. China's Administrative Litigation Law offers a prominent example, but it is far from unique. As Fu and Dowdle note concerning China, such measures work symbiotically with other legal measures that stunt civil society.

Lawsuits nominally not involving the state can present variations on this theme. Mass tort cases, such as those over melamine-tainted milk poisonings or earthquake-collapsed buildings or other public interest and potential "impact" litigation in contemporary China (which the regime has viewed with wariness and hostility), and environmental pollution and other social justice cases in Japan during the early decades of democratic legality (when, Nakano Koichi argues in his chapter, legacies of bureaucratic authoritarian legality lingered), can divert potentially disruptive political issues – principally state failures to regulate – into the state's legal institutions.[15] Legal doctrines and administrative orders limiting class actions or suits with large numbers of plaintiffs reduce the risk that lawsuits will become vehicles for larger political movements, making litigation less threatening to authoritarian regimes. As the Chinese mass tort cases and Japanese pollution cases illustrate, the state also can preempt, or truncate, impact litigation by offering state-brokered or state-run

Constitutionalism and Socialist Asia," *Loyola of Los Angeles International and Comparative Law Review* 37 (2015): 67–116.

[15] See, generally, Frank K. Upham, *Law and Social Change in Postwar Japan* (Cambridge, MA: Harvard University Press, 1987); Jing-Huey Shao, "State Power in Disguise – Addressing Catastrophic Mass Torts in the United States, China, and Taiwan," *Tulane Journal of International and Comparative Law* 24(1) (2015): 175–204; Jacques deLisle, "Law and the Economy in China," in Gregory C. Chow and Dwight H. Perkins (eds.), *Routledge Handbook of the Chinese Economy* (Abingdon, UK: Routledge, 2015), 264.

initiatives that provide ad hoc or discretionary relief without creating more state-constraining, legally enforceable rights.

Fifth, legality can solemnize, and thus make more credible and effective, an authoritarian regime's efforts at accommodation in ethnically mixed and potentially conflict-ridden societies.[16] Singapore's deeply legally entrenched communal pluralism, to limit domination by the ethnic Chinese majority, is a notable example. China's constitutionally based system of "autonomous regions" for national minorities, and laws granting privileges or exemptions to ethnic minorities (including from once-draconian population control policies) are examples – although overshadowed by harsh and repressive measures, especially in Xinjiang and Tibet – of an authoritarian regime's appreciation for this aspect of legality.

Finally, legality can help contain threats to political order and regime stability from upper reaches within authoritarian regimes. By mandating means for orderly and predictable succession, promising former leaders will face only lawful punishment for crimes such as corruption (rather than political reckoning after a political struggle), and so on, legal rules can hold out hope of ameliorating "winner takes all" and "I live, you die" struggles in elite politics. Unmitigated, such dynamics can impede regime functioning. They impel leaders to divert attention from policy priorities to factional politics, possibly spawning social conflict and imperiling regime stability. The absence of such retribution-limiting law also can feed top-level resistance to transition from authoritarian rule.[17] Post-Mao China's rules to limit leaders' tenure in office and to address official corruption offer examples of this dimension of legality's potential appeal and value for authoritarian regimes – albeit within limits, given that the mechanisms have been only partly law-based and have been shaken by, for example, moves in 2018 to eliminate constitutional term limits for the president and to create a state supervision commission entwined with party disciplinary mechanisms and wielding powers formerly belonging to prosecutors. In this book, Tom Ginsburg's

[16] See Hurst Hannum, *Autonomy, Sovereignty and Self-Determination* (Philadelphia: University of Pennsylvania Press, 1990); Crawford Young, *The Politics of Cultural Pluralism* (Madison: University of Wisconsin Press, 1977), 66–97; Roberto M. Unger, *Law in Modern Society* (New York: Free Press, 1976), 66–76.

[17] Ginsburg's analysis of the roles of constitutional courts, judicial review – and, by implication, legality – in Asian states that transitioned to democracy is consistent with this phenomenon. See Tom Ginsburg, *Judicial Review in New Democracies: Constitutional Courts in Asian Cases* (Cambridge, UK: Cambridge University Press, 2003).

account of Japan depicts an analogous phenomenon, characterizing the Meiji constitution as a "grand bargain" among the emperor and factions of oligarchs to manage potentially destabilizing elite conflicts.

1.2.2   Fostering Economic Development

Legality can be attractive to authoritarian rulers because it promises to promote economic development. From Meiji and Qing reformers, through the rise of the four "tiger" economies of Korea, Taiwan, Hong Kong, and Singapore and their would-be imitators in the region, to reform under socialism in China and Vietnam, East Asian authoritarian states have been developmental states in which delivering economic prosperity has been a policy priority, and source of legitimacy.[18]

Leaders in East Asian authoritarian regimes have seen law and legal institutions – particularly those borrowed from economically advanced nations – as promising, perhaps necessary, means to economic development. For reformist elites in Meiji Japan and late Qing China, adopting or adapting Western legal and law-related institutions was a strategy for national technological advancement and economic dynamism, and, thus, security against foreign, largely Western, encroachment. (Japan was both an additional model and an additional threat for some.) For newly industrializing, politically authoritarian entities in postwar East Asia as well, Western-based models of law and legal institutions were part of the machinery for development. For Singapore and Hong Kong, high-quality legal orders for the economy, established by colonial governments and sustained after the end of British rule, are widely and plausibly credited (including by David Campbell and Richard Cullen in this book) for remarkable economic success. For Hong Kong, Singapore, Taiwan, and Korea in the early postwar decades and China and Vietnam during their socialist reform eras, a central element in the recipe for economic development was engaging in international trade and – especially for China and Vietnam – welcoming foreign investment. Those economic policies

---

[18] See, generally, Chalmers Johnson, *MITI and the Japanese Miracle* (Palo Alto, CA: Stanford University Press, 1982); Stephan Haggard, *Pathways from the Periphery* (New York: Cornell University Press, 1990); Meredith Woo-Cumings (ed.), *The Developmental State* (New York: Cornell University Press, 1999); Atul Kohli, *State-Directed Development* (Cambridge, UK: Cambridge University Press, 2004); S. Philip Hsu, Suisheng Zhao, and Yu-Shan Wu (eds.), *In Search of China's Development Model: Beyond the Beijing Consensus* (Abingdon, UK: Routledge, 2011).

entailed – and perhaps required – adopting and implementing laws based on foreign models and convergent with international standards.

Many academic theories and much policy advice, based partly on East Asian experiences, have asserted that law (with market-consistent content) is important for economic development. This thread runs through the "law and development" literature of the 1970s; formulations of the "East Asian Model" in the 1980s; the Washington Consensus (with prescriptions for strong property rights and international economic openness that imply legal agendas); and the World Bank's touting the rule of law as an element of good governance and a pillar supporting economic development.[19]

The view that legality contributes significantly, perhaps indispensably, to economic development may recognize a "universal truth" of modernization. Or it may indicate path-dependency: although other routes to development are possible, the goal is more easily and reliably attainable for later-developing states through engagement with an outside world that expects or demands legality (or imposes big risk premiums in its absence) and that offers tested models for emulation. Or it may reflect lessons mistakenly derived from now-developed countries' pasts, which may represent a path that is neither necessary nor replicable. Or it may, particularly in postcolonial cases, be a legacy of "legal transplants," with once-foreign law and legal institutions taking root and closing off alternative paths.

Whatever the origins or accuracy of the view that law promotes development, the idea seemingly has persuaded authoritarian regimes in East Asia. To varying but significant extents, authoritarian rulers of East Asian developmental states have turned to laws and legal institutions to promise security of expectations to economic actors (in the form of private property, contract law, and so on), provide broadly market-conforming rules for the economy (including laws on corporate

---

[19] See David Trubek and Mark Galanter, "Scholars in Self-Estrangement: Some Reflections on the Crisis in Law and Development Studies in the United States," *Wisconsin Law Review* 4 (1974): 1062; Kevin Davis and Michael Trebilcock, "The Relationship between Law and Development: Optimists vs. Skeptics," *American Journal of Comparative Law* 56 (2008): 895; deLisle, "Development without Democratization?"; John Williamson, "What Washington Means by Policy Reform," in John Williamson (ed.), *Latin American Readjustment: How Much Has Happened?* (Washington, DC: Institute for International Economics, 1989); John Williamson, "What Should the World Bank Think about the Washington Consensus?," *World Bank Research Observer* 15(2) (2000): 251; Daniel Kaufmann and Aart Kraay, "World Bank Worldwide Governance Indicators," World Bank, info.worldbank.org/governance/wgi/index.aspx#home

structures, capital-raising mechanisms, competition policy, and the like), align with international standards for economic engagement (particularly international trade and foreign investment), and check state predation (including through legal protection of citizens' economic rights and administrative or criminal law constraints on state actors). Law's perceived role in development does much to account for the gap between law for the economy and law for more political matters that has been a common pattern in East Asian authoritarian regime.

1.2.3   Strengthening State Capacity

Another reason legality can have a powerful allure for authoritarian regimes is law's potential to enhance state power and effectiveness. All regimes seek authority, and authoritarian regimes – as their name suggests – are no exception.[20] Robust capacity to govern is a precondition for successful developmental states, which have been prevalent in authoritarian East Asia. The state-strengthening imperative may be potent in East Asia also for historical reasons: deep-seated memories and fears of internal fragmentation (e.g. in rebellion-prone China or feudal Japan) and external vulnerability (including colonial or quasi-colonial subjugation in the nineteenth and twentieth centuries, or recent threats from powerful and hostile neighbors or unforgiving international economic and political environments).

The paradox of authoritarian legality can seem especially acute in the context of legality's contribution to state capacity: law concerning state institutions and actors is often – and often rightly – seen as constraining state power. But such law also can be state-empowering. Even ostensibly state-limiting law can be Janus-faced, enhancing state efficacy even as it limits state actors' discretion.

As authoritarian rulers and elites in East Asia and elsewhere appear to have realized, constitutions serve formally to confer and confirm state powers, not just to limit them. Constitutions are literally – and can be functionally – "constitutive" of the state and its authority. The idea that laws defining the powers of institutions and officials are vital to creating a strong and capable state has ancient roots, prominently in Chinese Legalist (*fajia*) thinking two millennia ago. Late-nineteenth-century

---

[20] Fu and Dowdle argue that in authoritarian legal regimes generally, and China in particular, law serves to enhance, not check, state power – in contrast to law's performing both functions in democratic states.

reformers saw constitutional borrowing from Western models as
a means to strengthen the state and China's capacity to protect itself
against threats from foreign powers. Here, Qing China was following
Meiji Japan, where, as Ginsburg discusses, the adoption of a "rule of law"
system with constitutionally structured legal and political institutions,
including parliament, a bureaucracy, and courts, contributed to development of a capable state.

  The constitution of the Republic of China, which became the charter
for the authoritarian KMT-led regime in Taiwan, reflected the thought of
Sun Yat-Sen, whose political theories extended the late Qing project of
seeking legal-institutional solutions to China's weakness. Sun, too,
sought a more capable government and a more powerful China through
a constitutional engineering project that looked to Western examples
while also adapting traditional Chinese institutions. During the PRC era,
China's rulers have adopted four new constitutions, each marking a new
political period – or repudiating the preceding one – characterized by
distinctive institutional arrangements consistent with a particular conception of the contours and bases of authoritarian state power.
Hong Kong's Basic Law – a mini-constitution for the Special
Administrative Region – is a variation on this theme. It delegates powers
in principle belonging to the central government, and instantiates an
executive-dominated, limitedly democratic system of governance.
Tellingly, the recurring and tumultuous battles over the limits, and
proper foundations, of governmental power in Hong Kong – recent
examples of which Davis analyzes – have been waged largely in terms
of interpreting the Basic Law.[21]

  The pattern extends to sub-constitutional levels. Throughout authoritarian East Asia, regimes have turned to emergency powers or state of
emergency laws to authorize and empower state actors to wield powers
more expansive than those accorded by ordinary law.[22] For Beijing, the

[21] See generally Brian Christopher Jones (ed.), *Law and Politics of the Taiwan Sunflower and Hong Kong Umbrella Movements* (Abingdon, UK: Routledge, 2017); Jacques deLisle and Kevin P. Lane, "Hong Kong's Endgame and the Rule of Law," *University of Pennsylvania Journal of International Law* 18 (1997): 195–264, 811–1047.
[22] Victor V. Ramraj and Arun K. Thiruvengadam (eds.), *Emergency Powers in Asia* (Cambridge, UK: Cambridge University Press, 2009); compare Kim Lane Scheppele, "Exceptions that Prove the Rule: Embedding Emergency Government in Everyday Constitutional Life," in Jeffrey Tulis and Stephen Macedo (eds.), *The Limits of Constitutional Democracy* (Princeton, NJ: Princeton University Press, 2010), 129–30 (law as "the way the state talks to itself"); Bruce Ackerman, "The Emergency Constitution," *Yale Law Journal* 113(5) (2004): 1029–91.

Hong Kong Basic Law is mere legislation, not a constitution, and thus underscores and implements central government authority in a special (and, for Beijing, vexing) part of China.

Among ordinary state-structuring laws, the insight of Max Weber (in *Bureaucracy*) points to a reason for authoritarian regimes to find aspects of legality attractive.[23] Legal rules – including ones that delineate institutions' authority, authorize officials to act, coordinate differentiated governmental powers, set forth limits to institutions' and officials' mandates, and govern who may hold official posts – can produce a more effective, efficient, and disciplined state. They can help constrain state agents' overreach, reduce state functionaries' shirking, and make the state's hands and feet more responsive to directives from its head. Law for the state thus can help redress problems such as: agency costs, local abuses of power, corruption, capture by the objects of state regulation, sloth, and paralyzing wariness about consequences of taking not-clearly-authorized but desirable and innovative measures or unpopular but necessary or obligatory actions.

Law concerning state organs has been an area of significant development in East Asian authoritarian regimes. Ginsburg addresses state-strengthening dimensions of Meiji constitutional reforms, including creating an autonomous administration and a civil service system, and centralizing power from the quasi-feudal pattern of the Tokugawa period. Nakano tellingly calls Japan a case of "bureaucratic authoritarian legality." The accounts of contemporary China in this volume by Fu and Dowdle and Pils see legality in contemporary China as heavily focused on pursuing party-state control and securing its foundations.

Especially for the remaining communist regimes in East Asia (and to some extent for the KMT-led regime in pre-democratization Taiwan), a mutation of Weber's point gives an impetus to seek elements of legality. Laws and legal systems are among a Leninist regime's "organizational weapons."[24] Although narrowly instrumentalist and far removed from "rule of law" ideals, a Leninist conception of legality is not inherently

---

[23] See Max Weber, "Bureaucracy," in Guenther Roth and Claus Wittich (eds.), *Economy and Society* (Berkeley: University of California Press, 1978), 956–1005.

[24] See, generally, Philip Selznick, *Leadership in Administration: A Sociological Interpretation* (New York: Harper & Row, 1957) (contrasting durable, "value-infused" institutions with expendable, instrumental organizations); Philip Selznick, *The Organizational Weapon* (New York: McGraw-Hill, 1952) (analyzing disciplined, mobilizational features of communist organizations). On contemporary China, see deLisle, "Rule of Law with Xi-Era Characteristics."

absurd, as the reform-era Chinese experience (including in the Xi era) suggests. Explicitly politicized laws providing for suppression and punishment of those deemed enemies of the party-state are welcome additions to the arsenal of a Leninist regime. Laws structuring state organs and defining state functionaries' ambits, and targeting indiscipline and corruption within the party-state, appeal to Leninists as well as Weberians – as the reform-era Chinese example vividly illustrates.

Even seemingly state-power-constraining features of legality can appeal to authoritarian rulers because, overall, they can strengthen state capacity. Anti-corruption laws address behavior by officials that departs from the leadership's agenda and erodes regime legitimacy. Citizen suits against the state can enlist the public to help authoritarian rulers keep underlings in line and on task. This function can be performed when members of the public turn to legal rules to seek redress, including in the form of invoking legal rules and rights when seeking state-provided informal and discretionary relief. Such legal or law-related mechanisms for engaging citizens in increasing the state's internal discipline holds the additional appeal to authoritarians of perhaps deflecting or delaying popular demand for democracy.[25]

Putting policies in legal form can serve the authoritarian state's quest for capability through mast-binding and signaling, perhaps most evidently in the context of efforts to promote regime policies pursuing economic development. Where the regime insists (credibly) that especially important or stable policies are put into legal form, and where law enjoys (some) social legitimacy such that relevant audiences view law as more serious or worthy of confidence than (mere) policy, using legal forms allows an authoritarian regime to make more persuasive, and, therefore, potentially effective and successful, policy commitments. Substantive laws – some concerning state behavior, and some nominally addressing nonpublic behavior (such as economic interactions in mixed-market economies) – can send important messages to the public about an authoritarian regime's policy commitments, the undermining of which by state actors then becomes an occasion for regime-sanctioned whistle-blowing, sometimes in the form of citizens' invoking legal rights and rules. Reneging on the commitments embodied in law could undermine

[25] See deLisle, "China's Legal System," 233–41; Neil J. Diamant, Stanley B. Lubman, and Kevin J. O'Brien (eds.), *Engaging the Law in China* (Palo Alto, CA: Stanford University Press, 2005) (esp. chs. 2–4); Carl F. Minzner, "Xinfang: An Alternative to Formal Chinese Legal Institutions," *Stanford Journal of International Law* 42 (2006): 103–79.

the regime's capacity to make self-interested credible commitments in the future.

Laws – including procedural laws that offer the public and stakeholders legitimate and stable opportunities for input into, or feedback about, legislation and regulation – can be potent information-gathering tools for the regime. They can generate better law (in terms of suitability and effectiveness in pursuing policy goals), and more socially accepted law (which is less likely to be resisted), and, thus, a state more capable of implementing its (law-embodied) policies.

1.2.4   Legitimating Authoritarian Rule

Legality, even when modest or shallow, can help legitimate authoritarian rule. The rule of law, and lesser forms of legality, have a curious and elusive, but potent, capacity to confer legitimacy. Legitimacy is a chronic concern for authoritarian regimes, especially during the postwar and post-Cold War eras when democracy has become a global standard for legitimate governance. Authoritarian regimes often invest significantly in touting their legal regimes to foreign and domestic audiences. That those claims are often hollow arguably confirms that their purposes include legitimation (rather than performance of more tangible functions discussed earlier in this chapter). Here, hypocrisy may indeed be the tribute that vice pays to virtue – a tribute worth paying because legality matters for legitimacy.

For East Asian authoritarian regimes, some level of legality has long been a means to seek legitimacy or acceptance internationally. For Meiji Japan and Qing China, reforming "barbaric" legal systems (as the West dubbed them) to resemble Western models was a price of admission to the club of "civilized" nations and, in turn, claiming full rights of states in the international system (including freedom from foreign powers' encroachments that threatened national security and sovereignty).

More recent global developments, also relevant in authoritarian East Asia, reprise these nineteenth-century patterns: Washington Consensus-based prescriptions for developing countries' domestic legal orders; post-Cold War rule-of-law and constitutional democracy norms as foci for global NGOs and Western powers' policies; and the expectations or requirements for domestic legal orders established by the WTO-centered regime for international trade and myriad bilateral investment treaties based increasingly on developed, capital-exporting country templates.[26] As Kellogg argues concerning China's Foreign NGO Law, and in a point that resonates broadly, China risks its already-modest soft power and international legitimacy when it adopts laws that turn China's back on pro-legality international norms and institutions.

The authoritarian's game may be to undertake relatively empty or cosmetic changes to satisfy foreign audiences. Modern East Asia authoritarian regimes offer examples of efforts to draw on the internationally legitimating power of legality to avoid or parry foreign critiques of repressive domestic orders. During the Cold War, superficially liberal-democratic, familiar-to-the-West constitutions and legal orders offered international political cover for dissent-intolerant regimes, and facilitated US support for authoritarian rulers, in Korea and Taiwan. For China, post-9/11 UN Security Council resolutions expounding international legal obligations for combatting terrorism, and the US's adoption of terrorism-focused national security laws, provided external law-related legitimation for harsh measures that China's regime has taken against ethno-religious and political dissent.[27] Authoritarian regimes in East Asia – including reform-era China, pre-democratization Taiwan, and post-reversion Hong Kong – have taken care to tell the world that what critics denounce as political persecution is ordinary prosecution consistent with due process and the state's lawful role in protecting itself and social order.

Law's capacity to bolter legitimacy – and legality's resulting appeal to authoritarian rulers – may be no less important when the forms or substance of legality are addressed to domestic audiences. Weber's account of political legitimacy, in which legal-rational authority becomes the form of legitimate authority in polities where charismatic authority is scarce and traditional authority has waned, speaks to situations that are common in East Asian authoritarian polities, especially amid the often relentless and successful pursuit of market-consistent economic development.[28] Fallow constitutions in authoritarian states (in East Asia and more generally) do little to shape exercises of state power, yet

---

[26] For an argument that China's WTO accession imposed requirements for significant legal change – and implied more fundamental political–legal transformation to satisfy those requirements – see Pitman B. Potter, "The Legal Implications of China's Accession to the WTO," *China Quarterly* 167 (2001): 592.

[27] Jacques deLisle, "Security First?: Patterns and Lessons from China's Use of Law To Address National Security Threats," *Journal of National Security Law and Policy* 4 (2010): 397.

[28] Max Weber, "The Three Types of Legitimate Rule," *Berkeley Publications in Society and Institutions* 4(1) (1958): 1–11; "Politics as a Vocation," in Hans Gerth and C. Wright Mills (eds.), *From Max Weber* (New York: Oxford University Press, 1947), 77–128.

they can strengthen authoritarian rule by enhancing its legitimacy. Walter Bagehot's insight concerning Britain's constitutional monarchy – that "dignified" constitutional institutions with little real power (or relation to how power is exercised) can contribute to the authority of "efficient" institutions that actually wield power – resonates with authoritarian constitutions' roles in East Asia, perhaps most pointedly (if not most potently) in reform-era China.[29] In Ha and Nicholson's account, Vietnam's limited move toward constitutionalism, with largely undiminished party dominance, suggests a broadly similar phenomenon. Su discusses a seemingly simple, but interestingly recursive, example of this phenomenon: Taiwan's authoritarian KMT regime adopted a law-governed structure for not-very-democratic elections, tapping the legitimacy of both law and democracy – although leaning more on legality (having law-governed elections) than on democracy (given the context of a Mainlander-dominated KMT ruling over a majority Taiwanese population).

A second pattern may be found in authoritarian regimes in Hong Kong and Singapore. The rule of law is a colonial legacy on which postcolonial regimes rely as a basis for legitimacy. Perceptions of erosion, or fragility, of legality are seen as blows to – or bases for challenging – the regime's legitimacy. This has been an increasingly prominent concern in Hong Kong (one that Davis emphasizes but that Campbell and Cullen suggest is overblown, given the resilience of what they call a broadly and deeply shared understanding of the socially beneficial nature of law). Kindred but lesser worries have arisen in Singapore, where the constitutional amendment to overturn the court decision limiting the government's use of detention powers drew significant criticism as a threat to the rule of law (criticism that Jianlin Chen concludes overstates the problem and misses constitutionalism-preserving aspects of the regime's action).

Another example is the lengths to which East Asian authoritarian regimes have gone to convince their publics that seemingly politically motivated moves targeting political dissidents are lawful sanctions for violating positivistically valid criminal laws, including those against ordinary antisocial behavior (destruction of property, evasion of taxes, breaches of the peace, and the like) or against threats to state security (sedition, disclosure of state secrets, and so on). As the reform-era Chinese approach illustrates, East Asian authoritarian regimes have

---

[29] Walter Bagehot, *The English Constitution* (London: Chapman & Hall, 1867).

other means at their disposal – including punishment outside the formal legal system and, in less legality-minded times, incarceration for "thought crimes." Yet, they often prefer to employ potentially more legitimacy-conferring (or legitimacy-protecting) mechanisms of ostensibly apolitical criminal law.

Another variation on this theme may be found in East Asian authoritarian regimes' emergency powers laws. The legitimating potential of legality is a possible answer to the puzzle of why a regime with nearly unlimited powers would find it necessary or desirable to put claims to exceptional powers into formal legal form. It also may explain why the Schmitt–Dyzenhaus discourse about the relative wisdom of making emergency powers intra-constitutional or extra-constitutional would be seen as warranting serious, if regionally distinctive, discussion in the context of authoritarian regimes in East Asia.[30]

The link between legality and legitimacy in authoritarian regimes may be – and in East Asia has been – reinforced by regimes' efforts to promote legality for instrumental reasons that concern downstream effects. When an authoritarian regime pledges to rely on laws to punish and deter state-disapproved behavior, encourage market-regarding economic activities, or define parameters of authorized and permissible actions by state or party-state actors, the regime may bind itself to the mast – even if not very tightly. To betray those promises by wantonly disregarding laws and bypassing legal institutions – or changing laws and restructuring legal organs too lightly, too often, or too self-servingly – is to undermine the credibility of regime commitments more generally, and, thus, to imperil the regime's legitimacy (as well as its more tangible capacity). To the extent that an authoritarian regime's promises about law tap into law's power to legitimate, the delegitimating impact of betrayal of those legality-linked pledges can be all the greater.

Last but not least, legality can contribute to legitimacy by partly transforming political conflicts into legal ones. When a regime tolerates administrative litigation, or civil lawsuits to address regulatory failure, it avoids potential threats to the state's authority by fragmenting discontents that might otherwise become foci for organized political challenges

---

[30] See Ramraj and Thiruvengadam, *Emergency Powers in Asia*; Carl Schmitt, *Four Articles: 1931–1938*, trans. Simona Draghici (Washington, DC: Plutarch Press, 1999); David Dyzenhaus, *The Compulsion of Legality* (Oxford: Blackwell, 2008). Pils discusses a Schmittian turn in the Chinese regime's view of law (see Chapter 3 in this volume).

to the state's right, or fitness, to rule and demands for political change. It also diverts those disputes into processes where outcomes disappointing to the discontented can be defended as legally legitimate – and thus made less threatening to regime legitimacy.

Constitutional law in authoritarian East Asia provides examples of law's potential utility in protecting regime legitimacy by reducing politicization of potentially threatening discontent. As Weitseng Chen notes in his chapter, Taiwan's Judicial Yuan helped defuse demands for democratic change during the authoritarian era by channeling challenges into protracted legal processes and issuing constitutional interpretations that upheld suspensions of democratic national elections as constitutional. In Hong Kong, the Basic Law-created roles for the Special Administrative Region Court of Final Appeal's powers of final review, and, above it, the National People's Congress Standing Committee's quasi-judicial power of formal interpretation, show an attempt to "legalize," and thereby defang, contentious political disputes. Beijing and its allies in Hong Kong portray rejection of calls for greater democracy not as reflecting political preferences or calculations by central authorities but, rather, as what a "proper" reading of the quasi-constitutional document dictates. Although not always successful, this approach seeks to sublimate pro-democracy or pro-autonomy popular politics into questions of legal–textual interpretation, which occurs through a process that Beijing has kept under its ultimate control and views in highly positivist terms.

This process presumably sought to reduce, and may have reduced, Occupy Central/Umbrella Movement-like mass actions that might otherwise have occurred. Campbell and Cullen's analysis is consistent with this reading of law's legitimating, stabilizing function. They find that political conflicts in post-reversion Hong Kong – centered primarily on constitutional issues – have been less disruptive than they were in the final years of colonial rule, and than many pundits had predicted for the post-1997 era, because the SAR had inherited a robust constitutionalism (of a Diceyan type) from British colonial rule. Davis is skeptical about the durability of this arrangement in a contemporary era of heightened conflict over, and social demand for, democracy in Hong Kong. Mobrand's analysis of Korea is broadly similar. He argues that a legalistic ethos, with roots early in the authoritarian era and reflected in laws governing party and electoral politics, supported authoritarian legality in the political sphere that underpinned a distinctive claim to legitimacy by the regime.

In the clearly authoritarian context of reform-era China, something similar has at times been afoot. Administrative litigation against state entities, other aspects of administrative law promoting some degree of government accountability, brief flirtations with making individual constitutional rights justiciable, anti-corruption drives that rely partly on law, other uses of law to address officials' abuse of citizens, and some tolerance for citizens' extrajudicial invocation of legal norms to seek discretionary redress (such as "letters and visits" to government offices) are examples of how law's (limited) legitimacy seemingly promises a means for the regime to enhance its (contested) legitimacy.[31]

1.2.5   Responding to Demand

Authoritarian regimes may accept greater legality in response to pressure from below, or from within. Such accommodation may be necessary for regime survival, and, in the more ordinary course, for securing the cooperation and acquiescence that even nondemocratic rulers need from their societies and their subordinates or near-peers in the ruling elite. This "demand for legality" can come – and in authoritarian East Asia has come – from diverse sources.

Social pressure for greater legality has been a challenge for many of the developmentalist authoritarian states in East Asia, especially when economic success has come through international openness and market-oriented policies. Whether or not substantial rule by law, or rule of law, is necessary for economic development (or economic development above a certain level), greater wealth can, and often does, lead to pressure for greater legality.[32]

In much of authoritarian East Asia, economic development has produced large middle classes. They have property interests that they want to see protected, and typically seek greater autonomy and control over their lives. Domestic and foreign investors – important to the economy, but

---

[31] See generally, Jacques deLisle, "Legalization without Democratization in China under Hu Jintao," in Cheng Li (ed.), *China's Changing Political Landscape* (Washington, DC: Brookings, 2008), 185–211.

[32] On contemporary China as an example, see Jacques deLisle, "Law and Democracy in China: A Complicated Relationship," in Shelley Rigger, Lynn White, and Kate Zhou (eds.), *Democratization in China, Korea and Southeast Asia* (Abingdon, UK: Routledge, 2014), 126–40; on the correlation between rule of law and economic development in East Asia, see Randall Peerenboom, *China Modernizes* (Oxford: Oxford University Press, 2007), 33–77.

often politically vulnerable in authoritarian states – have similar aims and worries.[33] Authoritarian regimes can address these concerns and demands through greater legality in the form of property law, contract law, environmental protection regulations, legal redress for expropriation or arbitrary behavior by state actors, relatively reliable courts, and so on.

Demands for greater legality also may come from economic "losers" in developing, economically rapidly changing, East Asian authoritarian states. Even in contemporary China, with its comparatively weak legal order, those who have not fared well during the reform era – peasants whose land is taken for development, poor urbanites whose houses are targeted for demolition and redevelopment, and victims of polluting factories, dangerous products, or abusive local officials – have turned to legal procedures or informally invoked legal norms to seek redress. In China, law may be the last resort of the desperate, or a slim hope for the otherwise hopeless, but it sometimes is seen as offering at least a weak weapon for the weak.

An analogous pattern can be found in more affluent East Asian societies. In Hong Kong and Taiwan, the legal norms set forth in constitutional documents took on normative force for the youthful protesters of the Umbrella and Sunflower movements, who saw threats to their economic futures and their political ideals, partly from authoritarian or authoritarianism-tinged politics. In Hong Kong, the Umbrella Movement, like many earlier political–economic protests, targeted the undemocratic Beijing and SAR governments. Although Taiwan is not authoritarian, Sunflower Movement protesters notably framed their actions as responses to resurgent authoritarian-style behavior by a government that tried to push a cross-Strait trade agreement through parliament. As Weitseng Chen argues, the Sunflower Movement fell within a tradition of activism by discontented students that dates to Taiwan's authoritarian era.

More broadly, authoritarian regimes' long-running endorsements of the rule of law and claims to operate rule-of-law government can raise social expectations about, and demands for, legality. In Hong Kong and Singapore, leaders and officials long have touted the rule of law as something that makes their polities special and successful. In reform-era China, massive campaigns to popularize legal knowledge and to proclaim a "socialist rule of law" system

---

[33] For this argument concerning China, see Yuhua Wang, *Tying the Autocrat's Hands: The Rise of the Rule of Law in China* (New York: Cambridge University Press, 2015).

or a commitment to "ruling the country through law" (terms with uncertain meaning and incomplete implementation) have had effects on social expectations. Regime actions can encourage, reinforce, or tolerate legality's normative pull in the societies they rule, and thereby increase social pressures to provide something more nearly approaching a rule of law. In China, frustrated efforts by individuals and social groups to deploy legal mechanisms promising government openness and accountability sometimes have provided new foundations, and capacity building, for those demanding more law-governed government.[34]

Legal elites can, and have, become sources of pressure for change that authoritarian regimes address through greater legality. In authoritarian East Asia, those educated in law and practicing law have become politically formidable critics of regimes and their excesses. They have done so, in part, due to regimes' own actions. In Taiwan, Weitseng Chen argues, traditions established under the Japanese colonial regime of authoritarian legality and continued by the postwar KMT regime – and Confucian notions of the political role of intellectuals – led to lawyers and legal arguments looming large in student-centered political activism during the final decades of authoritarian rule. Reform-era PRC authorities long have proclaimed commitments to building the "rule of law" (albeit with Chinese socialist characteristics), which has created political space for legal elites to push a pro-legality agenda, in ways that range from quotidian pursuit of a legal environment consistent with their professional self-image, to high-profile moves by legal academics to trigger constitutional review of problematic legal rules, to calls for radical political change.

Many of contemporary China's most prominent public intellectuals are lawyers and law professors who call for greater rule of law. Many of the most eminent and potent critics of the SAR government and central government policies in Hong Kong are lawyers, law professors, and law students. Turning points in the erosion of authoritarian rule in Taiwan and Korea were reactions against highly political uses of criminal justice against pro-democracy and pro-legality dissidents for incidents in Kaohsiung and Kwangju and, later, the eve-of-full-democratization student protests in Taipei that led to the repeal of two special laws from the martial law period. A leading lawyer for the Kaohsiung defendants (Chen Shui-bian) would become Taiwan's first democratically elected president

---

[34] See, for example, Greg Distelhorst, "The Power of Empty Promises: Quasi-Democratic Institutions and Activism in China," *Comparative Political Studies* 50(4) (2017): 464–98.

from the opposition Democratic Progressive Party, which had grown out of a movement opposing authoritarian rule. Sometimes, idiosyncratic and path-dependent features are significant. For example, Weitseng Chen argues, student activists and their scholar allies stressed legality, and law-focused means, partly because more purely political approaches had been claimed by the DPP.

Absent concessions to legal elite and broader public calls for greater legality, more fundamental challenges to authoritarian regimes may arise. Discontent might fester into demands, and social movements, for system-transforming reform. As authoritarian leadership groups across East Asia appear to have recognized (as far back as the Meiji constitution-makers, Ginsburg argues, and carrying through to China today), legality holds some promise of substituting for – and preempting – more fundamental democratic change.[35] Many of the functions that make democracy appealing to publics and (sometimes) an effective form of governance might be performed by law, legal procedures, and legal institutions within an authoritarian political order. These include: holding wayward state actors to account (including through a somewhat independent judiciary), communicating popular views about failed or disliked government policies to ruling elites (including as expressed through law-governed mechanisms such as litigation and not-fully-democratic parliaments or elections), and implementing, through law, policies that align with preferences and interests of politically salient social groups. Perhaps partly reflecting such verities, or East Asian authoritarian rulers' perception of them, cotemporary East Asian authoritarian states score higher on "rule of law" indices than on indices of democracy, and their rule of law scores are generally dragged down by weaker performances law's democracy-related aspects.[36]

Movement toward legality may come from within the regime, including legal elites inside the state. In some East Asian authoritarian regimes, lawyers who staff state institutions – including courts – have been key proponents of greater legality, albeit with mixed results. Taiwan's constitutional court played a key role in the transition to constitutional, democratic governance, including by requiring election of parliament by the Taiwanese public. Established under the U.S. Occupation-imposed democratic-regime-establishing constitution, Japan's Supreme

---

[35] See generally, deLisle, "Law and Democracy in China."
[36] Kaufmann and Kray, *World Bank Worldwide Governance Indicators*; Peerenboom, *China Modernizes*, 26–81.

Court in its early days began issuing rulings that upheld constitutional rights associated with democratic governance, sometimes looking to international norms.

In Hong Kong, the Court of Final Appeal sought to expand judicial power in an early post-reversion case concerning the right of abode (wherein the CFA asserted authority to interpret national-level law), only to be rebuffed by central authorities in collaboration with the local government. Two decades later, preemption of SAR judicial proceedings – against the backdrop of broader concerns about the erosion of judicial autonomy – became a focal point in the controversy surrounding an NPC-Standing Committee Interpretation of the Basic Law that led to the ouster of two pro-autonomy legislators-elect.

Even in the PRC, courts sometimes have pushed to expand law's empire. The Supreme People's Court issued a short-lived decision (in the Qi Yuling case) approving direct judicial application of a constitutional provision on individual rights, and a provincial high court (in the Henan Seeds case) asserted powers akin to judicial review to treat as invalid local rules for nonconformity to higher law. More broadly, reformers within the Chinese judicial system, including presidents of the Supreme People's Court, have sought to expand law's ambit through greater insulation of judicial decision making from political intervention.

Judges have not been the only actors within the state favoring legality in authoritarian and transitional regimes in East Asia. Especially where Weberian rational authority – cast partly as legality – has grown within the state, officials and functionaries can, and do, become constituents for increased legality. Some perform distinctively legal work. Others understand their not-specifically-legal functions as structured – and facilitated – by law or law-like rules. Legality thus can become a habit or take on a high degree of normativity within the regime.

Many who staff the state in Hong Kong and Singapore have seen no insoluble contradiction between strong commitment to the rule of law and serving in an authoritarian government. Su presents an intriguing example of this phenomenon in authoritarian Taiwan's law-governed elections, attributing the success of election law, and finding foundations for later law-governed democratic governance, in the habits instilled in state staff who performed such seemingly mundane tasks as operating polling stations and counting ballots. Mobrand offers a broadly analogous, but less benign, account of how the operation of laws and institutions regulating elections in pre-1987 Korea created expectations and habits of legality in the political sphere that persisted within the state and among political elites into the democratic era.

Authoritarian rulers' choices about reforms may reflect their own subjective preferences for legality, apart from (and even contrary to) calculations of self-interest. It may be less common for rule of law, or pro-legality, norms to gain normative force with top leaders in an authoritarian regime than among the populace or state institutions. But, as Mark Tushnet has argued, it can – or at least could – happen as a feature of "authoritarian constitutionalism."[37] Tan's and Chen's accounts of Singapore depict a regime that is generally consistent with that paradigm.

Legality's appeal to those at or near the apex of power in authoritarian regimes may also reflect law's potential to preserve more tangible self-interest. Legal or law-like restraints on political contestation – factional conflict, succession struggles, appointment and advancement decisions, and the like – can be attractive to all but the most reckless and ambitious among authoritarian elites. A striking case may be reform-era China, where traumatic experiences of life-and-death conflicts for political power at many levels of the party-state during the Cultural Revolution cast a long shadow. Much of the impetus for the turn to law and the promises of enhanced legality may be reactions to the final decades of the Mao era. Xi's constitutional amendment eliminating term limits has been so fraught partly because it seems to question that historical lesson. Less dramatically, some groups within an authoritarian ruling elite may gain, relative to their rivals in intra-elite competition, from greater legality, as Su finds in considering election law in Taiwan.

Finally, support or demand for greater legality may come from abroad. Rule-of-law ideals – instilled through education abroad, carried by transnational flows of ideas (including by the global NGOs that Kellogg examines), bequeathed by colonial rulers, or disseminated through other means – have taken root in authoritarian polities across East Asia.

Sometimes a system supporting a high level of legality can be imposed by a foreign power. Japan's liberal and democratic postwar constitutional order was founded under an occupation regime after toppling authoritarian regime. The PRC-U.K. Joint Declaration made treaty-like commitments (implemented through the PRC-enacted Basic Law) to preserve and in some ways enhance (particularly in democracy-related and civil liberties-related areas) a legal order for Hong Kong that had been built by British colonial authorities and that was much more liberal

---

[37] Tushnet, "Authoritarian Constitutionalism."

and state-power constraining than Beijing allowed in the rest of China. The chronic controversies over interpretation and implementation of those promises is a testament to how important they are to both sides. Singapore has sustained a robust (if uneven) rule of law that was created by a now-departed colonial ruler that, like its successor, was an authoritarian regime.

Less direct foreign influence may push authoritarian regimes in the same direction. Pressure from Washington and perceptions of the need to shore up US support (especially as the Cold War waned) supported legal reforms for democratic elections in Taiwan and Korea. In the nineteenth century, Western powers' preconditions for treating China and Japan as juridical equals helped drive Western-style domestic legal reforms in Japan and China. Nationalist, modernizing reformers in Meiji Japan and Qing China saw laws and related institutions based on Western models as vital to their quest for power (and even national survival) and wealth (now called development). Latter day echoes of these phenomena have persisted as reform-era China and, later, Vietnam adopted laws and supporting institutions attuned to global capitalist standards, and the expectations of foreign investors and trading partners, in pursuing economic development.

Accommodating impetuses – from society, elites, foreign sources, or ruler preferences – for more legality is not without risk or cost for authoritarian regimes. But it may be preferable to alternatives. Heeding middle-class calls to protect economic interests and personal autonomy, offering law-based relief to desperate or anxious citizens, giving those who have absorbed pro-legality values more of a place and a stake in the system, acceding to demands and preferences of pro-legality constituencies within the regime, or acquiescing in externally imposed or demanded legality need not pose an immediate or existential threat to authoritarian rule, and can mitigate other, possibly greater dangers to the regime.

Authoritarian rulers' moves toward greater legality need not be (and in East Asia have not always been) so calculating. Powerful forces for legality can build gradually, sometimes encouraged by the regime's tolerance for modest development of law or by an inherited rule-of-law legacy, sometimes emerging from the lived experience of social groups and elites inside or outside the regime. These phenomena may help explain why regimes make choices about legality that, often unwittingly, put authoritarian rule at risk, and why discerning the prospects for authoritarian legality is difficult.

1.3 Whither?

How sustainable is authoritarian legality in East Asia? The variations in authoritarian legality across countries, aspects of legality, and over time in East Asia suggest that several pathways are possible. The chapters in this book offer examples of, and arguments for, some of them.

First, authoritarian regimes with significant legality may prove durable and adaptable. Ginsburg points out that the authoritarian constitutional order established under the Meiji endured until the troubled democracy of the Taisho era, and did not fully disappear until World War II. Hong Kong and Singapore have impressive, longstanding, and ongoing track records of legality. Campbell and Cullen find in post-reversion Hong Kong remarkably resilient and effective constitutionalism and legality that had been established under authoritarian colonial rule (and thrived because they proved congruent with local society). In the British and SAR periods, they argue, the legal order withstood numerous political stresses, largely because Hong Kong had achieved a robust rule of law, fairly distributed prosperity, political stability, and a legitimate nondemocratic political order (and partly because, to many Hong Kongers, pro-democracy advocates seemed to endanger those accomplishments). Even for those who, like Davis, reject so sanguine an account, the durability of authoritarian legality through a tumultuous history and wrenching change of sovereignty is striking, as is the backhanded compliment paid to legality by the adherence to the legal forms of Basic Law interpretation by the NPC Standing Committee during heated controversies concerning democratic reform.

Tan argues that Singapore has achieved a hardy form of constitutionalism in the absence of (over-idealized) liberal democracy. Jianlin Chen discerns in the judicial invalidation of detention without trial and constitutional amendment to permit similar practices, an illustration of the regime's commitment to constitutionalism along with maintaining authoritarian rule. In Chen's account, it is significant that the regime followed lawful procedures of constitutional amendment and minimized harm to judicial independence and autonomy consistent with achieving the government's goals. Weitseng Chen and Su find, in Taiwan's legal history, a growing normativity of law within the authoritarian KMT order that appears to have helped sustain authoritarian legality, even as that same legal normativity laid foundations for democratic transformation.

On some readings, reform-era China's legal development holds out the prospect of continuing authoritarianism with a level of legality that is significant, and perhaps ultimately rising, despite unevenness, limitations, and vulnerability.[38] As Fu and Dowdle see it, authoritarian legality and the authoritarian state are mutually reinforcing in China (and elsewhere). Vietnam – where efforts to increase legality, governance under law, and constitutionalism have not encountered some of the impediments and setbacks that have occurred in China, and where Confucian, colonial, and even Soviet traditions of authoritarian legality were less thoroughly repudiated – may offer a more hopeful variation on the same theme, as Ha and Nicholson's account suggests.

Second, authoritarianism may transform, and be replaced by democratic governance coupled with impressive legality, including full-fledged liberal rule of law. That was the trajectory in Japan (punctuated by wartime defeat) and Taiwan and Korea (where the transition was less wrenching). Tan argues that Singapore is already close to the line separating authoritarian and liberal democratic rule, and that its electoral system and relatively modest restrictions on political speech and media leave open the possibility of an opposition party victory. Gradual and peaceful transition toward full-fledged democracy, with continuingly robust legality, remains a hope of advocates for political change, and a possibility suggested by optimistic analysts, in Singapore and Hong Kong.

Choices by authoritarian regimes can set a polity with a relatively high level of legality along this path. Su's account of the regime's implementation of authoritarian-era election laws in Taiwan is consistent with this paradigm. Growing fears in Beijing about pressure for political democratization in Hong Kong or, more remotely, the Chinese mainland if high levels of legality are maintained (Hong Kong) or created (the PRC) reflect a sense that such a trajectory is plausible. Authoritarian rulers and their regimes may be akin to frogs in boiling water, or prison escapees who have reached the edge of a cliff: had they appreciated the trajectory, they might have resisted the moves toward greater legality and political change that now spell mortal peril – whether they now recognize the danger or not.

The role of the constitutional court in advancing democratization in Taiwan, the transformational impact of the US-imposed constitution in

---

[38] See, generally, Peerenboom, *China Modernizes*, esp. 257–81; Peerenboom, *China's Long March*; deLisle, "Law and Democracy in China."

postwar Japan, and the impetus for democracy that came from political prosecutions of dissidents after mass pro-democracy incidents in Taiwan and Korea, are disparate examples of how legal institutions and social movements can push systems of authoritarian legality toward liberal-democratic politics and legality. In a similar vein, Weitseng Chen argues that Taiwan's tradition of law-centered student political activism contributed to constitutionalist, democratizing political change (without a loss of legality). Su and Mobrand argue that laws governing political parties and elections during the authoritarian eras in Taiwan and Korea framed transitions to democracy (with the law-on-the-books in Korea undergoing strikingly little change). In Mainland China and Hong Kong, politicians, public intellectuals, and activists drawn from the ranks of lawyers, or those who have made the rule of law a defining element on agendas for democratic reform, have been principal advocates for less authoritarian governance – albeit with limited success so far.

Each of the five functionalist promises of legality for authoritarian regimes contains a threat to those regimes and, in turn, an opening for movement toward liberal democracy and the rule of law. The tools law provides to maintain social order and suppress actual, potential, or imagined opponents can create martyrs and alienate broader publics who see such uses of law as cynically political or personally threatening. An authoritarian regime's embrace of law for its own purposes can lead people to expect, and demand, more of the law, including greater fairness, restraints on state (or party) powers, and public input into laws' content. Cross-national correlations among affluence, the rule of law, and democratic politics – and the trajectory of Korea and Taiwan and, more incipiently, Hong Kong, Singapore and, perhaps, China's better-off urban areas – point to pressures for political change that may follow from a turn to legality in the successful pursuit of economic development.

Attempts to increase Weberian, or Leninist, discipline within the state or party-state to strengthen the sinews and the neural pathways of authoritarian rule can backfire. Moves in China to combat corruption and impose systems of "responsibility" for officials (including judges) – accelerating under Xi but with earlier roots – have spawned problems of state weakness: officials shirk duties to avoid "errors" that could devastate their lives and careers; or they cave in to the local public's – or "the mob's" – demands and preempt complaints to higher levels that could spell trouble for local officials; or they try to pass all decisions – and thus responsibility for "wrong" choices – up to higher levels. Amid such dysfunction, pressures for still-greater legal accountability and political change easily mount. Success in building a more law-governed and, thus, more capable state does not mean an authoritarian regime will not face formidable demands for deeper political reform. Now-democratic Taiwan and Korea, perhaps-increasingly-democratic Singapore, and now-pressed-to-democratize Hong Kong all once fared well as stable, law-governed authoritarian polities.

Efforts to tap law's legitimating power risk making laws, legal institutions, legal elites, and law-oriented thinking more legitimate in a society under authoritarian rule, with attendant perils for the regime. This dynamic of legitimation is likely part of what lies behind the significant roles of courts, lawyers, legal intellectuals, and law-invoking citizens in achieving democratic change in East Asian states that have transitioned from authoritarianism, or that may be on the path to doing so. Jianlin Chen suggests that even measures that seem questionable from a constitutionalist or rule-of-law perspective (such as the Singapore government's amending the constitution to overcome an adverse judicial ruling) can help to lay a rule-of-law foundation for more democratic rule. Kellogg argues that the PRC regime today may be losing legitimacy at home and abroad because of its repressive legal regime for NGOs, many of which have agendas that align with liberal legality. Pils's account of contemporary China discerns a surprising persistence of liberal constitutional discourse in an increasingly hostile ideological environment under Xi, perhaps because of the regime's earlier efforts to build up, and draw upon, law's legitimacy. Ha and Nicholson discern a broadly similar pattern in Vietnam's modest discourse on constitutionalism.

An authoritarian regime's turn to law to address mounting demand for public participation in politics can empower civil society (to the regime's chagrin, as Kellogg and Fu and Dowdle address) and create prototypes for polity-wide democracy (as illustrated by competitive elections for posts with limited power that Su examines in Taiwan). More broadly, an authoritarian regime's use of law to address pressure for public input or accountability can raise legal competencies, commitments to legality, and expectations of legality in society, among legal elites, and within the regime that create constituencies for more robust rule of law and democratic political change. Kellogg's account of NGO law provides a glimpse into such phenomena, and regime worries, in China.

Third, an authoritarian political order can decay, taking whatever legal order – usually a limited and fragile one – down with it. This is one possible outcome when the double-edged sword that legality presents to authoritarian regimes cuts sharply against those who wield it to try to preserve themselves. Or any number of perils – many having little connection to law – from within or abroad may lead to political disorder and systemic failure in an authoritarian regime. China in the decades preceding the foundation of the People's Republic, and Cambodia during its most troubled post-Indochina War period, are stark examples of what can happen to politics and law amid degeneration of an authoritarian regime. In the more hyperbolic accounts of pro-regime critics, the Umbrella Movement in Hong Kong (as Davis discusses) and the Sunflower Movement in Taiwan raised the prospect that groups calling for greater democracy, and criticizing perceived erosions of legality, would undermine law and political order in one polity that was undemocratic and another that was a recently consolidated, post-authoritarian democracy.[39]

Fourth, authoritarian rule may persist while legality wilts (or fails to bloom) in inhospitable environments of illiberal, undemocratic politics. In Hong Kong, as Davis notes, worries abound that the rule of law may be declining. Economic integration with the Mainland and its less rule-of-law-oriented business order, and repeated rejection of aspirations for democratic political progress (by Basic Law interpretations, among other means) are, to Hong Kong critics (many of them pro-democracy lawyers, lawyer-politicians, law professors, and law students), signs of a future that will remain politically authoritarian but become less law-governed.

Concerns about, and critiques of, limits to the rule of law, or rule by law, in China have been constant refrains throughout the reform era.[40] Recent developments – particularly under Xi – have made more vivid and pressing the specter of persisting or resurgent authoritarianism with crabbed or declining legality. Examples include: enacting an expansive national security law giving state authorities extensive power and discretion; imposing more strict and potentially arbitrary legal limits on foreign and domestic NGOs; cracking down severely on rights protection lawyers; restricting law-centered mechanisms (including collective litigation) to pursue society-driven changes; charging political activists with "pocket offenses" (for minor, vaguely defined disruptive activities);

---

[39] See Jones (ed.), *Law and Politics*.

[40] See, for example, Minxin Pei, *China's Trapped Transition* (Cambridge, MA: Harvard University Press, 2006), 66–72; Yuanyuan Shen "Conceptions and Receptions of Legality," in Karen G. Turner, James V. Feinerman, and R. Kent Guy (eds.), *The Limits of the Rule of Law in China* (Seattle: University of Washington Press, 2000), 20–44; Jiangyu Wang, "The Rule of Law in China," *Singapore Journal of Legal Studies* (2004): 347–89.

relying heavily on extralegal procedures by party or hybrid party-state supervision organs to address official corruption; increasing traditional and social media censorship (as Fu and Dowdle describe); marginalizing *tizhnei* ("inside the system") legal reformers and intellectuals; fostering (albeit not by design) a sense that the legal system will tolerate indefinitely an economic playing field tilted in favor of state-linked and well-connected firms; reemphasizing "stability maintenance" and "social management" over legal rights and procedures; adopting martial law-like, human rights-violating responses to ethnic unrest (or potential unrest); and eliminating presidential term limits.

Authoritarian legality faces the compound problems of ambivalent regime commitments to pursuing an inherently difficult task. It may prove untenable for the autocrat to tie his own hands with legal restraints, and this may place beyond reach the order-preserving, state capacity-supporting, economic development-promoting, and legitimacy-building contributions that law and legal institutions can, in principle, offer. For Singapore, Jianlin Chen cautions against unrealistically idealistic expectations about the role an authoritarian government will cede to courts in politically sensitive matters, and argues that premature or overreaching efforts by courts to resolve political matters can bring destructive blowback from an authoritarian regime. For Hong Kong, Davis argues that the preexisting rule of law regime and Beijing's promises in the Basic Law and Joint Declaration may not survive post-reversion erosion. In Vietnam, Ha and Nicholson find, continuing party dominance has fundamentally compromised efforts at constitutionalism. As recent PRC experiences with courts that bow to public pressure in high-profile criminal (and even civil) cases appear to show, steering political disputes or politically fraught issues to courts may yield not more legitimate outcomes but more delegitimized courts.

In China, and other authoritarian polities in East Asia, a regime's narrowly instrumentalist legalism may be doomed from the start, or too thin to survive the resulting stresses, when law appears to falter in fulfilling expected roles in advancing regime goals.[41] For Fu and Dowdle, "zones of exception" that place essential – often political – matters beyond law's reach, reliance on alternative institutions that deprive legal institutions of their jurisdiction, subordination of legal institutions

[41] deLisle, "Rule of Law with Xi-Era Characteristics"; Benjamin L. Liebman, "China's Law and Stability Paradox," in Jacques deLisle and Avery Goldstein (eds.), *China's Challenges* (Philadelphia: University of Pennsylvania Press, 2014), 157–77.

to political rule, and a debilitating gap between the law on the books and law in practice are not bugs, but features, of legality under authoritarian rule – ones inconsistent with all but the thinnest form of legality. Pils points to the waning of a somewhat legal-liberal and rationalist conception of law relative to a "rule by fear" technique that subdues not only its immediate targets but also others who might criticize, or seek to change, the regime. In these conditions, law may be a weapon wielded by the regime, but it lacks the autonomy and distinctiveness needed for rule by law and, in turn, conditions for legality to provide the support that it might offer an authoritarian regime.

Alternatively, legality may not prove necessary, or even very useful, for authoritarian rulers. This might be true for any of authoritarian legality's five functional virtues. The use of show trials by totalitarian or nearly lawless regimes (arguably exemplified by China through the dawn of the post-Mao era) to destroy and deter political opposition shows that legal forms can advance regime ends without accepting even the limited constraints of weak forms of authoritarian legality.[42] Sometimes, even thin pretenses of legality are eschewed when suppressing dissent and maintaining order. Analyses of reform-era China's remarkable economic progress under authoritarian rule that conclude that law has made little contribution, and that weak legality facilitated development, reject strong links between law and development. On many accounts, other exemplars of the East Asian Model relied much less heavily on the rule of law for the economy than did Hong Kong and Singapore.[43]

Leninist regimes, and perhaps softer authoritarian regimes as well, may be able to rely on nonlegal means to discipline state actors and strengthen state capacity. That appears to be an expectation inherent in Chinese Communist Party drives against corruption, including the aggressive one launched under Xi, with criminal law and courts playing marginal roles in a process dominated by intra-party or merged party-state disciplinary

---

[42] See Judith N. Shklar, *Legalism: Law, Morals and Political Trials* (Cambridge, MA: Harvard University Press, 1986), 164, 209–19; *A Great Trial in Chinese History* (Beijing: New World Press, 1981) (trial of the "Lin Biao Clique" and the Gang of Four at the dawn of China's reform era, melding elements of communist "show trials" and incipient claims to positivist legality in criminal law).

[43] See, Clarke, "Economic Development and the Rights Hypothesis"; Upham, "From Demsetz to Deng"; Katharina Pistor and Philip A. Wellons, *The Role of Law and Legal Institutions in Asian Economic Development, 1960–1995* (New York: Oxford University Press, 1999); Tom Ginsburg, "Does Law Matter for Economic Development? Evidence from East Asia," *Law and Society Review* 34(3) (2000): 829–56.

bodies.[44] A kindred expectation may underlie the Chinese regime's apparent preference for informal and nonjudicial mechanisms: seeking expert
input, receiving ad hoc citizen complaints, tolerating (limited) muckraking
journalism, and combining selective severe punishment (especially of
leaders) with side-payments and cooptation of mass protestors or incipient
social movements.

Law may not be indispensable, or very important, for legitimation for
some authoritarian regimes. Observers have noted a "turn against" law in
China in recent years that implies a belief that legality is not necessary for
legitimacy and may be corrosive of legitimacy.[45] Economic performance-
based legitimacy has had an impressive run in reform-era China and
economically more advanced authoritarian polities in East Asia.
Nationalism – particularly in the form of authoritarian regimes portraying themselves as guarantors of success or survival in a challenging or
hostile world – has offered an alternative, non-law-related basis for
legitimacy to some East Asian authoritarian regimes. Other alternatives
to partly law-based legitimacy can be found in varied East Asian authoritarian cases: Singapore's model of government by meritocratic technocrats and chilliness toward Western-style litigious and individualist
conceptions of rights; China's embrace – especially under Xi – of
a muscular foreign policy that challenges the existing international
order and a domestic governance model that rejects Western legal and
political values; and the besieged nationalism, with extremely low legality, of North Korea. As Pils details, Xi's China has returned to identifying
and targeting "enemies" – stressing reasons to fear them and the need to
defeat them – to legitimize authoritarian powers and justify harsh measures that do not differentiate clearly between legal and extralegal means.

Social demand for liberal-democratic and rule-of-law governance may
prove fragile or manageable. Although Hong Kong has had mounting
troubles in law and politics, Singapore remains stable, maintaining
legitimacy amid relatively modest pressure for political reform (as Tan
and Jianlin Chen address). Surveys of East Asian states that have transitioned to democracy (including Japan, Korea, and Taiwan) show low
trust in government officials (19–39 percent), middling satisfaction with
how democracy works (56–68 percent), and weak agreement that
democracy is always preferable to other forms of government

---

[44] Jacques deLisle, "Xi Jinping's Impact on China's Legal Development," *Asan Forum* 4(5)
(2016).
[45] Minzner, "China's Turn against Law"; Benjamin L. Liebman, "Legal Reform: China's
Law–Stability Paradox," *Daedalus* 143(2) (2014): 96–109.

(46–65 percent).[46] At East Asia's southern fringe, Duterte's Philippines suggests the vulnerability of commitments to liberal legality and the potential appeal of a populist leadership style reminiscent of past authoritarian rule – a pattern familiar from Eastern and Central European states. Ostensibly populist politics and democratic disillusionment in the United States and Western Europe point to possibly analogous trends in states that have been models – in both the political–aspirational and scholarly–analytical sense of the term – for reformists in East Asian authoritarian states.

Fifth, traces of authoritarianism may endure in a legal order even after a democratic transition. Courts, other legal institutions, and legal doctrines may maintain authoritarian mindsets and approaches after the political regimes that shaped them have transformed. In important respects, legal change may lag political change. Such tendencies are not ubiquitous or pervasive, as is illustrated by assertive, pro-liberal-rights stances of judicial decisions in post-reversion Hong Kong, and democracy-promoting and liberal-rights-protecting judicial interpretations by Taiwan's constitutional court. But they are important phenomena, possibly manifested in the deference and protection courts in post-authoritarian East Asian states sometimes accord to state power and discretion. Nakano and Mobrand argue that aspects of authoritarian legality linger in contemporary Japan and Korea. Nakano finds a "bureaucratic authoritarian legality" rooted in the prewar order and persisting – thanks to continuities in institutions, personnel, and political habits – until administrative-legal reforms of the 1990s, and – more controversially – a "neoliberal authoritarian legality" that blunts political democracy today. Mobrand describes Korea as retaining "authoritarian legality after authoritarianism" in laws on elections and political parties that have remained largely unchanged despite democratization in the late 1980s. A broadly similar but more limited argument might hold for Taiwan, where the constitutional court has been restrained in striking down decisions by the political branches, even when it has found state actions constitutionally troubling (e.g. when ruling on the issue of one person simultaneously serving as vice president and premier).

That post-authoritarian legality should remain, to some degree, residually authoritarian should not be surprising. Courts and other legal

---

[46] Asian Barometer Survey (third wave), www.asianbarometer.org/survey/survey-results. Data for the Philippines is similar, generally at the lower end, except for a higher (51 percent) level of trust in government officials.

institutions often avoid direct subjection to the wrenching changes that affect the organs of the state that are more often the immediate targets of demands for political change. Also, law and legal institutions are, in important respects, conservative institutions for which radical change is not the norm – a trait that is part of what makes legality appealing to authoritarians (as well as to some proponents of the rule of law).

Other logical possibilities exist, but the patterns described here have solid grounding in East Asian experiences. Past and possible future trajectories suggest that "authoritarian legality" remains tenable in some forms and under some conditions in East Asia. But authoritarian regimes' likely ambivalence toward legality, the difficulty of achieving and sustaining authoritarian legality, pressures exerted by economic and social change, and demands from social and political forces, present serious challenges. Authoritarian legality's viability also surely varies by national and historical circumstances and the version of authoritarian legality that an East Asian regime pursues or achieves.

PART II

Authoritarian Legality

Past and Present

Showcase of Authoritarian Legality and Its Potential Erosion

China

The Concept of Authoritarian Legality

The Chinese Case

HUALING FU AND MICHAEL DOWDLE

2.1 Introduction

Authoritarian legality can be defined narrowly to mean legal norms of authoritarian states and the process in which those legal norms are implemented. It is common ground that, in authoritarian states, there is no formal mechanism for meaningful competition for political power and that authoritarian leaders monopolize political power and are ready to use repression, co-optation, and other means to ensure regime survival.[1] Authoritarian leaders control political discourse and limit the scope of political expression and laws are frequently used, strategically and instrumentally, for the purpose of political repression and co-optation.[2] The hallmark of authoritarian legality, in Tushnet's terms, is that leaders make decisions without meaningful legal accountability.[3]

An authoritarian political system creates authoritarian legality, and it also evinces a distinctive legality in the otherwise authoritarian state (i.e. a unique normative and epistemic structure of the legal system and the way it interacts with the rest of the state and society). Authoritarian legality is, thus, an attribute and a subset of the authoritarian state, which is used to prevent and manage political challenges and to punish

---

[1] Jennifer Gandhi and Adam Przeworski, "Cooperation, Cooptation, and Rebellion Under Dictatorships," *Economics & Politics* 18(1) (2006): 1. For scholarship on state repression under authoritarian rule, see Milan W. Svolik, *The Politics of Authoritarian Rule* (Cambridge, UK: Cambridge University Press, 2012); Sheena Chestnut Greitens, *Dictators and Their Secret Police: Coercive Violence* (Cambridge, UK: Cambridge University Press, 2016).

[2] Steven Levitsky and Luan A. Way, *Competitive Authoritarianism: Hybrid Regimes after the Cold War* (New York: Cambridge University Press, 2010).

[3] Mark Tushnet, "Authoritarian Constitutionalism," *Cornell Law Review* 100(2) (2015): 391.

political enemies, real or imagined. While the law serves both the role of limiting state power and enhancing state powers in both democracies and authoritarian states, the use of law to enhance and legitimize state power and to control society is often regarded as the defining feature of authoritarianism. The line that demarcates permissible political space is more fluid, much less rules-based, and more uncertain in authoritarian states than in democracies.[4]

There is also a broader definition according to which authoritarian legality can develop characteristics of its own, independent of regime type. There is, thus, the possibility of a rise of authoritarian legality in democracies, where individual rights and freedom are limited in various degrees in the name of public order and state security. Here, authoritarian legality is used to capture an overwhelming illiberal or anti-liberal tendency that, in an "oppressive way," subordinates individual rights and freedom to statist and public interests, and is regarded as authoritarian because the new trend represents a significant departure from a rights-based and autonomous legal system.[5]

This chapter, using China as an example, aims at identifying the core features of authoritarian legality and its implementation and at studying the process of mutual reinforcement between the authoritarian state and authoritarian legality. It seeks to locate authoritarianism in Chinese law and discover authoritarian legality's wider and more nuanced spectrum and layers.

2.2   Framing Authoritarian Legality

It is now well established that authoritarian regimes are not necessarily hostile to legality and indeed have often embraced them strategically and used law proactively to meet internal and external needs. Commentators have studied the instrumental use of law to attract foreign investment; to facilitate market transactions; to create regime credibility and legitimacy; and improve governance broadly defined to include coordination of central–local relations, anti-corruption enforcement, and effective and predictable dispute resolution.[6] Law, therefore, interacts with authoritarian states at multiple entry points.

---

[4] Peter H. Solomon, "Courts and Judges in Authoritarian Regimes," *World Politics* 60(1) (2007): 122.

[5] Turkuler Isilesel, "Between Text and Context: Turkey's Tradition of Authoritarian Constitutionalism," *International Journal of Constitutional Law* 11(3) (2013): 702.

[6] Tom Ginsburg and Tamir Moustafa, *Rule by Law: The Politics of Courts in Authoritarian Regimes* (Cambridge, UK: Cambridge University Press, 2008); Tamir Moustafa, "Law and

Resorting to law in authoritarian states is often said to be "instrumental," "half-hearted," and "partial" in the sense that these regimes make selective use of law to suit a particularistic agenda. There is little or no normative commitment to law and legality. The particular function of legality adopted by different authoritarian regimes at different historic times may vary, but ultimately serves the overriding function of regime survival and the extension of power. It is partial because the commitment to legality is a limited one and the regime is consistently aware of the possibility that law, when put to use by civil society forces in an organized manner, may evolve into a social movement creating a cascading effect that may eventually spin out of control. In the same vein, legal institutions, when empowered and given a degree of autonomy, may develop a life of their own and change from its role of facilitating regime building to that of undermining the credibility and effectiveness of the regime. Gallagher points out that "[a]uthoritarian legality as an instrumental play for power and political stability is ultimately contradictory; as such 'rule of law' in autocracies is bounded, limited, and unstable."[7] A regime survival mentality requires flexibility, discretion, and a pragmatic approach to meet crises, real or perceived, but legality requires institutionalization, predictability, and certainty, which all function to tie the hands of autocrats. Authoritarian regimes, therefore, are torn between the two imperatives.[8] How have they managed the tension?

The spectrum of authoritarian legality is a long one, ranging from regimes with "sham constitutions"[9] that reduced law to irrelevance, to ones that give law a high degree of autonomy.[10] In Solomon's study of courts in authoritarian states, for example, there are four ideal types of courts according to their independence and the power that they wield. First,

Courts in Authoritarian Regimes," *Annual Review of Law and Social Science* 10 (2014): 281; Tushnet, "Authoritarian Constitutionalism," *Cornell Law Review*, 391. See also Chapter 1 in this volume.

[7] Mary E. Gallagher, *Authoritarian Legality in China: Law, Workers, and the State* (Cambridge, UK: Cambridge University Press, 2017), 62.

[8] See also Unger's classical study of the paradox of revolutionary legality: Roberto M. Unger, *Law in Modern Society* (New York: Free Press, 1976).

[9] Tom Ginsburg and Alberto Simpser, "Introduction: Constitutions in Authoritarian Regimes," in Tom Ginsburg and Alberto Simpser (eds.), *Constitutions in Authoritarian Regimes* (Cambridge, UK: Cambridge University Press, 2013); 1; David S. Law and Mila Versteeg, "Sham Constitutions," *California Law Review* 102(4) (2013): 863.

[10] Gordon Silverstein, "Singapore's Constitutionalism: A Model, But of What Sort?," *Cornell Law Review Online* 100 (2015): 1, cornelllawreview.org/clronline-issue/volume-100-october-2015; Tushnet, "Authoritarian Constitutionalism," 391.

there are the politically marginal courts, which encounter "multiple lines of dependency" and as a result are limited to resolving private disputes among ordinary citizens.[11] Courts have little role to play in limiting government powers. Chinese courts and those under the former and existing Communist system are representative of this category. Second, there is what the author refers to as "the Spanish solution," which is the creation of a fragmented court system where matters of importance to government are left to separate tribunals that are more vulnerable to political control, leaving an independent and strong judiciary with little to do.[12] The fate of regular courts in the Third Reich is a good example of this process. While the traditional courts retained a degree of professionalism and independence under Nazi rule, their jurisdiction was gradually taken away by the creation of tribunals, such as the People's Court and the Special Court that were under direct political control.[13] Similar practices were used in other authoritarian regimes to suppress political challenges.[14] A third model includes autonomous courts battling with authoritarian rulers and facing consequences. In this model, autonomous law and authoritarianism coexist during particular historical circumstances, leading ultimately to either judicial triumph or judicial defeat.[15] The periodical confrontation between lawyers and judges on the one hand and the regime on the other, as has occurred in Pakistan[16] and Malaysia,[17] offers excellent examples of courts in a struggle for autonomy in a larger authoritarian system. Finally, there are courts under authoritarianism with a relatively light touch[18] that are

[11] Solomon, "Courts and Judges," 430.

[12] Jose Toharia, "Judicial Independence in an Authoritarian Regime: The Case of Contemporary Spain," *Law and Society Review* 9(3) (1975): 475.

[13] Ingo Muller, *Hitler's Justice: The Courts of the Third Reich* (Cambridge, MA: Harvard University Press, 1991), 10; Hans Petter Gracer, *Judges against Justice: On Judges When the Rule of Law Is Under Attack* (Heidelberg: Springer, 2014).

[14] Ginsburg and Moustafa, *Rule by Law*; Richard Abel, *The Politics of Informal Justice, Volume Two* (New York: Academic Press, 1981).

[15] Peter H. Solomon, "Law and Courts in Authoritarian States," *International Encyclopedia of the Social & Behavioral Sciences* 2 (2015): 427.

[16] Human Rights Watch, *Destroying Legality: Pakistan's Crackdown on Lawyers and Judges*, vol. 19, no. 19, 2007 ed., www.hrw.org/sites/default/files/reports/pakistan1207web.pdf; Sahar Shafqat, "Civil Society and the Lawyers' Movement of Pakistan," *Law & Social Inquiry* 43 (2018): 889; Anil Kalhan, "'Gray Zone' Constitutionalism and the Dilemma of Judicial Independence in Pakistan," *Vanderbilt Journal of Transnational Law* 46(1) (2013): 1.

[17] Amanda Whiting, "Anwar Ibrahim's Conviction Lowers the Bar on the Malaysian Legal System," East Asia Forum, www.eastasiaforum.org/2015/04/13/anwar-ibrahims -conviction-lowers-the-bar-on-the-malaysian-legal-system

[18] Tushnet, "Authoritarian Constitutionalism," 391.

formally independent and powerful, but are subject to informal but effective political control in sensitive cases to ensure judicial compliance. For example, the heads of courts may use negative assessment of performance to ensure political obedience.[19]

These models capture broadly a wide spectrum of types of authoritarian legality and represent a horizontal variation in the degrees of authoritarianism. Moving into any particular authoritarian state and further pluralizing authoritarian legality,[20] one finds a hierarchical variation in a single authoritarian state. There are multiple narratives in the characterization of authoritarian legality. These narratives follow different logical paths, develop different institutional practices, and create different impacts on society and individuals in different areas of laws in different ways. They coexist even though they are internally contradictory.

2.3   Authoritarian Core

Authoritarian states that embrace law also create exceptions to law. In the name of state security broadly defined, authoritarian states carve out a zone of exception in which law is marginalized and legal rules are reduced to irrelevance or mere window-dressing. Political expedience governs what happens in the zone of exception. A defining characteristic of authoritarian legality is the existence of a dual system – the coexistence of a normative state where legal rules matter and a prerogative state where politics trumps.[21]

While the dual-state conceptualization is based on a concern for the security of the state, it has many variants and can be justified on particularistic grounds that reflect national characteristics. A dual state could be based on race (South Africa under apartheid); religion (Nazi Germany); or class (China and other communist states). There are different institutional designs to maintain the dual system. The best example is the internal security regime in some of the former British colonies such as Singapore;[22]

---

[19] Peter H. Solomon, "Judicial Power in Authoritarian States: The Russian Experiences," in Ginsburg and Moustafa (eds.), *Rule by Law*, 261; Peter H. Solomon, "Authoritarian Legality and Informal Practices: Judges, Lawyers and the State in Russia and China," *Communist and Post-Communist Studies* 43(4) (2010): 351.

[20] Tushnet, "Authoritarian Constitutionalism," 391.

[21] Ernst Fraenkel, *The Dual State: A Contribution to the Theory of Dictatorship* (New York: Oxford University Press, 2017); Carl Schmitt, *Political Theology: Four Chapters on the Concept of Sovereignty* (Chicago, IL: University of Chicago Press, 2005).

[22] Michael Hor, "Singapore's Anti-Terrorism Laws: Reality and Rhetoric," in Victor V. Ramraj, Michael Hor, Kent Roach, and George Williams (eds.), *Global Anti-Terrorism:*

and military jurisdiction over security cases involving subversion and terrorism, as documented in Taiwan,[23] South American countries before their democratization, and Egypt.[24] An authoritarian regime's attempt to perpetuate its monopoly of political power creates its own dissenters, and without exception, authoritarian rulers suppress and prohibit political opposition and often set up a separate, exceptional system outside the regular legal system to suppress their political enemies, whoever they may be.

In this carved-out zone, political or executive orders carry much more weight than legal rules, if such rules exist at all. Autocrats who worry about regime survival are bound to exert more hands-on control over their political opponents. While autocrats may leave the enforcement of legal norms with respect to conventional cases, such as contract or tort, to legal experts, they take personal interest in cases of political dissent where the pronouncement or instructions from leaders often take precedence over legal rules.[25] The exercise of power in the zone of exception is largely beyond the reach of state laws. In that sense, it is extralegal with a clear policy objective of diminishing and even bypassing the reach of normal legal protection. The creation of a prerogative state in China that operates lawlessly in the zone of exception forms the first tier of China's authoritarian legality. In a system where there is little possibility of effective political participation, the law has become a crucial site of contention in pushing back authoritarian overreach, and the creation and expansion of the zone of exception has become particularly detrimental to an emerging rights-based resistance.

The dual system is not new to communist China of course. After all, the Chinese Constitution in its opening Preamble expressly states that China is a "democratic dictatorship,"[26] which is commonly interpreted as democracy for the "people" (who support the regime) and dictatorship

---

Law and Policy (Cambridge, UK: Cambridge University Press, 2012), 271–89; Chapter 10 in this volume.

[23] See Chapter 12 in this volume.

[24] Anthony W. Pereira, *Political (In)Justice: Authoritarianism and the Rule of Law in Brazil, Chile and Argentina* (Pittsburgh, PA: University of Pittsburgh Press, 2005); Tamir Moustafa, *The Struggle for Constitutional Power: Law, Politics and Economic Development in Egypt* (Cambridge, UK: Cambridge University Press, 2007).

[25] Solomon, "Law and Courts," 427.

[26] Constitution of the People's Republic of China, adopted December 4, 1982, www .npc.gov.cn/englishnpc/Constitution/node_2825.htm

for the "enemy."[27] In Fukuyama's terms, China has a long history of a strong centralized state that decides where, when, and how legal rules apply or, more importantly, do not apply.[28]

Matters that are subject to direct political control have varied historically according to the nature of threats that the state is facing, real or perceived. In the first three decades of the People's Republic, the principal enemies included the so-called five elements: the "landlords," "capitalists," "counter-revolutionaries," "bad elements," and the "rightists," who received systematic and brutal persecution largely because of their status or political expression. In the post-revolutionary era after China initiated a reformist policy, the categories of enemies have also shifted from the traditionally class-based classification to one that is based on new threats to the regime in the new circumstances.[29] Devoid of a fixed class status, the new enemies are more fluid and harder to categorize and define, as explained below.

While China, like other authoritarian states, is faced with its own dissidents, political, religious or otherwise, it has not created a separate institution *de jure* for political control that is separate from and independent of the regular criminal process. In fact, the same judges handling shoplifting cases are also in charge of convicting political dissidents, separatists, and other enemies of the state. However, the judges are all well versed in the politics of justice and ready to comply with political instructions in politically sensitive cases. A compliant judiciary compensates for the lack of an alternative institution for political justice. The legal system has both prerogative and normal components serving a dual function.

China has undergone a systematic political crackdown since 2013. The crackdown has been conducted in the name of safeguarding China's national security as perceived and defined by the Chinese Communist Party (the party), including the suppression of ethnic populations in Xinjiang and Tibet; and of political dissents, religious offenders, and

---

[27] Donald C. Clarke and Jim V. Feinerman, "Antagonistic Contradictions: Criminal Law and Human Rights in China," *China Quarterly* 14 (1995): 135; see Chapter 3 in this volume.

[28] Francis Fukuyama, *Political Order and Political Decay: From the Industrial Revolution to the Globalization of Democracy* (London: Profile Books, 2014), 354.

[29] James Brady, *Justice and Politics in People's China: Legal Order or Continuing Revolution?* (London: Academic Press, 1982); Leng Shao-chuan. "The Role of Law in the People's Republic of China as Reflecting in Mao Tse-Tung's Influences," *Journal of Criminal Law and Criminology* 68(3) (1976): 356; Leng, Shao-chuan and Hungdah Chiu, *Criminal Justice in Post-Mao China: Analysis and Documents* (Albany, NY: State University of New York, 1985).

other civil society activists engaging in social–legal mobilization–such as journalists, human rights lawyers, feminists, and labor activists.[30] It is important to put the recent crackdown in perspective, however.[31] Repressive episodes are recurring events in the post-Mao era, and each generation of communist leaders in China have had repressive moments during their terms and have created their own political enemies. Deng Xiaoping suppressed the democratic movements in 1979 and 1989 and sentenced Wei Jingsheng, Wang Dan, and many others to long prison terms for counter-revolutionary propaganda and subverting state power. Jiang Zemin smashed the Falun Gong and sent tens of thousands of believers into labor camps without trial, instituting the longest persecution to date in post-Mao China. Jiang also wiped out the China Democracy Party (CDP), sending most of the CDP members to lengthy prison terms or exile. Under Hu Jintao, there was the crackdown of the chartist movement in 2009 leading to the lengthy incarceration of Liu Xiaobo and the forced disappearance of many public interest lawyers and other advocates in 2011 in the aftermath of the Color Revolutions in Tunisia and Egypt. The current crackdown on human rights lawyers and civil society activists, while moving decisively beyond the "usual suspects," does not break any new ground in its nature and, indeed, it actually pales in comparison with the brutality of its precedents such as the one against Falun Gong, although the most recent campaign under Xi is characterized by its systematic destruction of independent civil society forces with the reliance on thinly defined legality to achieve its political goal.

The categories of the new enemies have become more clearly defined since the amendment of the Criminal Procedural Law in 2012.[32] The amendment creates new prolonged and secretive detention powers for three types of offences: national security offences, major corruption offences, and terrorist offences. These three types of offences clearly fall under separate rules under the criminal investigation regime.[33] The offences of endangering national security and terrorism are ill-defined

---

[30] International human rights NGOs have documented the recent waves of political repression and prosecution. See Human Rights in China, www.hrichina.org/en; China Human Rights Lawyers Concern Group (CHRLCG), www.chrlawyers.hk/en; Weiquan wang [human rights website], www.wqw2010.blogspot.hk

[31] See Chapters 3 and 4 in this volume.

[32] Criminal Procedure Law of the People's Republic of China, effective January 1, 1980, www.npc.gov.cn/englishnpc/Law/2007–12/13/content_1384067.htm

[33] Joshua Rosenzweig, "Residential Surveillance: Evolution of a Janus-faced measure," in Eliza Nesossi, Sarah Biddulph, Flora Sapio, and Sue Trevaskes (eds.), *Legal Reforms and Deprivation of Liberty in Contemporary China* (Abingdon, UK: Routledge, 2016).

THE CONCEPT OF AUTHORITARIAN LEGALITY: CHINA   71

under Chinese criminal law, and include mainly the offence of subverting state power and the related inchoate offence of incitement, vaguely defined, if at all, to commit the aforesaid offences.[34] Politically, the law is targeted at what is referred to as the new "five elements," an informal categorization of new enemies that are barriers to China's rise. They include human rights lawyers, house churches, political dissidents, opinion leaders, and economically disadvantaged groups.[35]

For many, Xi's government is, so far, defined by repression and the imposition of fear.[36] The party has always demonstrated its clear resolve to eliminate new threats on the horizon that may pose challenges to its political power. This time, old enemies, such as the Falun Gong, have largely been left alone and the party has found its new enemies in law firms, NGOs, and the heart of mainstream society. Indeed, the current crackdown is particularly shocking and attracted wide attention in part because the targets have shifted from the traditional enemies to opinion leaders, feminists, journalists, lawyers, and activists who work on mainstream public interest projects in the name of the rule of law and accountability. Yet, as distinct as it is, the ongoing crackdown is a continuation, reinforcement, and escalation of China's authoritarian state.

It is also important to note that China's repression of political dissent in the mostly Han Chinese regions also pales significantly in comparison to the repression of the perceived separatists in Tibet and Xinjiang. In relative terms, the party that previously demonstrated a degree of restraint in its surgical repression against proponents of regime change has become much harsher and far less rule-bound in dealing with secessionist threats otherwise known as "the three evil forces" (i.e. terrorism, separatism, and fundamentalism) in the minority regions.[37]

---

[34] Hualing Fu, "Responses to Terrorism in China," in Victor V. Ramraj, Michael Hor, Kent Roach, and George Williams (eds.), *Global Anti-Terrorism Law and Policy* (2nd ed.) (Cambridge, UK: Cambridge University Press, 2012), 334.

[35] In Chinese, they are "*weiquan lvshi, dixia zongjiao, yijian renshi, wangluo lingxiu, ruoshi tunti*"; see "China Facing Real Challenges in the Next 5 to 10 Years," *People's Daily (Overseas Edition)*, August 1, 2012, finance.ifeng.com/stock/zqyw/20120801/6853120 .shtml

[36] See Chapter 3 in this volume.

[37] Hualing Fu, "Counter-Revolutionaries, Subversives, and Terrorists: China's Evolving National Security Law," in Hualing Fu, Carole J. Petersen, and Simon N. M. Young (eds.), *National Security and Fundamental Freedoms: Hong Kong's Article 23 under Scrutiny* (Hong Kong: Hong Kong University Press, 2005), 63; Hualing Fu, "Responses to Terrorism in China," 334; Hualing Fu, "Politicized Challenges, De-politicized Responses: Political Monitoring in China's Transitions," in Fergal Davis, Nicola McGarrity, and

Politically motivated prosecutions abound under authoritarian legality. Political offences are different from ordinary criminal offences in that
the former challenges the constituted political authority and the latter
violates legal rules.[38] As such, political prosecution and legal prosecution
follow different logic and manifest fundamental differences: whereas
criminal prosecution is based on action, political prosecution, in relative
terms, focuses on actors and is status-based and triggered by the political
positioning of a person and an assessment of political risks that the
person may pose to political authorities. In the first thirty years of the
People's Republic, the "enemy" status was largely inherent – one
belonged to an "enemy" class because of family ties.

Criminal prosecution is based on an act or omission. While the
individuality of an offender is prominent in political prosecutions, it is
the narrowly focused "*mens rea*" and "*actus reus*" that are the focal points
of the criminal process in which the personal traits of defendants fade
into background. In political prosecution, because of the focus on an
actor's political risk, criminal law is used, instrumentally, to achieve
a political aim. A typical political prosecution is, therefore, often based
on "trumped-up charges" in the sense that a person is first assessed as
politically risky meriting punishment and, following such political determination, a legal process is then summoned to figure out how that
political agenda can be achieved through legal means. The traditional
criminal process that transits from action to actor is reversed from actor
to action in a political prosecution. In a political process, a person is
determined guilty before a legal process starts and the only remaining
issue is what the person should be guilty of and how severe the punishment should be, which are all negotiable, as the current crackdown in
China has amply demonstrated.[39]

Political prosecution, thus, differs from criminal prosecution in that
the former is fundamentally an assessment of future political risk and the
latter is essentially the judgment of a past wrong. The criminal law is well
developed to scrutinize past acts and the corresponding state of mind,
based on facts that have been gathered through a legal process. There is
a high degree of certainty and accuracy in the regular criminal process.

George Williams (eds.), *Surveillance, Counter-Terrorism and Comparative Constitutionalism*
(Abingdon, UK: Routledge, 2014), 296.

[38] Ronald Christenson, "A Political Theory of Political Trial," *Journal of Criminal Law and
Criminology* 74(2) (1983): 547.

[39] Hualing Fu, "The July 9th (709) Crackdown on Human Rights Lawyers: Legal Advocacy
in an Authoritarian State," *Journal of Contemporary China* 27(112) (2018): 554–68.

Assessing future political risk is of a different nature. Risk is a perception in the eyes of the beholder and such perception differs significantly in different regime types and in different historical places and times. Even if one tries to introduce a degree of objectivity and rationality into the system, predicting future consequences necessarily involves a high degree of speculation, approximation, and uncertainty, and, in doing so, one has to engage in a broad scan of the available information, including information that would never be considered admissible or relevant to the legal process. Unlike ordinary criminal offences that are defined with relative clarity in terms of their components, political offences are not defined with any clarity and involve multiple acts. Each of the acts on its own may be entirely innocent but the combination of particular acts and/or their accumulating effects may be deemed politically risky and hence lead to prosecution. At the end of the day, it is who they are, not what has been done, that matters the most in political prosecution.

As it happens, there is often extensive political monitoring of those who are perceived to pose a threat to national security before the prosecution takes place and, in the process, there is also intensive coercion and intimidation. Political offenders tend to have a long record of dissent and have a lengthy history of interacting with the security apparatus. Dissidents, either as lawyers, journalists, or ordinary citizens, have often received lengthy periods of harassment, warnings, interrogation, and detention before a formal prosecution finally commences. Indeed, those who are politically prosecuted are often well-known dissidents, and, in the eyes of the authorities, are beyond redemption. There is a sliding slope in which the authorities have exhausted other means of persuasion to prevent harm before resorting to criminal punishment.[40]

Due to the different objectives involved in the punishment of a past wrong compared with the prevention of a future risk, the measures used, and processes involved to achieve the objectives are also distinct. To achieve a political agenda through the legal process is more time-consuming and is subject to multiple layers of approval in order to ensure the legality of the action, which is often an impossible mission. This explains why investigative detention is lengthy, as adequate information must be gathered and confirmed for risk assessment beyond simply securing a criminal conviction. Given the political sensitivity, the investigative process has to be secretive, and outsiders, in particular

---

[40] Victor Li, *Law without Lawyers: A Comparative View of Law in the United States and China* (Boulder, CO: Westview Press, 1977).

independent lawyers retained by families of the detainees, have to be denied access during the lengthy detention.

To achieve a preventative agenda, the state does not only condemn and denounce the offenders in public, but also it requires them, through force or otherwise, to confess their crime and/or denounce their comrades-in-arms and supporters in public. Public confession has become the most dramatic feature in China's new political trials. If political crime is defined as an open challenge to the authorities, then political justice can only be achieved through public humiliation and submission of the offenders. In a highly contentious political crackdown, the party, in order to win credibility in the eyes of the general public, has to do more than show its might. It has to show it is right. Beyond using legal power arbitrarily to intimidate those offenders and mobilizing state-controlled media to conduct a smear campaign, the "enemy" has to be brought to its knees. That can be best done through confession and the expression of remorse in public. There is an element of admission of one's guilt, willingly or not, and there is also an element of shaming. But, at the end of the day, as Bandurski puts it, "[i]t is about dominance and submission."[41] The defeat of those who challenge the state must be widely seen in public.

The politicization of the legal process does not necessarily mean increased severity of the punishment imposed by the courts. When political expedience is required, a political offence that was regarded as serious during the investigation could be given lenient treatment after a torturously lengthy detention if other political needs are satisfied. Wang Yu, one of the key targets of the "709" crackdown, received a suspended sentence in exchange for her publicized confession showing her remorse and condemnation of others. Conversely, even for a relatively minor offence, if a person resists and shows contempt for authority, that person may receive a lengthy prison term as the case of Xia Lin powerfully illustrates. Xia received a twelve-year prison term in 2016 for his well-known failure to confess. It is also commonly understood that Wu Gan and Wang Quanzhang have been detained for more than three years largely due to their refusal to confess and submit.

Finally, the grounding of political prosecution in law is achieved, if at all, through the subservience of law and sacrifice of legal principles. Legal rules are often distorted if not blatantly violated when law is used as an instrument for political prosecution. Independent

---

[41] David Bandurski, "Fifty Shades of Xi: China's Confessional Politics of Dominance," *Medium*, March 30, 2015, www.medium.com/@cmphku/fifty-shades-of-xi-c3277e91f94c

lawyers are banned from participation in the legal process; investigative detention is prolonged over and again without precise legal justification; those who are released on parole are never seen in public; and the entire process is opaque and secretive. Essentially, the law merely sets a trapdoor to bring political cases into the legal system; but, once placed in the system, political prosecution develops a life of its own without legal accountability that is demanded in the prosecution of regular cases.

2.4   Authoritarian Institutions

The difficulty with the dual-state conceptualization is that the line between the normative state and the prerogative state is vague and flexible. As the Chinese experience shows, one knows where the line is located only after crossing it. Political norms and expedient measures, supposedly existing only in the zone of exception, effective permeate the entire legal system. For example, when dissidents were convicted with seditious libel, the prosecution resulted in a chilling effect on the wider community of journalists, academics, and citizens. As a result, censorship gained momentum in society, which in turn led to pervasive self-censorship. When the Falun Gong was persecuted as a (evil) cult, other religious and quasi-religious practices vanished quickly – the larger environment became so hostile to religion that the ground for religious belief and practices disappeared. In the most recent prosecution of human rights lawyers and rights activists, while the prosecution itself might have been limited in scope, its impact was much larger and felt widely across the entire legal profession. For the half dozen or so prosecuted, more than 300 lawyers were detained, interviewed, or otherwise warned; public interest lawyering was forced to retreat, and the entire profession was put on notice, with drastic measures being considered or imposed to rein in the profession. In such situations, special powers that are authorized for the purpose of handling national security cases might be extended to ordinary cases. What happens within the zone of exception then creates an impact in the zone without.

Whether some authoritarian states can better contain and quarantine political repression to a tightly confined zone may be an empirical question. While some authoritarian states may be able to maintain a parallel system of political repression and a fair legal system to provide justice, contemporary China is clearly not such a case. Just as a liberal rule of law needs a support structure,[42] authoritarian repression also requires pillars of support to be sustainable. This is the second tier of authoritarian legality. These pillars of support include: (1) the wide use of censorship of political speech and widespread self-censorship; (2) broad policing power with limited legal accountability in exerting social and political control; and (3) the establishment of alternative institutions to marginalize the judicial system. With little exception, if at all, authoritarian states subscribe to the universal value and practice of censorship just as democratic states are committed to the value of free speech. They also create powerful policing powers and rely extensively on them to exert political control. This part of the chapter examines this second tier, a subsystem in which power is neither directly derived from proper constitutional authority nor subject to independent oversight (judicial or legislative).

The first strategy involves extensive censorship and the marginalization and irrelevance of law in media governance, including the governance of social media. Media governance is essentially a lawless business in China, and China's legislature has yet to pass a single law to govern the media. Traditional media is state-owned and controlled tightly by the party. There is a well-established political mechanism, armed with strong organizations and detailed procedures, to guide and manage all media outlets in China on an ongoing basis. Media governance is an area in particular in which party norms and organs, instead of legal rules and institutions, are the ultimate authorities.[43] The party has achieved three major successes in media governance. First, it has managed the commercialization of the press without liberalization.[44] The party has since the 1990s made its vast media outlets, including newspapers, television, and radio stations, financially profitable, socially acceptable, and politically reliable. Essentially, media outlets operate like businesses but are controlled as government departments. The party has tamed the media market through political censorship. With the exception of some localized variations, commercialization

---

[42] Charles R. Epp, *The Rights Revolution: Lawyers, Activists, and Supreme Courts in Comparative Perspective* (Chicago, IL: University of Chicago Press, 1998), 3.

[43] Richard Cullen and Hualing Fu, "Seeking Theory from Experience: Media Governance in China," *Democratization* 5(2) (1998): 155.

[44] Ibid.; Anne-Marie Brady, *Marketing Dictatorship: Propaganda and Thought Work in Contemporary China* (Lanham, MD: Rowman & Littlefield, 2008).

and economic growth in general have not brought about liberalism in the Chinese media.[45]

Second, the authoritarian state has effectively extended its control to information technology and social media. When the Internet first arrived in China, there was high expectation that as a "liberation technology,"[46] with its anonymity, speed, interactivity, and autonomy, it would pose a significant, though uncertain, challenge to authoritarian leaders.[47] As it happened, the Internet did help the creation of a vibrant civil society and expand the realm of freedom.[48] Yet, through the criminal punishment of rumor-mongering and defamation, smart regulation, proactive use of social media, and pervasive censorship, the party has been able to place the cutting edge of social media under effective control. There has been an ongoing battle between the government and civil society forces in shaping public opinion and influencing decision-making, but the battle has not placed the party's legitimacy at any significant risk.[49]

Finally, the party has been able to fend off the influence of foreign and overseas media through the "Great Firewall," filtering, blockage, deletion, and other measures. China might have become the most dedicated internationalist in promoting free trade as the driving force for the "One Belt One Road" initiative, but it remains hostile to liberal political values as the ongoing crackdown on Western values clearly illustrates.[50] China is one of the most heavily censored societies in the world, where foreign media has the lowest levels of penetration and degree of influence.[51] The blockage of foreign and allegedly hostile voices is a key

[45] Ya-Wen Lei, "Freeing the Press: How Field Environment Explains Critical News Reporting in China," *American Journal of Sociology* 122(1) (2016): 1.
[46] Larry Diamond, "Libertarian Technology," *Journal of Democracy* 23(3) (2010): 69.
[47] Nicholas D. Kristof, "Death by a Thousand Blogs," *New York Times*, May 24, 2005, www.nytimes.com/2005/05/24/opinion/death-by-a-thousand-blogs.html
[48] David Herold, "Introduction: Noise, Spectacle, Politics: Carnival in China's Cyberspace," in David Herold and Peter Marolt (eds.), *Online Society in China: Creating, Celebrating and Instrumentalizing the Online Carnival* (Abingdon, UK: Routledge, 2011), 2; Daniela Stockmann, *Media Commercialization and Authoritarian Rule in China* (Cambridge, UK: Cambridge University Press, 2013); Guobin Yang, *The Power of the Internet in China: Citizen Activism Online* (New York: Columbia University Press, 2011).
[49] J. Sullivan, "China's Weibo: Is Faster Different?" *News Media & Society* 16(1) (2014): 24; James Leibold, "Blogging Alone: China, the Internet, and the Democratic Illusion?" *Journal of Asian Studies* 70(4) (2011): 1023.
[50] Thomas E. Kellogg, "Arguing Chinese Constitutionalism: The 2013 Constitutional Debate and the 'Urgency' of Political Reform," *University of Pennsylvania Asian Law Review* 11(3) (2017): 1.
[51] Committee to Protect Journalists (2015) "10 Most Censored Countries," https://cpj.org/2015/04/10-most-censored-countries.php

component of information management and a key plank of China's authoritarian efficiency.

In sum, the Chinese economy has been growing and its society has been changing, but these changes have only little impact on pervasive political censorship. The commercialization of state media, the growth of social media, and the growth of foreign influence have in combination enlarged the sphere of freedom in social and economic matters. The Chinese media is now decisively more diverse and vibrant. But political censorship is indispensable for any authoritarian system that seeks to perpetuate its monopoly of political power. Firmly in the hands of the party, the media in China, including social media, continues to represent one interest and speak with one voice on significant political issues. The limited freedom of the media bolsters the party's legitimacy and strengthens its political control over society.

The second strategy for maintaining authoritarian resilience involves the use of broad police powers. The police occupy a unique place in China's political and legal system and has a contentious relationship with law and legal institutions.[52] As a general rule, an authoritarian system creates and relies extensively on a police force that is politically influential and legally powerful and there is good reason to describe such a state as a police state. When an authoritarian regime undergoes a democratic transition, one of the first reforms is to tame excessive police power and to place the police under greater legal and democratic control, as the cases in Taiwan and elsewhere demonstrate.[53] The police in China are authoritarian in multiple ways. First, the police have the power to punish without meaningful judicial supervision. Due to ideological commitment and historical legacy, criminal law punishes only "serious offences," leaving "minor offences" as a prerogative of the police. While approximately one million criminal cases go through the criminal justice process each year, minor offences of different severity and nature, and which number ten times larger, are dealt with administratively by the police in the name of punishment, treatment, or rehabilitation. The hodgepodge of administrative penalties

[52] Hualing Fu, "A Bird in the Cage: Police and Political Leadership in PRC," *Policing and Society* 4 (1994): 277; Hualing Fu, "Zhou Yongkang and Recent Police Reform in China," *Australian and New Zealand Journal of Criminology* 38(2) (2005): 241; Hualing Fu, "Autonomy, Courts and the Political–Legal Order in Contemporary China," in Cao Liqun, Ivan Sun, and Bill Hebeton (eds.), *Handbook of Chinese Criminology* (Abingdon, UK: Routledge, 2013), 76.

[53] Jerome A. Cohen and Margaret K. Lewis, *Challenge to China: How Taiwan Abolished Its Version of Re-education through Labor* (Barrington, MA: US–Asia Law Institute, NYU School of Law, 2013).

THE CONCEPT OF AUTHORITARIAN LEGALITY: CHINA   79

targets prostitutes, drug addicts, and a wide range of minor offenders, and the penalties may vary from a verbal warning to lengthy incarceration (such as in the form of compulsory drug rehabilitation). This administrative punishment regime is characterized by the relative severity in penalties, lack of representation and due process, and uncertain legislative authorization.[54] By replacing criminal law with administrative law, China has been able to define away most crimes and, hence, create a society of one of the lowest crime rates globally.

On top of administrative penalties, the police enjoy extensive criminal law powers to interrogate, detain, search, and seize without any external authorization. The power to detain suspects is so flexible and open-ended that it is virtually unlimited. Due to the extensive powers of questioning, interrogation, and detention, coupled with the lack of external oversight by lawyers, NGOs, or the judiciary, the police have ample opportunities to coerce confessions in order to secure convictions. Chinese courts rely, nearly entirely, on affidavit evidence and whatever case the police make is, as a matter of routine, relied upon by the subsequent actors.[55] As a result of the direct political control exercised by the Communist Party, the police play a predominant role in shaping the criminal process to a degree that the entire criminal justice system can be said to be police-centered.

While media governance is now entirely extralegal, and there is no sign of any relaxation of political censorship, serious efforts are being made to place police power, both administrative power and power in the criminal process, under more direct judicial control. Two changes highlight the retreat of police power and the rise of judicial authority over crime and punishment. In a decisive move in 2013, China abolished the infamous institution of Reeducation through Labor (RTL), which allowed the police to imprison minor offenders for up to three years without trial. RTL was well known as an instrument for the political prosecution of religious offenders and others who disturbed public order.[56] Legal reformers in China, supported by the international human rights community, had advocated its abolition for decades. The abolition of RTL reflects

---

[54] Sarah Biddulph, *Legal Reform and Administrative Detention Powers in China* (Cambridge, UK: Cambridge University Press, 2007); Hualing Fu, "Re-education through Labour in Historical Perspective" *China Quarterly* 184 (2005): 811.

[55] Mike McConville, *Criminal Justice in China: An Empirical Inquiry* (Cheltenham, UK: Edward Elgar, 2011).

[56] Sarah Biddulph, "Punishments in the Post Re-education through Labor World: Questions about Minor Crime in China," in Zhao Yun and Michael Ng (eds.), *China's Legal Reform and the Global Legal Order: Adoption and Adaptation* (Cambridge, UK: Cambridge University Press, 2017), 15.

a larger trend in China that the party is trying to tame the police in their routine interaction with citizens so that the personal freedom of ordinary people is respected.[57]

The other example is the empowerment of courts in assessing prosecution evidence and excluding evidence that is unlawfully obtained, raising the possibility of finding a defendant not guilty based on the legality and strength of evidence. While the party is launching its ferocious campaign against human rights lawyers and citizen activists, it has simultaneously instituted yet another legal reform, unprecedented in its scale and depth in creating autonomy and effectiveness for legal institutions and with the express objective of creating a trial-centered criminal process.[58] A series of not-guilty verdicts in several high-profile criminal cases, with the direct involvement of the Supreme People's Court, have sent an encouraging sign that, with more judicial autonomy and effective defenses, criminal justice for ordinary cases may improve.[59]

The third strategy for maintaining authoritarian resilience involves the establishment of alternative institutions in quasi-security areas outside the regular legal framework. The party's monopoly over media governance, as mentioned above, is one example and its exclusive jurisdiction over religious affairs is another.[60] The best example is anti-corruption enforcement – an in-house disciplinary mechanism of the party which openly challenges China's legal foundations. The party's disciplinary mechanism was initially designed to investigate and punish party members for misconduct and to reinforce political loyalty, but it has morphed into a powerful anti-corruption institution. Legal institutions were openly made subordinate and accountable to the party's political mechanism.[61] The now superseded disciplinary detention measure (*"shuanggui"*) was the

---

[57] Ibid.
[58] Margaret K. Lewis, "Controlling Abuse to Maintain Control: The Exclusionary Rule in China," *International Law and Politics* 43 (2011): 629; Guo Zhiyuan, "Torture and Exclusion of Evidence in China," *China Perspectives* 1 (2019): 45–53.
[59] Hualing Fu, "Building Judicial Integrity in China," *Hastings International and Comparative Law Review* 39(1) (2016): 167.
[60] Fenggang Yang, "The Red, Black, and Gray Markets of Religion in China," *Sociological Quarterly* 47 (2005): 100; Carl Hollan, "A Broken System: Failures of the Religious Regulatory System in the People's Republic of China," *Brigham Young University Law Review* 3 (2014): 755.
[61] Hualing Fu "The Upward and Downward Spirals in China's Anti-Corruption Enforcement," in Mike McConville and Eva Pils (eds.), *Comparative Perspectives on Criminal Justice in China* (Cheltenham, UK: Edward Elgar, 2013), 390.

most controversial issue in relation to the party's disciplinary authority over its membership. *Shuanggui* allowed the party to detain its members for interrogation for a virtually unlimited period of time. While there had been an attempt to legitimize disciplinary detention on political and constitutional grounds,[62] it remained far-fetched to justify the practice under the existing constitutional and legal framework as it was understood. On anti-corruption enforcement matters, the party's in-house disciplinary regime initiated investigations in important cases and took action with the legal system operating in its shadow and playing a supporting and legitimizing role.[63]

The creation of a new constitutional body, the National Supervisory Commission (NSC),[64] to take charge in anti-corruption work demonstrates the vulnerability and fragility of authoritarian legality. The use of party's disciplinary mechanism to exercise the public law power has a clear legality deficit. The creation of the NSC is expected to provide much-needed legality, which in turn legitimizes and solidifies party's anti-corruption mechanisms. On March 11, 2018, the NPC amended the Constitution to establish the NSC,[65] forming a new constitutional power under the NPC.[66] On March 23, 2018, the NPC enacted the National Supervision Law.[67] The law confirms the leadership of the party over anti-corruption work and establishes the NSC for the purpose of "creating a centralized, unitary, authoritative and highly

---

[62] Larry Backer and Keren Wang, "The Emerging Structure of Socialist Constitutionalism with Chinese Characteristics: Extra-Judicial Detention (*Laojiao* and *Shuanggui*) and the Chinese Constitutional Order," *Pacific Rim Law & Policy Journal* 23 (2014): 251; Flora Sapio, "Shuanggui and Extralegal Detention in China," *China Information* 22 (2008): 7.

[63] Hualing Fu, "China's Striking Anti-Corruption Adventure: A Political Journey towards the Rule of Law?," in Weitseng Chen (ed.), *The Beijing Consensus? How China Has Changed the Western Ideas of Law and Economic Development* (Cambridge, UK: Cambridge University Press, 2017), 249.

[64] Lin Feng, "2018 Constitutional Amendments: Significance and Impact on the Theories of Party–State Relationship in China," *China Perspectives* 1 (2019): 11.

[65] NPC Observer, "Annotated Translation: 2018 Amendment to the PRC Constitution (Version 2.0)," https://npcobserver.com/2018/03/11/translation-2018-amendment-to -the-p-r-c-constitution

[66] They are executive power of the State Council, the supervisory power of the National Supervision Commission, judicial power of the Supreme People's Court, and procuratorial power of the Supreme People's Procuratorate.

[67] The National People's Congress of the People's Republic of China, "People's Republic of China Supervision Law," www.npc.gov.cn/npc/xinwen/2018-03/21/content_2052362 .htm

efficient supervisory system with Chinese characteristics."[68] It is common ground that the NSC creates a degree of legality and legitimacy for the party's anti-corruption enforcement, but on closer examination it places the supervision commissions under the firm and near exclusive control of the party's disciplinary mechanism – demonstrating a high degree of continuity between the old and new regimes. As a self-claimed "political organization," the supervision commissions enjoy all the legal powers with little legal accountabilities that may exist in Chinese law. De facto, the anti-corruption mechanism, while wearing a thin legal veil, remains extralegal. So *Shuanggui* is replaced by *liuzhe* in name, a secretive detention for three months, renewable for another three months,[69] and nothing else changes.[70]

2.5 Authoritarian Legality

Moving further beyond the authoritarian hard core and the supporting institutions, how authoritarian is Chinese legality in general? In the shadow of a repressive, highly politicized prerogative state, there is a normal legal system, rule-based, institutionalized, and semi-autonomous in performing a dispute resolution function. Private law in post-Mao China, for example, has prospered, growing in form and substance, with courts internalizing political factors and operating in a large realm of freedom within the parameters set by the party.[71] How does the authoritarian political system leave its footprints in the Chinese legal system? If the authoritarian impact on criminal law, constitutional law, and administrative law is visible, does Chinese labor law, anti-discrimination and equality law, environmental law, or even family law have some authoritarian manifestations? This section will identify three foundational blocks of China's authoritarian legality: (1) its statist nature and the resulting centralism; (2) the lack of autonomous institutions and professionalism; and (3) the disaggregating and individualizing force of law.

[68] Art. 2, National Supervision Law.
[69] Ibid., art. 43.
[70] Li Li and Wang Peng, "From Institutional Interaction to Institutional Integration: The National Supervisory Commission and China's New Anti-corruption Model," *China Quarterly* 240 (2019): 967–89.
[71] Hualing Fu, "Duality and China's Struggle for Legal Autonomy," *China Perspectives* 1 (2019): 3.

Chinese law is statist with limited meaningful contributions from independent non-state actors. A key principle of China's authoritarian rule is the identification principle, according to which the interest of the party and that of the people are ideologically presumed to coincide. Reinforced by Chinese paternalism, the communist vanguard mentality ensures that law, in its entirety, reflects the will of the party.[72] Given the nature of the rigid Leninist political system, there are few institutionalized channels for political participation, either in terms of election, lobbying, or citizens' petitioning, rendering the bottom-up forces of civil society feeble and unsustainable. Authoritarian legality, therefore, envisages a hierarchical order in which rules are imposed through a top-down process with little bottom-up participation in lawmaking, monitoring, or enforcement. In that system, the party-state serves as the sole representative of the people and independent articulation of interests and monitoring from society is strictly prohibited. Where consultation is allowed, the system is absolute and top leaders have absolute veto power (i.e. absolute constitutionalism in Tushnet's terms).[73] There is no institutionalized veto in the Chinese political–legal system outside the party-state.

The statist nature produces a significant impact on Chinese law and orients it toward an authoritarian direction in five ways. First, China's authoritarian legality prioritizes the supply side of the legal system, which includes the enactment of new legislation, improvement in legislative procedure, and drafting skills. It also includes enhanced institutionalized capacity of the judiciary for the application of law and judicial professionalism. The supply side of the rule of law prioritizes the promulgation and application of legal rules and largely marginalizes the demand side of the legal system, which includes citizen participation, civil society input in lawmaking, monitoring of law enforcement, an autonomous legal profession, and prevents it from channeling grievances into the legal system and demanding fair and effective resolution. In such a system, civil society forces, which form an indispensable support structure for a liberal legal order,[74] are either co-opted by the state or are tightly controlled, and, therefore, cannot play an independent and forceful role in holding the state accountable to its legal rhetoric. Rights-based NGOs are tightly controlled, if allowed to exist at all, and to the degree that

[72] Andrew J. Nathan, *Chinese Democracy* (Berkeley: University of California Press, 1986).
[73] Tushnet, "Authoritarian Constitutionalism," 391.
[74] Epp, *Rights Revolution*.

NGOs are allowed to function, they are limited to providing services on behalf of, and according to the instructions of, the government.[75]

Second, it is with this statist nature that one appreciates the proposition that the Chinese rule of law is a thin one.[76] In the thin-rule-of-law discourse, rule of law is largely defined as following commands, and the internal quality of such commands, in both substantive and procedural senses, is the core concern of legality. In this narrow rule of law, the focus is clearly to use law more effectively as a governance tool to empower state agencies to exert control. The focus of the statist view of law, in its totality, is little more than a duty to obey on the part of the citizens.

This is not to say that a Chinese rule of law does not reflect values, as it is often assumed that a legal system cannot exist in a political and moral vacuum, and, invariably, reflects a certain value system. In the Chinese case, while scholars agree that the value that underpins the Chinese legal system is decisively illiberal or even anti-liberal, they disagree on what these illiberal or anti-liberal elements are and have offered a wide range of alternatives, including communitarian values with a Confucian spin, statist values, or a socialist value system.[77] A common theme in scholarly deliberation is that the state is powerful in shaping what values are to underpin the legal system. The Chinese legal system prioritizes state interest and is firmly anchored in centralism.[78]

Third, partly due to authoritarian centralism and partly reflecting China's civilian legal tradition, Chinese law prioritizes substantive justice in constructing its legal system and marginalizes procedures in the implementation of rules. The lack of procedural protection has weakened legal protection of property and personal rights and renders legal rules an instrument of state control.[79] In the Chinese case, there is a well-documented debate on the respective value of substantive justice and procedural justice in Chinese law and the consensus is that a key piece that is missing in the Chinese legal puzzle is procedural justice, the absence of which has led to inestimable human injustice in the criminal

---

[75] See Chapter 4 in this volume.

[76] Randall Peerenboom, *China's Long March toward Rule of Law* (Cambridge, UK: Cambridge University Press, 2002).

[77] Ibid.

[78] An understudied area is the impact of socialism, as a normative commitment, on Chinese law and its legal system. For a preliminary study, see Hualing Fu, John Gillespie, Pip Nicholson, and William Edmund Partlett (eds.), *Socialist Law in Socialist East Asia* (Cambridge, UK: Cambridge University Press, 2018).

[79] Daniel Treisman, "The Cause of Corruption: A Cross-National Study," *Journal of Public Economics* 76(3) (2000): 399.

process. In the government's relentless pursuit of the "right result," there are few procedural and evidential hurdles in place to constrain official power. Most of the abuses happen in a hasty pursuit of "justice."

Fourth, centralism demands institutional dependence. A classic example of an authoritarian system is the lack of an independent and effective judiciary to make the state legally accountable. China's politically compliant judiciary fits well into that model. Since law is a subset of politics and legal institutions are effectively absorbed into a broad political–legal community, judicial professionalism, along with professional ethics, identity, and interest, are at best tolerated but not encouraged. The party may accept a distinct judicial identity in a functional sense and as part of the division of labor within the political–legal system, but it has not allowed a separate legal identity to develop independent of its political identity. Fundamentally, the party is suspicious of the formation of judicial professionalism without politics and is vigilant in guarding any political challenges based on professional commitment and institutional autonomy and neutrality.

Ordinary justice in China has improved significantly outside the zone of exception and one might even argue that judging by the courts' adjudication of ordinary civil and commercial cases, China resembles a more mature legal system at least compared with its recent past. However, such autonomy is not institutionalized. It is delegated by the party and can be taken away by the party as quickly as it is given, as past experiences of judicial reform clearly shows.[80] The party has the power to decide when a simple labor case, gender equality case, or environmental protection case becomes politically sensitive and intervenes accordingly. The political leash placed on the courts is, therefore, a short one.

Finally, the lack of institutional space is not limited to courts: control extends to all judicial fields of any significance. Social and economic rights in the broad sense are protected in law and in practice, but independent agencies such as an Equal Opportunity Commission, an Ombudsmen, civilian oversight over police, or equivalent agencies are barely allowed to exist. Indeed, the party has effectively colonized traditional social fields, such as youth, women, labor, and disability representation, by establishing administrative control in areas where contention is

[80] Carl F. Minzner, "China's Turn against Law," *American Journal of Comparative Law* 59 (4) (2011): 935; Carl F. Minzner, *End of an Era: How China's Authoritarian Revival Is Undermining Its Rise* (New York: Oxford University Press, 2018).

most likely to occur. Social–legal activism in civil society, which is regarded as the most effective and often indispensable way of protecting legal rights, is critically missing in China. Abused and harassed women, mistreated workers, and people with systemic grievances cannot organize themselves or lean on NGOs as they can do in democracies. Rather than serving to protect civil society from the abuse of the state, the legal system shows a pronounced tendency to protect the state from civil society. The criminal justice system, in particular, is routinely used to punish and humiliate civil society activists, thereby discouraging and suppressing the attempts of civil society to use law to challenge questionable exercises of power. Without an effective support structure as defined by Epp,[81] isolated individual victims cannot utilize the law and claim their legal rights with any effectiveness. In that sense, reliance on law without freedom to organize is an "anti-solidarity" enterprise, as Lee and Shen point out.[82]

This brings us to the individualizing impact of authoritarian legality. During China's social and economic transitions, conflict was often collective: farmers against local authorities in land takings; hepatitis B virus carriers against their potential employers in hiring discrimination; pneumoconiosis patients against factory owners for compensation; migrants workers against their employers and official unions fighting for various labor rights; and residents against management companies for taking back owners' rights. The list goes on and touches on issues relating to environmental protection, educational rights, gender equality, and many others.

While Chinese law provides legal rights and allows legal action by individual actors to make their own claims, it generally restricts and even prohibits collective action by group actors.[83] Access to justice is provided on the condition that disputes are fragmented and collective action is disaggregated. While class action or representative litigation is permissible under civil procedural law, Chinese courts have never allowed collective litigation and insist on breaking collective disputes down into individual cases.

---

[81] Epp, Rights Revolution, 2.

[82] Ching Kwan Lee and Shen Yuan, "The Anti-Solidarity Machine? Labor Nongovernmental Organizations in China," in Sarosh Kuruvilla, Ching Kwan Lee, and Mary E. Gallagher (eds.), *From Iron Rice Bowl to Informalization: Markets, Workers, and the State in a Changing China* (Ithaca, NY: Cornell University Press, 2011), 173.

[83] Hualing Fu, "Mass Disputes and China's Legal System," in Teresa Wright (ed.), *Handbook of Protest and Resistance* (Cheltenham, UK: Edward Elgar, 2019).

This individualizing of disputes is pervasive throughout the entire legal process. For instance, petitioners are prohibited from making their complaints in a group that is more than five persons. According to the 2005 Petition Regulations, mass grievances must be petitioned through representatives and no more than five representatives are allowed in making representations in each grievance.[84] Lawyers are advised to take caution in representing so-called mass cases – defined as cases involving more than ten individuals in relation to a common legal issue – and are required to report to the professional body, the Lawyers' Association, for the record,[85] and to communicate with the competent government authority promptly and fully.[86] Courts have habitually broken down collective cases that they have accepted into multiple individual cases and rendered separate decisions to individual claimants, which is most commonly observed in the judicial management of labor disputes.[87] While social media in China, with its networking power, amalgamates individual grievances into an incremental force for collective protest,[88] the law serves to isolate grievances and to individualize disputes, which renders them merely individual matters distinct from a larger collective or class background.

Based on this foundation, one observes a wide gap between the legal rules and the legal practices that define authoritarian legality. There are different academic takes on the gap. For Solomon, in discussing the authoritarian nature of Russian law, this gap manifests itself in the sharp difference between formal rules and informal practices.[89] While formal rules and legal rights offer legitimacy for the government and have often been used by the regime to claim credibility, vast discretion and selective enforcement are the norm, and rules and rights are, therefore, effectively canceled out at the implementation level. For Gallagher, in her examination of Chinese labor law and relations, it is the difference

---

[84] Article 18 of the Regulation on Complaint Letters and Visits, effective May 1, 2005, www.lawinfochina.com/display.aspx?lib=law&id=3920&CGid
[85] All China Lawyers' Association, Guidance Opinions on Lawyers' Handling of Mass Cases, passed by the Standing Committee of All China Lawyers' Association on March 20, 2006, s. 3(1).
[86] Ibid., s. 2(3).
[87] Feng Chen and Xin Xu, "'Active Judiciary': Judicial Dismantling of Workers' Collective Action in China," *China Journal* 67 (2012): 87; Hualing Fu, "Bring Politics Back in: Access to Justice and Labor Dispute Resolution in China," in Flora Sapio et al. (eds.), *Justice: The China Experience* (Cambridge, UK: Cambridge University Press, 2017).
[88] Yang, Power of the Internet in China.
[89] Solomon, "Law and Courts," 427.

between "high standard" and "self-enforcement" that makes Chinese labor law authoritarian.[90] Worker-friendly laws are passed to expand the scope of workers' rights and to allow the state to proclaim the socialist nature of Chinese law, but weak official implementation of the laws leave workers at the mercy of ruthless exploitation in an emerging socialist market. Since formal legal rights depend principally on workers to enforce them in an individual capacity, they are regarded as remote, empty, and largely irrelevant given the social and economic constraints that workers face. In sum, while a gap between law on the books and law in practice is common in all legal systems, authoritarian states create formal rights to achieve political legitimacy and then selectively enforce them according to evolving political demands to maximize the political impact of decisions.

2.6 Conclusion

The chapter attempts to provide some background to China's authoritarian legality and to explain what makes Chinese law authoritarian. Horizontally, the chapter tries to locate China within the wide spectrum of authoritarian legality and, hierarchically, to identify what has happened to Chinese authoritarian legality in its core. China's authoritarianism differs significantly from that elsewhere and these differences make China's authoritarian legality and the struggle against it unique. The state owns and controls the mass media. Before the arrival of the Internet and social media, dissenting voices were virtually nonexistent in the public sphere. Tight censorship, however, has ironically made social media in China particularly vibrant, politicized, and hard to control. China does not permit the existence of autonomous social organizations, especially those advocating religious freedoms, labor rights, or equality. Unlike other authoritarian states, China does not permit independent unions, independent churches, or an independent legal profession. However, the lack of official recognition of organized civil society forces has not reduced them into irrelevance. Instead of disappearing, they hide and operate underground. The sheer size of the house churches and other underground religions present a significant challenge to the party's religious control. China's timid legal system and its compliant judiciary have been regularly criticized, but such timidity has rendered it unnecessary for the police to resort to extralegal violence. In general, the

---

[90] Gallagher, Authoritarian Legality in China, 21.

heavily politicized police in China, while politically repressive, are placed under effective political control and behave better than those in democratic Brazil and Russia.[91]

Authoritarian legality, like its liberal component, ebbs and flows in both authoritarian and liberal states. In the Chinese case, the authoritarian foundation is shifting and has faced challenges. Frustrated by the law's individualizing impact, workers, abused women, and other members of vulnerable groups, often led by lawyers, are realizing their common interest, developing a common identity, and forming collective entities in their struggles against political power. The demand for rights and freedom has been so strong that it has forced the state to respond actively. Indeed, the current crackdown on lawyers and activist citizens is a sign that the party is taking the vibrancy and aggressiveness of civil society seriously.

As part of its response, the party is reshaping the pillars of its authoritarian rule. We are, therefore, witnessing an increasingly nuanced picture. While the party is reinforcing censorship and is more hands-on in media management, it is also embracing more effective judicial control over the police and plans to create a criminal justice system that is court centric. While concurrently hardening its authoritarian core and using harsher measures to deal with what the party regards as its political enemies, including separatists, terrorists, or subversive elements, all vaguely defined, the party has largely left legal issue in the expansive social and economic spheres to legal institutions for a rule-based resolution. Thus, we are witnessing dual institutionalization of both political repression and a normal legal system as the Chinese authoritarian state continues to mature.

---

[91] Matthew Light, Mariana Mota Prado, and Yuhua Wang, "Policing Following Political and Social Transitions: Russia, Brazil, and China Compared," *Theoretical Criminology* 19(2) (2015): 216.

3

Rule-of-Law Reform and the Rise
of Rule by Fear in China

EVA PILS

3.1 Introduction

In 1989, Judith Shklar published an essay arguing that liberalism's most central concern was to avoid, oppose, and overcome a particular kind of political fear, or fear of state violence and cruelty, deployed as a tool of governance by rulers to stay in control. She called her version of liberalism "the liberalism of fear."[1] In calling for a system of protection from state terror, her argument reflected twentieth-century experiences of totalitarianism at the very end of the Cold War era, just as the Soviet Union and its satellite states were collapsing. Yet, the concerns Shklar addressed were not limited to totalitarian systems. On the contrary, one of her points is that liberals need to expect – and be prepared to oppose – cruelty and violence from any state.

While the argument for a liberalism of fear during the two decades following Shklar's essay might have seemed to belong to a distant historical era, we now have good reason to revert to it, as renewed academic and media discussion of the "politics of fear,"[2] "post-truth politics,"[3] populism,[4] and

3

The author wishes to thank the participants of the workshops held at National University of Singapore in December 2016, Columbia Law School in April 2017, and Freie Universität Berlin and Oxford University in May 2017, especially to my discussants Mike Dowdle, Kate Jackson, and Madhav Kosla for their very helpful comments on the earlier drafts.
[1] Judith Shklar, "The Liberalism of Fear," in Nancy Rosenblum (ed.), *Liberalism and the Moral Life* (Cambridge, MA: Harvard University Press, 1989), 21.
[2] Human Rights Watch, "World Report 2016: 'Politics of Fear' Threatens Rights," January 27, 2016, www.hrw.org/news/2016/01/27/world-report-2016-politics-fear-threatens-rights
[3] William Davies, "The Age of Post-Truth Politics," *New York Times*, August 24, 2016, www.nytimes.com/2016/08/24/opinion/campaign-stops/the-age-of-post-truth-politics.html
[4] Jan-Werner Müller, *What Is Populism?* (Philadelphia, PA: University of Pennsylvania Press, 2016).

the possibility of a global authoritarian resurgence well illustrate.[5] The changes that China has undergone over the past decade, especially since Xi Jinping came into power in late 2012, are part of this broader change. Taking some of the ideas that moved Shklar as a starting point, this chapter focuses on understanding how and why China has intensified state-directed terror, not only through harsher measures against individuals and individual groups (including forced "medication" as a form of mind control), but also by sophisticated mass propaganda portraying its victims as enemies of the state. The repression and terror of the Chinese government have also increasingly reached beyond China's borders and in parallel with these developments, there has been a shift toward different and – as it will be seen here – darker conceptions of law and power.

3.2 Party Leadership and "Legality" in the Reform and Opening Era

Deng Xiaoping's post-Mao "reform and opening" policies were at least in part based on the notion that the destructive, revolution-perpetuating bent of the system must be reversed and that law could serve the function of recreating order, stability, and prosperity. This gave rise to a particular optimistic perspective on reform.[6]

Cautiously, the party adopted and promoted the belief that well-enforced laws protecting economic and other liberties were necessary to promote economic growth.[7] The judiciary, the procuracy, and the police, as well as the Ministry of Justice were rebuilt. Laws were enacted and training for legal professionals, as well as *pufa* ("law dissemination"), were introduced. The idea of *yi fa zhi guo* ("ruling the country in

---

[5] Alexander Cooley, "Authoritarianism Goes Global: Countering Democratic Norms," *Journal of Democracy* 26 (2015): 49, www.journalofdemocracy.org/article/authoritarianism-goes-global-countering-democratic-norms; Larry Diamond, "Facing up to the Democratic Recession," *Journal of Democracy* 26 (2015): 141, www.journalofdemocracy.org/article/facing-democratic-recession; Steven Levitsky and Lucan Way, "The Myth of Democratic Recession," *Journal of Democracy* 26 (2015): 45, www.journalofdemocracy.org/sites/default/files/Levitsky-26-1.pdf; Jacob T. Levy, "Who's Afraid of Judith Shklar?," *Foreign Policy*, July 16, 2018, foreignpolicy.com/2018/07/16/whos-afraid-of-judith-shklar-liberalism

[6] Tom Ginsburg and Alberto Simpser, "Introduction," in Tom Ginsburg and Alberto Simpser (eds.), *Constitutions in Authoritarian Regimes* (Cambridge, UK: Cambridge University Press, 2013), 11.

[7] Beijing Review, "Communiqué of the Third Plenary Session of the 11th Central Committee of the Communist Party of China (1978)," October 10, 2008, www.bjreview.com.cn/special/third_plenum_17thcpc/txt/2008–10/10/content_156226.htm

accordance with law"),[8] in particular, seemed to indicate a promise on behalf of the authorities that the law would bind the government as well as ordinary citizens.[9] Part of this development was the policy announced at the Thirteenth Party Congress that there would be a clearer separation of party and state (or government), a move that would forestall excessive power concentration in the hands of the party.[10]

Yet, from when it was first introduced in the 1950s, "socialist legality" was a conflicted idea. The party's organization, based on Leninist principles, and its undefined role in the constitutional framework accentuated this conflict, which could also be gleaned from a quick read of the "reformist" Constitution of the People's Republic of China adopted in 1982. The liberal principles articulated in Chapter 2 of the 1982 Constitution sharply contradicted the authoritarian principles of Chapters 1 and 3,[11] which contain the principles of democratic centralism ("*minzhu jizhongzhi*"),[12] the "People's Democratic Dictatorship,"[13] and the democratic "mass line,"[14] enshrining a principle of rule by theoretically undivided power.

In fact, even if in comparison with the Mao era, the Marxist–Maoist belief that law was an "instrument of oppression of the antagonistic

---

[8] Yang Deshan (杨德山), "Yifa zhiguo, yide zhiguo" [Ruling the country in accordance with law, ruling the country in accordance with virtue], *Xinhuanet*, September 6, 2002, http://cpc.people.com.cn/GB/64162/64171/4527669.html

[9] The PRC Administrative Procedure Law played an important role in this. *Zhonghua renmin gongheguo xingzheng susongfa* [Administrative Procedure Law of the People's Republic of China], adopted and promulgated on April 4, 1989 and effective as of October 1, 1990, http://english.court.gov.cn/2015-09/11/content_21845451.htm

[10] For a succinct discussion, see Wu Wei, "Shisanda hou de dangzheng fenkai gaige" [The Post-Thirteenth Congress Policy of Separating Party and Government], *New York Times Chinese Edition*, September 30, 2014, cn.nytimes.com/china/20140930/cc30wuwei31. On the move from using policies to using legal rules, see Timothy R. Heath, *China's New Governing Party Paradigm: Political Renewal and the Politics of National Rejuvenation* (Burlington, VT: Ashgate, 2014), 34.

[11] For example, see Teng Biao, "Rights Defence, Microblogs, and the Surrounding Gaze: The Rights Defence Movement Online and Offline," *China Perspectives* 3 (2012): 29.

[12] Stephen C. Angle, "Decent Democratic Centralism," *Political Theory* 33 (2005): 518.

[13] Renmin minzhu zhuanzheng [The Communist Party of China and state represent and act on behalf of the people, but may use dictatorial powers against reactionary forces]. In Chinese, the word used for "dictatorship" (*zhuanzheng*) does not have negative connotations, unlike "dictator" [*ducai(zhe)*] or "hegemon" [*bawang*].

[14] Xu Chongde (徐崇德), Zhonghua remin gongheguo xianfa shi [A constitutional history of the People's Republic of China] (Fuzhou, China: Fujian People's Press, 2003), 309.

classes" was weakened,[15] the party continued to control all the institutions of the state. It controlled what state laws and regulations were made and even after the enactment of the Law on Legislation in 2000, party-issued documents retained enormous, albeit uncodified, de facto power within the legal–political system.[16] The party also controlled the state administration, law enforcement, and the operation of the judicial system. It continued to exert a high degree of control over the economy, and it retained control over appointments in entities as diverse as state-owned enterprises (SOEs), academia, and the official media, and thus over economic actors and individuals and organizations increasingly seen as part of an emerging civil society.

Although they were reluctant to relinquish control, the authorities themselves seemed intent on sustaining the rhetoric of gradually constructing and improving the rule of law. They nurtured this belief through, inter alia, the official recognition of human rights.[17] They quoted the preamble of the International Covenant on Economic, Social and Cultural Rights, which states that "the ideal of free human beings enjoying freedom from fear and want can only be achieved if conditions are created whereby everyone may enjoy his economic, social and cultural rights, as well as his civil and political rights," implying that theirs was a long-term reform goal of realizing *all* human rights.[18] It was "[e]conomic reforms first, political reforms later," in the words of one of the Chinese scholars of the "Chinese model."[19] In comparison with countries where system transition had followed power transition, the

[15] Carlos Lo, "Socialist Legal Theory in Deng Xiao-ping's China," *Columbia Journal of Asian Law* 11 (1997): 469. As discussed below, the Maoist theory of contradictions is being revived.

[16] The PRC Law on Legislation was promulgated on March 15, 2000 and last revised on March 15, 2015. Zhonghua renmin gongheguo lixianfa fa [Legislation Law of the People's Republic of China], effective July 1, 2000, www.npc.gov.cn/npc/dbdhhy/12_3/2015-03/18/content_1930713.htm (translation by China Law Translate, www.chinalawtranslate.com/2015lawlaw/?lang=en#_Toc414358117).

[17] The first White Paper on human rights was issued in 1991. State Council Information Office, *White Paper on Human Rights*, Preface, November 1991, www.china.org.cn/e-white/7/index.htm

[18] China Human Rights Studies Association (中国人权研究会), "Geren renquan yu jiti renquan, gongminquanli, zhengzhiquanli yu jingji, shehui, wenhua quanli tongdeng zhongyao" [Individual and collective human rights, civil and political and social, economic and cultural rights are equally important], *People's Daily*, June 20, 2005, theory.people.com.cn/GB/49150/49152/3481073.html

[19] Zhang Weiwei, "The Allure of the Chinese Model," *International Herald Tribune*, November 2, 2006, www.sinoptic.ch/textes/articles/2006/20061102_zhang.weiwei_chinese.model-en.pdf

expectation was apparently that in China, political liberalization would be a self-initiated, gradual, and ordered process. This belief came to be referred to as *jianjin gaige zhuyi* ("reform incrementalism"),[20] and it was an important part of government rhetoric especially after the failure of the democracy movement culminating in June Fourth.

The reformist and developmental rhetoric was in many ways effective. From the 1990s onward, there was a widely shared belief that the ongoing legal reform process was going in a liberal direction – that China was moving, as Xiao Yang put it in 1999, "Toward an Age of Rights."[21] There was a widely shared belief that the system could approximate to the rule of law, and that civil society, as it gradually liberalized and became more active, would exert pressure on the system to democratize step by step. In this process, not only the party-state, but also citizens could play an active role by helping the system transform itself, as advocates would sometimes put it, by educating the officials about the values and principles the Chinese system had now committed to.[22] Rights defense would allow people to overcome *kongju* ("terror"), as Yuan Hongbing put it in 2005.[23]

Even outside China, those who saw the emergence of the rule of law and further political transition as a function of economic growth[24] supporting a growing middle class that would naturally demand further liberalization could have little doubt that the economic and political structures would eventually become more liberal, open and democratic. The notion that economic growth might one day come to support political tightening and more stringent state control of society and the

---

[20] Overseas Chinese scholars such as Wang Tiancheng, Teng Biao, and Mo Zhixu have rejected approaches of "reform incrementalism" in their academic writings. Wang Tiancheng (王天成) is critical of reform incrementalism (渐进改革主义) in *Da zhuanxing – Zhongguo minzhuhua zhanlve yanjiu kuangjia* [The great transition – a framework for studying strategies of democratization in China] (Hong Kong, 2012), esp. chs. 5, 7, 8.

[21] *Zou xiang quanli de shidai: Zhongguo gongmin quanli fazhan yanjiu* [Toward a Time of Rights: A Perspective of the Civil Rights Development in China], ed. Xia Yong (夏勇) (Beijing: China University of Politics and Science Press, 1999).

[22] Teng Biao, "What Is Rights Defence," in Stacy Mosher and Patrick Poon (eds.), *A Sword and a Shield: China's Human Rights Lawyers* (Hong Kong: China Human Rights Lawyers Concern Group, 2009), 122.

[23] Yuan Hongbing (袁红冰), "人们正在逐步走出恐惧－袁红冰教授声援高智晟律师 Renmen zhengzai zhubu zouchu kongju – Yuan Hongbing jiaoshou shengyuan Gao Zhisheng lvshi" [People are gradually leaving fear behind – Professor Yuan Hongbing expresses support for lawyer Gao Zhisheng], *Epoch Times*, January 16, 2005, www.epochtimes.com/gb/5/1/16/n782007.htm

[24] Randall Peerenboom, *China's Long March toward Rule of Law* (Cambridge, UK: Cambridge University Press, 2002).

economy would have seemed absurd from this perspective, since the success of the reform era (in terms of the increase in GDP) was by most observers ascribed to marketization and liberalization.[25]

Sociological work on changes in social attitudes and public opinion has suggested, moreover, that the Chinese people were becoming more liberal (in a broad sense of the term), and that rule-of-law progress, or "governing the country in accordance with law" was the foundation of ordinary people's support for the party-state in the reform era. Presented in a descriptive mode, such analyses tend to emphasize the Chinese system's ability to engender some form of social acceptance. The majority view that an existing system is appropriate (or should not be opposed) can be taken as an indication of regime legitimacy understood in a sociological and descriptive sense, referring to "people's beliefs about political authority and, sometimes, political obligations" in a detached way, not committed to a view on the truth of the beliefs thus described.[26] A predominantly descriptive conception of political legitimacy has played an important role in advancing the idea of "authoritarian legality." For example, drawing on a significant body of earlier writings by other scholars, Whiting has argued that "the Chinese state's project of legal construction powerfully shapes the legal consciousness of ordinary rural citizens and that state-constructed legal consciousness enhances regime legitimacy."[27] In Tanner's words, "the Communist Party is trying to create clear, explicit rules for cases that are not politically sensitive, in which people who are not involved in politics are more likely to get some measure of protection."[28]

Comments like these stop just short of endorsing "authoritarian legality" by embracing a normative conception of the legitimacy of legal norms and institutions in authoritarian systems. Yet despite their

[25] This linear developmentalist view has been criticized by Weitseng Chen ("Twins of Opposites – Why China Will Not Follow Taiwan's Model of Rule of Law Transition toward Democracy," *American Journal of Comparative Law* 66 (2018): 481).

[26] Fabienne Peter, "Political Legitimacy," entry in *Stanford Encyclopedia of Philosophy* (esp. section 1 "Descriptive and Normative Concepts of Legitimacy"), revised April 24, 2017, https://plato.stanford.edu/entries/legitimacy

[27] Susan Whiting, "Authoritarian 'Rule of Law' and Regime Legitimacy," *Comparative Political Studies* 50 (2017): 1 and 28, citing numerous further scholars including Diamant, Epstein, Landry, Lee, Massoud, Rajah, Stockmann, and Gallagher in support of idea that "the Chinese state, like other authoritarian states, promotes rule by law to enhance its legitimacy."

[28] Tim White, interview with Murray Scot Tanner, "Rule of Law in China: An Essential Component of U.S.–China Relations," National Bureau of Asian Research, May 17, 2017, www.nbr.org//research/activity.aspx?id=776

descriptive framing, such statements can be taken to suggest that legality, understood as a morally attractive value, can be promoted through legal reforms in politically authoritarian contexts. They thus provide support for what Carothers has termed the "unhelpful temptation" of "sequentialism," namely, "the doctrine that a country should establish an environment conducive to economic investment first – it should secure the Rule of Law and provide a relatively risk-free environment for economic investment first, and then worry about setting up elected legislatures and other democratic institutions later."[29] They suggest that law and order, even if limited to certain aspects of life, lead to social acceptance of government, which in turn indicates political legitimacy – the majority's apparent acceptance of the system is taken to indicate that the system is good, or at least getting better.

The developmental, gradualist, sequentialist rhetoric can – and in China, did – have a problematic implication: it became the basis for toning down criticism. It could justify the rejection of certain topics of discussion or reform efforts as "too radical," and the exclusion from debates and exchanges of those individuals or groups whose contributions (or mere presence) might upset Chinese partners anxious not to cross (perceived) red lines of (self-)censorship. If the end point of legal reforms was a more liberal, more acceptable system, why spoil the process by rushing it? If certain participants, perceived as too impatient and radical critics of the system, made a Chinese project partner uncomfortable, why insist on inviting these particular individuals? If advocacy for human right x or group A was regarded as too sensitive, why not focus on right y or group B instead? Challenges to authoritarianism had to remain limited and were inherently risky, as they threatened to provoke the authoritarian ruler,[30] an entity whose potential to be wise and good must be assumed.[31]

Following the logic of sequentialism, the party-state's most egregious rights violations were often omitted from exchange and reform programs and left to be brought up in other forums via other mechanisms. The persecution and occasional criminal prosecution of prominent rights defenders and political dissidents are emblematic of this approach. For

---

[29] Thomas Carothers, "Rule of Law Temptations," *Fletcher Forum of World Affairs* 49 (2009): 55.

[30] Hualing Fu, "Challenging Authoritarianism through Law: Potential and Limits," *National Taiwan University Law Review* 6 (2011): 339, www.law.ntu.edu.tw/ntulawreview/articles/6-1/12-Article-Fu%20Hualing_p339-365.pdf

[31] Carothers, "Rule of Law Temptations," 56.

example, when repeatedly asked about the fate of the internationally well-known human rights lawyer Gao Zhisheng, disappeared by the authorities, the government said on various occasions that they did not know who he was; that they did not know where he was and that he was "where he should be."[32] At one point, local officials even told Gao's brother that Gao had "gone missing while in detention."[33] (Shortly afterward, the author met Gao and heard his story of continued abuse at the hands of the party-state.)[34]

By the end of the Hu–Wen leadership (2002–12), many principles of public international law had been officially recognized, strategic concessions had been made toward the global constitutional law model, and legal reforms had introduced procedural and substantive laws largely modeled on liberal ideas. The system appeared to have reached a stage of concurrent "denial" and some norm "contestation," in the terms of political scientists Risse, Ropp, and Sikkink's optimistic "spiral model" of gradual achievement of human rights treaty compliance.[35] Yet, the passage of time spent in supposed "transition," without political liberalization, the unconvincing emptiness of party-state rhetoric, and the gradual diversification of domestic criticism of the system increasingly presented challenges to the maintenance of the transition narrative. Some of the newer scholars of "authoritarian legality" in China – a concept whose very purpose is to claim that authoritarian legality can be articulated and practiced in contradistinction to liberal legality as its apparent opposite – turned against what was considered the liberal mainstream

3.3   The Repurposing of Law in the Xi Era

Xi Jinping's more forceful personality and seemingly more approachable, jovial demeanor led some to hope he would be a better leader than Hu Jintao, who had ruled in a technocratic fashion; it was even thought that Xi's experience of terror in the Cultural Revolution could have turned him into a closet liberal.[36] Yet as Willy Lam has pointed out, Xi Jinping

---

[32] Michael Bristow, "Mystery of Missing Chinese Lawyer Gao Zhisheng," *BBC News*, January 29, 2010, news.bbc.co.uk/2/hi/asia-pacific/8482413.stm

[33] Kerry Brown, "Gao Zhisheng and China's Question," *openDemocracy*, February 4, 2010, www.opendemocracy.net/kerry-brown/gao-zhisheng-and-chinas-question

[34] Eva Pils, "Asking the Tiger for His Skin: Rights Activism in China," *Fordham International Law Journal* 30 (2007): 1209.

[35] Thomas Risse, Stephen C. Ropp, and Kathryn Sikkink, *The Persistent Power of Human Rights* (Cambridge, UK: Cambridge University Press, 2013).

[36] Willy Wo-Lap Lam, *Chinese Politics in the Era of Xi Jinping* (New York: Routledge, 2015).

was not attracted to liberal ideas; rather, he had learned through his father's terrifying example how dangerous holding such ideas could be for a party member.[37]

Changes that appeared to accelerate from Xi's assumption of his current post suggest that the party-state wishes to establish a system in which law still plays a centrally important role, unlike in the Mao era; but unlike in the reform and opening era, it is understood in explicitly anti-liberal terms.

First, in the new era, power concentration in the hands of the leadership is emphasized and celebrated, not obfuscated. It is no longer seen with any skepticism and the ideas of law and the legal process are remodeled to allow feeling and sentiment to take precedence over rationality. In the Xi era, the system has rejected until recently still (at least) debatable ideas such as judicial independence and what it skeptically refers to as "so-called 'universal values'" and constitutionalism ("*xianzheng*"), and it now clearly subordinates law ("legal governance") to party leadership.

> Party leadership and socialist rule of law are identical; only when we adhere to Party leadership can we realize [the principle of] letting the People be the masters, and systematically organize the state and social life; only then can legal governance [*fazhi*] be promoted in an orderly manner.[38]

On this basis, law and democracy can be defined along clearly illiberal lines. Gone is the hope, so important in the 1980s, of separating the party from the state, and largely gone too is the expectation of rendering the practice of law more autonomous by strengthening the law as a set of social practices limiting power. The preferred mode of governance instead is one of enhanced power and influence of the party. As it concentrates, this approach also romanticizes power – it advocates a felt unity between the people and the party that neither allows nor requires rational analysis and justification, and in which feeling and power often take precedence over reason and law.

For example, conceptions of good adjudication propagated under Xi suggest that there is emotional, romantic value in the subjection of the legal process to the will of the party and/or the people,[39] without strict

---

[37] Ibid.

[38] Xi Jinping, "Xi Jinping lun fazhi" [Xi Jinping discusses rule of law], *People*, January 7, 2014, http://cpc.people.com.cn/xuexi/n/2015/0511/c385475-26978527.html

[39] Liu Xiaofeng (刘小枫) interprets "renmin" as a homogeneous category, people who must be subordinated to the national goal of remaining as a competitive nation. See Qi Zheng, "Carl Schmitt, Leo Strauss and the Issue of Political Legitimacy in China," *American*

adherence to legal rules. Official eulogies praise individual judges for possessing a "public sentiment barometer,"[40] and demand that they "must have a mindset that is close to the People, love the People, and benefit the People."[41] "The People" as invoked here is not a reference to a critical public providing scrutiny of the legal process; rather, they are an abstract entity in whose service the judicial process must overcome the rationality of rules when necessary. This approach is compatible with the stated goal of the leadership of achieving better discipline by officials, as long as one remembers that obedience, under such a model, is primarily owed to political leaders, not the law.

The concentration of political control of legal processes is accompanied by technologically updated systems of surveillance and control of widening society circles. An example is the party-state's announced plans, as of 2016, to create what is described as a system of "social credit governance."[42] Preceded by the more modest systems for "education and discipline" already being implemented through the party-dominated associations and federations for workers, women, lawyers, and so on, and functioning rather like a credit score check writ large, it would assemble vast amounts of information about each Chinese citizen in one database to assess their trustworthiness or "social credit." On the basis of their social credit assessment the individual citizen might be eligible for being issued with a passport (or not); they might (or might not) have a high enough score to get a loan or to place their child in

---

Foreign Policy Interests 35(5) (2013): 257. On judicial dependence, see Ling Li, "The Chinese Communist Party and People's Courts: Judicial Dependence in China," *American Journal of Comparative Law* 64(1) (2016): 28, ssrn.com/abstract=2551014

[40] Guo Shuxun (郭树勋) and Zhu Jianfeng (朱建锋), "Li Yuxiang faguan de 'minqing qingyubiao'" [Judge Li Yuxiang's "Popular Sentiment Weather Barometer"], Higher People's Court of Xinjiang Province website, July 25, 2013, www.xjcourt.org/public/detail .php?id=7119

[41] Zhang Dejin (张德金), Liu Bing (刘冰), and Tong Yuping (董玉萍), "Yi pian danxin xi mingqing – ji Heilongjiang sheng Daqing shi Chengfeng fating futingzhang Zhu Dan" [Full devotion to the people – remembering vice division president of ChengFeng district court in Daqing, Heilongjiang Province], *Guangmingwang*, March 19, 2013, court .gmw.cn/html/article/201306/19/130580.shtml

[42] 国务院关于建立完善守信联合激励和失信联合惩戒制度加快推进社会诚信建设的 指导意见 China Copyright and Media, "State Council guiding opinions concerning establishing and perfecting incentives for promise-keeping and joint punishment systems for trust-breaking, and accelerating the construction of social sincerity," October 18, 2016, translation by Rogier Creemers, available at https://chinacopyrightandmedia.word press.com/2016/05/30/state-council-guiding-opinions-concerning-establishing-and-per fecting-incentives-for-promise-keeping-and-joint-punishment-systems-for-trust-break ing-and-accelerating-the-construction-of-social-sincer

a good school, for example.[43] As Chen and Cheung point out, the principle is that "those who gain credit will everywhere reap benefits; those who lose credit will be impeded at every turn."[44] In conjunction with this program, further systems to "strengthen" propaganda and education, as well as "joint incentives and joint punishments" are envisaged to be implemented.[45] While party loyalty (*dangxing*) is framed as a patriotic virtue, it is thus also enforced by ever-more invasive techniques.

Second, the legal process is dedicated to the project of crushing the system's (or the People's) enemies and, in this process, making both these enemies and the party, as protector of peace and order, more visible. A raft of new legislation reflects this purpose. For example, the 2015 National Security Law suggests that potential enemies are everywhere, and that every citizen's assistance may be called upon to fight these enemies. It defines national security in very broad terms as "the relative absence of international or domestic threats to the state's power to govern, sovereignty, unity and territorial integrity, the welfare of the people, sustainable economic and social development, and other major national interests, and the ability to ensure a continued state of security" (article 2). It empowers officials as well as others "assisting" officials to take measures to protect national security based on these broad terms.[46] It also explicitly refers to the "People's Democratic Dictatorship," a principle that had survived in all the texts of the Constitution, but was rarely employed elsewhere. Other examples of such legislation

[43] Yongxi Chen and Anne S. Y. Cheung, "The Transparent Self under Big Data Profiling: Privacy and Chinese Legislation on the Social Credit System," *Journal of Comparative Law of the University of Hong Kong* 12 (2017): 356; Jeremy Daum, "China's Social Credit System," *China Digital Times*, January 18, 2018, chinadigitaltimes.net/2018/01/giving-credit-jeremy-daum-chinas-social-credit-system; Mirjam Meissner, "China's Social Credit System," China Monitor Analysis Report (MERICS, 2017), www.merics.org/en/microsite/china-monitor/chinas-social-credit-system; Simon Denyer, "China Wants to Give All of Its Citizens a Score – And Their Rating Could Affect Every Area of Their Lives," *The Independent*, October 22, 2016, www.independent.co.uk/news/world/asia/china-surveillance-big-data-score-censorship-a7375221.html

[44] Chen and Cheung, "Transparent Self under Big Data Profiling."

[45] China Copyright and Media, "State Council guiding opinions."

[46] Similarly, the revision of the Criminal Procedure Law in 2012 purported to legalize "non-residential residential surveillance" by providing for incommunicado detention of criminal suspects in certain cases affecting "national security." Joshua Rosenzweig, Flora Sapio, Jiang Jue, Teng Biao, and Eva Pils, "The 2012 Revision of the Chinese Criminal Procedure Law: (Mostly) Old Wine in New Bottles," CRJ Occasional Paper (Centre for Rights and Justice, 2012), www.law.cuhk.edu.hk/en/research/crj/download/papers/2012-CRJ-OccasionalPaper-CPL.pdf

enacted between 2015 and 2017 include the Foreign NGO Management Law, the Anti-Espionage Law, the Cyber-Security Law, and the National Intelligence Law.[47]

Moreover, as anticipated, specific party-state crackdowns on perceived enemies continued and were integrated into the party-state system. The *fanfu* anti-corruption drive initiated in 2013, for example, targeted powerful actors within the party-state system, initially using the *shuanggui* system of party-administered investigation detention, which has no basis in state law.[48] *Shuanggui* had long been a tool the party had used to investigate its members (see Chapter 2 in this volume). Like other forms of extralegal incommunicado detention, it routinely involved torture.[49]

Under Xi Jinping, this system was renamed *liuzhi* and a new institution put in charge of it, the Supervision Commission, was written into the Constitution. In a complete reversal of the reform-era approach of separating party and state, this constitutional reform is clearly intended to fuse party and state back together, and to reentrench the Mao-era practice of "self-criticism" ("*jiantao*") under conditions of duress. When the creation of this new system was announced, it was stipulated, inter alia, that party-internal supervision must include "frequent criticism and self-criticism through conversations and letters so as to make 'red and sweaty faces' the norm."[50] The Supervision Commission has thus become an embodiment of the now-strengthened party-state principle and allowed the party to acquire a more visible presence in the legal system.[51] Concurrently,

---

[47] Elizabeth Lynch, "A Slow Death? China's Draft Foreign NGO Management Law," *China Law and Policy Blog*, May 10, 2015, www.chinalawandpolicy.com/2015/05/10/a-slow-death-chinas-draft-foreign-ngo-management-law; Bethany Allen-Ebrahimian, "The Chilling Effect of China's New Cybersecurity Regime," *Foreign Policy*, July 10, 2015, www.foreignpolicy.com/2015/07/10/china-new-cybersecurity-law-internet-security; Christian Shepherd, "China Activists Fear Increased Surveillance with New Security Law," *Reuters*, June 5, 2017, www.reuters.com/article/us-china-security-idUSKBN18M09U

[48] Human Rights Watch, "Special Measures: Detention and Torture in the Chinese Communist Party's Shuanggui System," December 6, 2016, www.hrw.org/report/2016/12/06/special-measures/detention-and-torture-chinese-communist-partys-shuanggui-system

[49] For a documentary featuring *shuanggui* [double regulation] torture survivors, see the interview by Zhiqiang Pu, on "Ningyuan Shuanggui" [Ningyuan Double Regulation] and translated by the HKU Media Project, www.vimeo.com/104070378

[50] Section 7 of "Zhongguo gongchandang dangnei jiandu tiaoli" [CCP Intra-Party Supervision Regulation], *Xinhuanet*, October 27, 2016, news.xinhuanet.com/politics/2016–11/02/c_1119838242.htm

[51] Ning Xin (宁馨), "Tushe jianchawei, wei zhenggai haishi wei Wang Qishan liuren" [The sudden establishment of the Supervision Commission: for political reform, or to keep

perceived enemies of the party-state in domestic and transnational civil society, including lawyers, journalists, and NGO workers, have also been persecuted in new and more visible ways.[52]

Third, in perhaps the most obvious break with the practices of the reform and opening era, the party-state has again taken to *displaying* political detainees, convicts, etc. in propagandistic fashion as enemies to be feared and crushed.[53] In doing so, it has heightened its own visibility and dominance. For example, a 2015 crackdown on rights lawyers, dubbed the "709" crackdown, was turned into a highly visualized and partly televised state media spectacle.[54] Several lawyers and legal assistants were shown on national television renouncing their former activism, as well as denouncing their colleagues, thanking and praising the authorities for protecting their legal rights and looking after them while detained, and admitting to having been goaded into advocacy by "hostile foreign forces."[55] Enhancing the effects of these measures, an officially circulated video clip cast human rights advocates as enemies, visually associating them with images of US warfare in Iraq and Syrian refugees stranded in Europe, suggesting that human rights advocates were part of a US-based plot to subvert China.[56] Other reports showed foreign supporters of such "enemy" figures also "confessing" to wrongdoing,[57] and cartoon videos from obscure sources provided fictional representations

Wang Qishan in post], *Voice of America* (Chinese Desk), December 9, 2016, www.voachinese.com/a/VOAWeishi-20161209-Pro-and-Con-2/3629772.html

[52] Orville Schell, "Crackdown in China: Worse and Worse," *New York Review of Books*, April 6, 2016, www.chinafile.com/nyrb-china-archive/crackdown-china-worse-and-worse

[53] Hualing Fu, "The July 9th (709) Crackdown on Human Rights Lawyers: Legal Advocacy in an Authoritarian State, *Journal of Contemporary China* 27 (2018): 554; Eva Pils, 'China's Turn to Public Repression: The Case of the 709 Crackdown on Human Rights Lawyers," *China Law and Society Review* 3 (2018): 1–47.

[54] Pils, "China's Turn to Public Repression," 1.

[55] Translated in Chris Buckley, "Week of TV Trials in China Signals New Phase in Attack on Rights," *New York Times*, August 5, 2016, www.nytimes.com/2016/08/06/world/asia/china-trial-activists-lawyers.html

[56] "[Y]ear after year, the western forces, led by the U.S., under the banner of democracy, freedom and rule of law, create social contradictions in targeted countries with the intention to overthrow governments. Their slogans are loud, their lies are beautiful; but they will not become facts" ("Yanse geming" [Color Revolution], YouTube, www.youtube.com/watch?v=8qBt-i9ErSY).

[57] Hong Kong Free Press, "State TV Confession: Peter Dahlin," YouTube, www.youtube.com/watch?v=whbgVz4xKww; Edward Wong, "Inside China's Secret 23-Day Detention of a Foreign Nonprofit Chief," *New York Times*, July 9, 2016, www.nytimes.com/2016/07/10/world/asia/china-ned-ngo-peter-dahlin.html

of the career of the "die-hard" legal advocate, depicted as an enemy of the people (and the party), transitioning from legal practice into prison.[58] Commenting on the wider effects of this campaign, a lawyer observed that "many ordinary people" might trust these official reports and believe that human rights lawyers had been working "under the direction of foreign anti-China enemy forces."

The changes discussed above, and the rhetoric accompanying them, call to mind many aspects of the Mao era, such as Mao's distinction between contradictions among the people and contradictions between the people and its enemies.[59] However, in the way these changes make law and the legal process a central, albeit subordinate, element of the political system, they also depart from Mao's China, especially Maoism during its more revolutionary periods. They strongly evoke the twentieth-century visions of the total state by Carl Schmitt,[60] and they do so for a good reason. Carl Schmitt has over the past decade received a significant reception among Chinese legal–political scholars[61] In some ways, the connection is obvious: Schmitt's theory defends the identification of the party with the people and the principle that party leadership must not be challenged, but it also provides an account of law that justifies reliance on the law to give effect to the will of the party .

For example, the idea of adjudication "close to the people" reflects a Schmittian, ultimately romantic conception of law. Schmitt's theory supports the recasting of the judicial decision as an exercise of *"gesundes Volksempfinden"* (i.e. "healthy popular feeling") rather than an exercise

---

[58] Bu xiashuo TV [Non-nonsense TV], "Sike de na dian shir – jiemi sike lvshi qunti de na dian xiao mimi" [This issue of "being diehard" – disclosing the secret of the "diehard lawyer" group], August 2, 2016, https://perma.cc/8MBH-A7SW

[59] Mark Selden, *The People's Republic of China: A Documentary History of Revolutionary Change* (New York: Monthly Review Press, 1979).

[60] Schmitt proposes a "total state" as "a state of identity of state and society." Carl Schmitt, *The Concept of the Political*, expanded ed. (1932), trans. G. Schwab (Chicago, IL: University of Chicago Press, 2007), 24. Later, he calls for the subjection of social organizations to *"Gleichschaltung"* or "coordination" by the party (ibid.); Reinhard Mehring, *Carl Schmitt: Aufstieg und Fall* (Munich: Beck, 2009), 320.

[61] Karl Marchal and Carl K. Y. Shaw (eds.), *Çarl Schmitt and Leo Strauss in the Chinese-Speaking World: Reorienting the Political* (Lanham, MD: Lexington Books, 2017); Flora Sapio, "Carl Schmitt in China," *China Story*, October 7, 2015, www.thechinastory.org /2015/10/carl-schmitt-in-china; Jean-Christopher Mittelstaedt, "Understanding China's Two Constitutions: Re-assessing the Role of the Chinese Communist Party," 10th ECLS Conference, "New Perspectives on the Development of Law in China" (Institute of East Asian Studies, University of Cologne, 2015), papers.ssrn.com/sol3/papers.cfm? abstract_id=2682609

in reasoning through legal rules and principles.[62] Importantly, this anti-rational conception of adjudication can be used to justify the subjection of the judiciary to party goals, even when they permit (and require) flagrant violations of law. More widely, Schmitt's theory is defensive of extralegal (arbitrary) use of power and grounded in the claim that "no legal norm ... can govern an extreme case of emergency or an absolute state of exception"[63] and that the sovereign is "he who controls the state of exception."[64]

A Schmittian conception of the political also explains attempted justifications of the crackdown on perceived enemies inside (party-state officials and other powerholders) as well as outside the system (e.g. human rights advocates). Schmitt's conception of the authority to rule is reductionist and relativistic, grounded in the simple historical fact of being the ruling party.[65] Under this theory, the ruling party does not need to identify its enemies by reference to the (inconvenient) notion of class. As in a Schmittian world, "the political" defines and determines all aspects of the legal–political order through its fundamental conception of the enemy,[66] turning against the party means turning into an enemy, who must be crushed in the name of the law, as well as of the party. This view is reminiscent of the idea of class struggle under Mao, but stripped of socialist or Marxist assumptions about law. As it integrates the legal process within the fight against enemies by simultaneously asserting the importance of law and law's subordination to the concept of the political, the party can claim to have devised

---

[62] The German criminal law was amended in 1935 to criminalize acts in violation of "the principles underlying an existing criminal provision and healthy popular feeling." Gesetz zur Änderung des Strafgesetzbuchs vom 28. Juni 1935 [Law to amend the Criminal Law of 28 June 1935] (RGBl. I 1935 S. 839).

[63] Lars Vinx, "Carl Schmitt," *Stanford Encyclopedia of Philosophy*, August 7, 2010, https://plato.stanford.edu/entries/schmitt

[64] This view was also captured in his comment piece justifying an instance of political assassination, "The Leader Protects the Law." See Carl Schmitt, "Der Führer schützt das Recht," [The leader protects the law], *Deutsche Juristen-Zeitung* 39 (1934): 945 which is discussed in Volker Neumann, *Carl Schmitt als Jurist* [Carl Schmitt as a lawyer] (Tübingen: Mohr Siebeck, 2015), 338. Schmitt dismissed the government's attempt to legalize these murders by means of retroactive legislation as unnecessary liberal legal formalism.

[65] Mittelstaedt, "Understanding China's Two Constitutions," which explores this through its analysis of three legal scholars, Chen Duanhong, Jiang Shigong, and Gao Quanxi, who associate themselves closely with Carl Schmitt.

[66] Carl Schmitt, *Political Theology: Four Chapters on the Concept of Sovereignty*, trans. George Schwab (Chicago, IL: University of Chicago, 2005), 5.

RULE-OF-LAW REFORM AND RULE BY FEAR 105

a successful new model of authoritarian legality suited to the conditions of illiberal democracy.[67]

3.4 The Rise of Rule by Fear in the Xi Era

Political control is not reconstituted merely by new rules and rhetoric. An important factor in engendering obedience and political control under Xi Jinping's "new normal" ("*xin changtai*") is the creation and propagation of fear – both the fear of political enemies, and the related fear of being made into an "enemy" by the state. While during the reform and opening era, it might plausibly be claimed that the system was working to overcome such fear, reduce its use, and enhance legal protections for everyone, China in the Xi Jinping era has increased its reliance on fear.

Some interlocutors who were keen and critical observers of the system, as well as victims of its fear techniques, were also at the receiving end of its persecution campaigns. They found themselves wheeled out on television, not only displaying contrition, but also in numerous instances quite visibly affected by their treatment in detention. Soon, it emerged that some had been subjected to the use of forced "medication"[68] This addition of a novel suppression technique might seem minor, yet it was significant: by forcibly drugging victims, the party-state introduced a new type of fear. As one interlocutor explained, being forced to take pills following patently invented diagnoses of illness was terrifying due to the total and absolute uncertainty of what these pills might do to him.[69] The fear generated by forced drugging was also a fear of being robbed of one's sanity, especially after one victim returned with a diagnosis of serious mental illness following weeks of forced drugging that affected his mental state.[70] Thus, forced drugging went to the heart of what some have described as the essence of torture: a loss of agency, of the power to think and act for oneself, the loss of language, and the loss of rationality.[71] Moreover, by *propagating* its victims'

---

[67] Müller, *What Is Populism?*

[68] Eva Pils, ChinaFile/Foreign Policy contribution to "Rule by Fear?," February 17, 2016, https://foreignpolicy.com/2016/02/18/chinas-new-age-of-fear-new-normal-under-xi-jinping; piece originally published as "The Rise of Rule by Fear," University of Nottingham China Policy Institute Blog, February 15, 2016.

[69] Pils, "China's Turn to Public Repression," 1.

[70] Ibid.

[71] As a rights defender who had gone through the experience of forced disappearance and torture in the 2010s commented, "Not only did they want to make you say *that* black was

"confessions," the party-state could multiply the fear it had generated. Victims talking about their contrition, gratitude to the Party, and desire to change their ways perfectly illustrate the Party's power through its capacity to make former opponents "fold" in this way, denouncing their ideals, their friends, and themselves before a television camera.

The fear engendered through these measures is a perfect example of the fear Shklar had in mind when writing "The Liberalism of Fear." Fear, as Shklar reminded us, is a mental as well as a physical reaction; it is "universal," as it is "physiological."[72] At its most basic, it is a mere "unpleasant emotion caused by the threat of danger, pain or harm."[73] As far as it is experienced, or felt, it may be possible to measure fear, or at least to measure fear of particular things such as cancer or burglary. Yet even if it can be measured in terms of psychological or neuro-scientific fact, such measures would not necessarily help us understand the specific fear of political violence or cruelty that Shklar had in mind; they would not directly answer the question of how to identify and assess politically relevant fear.

Shklar had an answer to this question. She argued that to decide what kind of fear is reprehensible, we need to determine how and why it is produced:

> A minimal level of fear is implied in any system of law ... and the liberalism of fear does not dream of an end to public coercive government. The fear it does want to end is that which is created by arbitrary, unnecessary, and unlicensed acts of force and by habitual and pervasive acts of cruelty performed by military, paramilitary and police agents in any regime.[74]

She defined cruelty as "deliberate infliction of physical and secondarily emotional pain upon a weaker person or group by stronger ones in order to achieve some end, tangible or intangible, of the latter."[75] In a similar

---

white. You also had to explain *why* black was white". Eva Pils, *China's Human Rights Lawyers: Advocacy and Resistance* (New York: Routledge, 2015), 189.

[72] Shklar, "Liberalism of Fear," 29.

[73] Fear is defined as an "unpleasant emotion caused by the threat of danger, pain, or harm" and its synonyms are terror, fright, fearfulness, horror, alarm, panic, agitation, trepidation, dread, consternation, dismay, distress. An example of the word "fear" used in a sentence: "I cowered in fear as bullets whizzed past" (*Oxford Dictionaries*, en .oxforddictionaries.com/definition/fear).

[74] Shklar, "Liberalism of Fear," 11. This distinction is echoed by Jon Elster's distinction between "prudential" and "visceral" fear ("Constitution-Making and Violence," *Journal of Legal Analysis* 4(1) (2012): 7).

[75] Shklar, "Liberalism of Fear," 11.

vein, Arendt has argued that as "terror is the essence of totalitarian domination," the essence of good government rests on the distinction between lawless and lawful, and legitimate and arbitrary power.[76] It is also in response to the experience of twentieth-century totalitarianism that political arguments for freedom from fear were developed,[77] and that the international human rights mechanisms including the Convention against Torture and Other Cruel, Inhuman or Degrading Treatment or Punishment, with its explicit inclusion of psychological torture, were introduced.[78]

On this basis, it would not be helpful or necessary to assess the rise or fall of fear experienced by the Chinese people in the aggregate; rather, it is important to understand how the authorities responsible create fear and how they justify their reliance on fear. In the contexts observed, the politically motivated creation of fear is directly related to the notion of political enemies, whose threatening existence is reflected, as noted earlier on, in the laws as well as the rhetoric of the "new normal."[79] The existence of enemies "justifies" what Shklar would describe as "arbitrary, unnecessary, and unlicensed acts of force" and "habitual and pervasive acts of cruelty." In the example just given, the application of this nexus is evident – the victims of fear creation were held on suspicion of "subverting" or "inciting to subvert" the party-state or other national-security-related crimes, and the party-state's propagandistic portrayals of these victims deliberately created visual associations with perceived external enemies of China, as discussed earlier.

Similar moves can be observed in other areas; for example, techniques of what Nussbaum would describe as "aggressive othering"[80] are applied to portray as enemies and even dehumanize Uighur Muslims in Xinjiang in order to "justify" an unprecedented mass detention campaign for

---

[76] Hannah Arendt, *The Origins of Totalitarianism* (New York: Harcourt Brace Jovanovich, 1973), 461.

[77] Other examples include Franklin D. Roosevelt's postulate of freedom from fear (of war) in the 41st State of the Union address in 1941, and Aung San Suu Kyi's interpretation of freedom from fear, including the fear of losing power.

[78] United Nations, Convention against Torture and Other Cruel, Inhuman or Degrading Treatment or Punishment (Geneva: UNTS, 1984), 85.

[79] An increased preoccupation with China's enemies has also motivated changes in military policy and international relations.

[80] Faced with the threats of resurgent populism in the twenty-first century, Martha Nussbaum has argued that fear, with its capacity of upsetting rational argument, leads to "aggressive 'othering' strategies" that must be challenged and overcome (*The Monarchy of Fear: A Philosopher Looks at Our Current Political Crisis* (Oxford: Oxford University Press, 2018), 2).

"education and conversion" purposes.[81] Like in the case of the "709" detentions and televised confessions, the reality of the camps is undeniable, and the goals of "Sinicization" of Islam among Uighur and other minorities in China have been openly propagated.[82]

To understand how fear comes to play such an important role in repressive systems, it is important to appreciate not only how it is deployed to control, but also how it is used to justify the obligation to obey the law, and the status of 'enemies' in such systems. The idea that having enemies entails a right to kill[83] runs through all Schmittian accounts of law's fundamental basis in "the political."[84] In so far as it claims an entitlement to rule through its capacity to protect from enemies, the sovereign power implicitly relies on fear. As McCormick has pointed out, such reliance has a longer intellectual history; not only Carl Schmitt, but also Hobbes have regarded fear as 'the source of political order.'[85]

In the Chinese context, the philosophical tradition of legalism comes to mind as in some ways similar to Hobbesian theory.[86] Obedience, at least on a Schmittian (if not a Hobbesian) account, cannot be reduced to a mere obedience to rules according to the old Austinian/

---

[81] Sophie Beach, *China Digital Times*, "Evidence of Abuses, Deaths in Xinjiang Camps Emerges," August 20, 2018, chinadigitaltimes.net/2018/08/evidence-of-abuse-deaths-in-xinjiang-camps-emerges

[82] Ibid.

[83] According to Schmitt, enmity as a political concept is the essence of the political and it is connected to a "right to kill" ("ius vitae ac necis"). Carl Schmitt, *The Concept of the Political* (expanded ed.), trans. G. Schwab (Chicago, IL: University of Chicago Press, 2007).

[84] Mittelstaedt rightly gives prominence to this distinction ("Understanding China's Two Constitutions," 4).

[85] John P. McCormick, "Fear, Technology, and the State: Carl Schmitt, Leo Strauss, and the Revival of Hobbes in Weimar and National Socialist Germany," *Political Theory* 22(4) (1994): 622. McCormick cites Schmitt, *Concept of the Political*, 52, in the claim that "protego ergor obligo'" is "the cogito ergo sum of the state."

[86] Jeffrey Riegel, "Confucius," *Stanford Encyclopedia of Philosophy*, plato.stanford.edu /entries/confucius; "Legalism," ibid., plato.stanford.edu/entries/ethics-chinese/#Leg; Ryan Mitchell, "Is 'China's 'Machiavelli' Now Its Most Important Philosopher?," *Foreign Policy*, January 16, 2015, thediplomat.com/2015/01/is-chinas-machiavelli-now-its-most-important-political-philosopher. In the evolution of liberal theory, reliance on fear by public power becomes more and more suspect. Hobbes's theory of the state still fundamentally rests the state's claim to legitimacy on fear; he dismisses the argument of "them that hold all such covenants, as proceed from fear of death or violence, void: which, if it were true, no man in any kind of Commonwealth could be obliged to obedience." Thomas Hobbes, *Leviathan* (1651). Descartes, in contrast, argues that rationality can and should overcome fear. René Descartes, *Les passions de l'âme* [Passions of the soul] (1649).

Benthamite conception; nor is it motivated merely by the rational "fear of sanctions" essential to some positivistic accounts of law. At least in the case of Schmittian theory, obedience is obedience to a law whose subordination to the political is part of the theory. It is also obedience to the power of the sovereign in the state of exception, and therefore it cannot simply be obedience motivated by the fear of rule infraction but has to be obedience more widely motivated by the power of the sovereign to do as he likes. In this way, Schmitt's *"protego ergo obligo"* is tied to the concept of the political – the law only offers protection to friends but not to enemies, and in the totalist state, fear is overcome only when the individual and her legal protections give way to total, willing subordination to the sovereign, who is engaged in a struggle against the enemy.

Enemy ideas are central not only to the rhetoric of the Xi-era party-state propagandists, but also to the contemporary Chinese scholars whose work they draw on in support of the "new normal." Already in 2004, Jiang Shigong commented that according to Schmitt:

> The primary problem in politics is to distinguish clearly between friend and enemy. Between enemies and friends, there is no question of liberties; there are only violence and conquest.[87]

Zhang Xundong, writing in 2005, argued that:

> A flaw of liberalism is precisely [to assume] that the "enemy" can be transformed or reconciled away – liberals believe in peace, reason, free debate and mutual exchange; but the innermost core of political issues is to "preserve one's own form of existence" and to "repel the enemy"; this can be a life-and-death struggle.[88]

This position further means that discussion, argument, and peaceful deliberation (or the "dictatorship of enlightened reason") as paths to resolving differences are weak ideas, leading to pretenses of peace characteristic of weak systems, and the rational procedures characteristic of the law should be rejected.[89]

---

[87] Jiang Shigong (强世功), "Wukelan xianzheng weiji yu zhengzhi duanjue" [Constitutional crisis and political decision in Ukraine], *21st Century World Economic Herald*, December 15, 2004, www.duping.net/XHC/show.php?bbs=11&post=483745

[88] See also Zhang Xudong (张旭东), "Shimite de tiaozhan – du "yihui minzhu zhi de weiji'" [Schmitt's challenge – reading "The Crisis of Parliamentary Democracy"], *Kaifang Shidai*, April 6, 2005, www.aisixiang.com/data/6350.html

[89] Carl Schmitt, *Dictatorship: From the Origin of the Modern Concept of Sovereignty to Proletarian Class Struggle*, trans. M. Hoelzl and G. Ward (Cambridge, UK: Polity, 2014).

More recent scholarship has applied these abstract insights to the justification of China's deepening authoritarianism. For example, in a comment piece discussing the 2018 constitutional revisions mentioned earlier, Tian Feilong defends the new policy of fusing, as opposed to separating, party and state ("*dangzheng ronghe*"). He argues that China's social elites must be disabused of their preference for and expectation of democratization and that they must get used to an authoritarian Chinese future.[90] The "futurism" ("*weilaizhuyi*") Tian also advocates shares with Schmittian theory a convenient lack of substance – if the belief in the future as such is embraced, that future can be filled with whatever the powers that be decide it should be filled with.[91]

It is in the context of the revival of fear techniques and their increasingly assertive official justifications that Shklar's account of liberalism acquires great contemporary significance.[92] Her account allows us better to grasp and analyze the Xi-era changes. According to Shklar, it is abusively created fear that would lead to the sort of society we rightly fear – "a society of fearful people." Societies governed by liberal principles had a better chance of curbing abuses and of allowing citizens to become persons acting responsibly in the public sphere, whose maintenance is another central concern of the liberalism of fear:

> Every adult should be able to make as many effective decisions without fear or favor about as many aspects of his or her life as is compatible with the like freedom of every adult . . . this is the original and only defensible meaning of liberalism.[93]

While the examples of detention and torture including forced drugging represent extreme fear creation techniques, other similar strategies and practices including those euphemistically termed "education" may also violate the principles of a "liberalism of fear" as Shklar envisaged. As she observed:

<hr/>

[90] Tian Feilong (田飞龙), "Xiuxian queli Zhongguo xianfa xinzhixu" [The constitutional revision consolidates China's new Constitutional order], *DW News*, March 31, 2018, http://blog.dwnews.com/post-1013159.html
[91] 'Futurism' echoes the twentieth-century futurism advocated, inter alia, by the Italian fascist Marinetti. See Umbro Apollonio (ed.), *Documents of 20th Century Art: Futurist Manifestos*, trans. Robert, Brain, R. W. Flint, J. C. Higgitt, and Caroline Tisdall (New York: Viking Press, 1973), 19–24, www.italianfuturism.org/manifestos/foundingmanifesto
[92] Levy, "Who's Afraid of Judith Shklar?"
[93] Shklar points out that the enabling aspects of her political theory set her apart from Isaiah Berlin's argument for a negative conception of liberty ("Liberalism of Fear," 28).

> The inviolability of personal decisions in matters of faith, knowledge and
> is still defended on the original grounds that we owe it to each other as
> a matter of mutual respect, that a forced belief is in itself false and that the
> threats and bribes used to enforce conformity are inherently demeaning.[94]

Returning to the examples of the social credit and 'education and conversion' systems discussed earlier,[95] it is evident that these policies rely on precisely what Shklar condemns. The social credit system, for instance, makes the fear of sanction and the desire for favors an explicit element of its policy, whose propagation is designed not only to instill fear among specific targets of repression, such as persecuted dissidents and rights defenders, but also ensure the dispersal of fear among wider communities, which goes beyond "relational repression."[96]

Shklar not only reminds us that the results of such policies tend to be incompatible with respect for moral autonomy. She also insists that the rule of law can be an important tool to overcome rule by fear.[97]

Indeed, legal argument has often reflected law's fundamental aversion to fear-induced coerced conformity as well as efforts to contain fear through legal regulation, in otherwise remote areas of legal doctrine. These include not only the prohibition on torture, but also the many rules designed to outlaw duress, as well as the law of freedom of expression and media freedom, an area where the problem of the "chilling effect" of unclear prohibitions on freedom of expression have long been recognized.[98] Together, these doctrines acknowledge fear's corrosive impact on the preconditions of autonomy and – at least in cases of visceral fear – rationality. They recognize the incompatibility of fear with liberty, rational argument, and the virtues of a genuinely rule-based system of governance, a system in which law cannot be "switched off."

To understand the significance of abuses such as detention and torture in the context considered here, we should therefore think of them not only as violations of specific rules and principles of law on a liberal

---

[94] Ibid., 23.

[95] The social credit system, discussed (above, p. 99), is intended to have nationwide application, whereas internment for the purpose of "education and conversion," discussed (above, p. 99) has been used primarily in the Xinjiang Uighur Autonomous Region.

[96] Yanhua Deng and Kevin O'Brien, "Relational Repression in China: Using Social Ties to Demobilize Protesters," *China Quarterly* 215 (2013): 533.

[97] Shklar, "Liberalism of Fear," 37.

[98] Frederick Schauer, "Fear, Risk, and the First Amendment: Unraveling the 'Chilling Effect,'" *Boston University Law Review* 58 (1978): 685.

conception, but also consider them as part of a scale of techniques that, when viewed together, are part of a rule by fear: a form of governance that is reverting to prominence in the legal–political system and that subverts the achievements of China's earlier, liberal-oriented rule-of-law reform process.[99] They suggest that narratives of "authoritarian legality" are mistaken, if they are taken to mean that law can be valuable when it does not serve as an instrument to restrain government.

This does not mean that rule-by-fear techniques are limited to systems explicitly rejecting liberal precepts. Rather, a second, central insight from Shklar's liberalism of fear is that we should "regard abuses of power in any regime with equal trepidation" and that we must not "take freedom for granted."[100] In a global situation in which societies and political systems interact in increasingly complex ways, this is all the more important, as the concurrent and related challenges of populism and authoritarian resurgence pose rising threats to liberal democracy.

3.5 Conclusions

In the light of skepticism about the ability of democracies to function well, models of "illiberal democracy,"[101] or of "smart authoritarianism" have gained traction[102] and the attractiveness of these models rests on the coherence of the notion of authoritarian legality. From the perspective taken here, however, the idea of authoritarian legality as deployed in Chinese contexts is inherently conflicted: The idea of legality assumes that there is a value in being governed by rules and (other) principles, whereas the authoritarianism practiced in China today rests on the party-state's increasingly explicit claim that it can ignore and suspend law as it deems expedient to crush its "enemies"; in order to maintain control, the

---

[99] As Fraenkel has argued in his discussion of the dual state, such a system cannot achieve the goal of rule of law in the sense of a system where power is in principle constrained by law interpreted based on reasonable principles. According to this account, neither the normative nor the prerogative parts or aspects of the dual state can achieve the rule of law. Ernst Fraenkel, *The Dual State: A Contribution to the Theory of Dictatorship*, trans. E. A. Shils (New York: Oxford University Press, 1941).

[100] Shklar, "Liberalism of Fear," 28, 36.

[101] See e.g. Hungarian President Orban's widely noted speech in 2014 at Băile Tuşnad (Tusnádfürdő), Budapest Beacon, www.budapestbeacon.com/public-policy/full-text-of-viktor-orbans-speech-at-baile-tusnad-tusnadfurdo-of-26-july-2014/10592

[102] Timothy Garton Ash, "Xi Jinping's China is the Greatest Political Experiment on Earth," *The Guardian*, June 1, 2015, www.theguardian.com/commentisfree/2015/jun/01/war-peace-depend-china-domestic-success

party-state must constantly create and propagate subliminal and visceral fear.

Shklar's account of the liberalism of fear provides a powerful, albeit implicit, argument against the claims of "authoritarian legality." If the values of legality are genuinely promoted in authoritarian systems, this can only make these systems less authoritarian, but mere claims to pursue an authoritarian (or indeed, totalitarian) model of legality while enhancing the use of fear techniques must be rejected as false.

This conclusion begs the further question of how to oppose rule by fear. In some contrast to her liberal contemporaries such as Rawls, Shklar's liberalism of fear does not rest its case on the design of political systems and their institutions. Shklar is particularly aware that liberal political institutions will not mechanically engender freedom from cruelty and violence, or from the fear of cruelty and violence, and that civic-minded action is required:

> If citizens are to act individually and in associations, especially in a democracy, to protest and block any sign of governmental illegality and abuse, they must have a fair share of moral courage, self-reliance, and stubbornness to assert themselves effectively.[103]

The changing, complex and less easily controlled structures of interaction that make China's current situation so different from the twentieth-century's repressive societies also suggest that it is now easier to find intellectual, communicative, and associative resources of resistance were not available in earlier systems, as people communicate and connect in many state-independent ways within and beyond China's borders. The very irrationality that allows the party-state to harness fear for control purposes also suggests that fear is an imprecise governance tool, that fear can be overcome, and that a transnational civil society can and must resist rule-by-fear techniques wherever they originate.

---

[103] Shklar, "Liberalism of Fear," 33.

The Foreign NGO Law and the Closing
of China

THOMAS E. KELLOGG

4.1 Introduction

On October 9, 2014, Chinese authorities detained leading activist and intellectual Guo Yushan. Guo was held for nearly a year in mostly incommunicado detention, and was finally released on September 15, 2015. Immediately after his release, Guo spent much of his time under house arrest. His contact with others was heavily circumscribed and closely monitored, despite the fact that, legally speaking, he had committed no crime.[1]

An economist by training, Guo has been at the heart of China's small and embattled human rights movement for more than a decade. In 2003, Guo, working with prominent lawyer-activists Xu Zhiyong and Teng Biao, founded the Open Constitution Initiative (OCI), one of China's first explicitly rights-based nongovernmental organizations (NGOs). OCI was forced to close its doors in 2009, after the group released a report critical of the Chinese government's Tibet policy.[2]

In 2007, Guo founded the Beijing-based Transition Institute (TI), a combination think tank, grassroots NGO, haven for beleaguered activists, and clubhouse-like salon for liberal intellectuals that surely ranks as one of the most unique and wide-ranging organizations ever founded in China. The organization produced policy research reports on oligopoly in China's taxi industry, corruption and inefficiency in China's state-run

---

[1] Andrew Jacobs, "China Releases Guo Yushan, Scholar Who Helped Activist Gain Asylum in U.S.," *New York Times*, September 15, 2015. Several interviews by this author with colleagues of Guo in the months following his release documented the limitations on his freedoms after his arrest.

[2] Tania Branigan, "China Officials Shut Legal Aid Centre," *The Guardian*, July 18, 2009.

energy sector, institutionalized discrimination under China's abusive *hukou* household registration system, and China's controversial Three Gorges Dam project, among other subjects.[3]

And yet, its steady stream of high-quality research reports aside, from its very first days, TI was more than just a high-profile liberal think tank. It also pursued an activist agenda. It raised funds for dissidents who had run into trouble with the authorities, worked with lawyers on public interest litigation, and engaged with university students on key economic and political reform debates. Guo himself is perhaps best known outside of China for his participation in the daring 2012 rescue of the blind rights activist Chen Guangcheng from long-term house imprisonment in his hometown in rural Shandong.[4]

Those activist interventions aside, from its first days, TI sought to position itself as a relatively moderate voice favoring gradual reform.[5] In contrast to other, more self-consciously rights-focused organizations like the OCI, TI believed in dialogue with the party-state, and in using its on-the-ground research to influence government policy.[6] And yet, TI could not survive in the Xi Jinping era: in July 2013, TI's offices were raided by dozens of municipal officials. The officials confiscated TI's publications, and ordered its immediate closure. Guo himself was detained just fifteen months later.

To outside observers, Guo's detention, and the forced closure of TI, might seem like just another story of political repression in China. But a closer examination of Guo's case suggests a deeper meaning: the closure of TI quite likely marks the end of the emergence of more cutting-edge and savvy rights-based organizations that seek to use inside-the-system tools to push for progressive change. It marks the end – for now at least – of groups that are self-consciously moderate, yet autonomous and

---

[3] For an example of TI's Three Gorges Dam Project advocacy, see Guo Yushan, "Things You May Not Know about the History of the Three Gorges Dam Project," *Probe International*, February 8, 2012. For an example of the vital role that TI played as a forum for public debate and discussion, see Zhang Dajun (ed.), *Selections from Civic Forum on Transition* (2009) [in Chinese], a self-published selection of transcripts of lectures given at TI, on file with author.

[4] Keith B. Richburg and Steven Mufson, "Chen Guangcheng, Escaped Chinese Dissident, Is Subject of Diplomacy with U.S., Activists Say," *Washington Post*, April 28, 2012.

[5] Zeng Jinyan, "Guo Yushan and the Predicament of NGOs in China," *Probe International*, May 21, 2015.

[6] For more on the OCI, see Eva Pils, "From Independent Lawyer Groups to Civic Opposition: The Case of China's New Citizen Movement," *Asian-Pacific Law and Policy Journal* 19(1) (2017): 110–52.

advocacy oriented, seeking to occupy the always tenuous middle ground in between state-affiliated NGOs and more assertive rights activists whose tactics are often more audacious and overtly political.

At the same time as it cracks down on advocacy organizations like TI, the party-state has also moved to tighten control over foreign NGOs operating inside China. In 2016, the Chinese government passed the Law of the People's Republic of China on Administration of Activities of Overseas Nongovernmental Organizations in Mainland China (hereafter, the Foreign NGO Law). The Law takes a largely state security-based approach to the activities of foreign NGOs, and burdens them with extensive registration, preapproval, and reporting requirements.

In this chapter, I argue that the closure of these rights-based advocacy organizations represents a key turning point in China's legal and political development. The CCP's efforts to limit the development of such organizations – or to eliminate them altogether – is part of a larger effort to reassert the authority and the primacy of the Communist Party in all key aspects of Chinese public life, and has very real implications for rule-of-law and political development in China.[7]

The crackdown on civil society has included both key organizations and top individual activists. Since Xi Jinping came to power in late 2012, a veritable who's who of Chinese liberalism has been jailed, forced into exile, or pressured into putting aside their public interest work. Prominent examples include rights lawyer Teng Biao, who fled into exile in 2014 after enduring years of harassment; award-winning journalist Chang Ping, who has spent the last several years in Germany; rights lawyer Wang Yu, who was detained for over a year, and has, since her release, largely stopped taking on rights cases; and lawyer and activist Xu Zhiyong, who was sentenced to four years in prison for disturbing public order in January 2014. Xu was released in July 2017.

Though difficult to quantify, the absence of these key leaders from the domestic scene has had a significant impact on the development of civil society in China. How much smaller is China's civil society sector today than it would have been otherwise? How many young men and women

---

[7] See generally Elizabeth C. Economy, *The Third Revolution: Xi Jinping and the New Chinese State* (Oxford: Oxford University Press, 2018). Economy notes that the core pillars of Xi's governance strategy include "the dramatic centralization of authority under his personal leadership; the intensified penetration of society by the state; the creation of a virtual wall of regulations and restrictions that more tightly controls the flow of ideas, culture, and capital into and out of the country; and the significant projection of Chinese power" (ibid., 10).

have lost the chance to take part in grassroots activism, and to be mentored by experienced and charismatic activists like Pu Zhiqiang and Xu Zhiyong?[8] How many Chinese citizens have had less access to liberal discourse – online, in classrooms, and even occasionally in print – as a result of the ongoing crackdown? Numbers can only be guessed at, but the total impact is no doubt very significant.

This chapter also attempts to link the closing of civil society space in China to broader theoretical debates on the development of authoritarian legality in Asia. Given the trends described above, one must ask whether China is still pursuing the authoritarian legality model in the same way as it has in decades past, or in the same way that other East Asian model countries have. I argue that the overall mix of authoritarianism versus legality has shifted, away from limited liberal legality and in favor of a greater emphasis on more traditional political authoritarian tools, including surveillance, coercion, violence, threats, and propaganda. China is also less reliant on law as a bridge to the outside world, one that can attract outside investment, expertise, and ideas. Increasingly, law is instead being used as a barrier, erected to keep at least some international actors out.

This chapter proceeds in four sections. In Section 4.2, I analyze the authoritarian legality framework, and its applicability to the Chinese context. In Section 4.3, I describe the rise and fall of advocacy NGOs in China, and analyze how the repression of such groups signals a significant departure from authoritarian legality. In Section 4.4, I analyze the Foreign NGO Law, and look at the ways in which the law presents a series of very difficult choices for foreign actors operating in China. In Section 4.5, I conclude by asking whether these moves to limit the development of civil society in China will in fact succeed.

4.2   Theoretical Concerns: China's Evolving Approach to the East Asian Model

For some time, scholars have recognized that authoritarian regimes might self-interestedly embrace certain elements of the rule of law.[9] In

---

[8] Two leading scholars of rights activism in China write, "[t]he ground that produced past leaders and activists no longer exist [sic], and the support structure that had gained strength is under stress and collapsing" (Hualing Fu and Han Zhu, "After the July 9 (709) Crackdown: The Future of Human Rights Lawyering," *Fordham International Law Journal* 41 (2018): 1135, 1139).

[9] Peter H. Solomon, "Courts and Judges in Authoritarian Regimes," *World Politics* 60(1) (2007): 122–45.

so doing, authoritarian rulers seek to selectively gain certain benefits that can be had from increased legalization. The potential benefits are many, including improved social control, stronger political legitimation, improved governance, increased ability to attract international investment, and the legalization of thorny political questions.[10] At the same time, authoritarian regimes generally want to avoid other, less attractive (from their perspective) aspects of the rule of law, including judicial protection of individual rights or legislative and judicial oversight of executive authority.[11]

As this dichotomy shows, the move to partially embrace legal values, norms, and institutions carries with it certain risks. How best can those risks be managed, and how does an authoritarian regime strike the right balance between the authoritarian and the rule-of-law elements of authoritarian legality? This question has vexed both Chinese scholars and Chinese officials alike since the reintroduction of legality as a core governance tool in the late 1970s.

Authoritarian legality has been characterized as using law to open to the outside world, while at the same time using legal tools to maintain more control over the domestic scene.[12] Some scholars have argued that the dichotomy between economic law and other areas of law best describes China's approach to authoritarian legality: Chinese officials have an interest in tying their own hands when it comes to commercial matters, so as to affirm to investors that their investment dollars would be protected by law, and enforced by strong legal institutions.[13]

For many would-be reformers in China, the hope was that economic and commercial law reforms would launch something of a virtuous circle of legal reform. The idea was simple: the development of legal institutions

---

[10] This list is drawn from Tamir Moustafa and Tom Ginsburg, "Introduction: The Functions of Courts in Authoritarian Politics," in Tom Ginsburg and Tamir Moustafa (eds.), *Rule by Law: The Politics of Courts in Authoritarian Regimes* (New York: Cambridge University Press, 2008), 2–11.

[11] Peter H. Solomon Jr., "Authoritarian Legality and Informal Practices: Judges, Lawyers and the State in Russia and China," *Communist and Post-Communist Studies* 43(4) (2010): 351–62.

[12] As deLisle put it, "Western-based models of law and legal institutions . . . were part of the machinery for economic development."

[13] Yuhua Wang, *Tying the Autocrat's Hands: The Rise of the Rule of Law in China* (New York: Cambridge University Press, 2015), 3. According to Wang, "I define the rule of law that exists in authoritarian regimes as a partial form of the rule of law in which judicial fairness is usually respected in the commercial realm, but not in the political realm." See also Randall Peerenboom, *China Modernizes: Threat to the West or Model for the Rest?* (Oxford: Oxford University Press, 2008).

to attract and manage international investment would spread. Over time, more and more citizens would demand the same legal protections that the state extended to private economic interests. Building on that private law foundation, rule-of-law values and practices could slowly be extended outward.

And in the early years of the reform era, this precarious balance did, more or less, describe China's approach. In the early 1980s, China set about resurrecting its legal system. A core goal was to create the legal conditions necessary to attract international investment. At the same time, the Party moved to apply legal values and processes to a growing number of noneconomic spheres, such as criminal justice. Many hoped that the CCP would allow itself, eventually, to be more tightly bound by a genuine constitutional order, and only exercise political power through legally bound government institutions.[14]

For many reform-minded legal scholars, lawyers, and Party officials, full-fledged liberal constitutional democracy along the lines of the United States or Western Europe seemed to be a bridge too far. Still, more-liberal-minded – compared to the PRC – authoritarian states like Singapore were thought to be a more politically feasible model. For many reformers, Singapore's strong court system, greater commitment to transparent, rule-based governance, its toleration of opposition political parties, and its willingness to hold regular elections – however imperfect – all signaled a potentially politically viable path forward.[15]

Experts differ as to when the Party shifted away from liberal legal reform as a key element of its overall reform package.[16] Still, there is general consensus that the trend has accelerated since Xi Jinping took office in 2012. China under Xi Jinping is still promoting the rule of law as part of its overall legitimation strategy. And it continues to invest in the development of legal institutions as a key tool of day-to-day

---

[14] Paul Gewirtz, "The U.S.–China Rule of Law Initiative," *William & Mary Bill of Rights Journal* 11 (2003): 603–21, 604.

[15] As two observers pointed out, the political tightening under Xi Jinping "is actually moving the country further away from rather than toward the Singapore model" (Stephan Ortmann and Mark Thompson, "China and the 'Singapore Model,'" *Journal of Democracy* 27(1) (2016): 40).

[16] For an excellent discussion of the shifts in Beijing's policy toward legal reform, see Carl F. Minzner, "China's Turn against Law," *American Journal of Comparative Law* 59 (2011): 935–84. See also Hualing Fu and Richard Cullen, "From Mediatory to Adjudicatory Justice: The Limits of Civil Justice Reform in China," in Margaret Y. K. Woo and Mary E. Gallagher (eds.), *Chinese Justice: Civil Dispute Resolution in Contemporary China* (New York: Cambridge University Press, 2008), 25–57.

governance.[17] That said, the trajectory of legal reform in China has shifted significantly since the early 2000s. The change of course on legal reform represents a dramatic shift in China's overall legal and political development trajectory since the early years of the reform era. On the whole, recent changes are all meant to centralize the Party's authority over the legal system, and in particular to increase the level of authority and control exercised by the top Party leadership under President Xi Jinping.[18]

In particular, the Xi regime has altered China's approach to authoritarian legality in four key ways: first, the regime has relied more heavily on Party organs over state ones on key aspects of day-to-day governance, and has moved to reassert central Party control over local-level state organs. Second, the regime has increased its already significant investment in law as a tool of social control, and has largely abandoned efforts to place legal limits on the use of state power to curb political dissent. Third, the CCP's commitment to rule of law as a means of attracting foreign investment has waned, as has its commitment to use law as a bridge to the international community more generally. And finally, the recognition of the limited role that civil society can play in enforcing laws, and even strengthening them through legal and policy advocacy, has been largely reversed, with the key exception of environmental civil society.

First and foremost, Xi has sought to remake the party-state bureaucracy in order to centralize power, and to strengthen the role of the Party in day-to-day governance. One of the primary tools that Xi has used to achieve these goals has been the creation of so-called Leading Small Groups (LSGs).[19] Such groups have been a part of Chinese governance almost since the founding of the People's Republic. During the early years of the reform era, the use of such groups waned somewhat, as the Party invested heavily in the building up of formal government structures that would take the lead in governing.

Since taking office, Xi has radically altered the division of labor between Party and state, using a mushrooming number of LSGs to both set and, in some cases, implement policies. Over the course of Xi's tenure, more than eighty such groups have been created since the 18th

---

[17] Taisu Zhang and Tom Ginsburg, "Legality in Contemporary Chinese Politics," *Virginia Journal of International Law* 58 (2019).

[18] Economy, *Third Revolution*, 10–11.

[19] Christopher K. Johnson and Scott Kennedy, "China's Un-Separation of Powers," *Foreign Affairs*, July 24, 2015.

Party Congress, covering virtually every major policy area, as well as more than a few minor ones.[20] LSGs allow Xi Jinping to circumvent often cumbersome state bureaucratic structures, to maintain a higher degree of responsiveness and flexibility in policymaking and formulation, and to ensure that all key policies bear his personal imprimatur.

Still, state organs and laws continue to play a vital role, often as a tool of social control. Criminal law, enforced by Chinese courts, is one area where Xi has leaned more heavily on state structures. In general, under Xi, law has become an even more crucial tool of social control. For rights lawyers, activists, and dissident intellectuals, repression through law has become an even more fearsome prospect, as the state moves to strip away even the most basic procedural protections for individuals accused of political crimes. Under Article 73 of the revised Criminal Procedure Law, state authorities have the power to detain individuals in secret locations for up to six months without charge or trial. This mode of detention is referred to in the law as Residential Surveillance in a Designated Location, or RSDL.[21] In practice, state security officials have used Article 73 to strip individual detainees of their rights to an attorney, to family notification, both of which are protected under Chinese law.[22]

Third, the Party has stopped using law to facilitate the flow of international goods – including not just investment capital, but also expertise, ideas, cultural products, and civil society contacts, among others – into China. Simply put, the Party no longer sees law as a bridge to the outside world. More often over the past five years, new laws have been used to limit or control international engagement.[23]

As noted above, authoritarian legality regimes generally tend to use law to facilitate international investment. Before it joined the WTO in 2001, the Chinese government engaged in a massive overhaul of its economic and trade laws, seeking to bolster China's status among international investors. The push to join the WTO in the late 1990s was preceded by an explosion of outward engagement in the 1980s, when China's thirst for external ideas was fueled in part by a desire to end the

---

[20] Christopher K. Johnson, Scott Kennedy, and Mingda Qiu, "Xi's Signature Governance Innovation: The Rise of Leading Small Groups," CSIS Commentary, October 17, 2017.

[21] Michael Caster, "RSDL and Enforced Disappearances, a Legal View," in Caster (ed.), *The People's Republic of the Disappeared: Stories from Inside China's System for Enforced Disappearances* (USA: Safeguard Defenders, 2017).

[22] Ibid., 140–3.

[23] Economy, *Third Revolution*. Economy notes that "enhanced Party control [under Xi] also extends to efforts to protect China's society and the economy from foreign competition and influence" (ibid., 11).

PRC's decades-long estrangement from the world, from 1949 to 1976. In many ways, the Party itself led the charge to deepen international engagement, adopting slogans like *zou xiang shijie* ("stride toward the world"), and *yu guoji jiegui* ("link up with the international").[24]

While there have been various periods of retrenchment over the years, nonetheless many international actors operating inside China – including multinational companies, American and European universities, Western philanthropic entities, and NGOs – assumed that, over time, China would indeed become more and more open to the global community.[25]

Many of the laws and policies introduced since 2012 have dashed those hopes. On the commercial side, Western companies are increasingly critical of new laws and practices that are seen as protectionist. Laws and institutions meant to facilitate corporate entry into China are less welcoming than they once were.[26] Many top international firms have expressed concern about growing protectionism in China, and some firms operating in particularly crucial sectors worry that they may be targeted by state regulatory bodies.[27] In an April 2017 report, the American Chamber of Commerce expressed concern that the business environment had reached its lowest point in decades, and lamented that "[t]he pace of economic reforms and market opening has been slow and faltering."[28]

Finally, since taking office in 2012, Xi has sought to recast the role of civil society organizations. Social scientists have long recognized the benefits that civil society organizations bring to authoritarian rulers: NGOs can make constructive policy recommendations, and can serve as a bridge between the authoritarian state and society. Through litigation and other mechanisms, NGOs can ensure better enforcement of laws that are vital to an authoritarian ruler's policy goals. By virtue of their very existence, such groups can enhance regime legitimacy.

---

[24] Carl Minzner, *End of an Era: How China's Authoritarian Revival Is Undermining Its Rise* (Oxford: Oxford University Press, 2018), 22.

[25] For a critique of this view, see James Mann, *The China Fantasy: How Our Leaders Explain Away Chinese Repression* (New York: Viking Penguin, 2007), 1–27.

[26] Michael Martina, "U.S. Lobby Says China Protectionism Fueling Foreign Business Pessimism," Reuters, January 18, 2017.

[27] As a result, many top Western corporations operating in China now favor a much tougher response to restrictive practices by Beijing. Jamil Anderlini, "American Executives Are Becoming China Skeptics," *Financial Times*, November 14, 2018.

[28] *Bloomberg News*, "U.S. Firms in China Face Worst Conditions in Decades: AmCham," April 17, 2017; Sui-Lee Wee, "As Zeal for China Dims, Global Companies Complain More Boldly," *New York Times*, April 19, 2017.

At the same time, such groups bring with them several risks: if left unchecked, such groups can grow quickly, and can challenge state authority in potentially damaging (again, to the ruler's authority) ways. They can force the ruling regime to make policy changes, for example, or even concessions on the approved use of political power, that the regime would prefer not to make.

No one knows better than the Party that a single spark can start a prairie fire. Therefore, the Party has long maintained a high degree of vigilance when it comes to Chinese NGOs, particularly advocacy-focused NGOs. Since 2012, however, the Party has shifted from vigilance and occasional repression to a much more overtly repressive stance. In pushing for the closure of several key advocacy groups, the CCP may well have taken care of what it sees as a genuine potential political threat. But it has also lost a key channel for policy feedback and public engagement, one that will be difficult to replace.

Taken together, these shifts constitute a major departure from the gradual reformist path that the CCP leadership had charted since the late 1970s. As one scholar of Chinese law has put it, China is facing the end of reform.[29] At the same time, a new governance model is emerging. While it's too early to say exactly what the new governance model will look like, it's clear that – if Xi has his way – China will look less and less like other authoritarian legality states like Singapore, and more and more like the PRC's own pre-reform-era governance model, updated for the twenty-first century. In adopting this new approach, the Party is seeking to ensure that China will avoid the democratic transitions that took place in former authoritarian legality states like Taiwan and South Korea.

4.2.1   A Paradigm Shift? Lessons for the Study of Authoritarian Legality

What does China's shift mean for the study of legal authoritarianism more generally? First, China's experience shows that the process is in fact reversible. At times, a certain inevitability has crept into some studies of legal authoritarianism in Asia.[30] Some scholars, perhaps having studied

---

[29] Minzner, *End of an Era*, 32.

[30] See, e.g., Randall Peerenboom, *China's Long March toward the Rule of Law* (Cambridge: Cambridge University Press, 2002), 4. At one point, Peerenboom suggests that "as legal reforms have progressed in China, the legal system has converged in many respects with the legal systems of well-developed countries; *and it is likely to continue to converge in the future*" (emphasis added).

relative success stories like Taiwan and South Korea too closely, have seemed to suggest that, once legal reforms are begun, they will inevitably deepen and expand outward.[31] To be sure, there was some basis for this relative optimism: jurisdictions like Singapore and Hong Kong have developed relatively strong legal regimes. Several years into the Xi Jinping era, China is more clearly – even self-consciously – defying the liberal evolutionary pattern of some other East Asian developmental regimes.

At the same time, China's de-emphasis of legal reform also reinforces some core elements of authoritarian legality theory: if, as the theory indicates, the authoritarian ruler's embrace of legal reform is opportunistic and instrumentalist, it makes sense that, as circumstances change, the ruler might rethink the costs and benefits of legal reforms. In other words, when the commitment to legality is contingent and provisional, rather than normative, it can be downgraded or even jettisoned at any time.[32] This conclusion points to the need for deeper study of the *why* of authoritarian legality – the more that we know about the political factors that push an authoritarian ruler to embrace authoritarian legality, the more that we might be able to tease out the factors that might lead him or her to reverse course.

Third, China's experience shows that *institutionalization* of legal reforms is key. Over the years, the CCP has resisted reforms that would be difficult to reverse, in effect keeping open the option of undoing certain reforms that ceased to serve the Party's interests. Calls for reforms that would have institutionalized a role for the courts in constitutional interpretation, for example, went nowhere, despite near-universal agreement among legal scholars and others that such reforms were urgently needed.[33]

---

[31] This linear view also overlooks other external factors, such as colonial legal legacy and international context, that partially account for the democratic transitions in Taiwan and South Korea. For a further discussion, see Weitseng Chen, "Twins of Opposites: Why China Will Not Follow Taiwan's Model of Rule of Law Transition toward Democracy," *American Journal of Comparative Law* 66(3) (2018): 481–535.

[32] As Mary Gallagher puts it, "authoritarian legality as an instrumental play for power and political stability is ultimately contradictory; as such, 'rule of law' in autocracies is bounded, limited, and unstable" (*Authoritarian Legality: Law, Workers, and the State in Contemporary China* (New York: Cambridge University Press, 2017)).

[33] See Thomas E. Kellogg, "Courageous Explorers? Education Litigation and Judicial Innovation in China," *Harvard Human Rights Journal* 20 (2007): 170–88; "Arguing Chinese Constitutionalism: The 2013 Constitutional Debate and the 'Urgency' of Political Reform," *University of Pennsylvania Asian Law Review* 11(3) (2017): 337–407.

Fourth, civil society plays an important role. For the most part, studies of authoritarian legality have focused more heavily on traditional legal actors, including courts, lawyers, and legislators. Still, as some studies have suggested, nongovernmental actors can play a key role in pushing for legal reforms within an authoritarian legality system when the moment of political opportunity presents itself.[34]

Groups like TI and Yirenping managed to achieve key political victories, even in a highly restrictive, authoritarian environment. Their suppression suggests that the CCP has become aware of the risks that such groups pose, and has acted accordingly. For international donors, the lesson is clear: support for rights advocacy organizations is a crucially important element of an overall legal reform and development strategy.[35]

Finally, more study is needed of the role that foreign actors play in transmitting liberal values within authoritarian systems. Over the past several years, a growing number of states have sought to use law to limit the influence and access of international groups to the domestic sphere.[36] In 2016, with the passage of the Foreign NGO Law, China joined that group, which suggests that it too wants to limit the role that foreign actors can play in China.

4.3   Closing Space: the Future of Civil Society Development in China

Since Xi Jinping came to power in late 2012, the party-state has moved to increase its control over virtually every important element of Chinese public life, including the media, the internet, academia, civil society organizations, rights activists and lawyers, the legal profession, and arts and culture. This wide-ranging reassertion of control has led to a precipitous decline in the political environment. Many observers, both domestic and international, have concluded that the situation has reached a low point not seen since the immediate aftermath of the 1989 Tiananmen Square crackdown.

---

[34] See Chapter 12 in this volume.

[35] Thomas E. Kellogg, "Western Funding for Rule of Law Initiatives in China: The Importance of a Civil Society Based Approach," *China Perspectives* 3 (2012): 43–9.

[36] In some ways, before the passage of the Foreign NGO Law, China lagged behind other authoritarian states in imposing legal restrictions on international support to domestic NGOs. For an in-depth assessment of the global trend, see Thomas Carothers and Saskia Brechenmacher, *Closing Space: Democracy and Human Rights Support under Fire* (Washington, DC: Carnegie Endowment for International Peace, 2014).

Thus far at least, the Party itself remains the top target of repression. Xi Jinping's anti-corruption campaign has been even more hard-hitting than his moves against civil society and the media. Certainly, with 750,000 Party members disciplined over the first three years of the campaign, there have been many more victims of the internal Party crackdown than there are victims of the external crackdown.[37] In fact, the anti-corruption campaign and the broader reassertion of control over society as a whole are likely interrelated: the newly installed Party leadership under Xi Jinping almost certainly knew that it would be more vulnerable to external threats as it moved forward with the anti-corruption campaign. In this context, moving to neutralize any external threats at the same time makes sense.

The timing of the crackdown is deeply unfortunate, in that it comes just as Chinese civil society was taking a crucial step forward: over the course of the 2000s, some NGOs began making the transition from service provision to policy advocacy, and to a greater attention to rights-based activism that, at times, challenged the Party's claim to full authority over its citizens.[38]

This small cadre of organizations, including such groups as TI, Beijing Yirenping, founded in 2006, and the Institute for Public and Environmental Affairs (IPE), also founded in 2006, built on the work of a prior generation of civil society activists and organizations, some of which were more service-oriented, and which were often affiliated with or even housed inside larger official entities which could provide a degree of political protection. Prominent examples included the Center for Women's Law Studies and Legal Services at Peking University, founded in 1995 by leading rights lawyer Guo Jianmei, and the Center for the Protection of the Rights of Disadvantaged Citizens at Wuhan University Law School, founded in 1992 by leading jurist – and eventual Supreme Court Justice – Wan E'xiang.[39] The pathbreaking HIV/AIDS advocacy organization Aizhixing, founded by former public health official Wan Yanhai in 1994, also served as a key model for many young activists,

---

[37] Hudson Lockett, "China Anti-Corruption Campaign Backfires," *Financial Times*, October 9, 2016, www.ft.com/content/02f712b4-8ab8-11e6-8aa5-f79f5696c731

[38] Kellogg, "Western Funding."

[39] Sadly, even these two more moderate groups have faced extreme political difficulties in recent years, as have several other university-based clinical programs. See, e.g., Tom Phillips, "Women's Rights Crackdown Exposes Deepening Crisis in Chinese Society," *The Guardian*, February 4, 2016, www.theguardian.com/global-development /2016/feb/05/china-womens-rights-crackdown-exposes-deepening-crisis-in-chinese-society

including Lu Jun, the founder of Yirenping. For more economics and policy-focused intellectuals, the Unirule Institute for Economics, founded by a group of prominent pro-market economists and intellectuals in 1993, was a key organization that many sought to emulate.[40]

In the early and mid-2000s, new groups emerged that were willing to take the work of this prior generation of organizations one step further. Because these groups were generally not affiliated with any official entity, they could adopt a more experimental approach, without having to worry about censorship from above. And because the staff of these organizations were generally younger – in many cases, less than 30 years old – they were both more open to the possibilities of what could be done, and had less on the line that the Party could threaten to take away.

These and other factors led some of these groups to experiment with advocacy approaches that, up to that point, were largely unknown in China. Such advocacy approaches included litigation, policy advocacy, public mobilization, media outreach, extensive and at times very savvy use of social media, and public protest, usually in the more politically feasible form of performance art. While such tools are the stock-in-trade of many NGOs outside China, these groups were extremely innovative in importing and adapting them for the Chinese context.

One of the most powerful tools that these groups developed was public mobilization. In stark contrast to the mass organizations whose work they sought to supplant, these groups placed a high premium on grounding their work in communities of affected people. Yirenping mobilized persons with hepatitis B, for example, encouraging them to think of themselves as a class of people, and to take action to fight for their rights.[41] They would mobilize their members to travel to courthouses to observe key cases brought by Yirenping-affiliated lawyers, signaling to local officials that the case carried with it very real social stability risks, and that it needed to be taken seriously. Other groups followed suit, and pathbreaking work with persons with disabilities, gays and lesbians, migrant workers, and women followed.

---

[40] In July 2018, Unirule was pushed out of its Beijing office, the latest in a series of repressive moves that put the future of the organization in grave doubt. See Chris Buckley, "In Beijing, Doors Shut on a Bastion of Independent Ideas," *New York Times*, July 11, 2018, www.nytimes.com/2018/07/11/world/asia/china-unirule-institute.html

[41] Thomas E. Kellogg, "Constitutionalism with Chinese Characteristics? Constitutional development and civil litigation in China," *International Journal of Constitutional Law* 7(2) (2009): 234–45.

Litigation has probably been the most effective tool developed by advocacy NGOs since the mid-2000s. Advocacy organizations quickly realized that litigation was a potent way to mobilize constituent groups, attract media attention, win allies in academia and the legal community, and highlight the need for policy change. Women's rights and LGBT rights groups, for example, have brought a number of gender discrimination and LGBT rights cases over the years, and won some initial victories in 2013 and 2014.[42] Groups working in other areas took note of these milestone wins, and sought to model their own litigation work on these victories.

This new generation of advocacy NGOs also sought to expand the use of other tools that the Party has made available in recent years, including Open Government Information regulations, strengthened notice and comment procedures for new laws, and revamped administrative reconsideration tools.

Perhaps the largest difference between the new generation of NGO activists and those that came before was the younger generation's embrace of the political tool of public protest, which many had long thought to be out of bounds in China. The new generation of advocacy-based NGOs sought to chip away at this prohibition by dressing up their public protest in the garb of what they called "performance art" – using costume, narrative, and other forms of public theater to turn their protest into more of a public-education display than a more traditional public rally. LGBT activists would engage in a public same-sex kiss-in, for example, or stage a mock same-sex wedding, in order to make a point about LGBT rights. Such performances, though frowned upon by the authorities, were nonetheless tolerated, at least until Xi Jinping took office. By claiming the right to engage in such public acts, the new generation of grassroots advocacy organizations expanded the space available to civil society as a whole.

As they adapted these new advocacy tools for their own ends, these groups highlighted for more conservative Chinese officials the double-edged nature of legal reform: it could be used to hold lower-level officials accountable, but it could also be used by activists to push the Party beyond its own often narrow comfort zone.

Though these new groups wanted to build the strength and the influence of civil society organizations in China, nonetheless they were very

---

[42] Joy L. Chia, "Rights Lawyering in Xi's China: Innovation in the Midst of Marginalization," *Fordham International Law Journal* 41 (2018): 1111, 1130.

thoughtful and deliberate, even careful, about their political position. Activists were fully committed to their liberal agenda, but they had no interest in getting arrested, or in seeing the government shut down the organizations that they had worked so hard to build. In other words, they sought to skate right up to the line of what was politically acceptable, but not to cross it. Almost without exception, the leaders of these groups were intensely engaged in constant political risk analysis, the better to ensure the long-term viability of the organizations they had founded, and to ensure the safety of their colleagues and collaborative partners.[43]

The fact that some of these groups have been shuttered over the past few years speaks to a shifting of the lines: what was once acceptable – if risky – during the Hu–Wen administration has become simply unacceptable during the Xi Jinping era. Many activists and lawyers believe that the space for civil society activism began to tighten 2008, and indeed there are some data points that point to a more difficult environment: Beijing University Women's Legal Aid Center was forced to dissociate with Beijing University in 2010, and longtime HIV/AIDS activist Wan Yanhai fled China for the United States that same year. Still, even after 2008, new groups continued to form, and the activist sector continued to grow: Yirenping, for example, continued to found sister organizations in other cities across China, many of them working on similar anti-discrimination and public health concerns.

After 2012, the repressive trend quickly became all too clear. Since Xi took office in 2012, several NGO activists have expressed the fear that the Party's goal may be to wipe out advocacy-based NGOs entirely, leaving only service-based groups still standing.[44] If that is indeed their goal, then the Foreign NGO Law might prove helpful in that regard, given that most advocacy groups receive the bulk of their funding from foreign sources.

Many scholars have pointed out that authoritarian legality regimes can benefit from the existence of rights-based advocacy NGOs that work within the system to advance progressive goals.[45] Such groups can perform a number of (from the state's perspective) beneficial functions: they can help the state solve pressing social problems, which in turn enhances the ruling Party's political legitimacy and adaptability. They can help the ruling elite to enforce national norms and laws at the local level, and can

---

[43] Author interviews.

[44] Ibid.

[45] Chloe Froissart, "Using the Law as a 'Harmonious Weapon': The Ambiguities of Legal Activism in Favor of Migrant Workers in China," *Journal of Civil Society* 10(3) (2014): 255–72.

alert the central leadership when its local agents resist implementation of those norms. They can inject new ideas into public discourse, allowing the ruling elite to gauge public reaction to those ideas in a relatively low-risk way.[46] Their mere existence can bolster the authoritarian ruler's reputation for tolerance, suggesting that he or she is willing to accept some autonomous political activity that indirectly challenges state policy.

At the same time, allowing such groups to form and to grow is by no means a risk-free proposition. NGOs can succeed in mobilizing the public to push for changes that the authoritarian ruler doesn't want, for example. They can channel discontent over governance shortcomings into outright political opposition to the regime. More broadly, NGOs can aid in the transition from authoritarianism to liberal constitutional democracy. As the risk of a political transition grows, they can force the state to show its more repressive side, thereby damaging the ruler's standing in the eyes of the public. Managing these risks requires authoritarian leaders to engage in a constant balancing act: risk and reward must be carefully weighed at all times. Authoritarian leaders must constantly monitor activist groups, and be ready to crack down when potential threats emerge.

Since 2012, the CCP's approach has been less about balancing risks and benefits, and more about the use of repression and other tools to alter the long-term trajectory of civil society development in China in ways that the regime perceives as favorable.[47] The regime has become much more rigid in its approach to civil society groups. It remains to be seen whether the new organizations that emerge in the coming years will be able to offer the same benefits – in terms of policy feedback, enhanced public discourse, and so on – as the groups that have been sidelined did.

4.4   The Foreign NGO Law

The Foreign NGO Law has proven to be one of the most controversial laws issued during the reform era. The final version of the law, passed by the Standing Committee of the National People's Congress on April 28, 2016,

---

[46] Successful efforts to limit state authority to institutionalize mentally ill individuals against their will – sometimes for years or even decades – is one example. See Stephen Hallett, "'Enabling the Disabled': The Growing Role of Civil Society in Disability Rights Advocacy," in Andreas Fulda (ed.), *Civil Society Contributions to Policy Innovation in the PR China: Environment, Social Development and International Cooperation* (London: Palgrave Macmillan, 2015), 186–7.

[47] The one partial exception is Beijing's approach to environmental advocacy NGOs, which have been granted a bit more political space to operate. As of 2018, most top environmental groups remain open, even as other advocacy NGOs have been shut down.

established the primary role of the Ministry of Public Security in overseeing foreign NGOs, largely sidelining the Ministry of Civil Affairs, which had previously been the lead actor in charge of regulating and overseeing foreign NGO activity. It also enshrined extensive registration and oversight requirements for all foreign NGOs operating in China.

The Foreign NGO Law was drafted and passed relatively quickly. In December 2014, the government announced that the National People's Congress Standing Committee would deliberate on a first draft of the law. The drafting of this new law likely began in April 2014, at around the time that the National Security Commission was established.[48] The second draft of the law was issued, and public comments solicited, in April 2015, and the final version was passed just one year later. In roughly twenty-four months, the Chinese government passed extensive new regulations which fundamentally altered the regulatory environment for foreign NGOs. By contrast, the Chinese government passed just one national-level regulation on foreign NGOs operating in China between 1989 and 2016, the 2004 Regulations on the Management of Foreign Foundations.[49] The Foreign NGO Law was the first national-level comprehensive *law* on foreign NGOs of the reform era.[50]

The core goal of the law is to bolster the state's hold over *domestic* civil society by tightening control over access to foreign funding and expertise. In fact, the Foreign NGO Law is one of several laws passed over the past three years meant to expand state power in order to improve China's domestic security, including the Counter-Terrorism Law (2015), the National Security Law (2015), and the Cybersecurity Law (2016). All four laws regulate the activities of foreign actors, and have drawn criticism from both foreign businesses and governments, as well as international human rights groups.[51] In that sense, all four laws are part of the trend of revising China's approach to outside actors: rather than using

[48] For an excellent account of the steps leading up to the passage of the Foreign NGO Law, see Shawn Shieh, "The Origins of China's New Law on Foreign NGOs," *Chinafile*, January 31, 2017, www.chinafile.com/reporting-opinion/viewpoint/origins-of-chinas-new-law-foreign-ngos

[49] The 2004 Regulations were followed by some lower-level Measures, which had a limited impact on most foreign foundations' operations in China. In 2009, new banking regulations, the Notice of the State Administration of Foreign Exchange on Issues Concerning the Administration of Foreign Exchange Donated to or by Domestic Institutions, did make grantmaking by international organizations to domestic groups more difficult, but it too was limited in its impact.

[50] Shawn Shieh, *China Philanthropy Law Report* (Washington, DC: International Center for Not-for-Profit Law, 2017), 15.

[51] Liza Lin and Yoko Kubota, "U.S. Tech Firms Spooked by China's Arcane Cybersecurity Law," *Wall Street Journal*, December 6, 2017, www.wsj.com/articles/chinas-blurry-cyber-

law as a tool to attract foreign investment and expertise, law is used to restrict entry.

For Beijing, the need for the new law was likely driven by the steady growth of international organizations operating in China, and by the explosive proliferation of domestic groups, many of them funded almost exclusively by foreign donors. Starting from a low base in the early 1990s, the number of domestic NGOs has grown over the past several years to the tens of thousands.[52] And yet, this rapid growth masks an important point. The number of genuine NGOs with some level of autonomy and capacity – ones that can educate and mobilize the public to change government policy, for example – remains quite small. One leading activist recently estimated that the number of such NGOs might be as small as a few hundred, or at most one to two thousand.[53] Sensing a latent threat from more sophisticated advocacy NGOs, Beijing took action: the Foreign NGO Law represents one of the most sophisticated and far-reaching attempts by the Party to date to curb, and to control, the growth of the domestic civil society sector.[54]

To be sure, the law does include some positive elements. Before the passage of this law, most foreign NGOs operating in China lacked legal status, and did not have a clear legal avenue to registration. The Foreign NGO Law provides such a pathway. Article 4 of the Law makes clear that "[o]verseas NGOs that carry out activities in the mainland of China in accordance with the law shall be protected by the law." In addition, under Article 8 of the law, the Chinese government is empowered to recognize foreign NGOs that "make outstanding contributions to the development of public welfare in China." And yet, on the whole, the negative elements of the law significantly outweigh the few positive aspects.

Perhaps most troublingly, as noted above, the Foreign NGO Law preserves the national security approach to regulation of foreign NGOs. Implicit in the law's regulatory approach is the suggestion that foreign NGOs should be viewed with suspicion, that they are guilty until proven innocent. As one Chinese commentator put it, the law's conceptual frame

laws-give-u-s-tech-companies-no-security-1512558004; "China: State Security, Terrorism Convictions Double," March 16, 2016.

[52] Kellogg, "Western Funding," 54.

[53] Kou Yanding, "Zhongguo daodi you duoshao "xiangyang de" minjian NGO?" [How many "decent" NGOs does China have?], *The Initium*, October 17, 2015, https://theini tium.com/article/20151017-opinion-trailwalker (accessed May 15, 2017).

[54] Xiaoguang Kang, "Moving Toward Neo-Totalitarianism: A Political–Sociological Analysis of the Evolution of Administrative Absorption of Society in China," *Nonprofit Policy Forum* 9 (2018).

for foreign NGOs treats them as akin to "public enemies, second-class citizens, (or) criminal suspects." Article 5, for example, warns that foreign NGOs should not "threaten China's national reunification and security or ethnic unity, nor harm China's national and social interests." Under Article 47, any foreign NGO that "engages in ... acts that endanger national security or harm[s] national or public interests" can have its registration revoked. Such elastic language has repeatedly been used by Chinese state actors to prosecute Chinese citizens for purely peaceful – and, under international human rights law, fully protected – political activity. Its inclusion in the Foreign NGO Law is cause for concern.

Indeed, some of the national security-related provisions of the law could all too easily be applied to core NGO activities. If, for example, a local NGO that receives funding from a foreign partner moves forward with a public protest against insufficient toilet facilities for women, might not such a move be considered an act of "inciting resistance to laws and regulations" by the foreign actor, assuming that the protest did not receive the necessary government approvals?[55] What about public protests organized by grassroots environmental NGOs against new plants that might harm the environment and damage public health?[56] Such acts of protest, always risky in the Chinese context, have nonetheless been established as useful NGO tools in China over the past decade.[57] The Foreign NGO Law will make it more difficult for international donors to support NGOs that use such edgy tools.

Almost certainly by design, the scope of the law is quite broad: it covers "the activities in the mainland of China of *all* overseas NGOs" (emphasis added). Overseas NGOs are defined under the law as "foundations, social groups, think tanks and other non-profit, nongovernmental social organizations legally established overseas." This broad definition – which on its face could cover Western universities, many of which have extensive

---

[55] Sharon LaFraniere, "For Chinese Women, a Basic Need, and Few Places to Attend to It," *New York Times*, February 29, 2012, www.nytimes.com/2012/03/01/world/asia/chinese-women-demand-more-public-toilets.html; Jess Macy Yu, "Demanding Toilet Justice for the Women of China," *New York Times*, November 19, 2014, news.nytimg.com/china/20141120/c20toilet/en-us

[56] For an excellent account of one of the earliest such protests, see Jonathan Ansfield, "Alchemy of a Protest: The Case of Xiamen PX," in Sam Geall (ed.), *China and the Environment: The Green Revolution* (London: Zed Books, 2013), 136–202.

[57] For a broad discussion of the use of these tools by environmental activists, see H. Christoph Steinhardt and Fengshi Wu, "In the Name of the Public: Environmental Protest and the Changing Landscape of Popular Contention in China," *China Journal* 75 (2016): 61–82.

collaborative programs in China; commercial lobbying groups like the American Chamber of Commerce; and top think tanks like the Brookings Institution and the Carnegie Endowment, both of which have offices in Beijing – gives the Ministry of Public Security a powerful legal tool to influence and investigate the activities of a wide range of Western entities that maintain a presence in China.

During the notice and comment period on the draft law, from the end of April to June 4, 2015, several Western actors urged the Chinese government to tighten the scope of the law, to exclude commercial lobbying or academic activity, for example.[58] And yet, with the exception of the addition of a single vague article tacked on to the end of the law,[59] Beijing largely refused to do so. In effect, the Party chose to keep its options open on the regulatory coverage of Western universities, leaving those entities in a regulatory gray zone – the very scenario that Beijing claimed the law was meant to avoid. For trade associations and think tanks, their efforts were largely for naught: they too faced the prospect of having to comply with the new law.

Extensive and intrusive registration and reporting requirements are at the core of the Foreign NGO Law. In order to operate in China, all Foreign NGOs must apply to register a representative office, and then, if they succeed, must have their full roster of activities and partners approved on an annual basis, both *ex ante* and *ex post*.

The law envisions a two-step registration process: first, foreign NGOs operating in China must find a willing sponsor, which the Law itself refers to as a Professional Supervisory Unit (PSU). Once a foreign NGO receives formal approval from an eligible PSU, that NGO can apply to the Public Security Bureau for formal registration.

Perhaps unsurprisingly, the text of the Law itself does not offer any guidance as to what sort of standard the authorities will use when evaluating an application for registration. This lack of information on what constitutes a successful application means that the Public Security

---

[58] Gillian Wong, "US Business, Professional Groups Sign Letter Opposing Draft China NGO Law," *Wall Street Journal*, June 4, 2015, www.wsj.com/articles/u-s-business-professional-groups-sign-letter-opposing-draft-china-ngo-law-1433440263
[59] Article 53 of the Foreign NGO Law does exempt exchanges between foreign and Chinese "schools, hospitals, natural sciences and engineering technology research institutes [and] academic organizations," but the nature and scope of the exemption remained unclear. And Western academic activities in China that do *not* include a Chinese counterpart would presumably be outside the scope of the Article 53 exemption.

authorities have more or less a free hand in either approving or rejecting applications from foreign NGOs.

In practice, however, much of the screening will take place at the level of PSUs. If a potential PSU is willing to take on a foreign partner, that willingness should bode well for eventual registration. That said, many potential PSUs have proven reluctant to enter into agreements with foreign NGOs, for the simple reason that the political risks inherent in doing so may well outweigh any potential benefits to the relationship. As of 2018, the difficulty of finding a suitable PSU has emerged as a major barrier to international NGO entry into China, so much so that state security authorities have publicly and privately urged potential PSUs to fulfill their role under the law, even as they remind PSUs of their monitoring responsibilities.[60]

PSUs will also view any potential collaboration through the prism of their own institutional interest, which means that even projects that address real concerns but might undercut a mass organization's political position – such as a project on the development of grassroots disability rights groups that are independent of the CDPF, for example – might prove untenable.

For those foreign NGOs that are able to register, the reporting and oversight provisions are very burdensome. Under Article 19, all representative offices of foreign NGOs must submit to their PSUs an annual activity plan, which the PSUs must then approve. Once the annual activity plan is approved by the foreign NGO's PSU, it is submitted to the public security authorities, who – at least on paper – merely receive the activity plan for their own files, and do not formally approve it themselves. That said, both the foreign NGO representative office and the Chinese PSU know that the authorities will eventually review the activity plan; both actors will no doubt plan their activities accordingly, rather than risk any unwanted negative commentary from public security.

In order to ensure full compliance, representative offices must submit annual end-of-year reports to both their PSUs and to the public security authorities. That report then forms the basis for public security authorities' annual inspection. Under Article 41, public security organs are granted extensive investigation powers, including the right to interview foreign NGO representatives; the right to search a foreign NGO's representative office; the right to review and make copies of relevant documents; and the right to seize property.

---

[60] Author interviews with international and domestic NGO administrators.

In practice, the submission and approval of activity plans and annual reports means that all foreign NGO activities are subject to official approval. Such an extensive approval and oversight regime raises real concerns about organizational autonomy for foreign NGOs operating in China. If all activities, partnerships, and expenditures are subject to Chinese government approval, then international NGOs are faced with an extremely unappealing dilemma: allow their programmatic work to be shaped by Chinese officials, or pull out of China altogether.

Given all of these strictures, what impact will the law have on civil society development in China? As of 2018, the impact has been significant. First and foremost, as noted above, work by foreign NGOs on topics deemed too "sensitive" – which in recent years has included such key mainstream topics as women's rights and labor rights – has been scaled back, as various international groups hold off on new projects and adopt a wait-and-see attitude toward the domestic regulatory environment. Some international groups, including some working on less sensitive issues, have decided to end their work in China altogether.

Second, international collaboration with grassroots civil society groups, many of which are completely unregistered or are registered as private companies, has become much more difficult. If a core goal of the law was to impede access for some domestic NGOs to sources of international funding, then the law must be counted as a success on this front.

On the positive side of the ledger, the government has taken some steps to make the new law operable in practice. It seems clear that the Party leadership and the Ministry of State Security do in fact want the new law to work. Their goal is not to force the majority of international NGOs to end their activities in China, but rather to bring those activities under state oversight and control.

In December 2016, for example, the Ministry of Public Security issued a list of eligible PSUs, including various government ministries and Party-controlled mass organizations, such as the All-China Federation of Trade Unions and the China Women's Federation. And since that initial list was published, additional PSUs have been added. The Ministry of State Security also informed some international organizations that they can propose other potential PSUs, as long as the would-be PSU agrees to be considered.

These efforts at limited bureaucratic flexibility have paid some initial dividends: in 2017 and 2018, several hundred international organizations successfully registered. Most of the groups that have registered thus far are focused on less controversial issues, including education, poverty alleviation, and international trade and commerce. Organizations focused on more politically sensitive work, including groups focused on legal development and human rights, have generally been less success-ful in registering, and some have had to pull out of China altogether.[61] The American Bar Association, for example, closed its Beijing office in December 2016, just days before the Foreign NGO Law went into effect.[62]

What are the implications of the new law in terms of China's approach to authoritarian legality? As noted above, over the past several decades, China has generally used law to attract foreign investment and expertise. The approach to foreign nongovernmental groups has been somewhat different: rather than creating new laws to facilitate entry, Beijing has largely stayed silent, issuing no new laws on foreign NGOs operating in China for years at a time.[63] Though they no doubt would have preferred a more welcoming framework, most international NGOs found that they could live with the government's hands-off regulatory approach. More and more international groups continued to enter China, and to seek out new partnerships with various Chinese actors. The lack of a legal frame-work facilitated entry, rather than blocking it.

The Foreign NGO Law casts this approach aside, in favor of a much more restrictive legal framework. In essence, international organizations are being treated in a fundamentally new way: they are being treated exactly the way that many domestic actors – including both domestic NGOs and many individual Chinese citizens – have been treated by the party-state for decades. They are being treated as objects of suspicion, whose operations must be closely monitored. By ending the special treatment of NGOs, Beijing has undertaken a substantial shift in its approach to authoritarian legality.

4.5   Conclusion

In this chapter, I have argued that, in many key ways, China is altering its approach to the authoritarian legality paradigm. Beijing's rethinking of

---

[61] Author interviews. See also Tom Hancock, "China Law Puts Foreign NGOs under Tighter Control," *Financial Times*, April 22, 2018, www.ft.com/content/a61994da-3ec1-11e8-b7e0-52972418fec4

[62] Terry Carter, "ABA Closes Office in China While It Measures the Impact of New Restrictions on NGO Activities," *ABA Journal*, March 2017.

[63] Shawn Shieh, "The Chinese State and Overseas NGOs: From Regulatory Ambiguity to the Overseas NGO Law," Nonprofit Policy Forum, April 2018.

its approach to authoritarian legality begs a more fundamental question: will it work? Will the new Foreign NGO Law curb international engagement on more "sensitive" issues, including human rights and rule of law? Given that the real targets of the Foreign NGO Law are domestic activists, will the decline of foreign funding force grassroots Chinese activists out of business? In general, how will frontline activists and lawyers respond to the rapidly evolving domestic political and legal environment?

There are no easy answers to these questions. To be sure, many activists will have to find new ways to sustain themselves, if and when international funding is significantly reduced. Some will no doubt be forced to leave the country, at least for some period of time. It seems likely, however, that many activists will continue with their work, even despite all of the new barriers that have emerged over the past several years.

In the weeks and months after Guo Yushan was released in September 2015, I asked mutual friends how Guo was doing. Reasonably well, considering the circumstances, I was told: he was still under heavy surveillance, and could only leave home with official permission. He was warned that he should be careful, and that he could be detained yet again at any time if he stepped out of line. Occasional visits with friends in Beijing were permitted, but in general he had to lay low. On my own visits to China, I refrained from calling him, worried that any contact with a foreign friend could make his life even more difficult.

So it came as a surprise when I came across a short piece written by Guo Yushan on September 19, 2016.[64] Guo broke his public silence to lament the pending sentence that would be handed down to his friend, the Beijing-based lawyer Xia Lin. He told the story of meeting and getting to know Xia Lin, and of working with him on various human rights cases over the years. He predicted – rightly as it turned out – that the brutality of the system would once again manifest itself in Xia Lin's sentencing. And he appealed to history as the ultimate judge of both his own and Xia Lin's work:

> We all know the fates we will come to assume in history. Both Xia Lin and myself, and so, so many of our colleagues, are all fated to be the stepping stones, the paving stones, for the age of the future. Accepting this humble place in history is our honor.[65]

---

[64] Guo Yushan, "Lawyer Xia Lin Will Be Sentenced on September 22, and It Will Have Nothing to Do with the Law," *Chinachange*, September 22, 2016, https://chinachange.org /2016/09/21/lawyer-xia-lin-will-be-sentenced-on-september-22-and-it-will-have-noth ing-to-do-with-the-law

[65] Ibid.

Looking back on it now, I should have known: Guo Yushan and hundreds of other Chinese activists will continue to struggle on behalf of fellow activists, and on behalf of the values they hold so dear, regardless of whether international groups are able to support them or not. In that most important sense, I believe that the Foreign NGO Law will fail in its ultimate goal.

City Jurisdictions with a Colonial Common Law Tradition

Hong Kong and Singapore

5

Understanding Authoritarian Legality in Hong Kong

What Can Dicey and Rawls Tell Us?

RICHARD CULLEN AND DAVID CAMPBELL[1]

If we accept this argument ... that all men everywhere, merely by virtue of being men, have certain fundamental rights, and among these is the right not to be governed by anyone who has not acquired authority over them by their consent, we have to conclude that only democracy ... is legitimate. No matter what the conditions of a people may be, no matter how urgent their need for effective government, no matter how little used they are to democracy, they must have it, for it alone is rightful government ... But this is absurd ... If we are to make a realistic case for democracy we must be content to argue that it is the best form of government only when certain conditions apply.[1]

5.1 Introduction

For more than 150 years, the British ran Hong Kong with no direct elections to any legislative or senior executive position. Between 1842 and 1997, the constitutionally omnipotent governor was simply appointed by London. Nevertheless, during this period, and especially after World War II, the British unarguably improved what was already a successful governance structure based on authoritarian legality, not least through the developed quality of its judiciary and civil service. The basic precepts of this system of authoritarian legality under British rule have continued to apply since July 1, 1997 when sovereignty over Hong Kong was resumed by the People's Republic of China (PRC) after the transition from British rule. On that day, Hong Kong became the Hong Kong Special Administrative Region (HKSAR) within the

---

[1] John Plamenatz, *Democracy and Illusion* (London: Longman, 1973), 8.

People's Republic of China. The principal indicator of this success is, of course, the Hong Kong economy which, though open to many criticisms, has plainly performed to the pronounced advantage of (almost all) the members of Hong Kong society.

The achievements of authoritarian legality under British rule were built on peculiarly British constitutional foundations. As is currently being rediscovered in constitutional scholarship, analysis of the largely unwritten and organically evolved British constitution must still, in considerable part, be based on A. V. Dicey's works.[2] But we will argue that Dicey should play an even larger role in the analysis of the Hong Kong polity under British rule. "Diceyan constitutionalism" was fundamental in shaping the governance institutions and operational procedures of British rule. These, in turn, worked remarkably well in conjunction with "Chinese familialism." The principal reason that Diceyan constitutionalism as a constitutional theory fell into disuse and indeed into a considerable degree of disrepute in the UK itself was that Dicey's views, which seem to have been essentially settled by the 1860s, are not merely undemocratic by contemporary British standards, but were highly suspicious of the growth of democracy which was, with industrialization, one of the two core features of Victorian Britain. In the end, the growth of democracy and the constitutional changes to which it necessarily gave rise led to the positive British constitution diverging from Dicey's account of that constitution, although it would be quite wrong to believe that all aspects of the divergence represented gain. Hong Kong under British rule did not, of course, until a late stage in its history, pose a similar difficulty for Diceyan constitutionalism, and indeed it was the maintenance of respect for the rule of law and for the

---

[2] The first edition of A. V. Dicey, *An Introduction to the Study of the Law of the Constitution* was published in 1885. The text was established in the 7th ed. of 1907, though a long and important new introduction was added to what proved to be the last edition by the author, the 8th of 1914. What has served as the standard edition is the 10th of 1959 by E. C. S. Wade, Wade's introduction to which is itself a work of significance in constitutional law, describing Dicey's influence at a time when it had only recently but nevertheless unarguably passed its zenith and a distanced perspective could be taken. A variorum edition by J. W. F. Allison has appeared as the first volume in a projected Oxford edition of Dicey: A. V. Dicey, *The Law of the Constitution* (Oxford: Oxford University Press, 2013). Dicey published a, by modern standards, small number of other works on British constitutional law and politics, but outstanding among these is his other great book: A. V. Dicey, *Lectures on the Relation between Law and Public Opinion in England During the Nineteenth Century* (Indianapolis, IN: Liberty Fund, 2008). First published in 1905, a second and last edition also appeared in 1914. Though not very substantially revised, this edition also contained a substantial and important new introduction.

public interest while eschewing pursuit of democracy that grounded the legitimacy of authoritarian legality.

How is it possible to claim that a constitution which in the postwar era avoided the pursuit of democracy was legitimate? Before we turn to our account of authoritarian legality in Hong Kong, we wish to establish a framework for evaluating this claim drawn from the political philosophy of John Rawls. We shall then describe the fundamentals of Diceyan constitutionalism within the Hong Kong context before proceeding to review how authoritarian legality has been regularly politically "stress-tested" over the course of Hong Kong's history, mainly focusing on the tests which have been undergone in the HKSAR. We conclude by reassessing the legitimacy of authoritarian legality in the HKSAR and more widely.

5.2 Rawls on the Legitimacy of Nondemocratic Societies

There has been, of course, a great deal of debate about the relationship, both in Hong Kong and the PRC, of economic success and political liberty, the basic issue having been taken to be whether the former will necessarily promote (perhaps by requiring) the latter. Both of the current authors have previously had their say on this.[3] We now wish to add to this debate by restating it in terms that, to our knowledge, have not previously been explored at length, terms derived from the earlier political philosophy of John Rawls which, we believe, provide a particularly strong basis upon which to evaluate authoritarian legality.

In our view, Rawls's principal achievement, writing against a background of general if hardly universal commitment to equality in liberal-democratic societies, has been to give inequality of outcome a legitimate basis. In *A Theory of Justice*,[4] Rawls argued that the justice

---

[3] Richard Cullen, "Hong Kong: The Making of a Modern City State," *Murdoch E-Law Journal* 13 (2006): 24, papers.ssrn.com/sol3/papers.cfm?abstract_id=2145140; Richard Cullen, "The Rule of Law in Hong Kong," Civic Exchange, Democracy 2004 Project, www.academia.edu /5156780/Rule_of_Law_in_Hong_Kong; David Campbell, "Economic Ideology and Hong Kong's Governance Structure After 1997," in Raymond Wacks (ed.), *Hong Kong, China and 1997* (Hong Kong: Hong Kong University Press, 1993), 87.

[4] References here will usually be to John Rawls, *A Theory of Justice* (rev. ed., Oxford: Oxford University Press, 1999). But we find certain passages of the first edition to be superior to the revised edition, certainly in terms of focusing on our concerns here, and we will refer occasionally to these passages, noting our use of this edition when we do so. John Rawls, *A Theory of Justice* (1st ed., Cambridge, MA: Belknap Press, 1971).

or otherwise of inequality is determined by what he called the "difference principle." That is to say, inequality is to be permitted to the extent that "it is to everyone's advantage," essentially by increasing economic welfare. The plausibility of the difference principle rests upon what, in later work, Rawls called the "realistic utopianism" of his approach.[5] The stability of an economy requires an acceptance that, on any plausible philosophic anthropology of economic action, there is a trade-off between equality and output. That an economic actor will normally be better incentivized by the prospect of personal betterment as the reward for personal effort rather than by having no such prospect, or even by the prospect of public betterment, is a particularly important relevant consideration on which we will focus in order to emphasize the difficulty of the judgments involved in acceptance of the difference principle.

Now, a very extensive trade-off indeed might satisfy the difference principle and thus legitimize a very profound degree of inequality. But those whose views are framed within the political consensus that makes liberal-democratic societies stable will conclude that, beyond a certain point, such a degree of inequality undermines the acceptability of the difference principle and so too the whole argument for the legitimacy of inequality. In what constitutes the superiority of his approach to political theories which in principle aim to maximize total welfare and so are inclined toward authoritarian paternalism, notably classical utilitarianism, Rawls conceived of the difference principle in a way which is intended to avoid this.

The possibility of very profound inequality we have just considered emerges from a trade-off conducted according to what Rawls called the "general conception of justice":

> All social values – liberty and opportunity, income and wealth, and the social bases of self-respect – are to be distributed equally unless an unequal distribution of any, or all, of these values is to everyone's advantage. Injustice, then, is simply inequalities that are not to the benefit of all.[6]

In the general conception, the difference principle applies, precisely, generally. Equality might in (almost) all its aspects and to (almost) any extent be sacrificed to economic welfare. But in a liberal-democratic society in which legitimacy rests on "justice as fairness," the difference principle is but the second of two principles of justice:

[5] John Rawls, *The Law of Peoples* (Cambridge, MA: Harvard University Press, 1999), 4–5.
[6] Rawls, *Theory of Justice* (rev. ed.), 54.

First principle: Each person is to have an equal right to the most extensive total system of equal basic liberties compatible with a similar system of liberties for all.

Second principle: social and economic inequalities are to be arranged so that they are ... reasonably expected to be to everyone's advantage.[7]

The order of these two principles is not arbitrary but expressive of the important priority of the first over the second, which Rawls pretentiously called the "lexical ranking" of the principles. Rawls's fundamental ethical commitment is to the (rationality and) autonomy of human beings as it is established by Kant, and justice as fairness is the principle of a political arrangement that is essential for such autonomy,[8] though it is intrinsic to the persuasiveness of Rawls's argument that he goes a long way toward accommodating the difference principle's consideration of total economic welfare within that arrangement. Inequalities can be arranged to maximize economic welfare, but only up to the point where this does not interfere with each citizen's basic autonomy. To take an extreme but hopefully therefore clear example:[9] it may be shown that economic welfare would be maximized by creating slavery, but this is not permissible as the welfare would be gained by erasing the autonomy of those who become slaves.[10]

Every aspect of justice as fairness has proven to be open to extensive but productive debate, the sure sign that it is a contribution of a very high order indeed. The aspect that is of interest here turns on Rawls's identification in the first principle of justice of equal basic liberties and his concentration on the institutions – the "basic structure" of a society – necessary to make these liberties actual. Rawls identified a person's possession of certain "primary" goods as conditions of the person's autonomy. Some of these are "natural," such as the "health and vigour," and some are "social," such as "rights, liberties ... opportunities and [a minimum level of] income and wealth."[11] A society which is just in the sense that its basic structure provides the conditions for respect for

---

[7] The difference principle is revised as the argument of *A Theory of Justice* progresses and in its final formulation "reasonably expected to be to everyone's advantage" becomes "to the greatest benefit of the least advantaged" (ibid., 53). The aspect of the principle of interest here is clearer in its first formulation (ibid., 266).

[8] Ibid., 452.

[9] Ibid., 55. Rawls expressly denies himself this example and focuses on more plausible ones.

[10] It is not a particularly difficult argument to show that the autonomy of the slave owners would also be erased, albeit in a different manner.

[11] Rawls, *Theory of Justice* (rev. ed.), 54.

autonomy must adequately provide these primary goods. One of Rawls's achievements has been to provoke debate about the detail of what is involved in providing primary goods, but we wish to focus on the general issue of what the provision of such goods implies for the relationship of justice as fairness to the general conception of justice.

Rawls regarded justice as fairness as a "special case" of the general conception.[12] If we put the abstract philosophical points to one side, justice as fairness is a special case in that it really can have acceptance only in affluent societies, and of these it really applies only to the liberal democracies because these are the only societies where there is a possibility of consensus over the value of autonomy. In the first instance, it is only affluent societies that can provide adequate social security to sustain a person's autonomy during periods of incapacity or unemployment. But, more than this, it is only affluent societies that can refuse to exploit possible trade-offs between increasing economic welfare and preserving autonomy.

We have noted that Rawls came to see his work as an account of a realistic utopia. Rawls saw liberal democracy as utopian in the sense that, accepting a philosophic anthropology which grounds autonomy but also accepts constraints of the sort we have mentioned in connection with economic issues, it is the best possible society. But, of course, not all societies are utopian in this way. In particular, some societies are not sufficiently affluent to adequately provide primary goods or indeed to refuse trade-offs which would be found unacceptable in liberal democracies. In such societies, the general conception of justice may legitimately obtain, even though basic liberties are sacrificed.

It is actually easier to accept the sacrifice of basic liberties in poor societies than it will at first seem to those who are members of liberal-democratic societies because, in a sense, there is little to sacrifice. In societies which are not sufficiently affluent to adequately provide primary goods, the formal existence of basic liberties may count for little as, in the absence of the requisite primary goods, a person may well lack the capacity to exercise those liberties. This argument draws upon the strength of Rawls's concept of the basic structure and its provision of

---

[12] Rawls, *Theory of Justice* (1st ed.), 63. In the revised edition of *Theory of Justice*, this language was somewhat altered as part, it would seem, of Rawls's retreat from a general theory of justice to an even greater focus on the political theory of liberal democracy culminating in John Rawls, *Political Liberalism* (New York: Columbia University Press, 1993) and John Rawls, *Justice as Fairness: A Restatement* (Cambridge, MA: Harvard University Press, 2001).

primary goods. However, it must be said that this aspect of this argument is a restatement of the core of socialism, though Rawls, incredibly really, seemed to be unaware of this in *A Theory of Justice*.[13] As T. H. Marshall put it in one influential formulation,[14] legal and political rights of citizenship will tend to be merely formal without a "social citizenship" conveying the capacity to exercise the otherwise formal rights. And, just as socialism implies that social citizenship should be developed in order to improve societies from which it is absent, Rawls's argument implies that in a poor society, increases in economic welfare may be pursued in accordance with the general conception through the trade-offs which are unacceptable in liberal-democratic society, but only so as to get to a position where the formerly poor society can provide primary goods and thus really establish an extensive system of total basic liberties. This is to say that economic policies may be justified by the general conception in societies other than liberal democracies because the result of those policies is that those societies will eventually become capable of transforming themselves into free societies. According to Rawls:

> It is only when social conditions do not allow the effective establishment of ... rights that one can concede their limitation; and these restrictions can be granted only to the extent that they are necessary to prepare the way for a free society. The denial of equal liberty can be defended only if it is necessary to raise the level of civilization so that in due course these freedoms can be enjoyed ... The serial ordering of the two principles eventually comes to be reasonable if the general conception is consistently followed. This lexical ranking is the long-run tendency of the general view.[15]

If one accepts Rawls's Kantian commitment to autonomy, then it is arguable, and we believe it is indeed the case, that he furnishes us, not only with a conception of a workable relationship of liberty and economic welfare in liberal-democratic society, but also with a workable

---

[13] Ibid., 148. When he turned to the socialist criticism of "merely formal" rights in later work, he did so rather gesturally, identifying the criticism with Marx. This was quite wrong as Marx was a "socialist" who thought such criticism was ultimately a mere distraction from the more profound criticisms he thought it necessary to make of capitalism. David Campbell, "The Critique of Bourgeois Justice After the Failure of Marxism," in Anton Kerner et al. (eds.), *Current Legal Issues in the Czech Republic and the United Kingdom* (Prague: Charles University Press, 2003), 9.

[14] T. H. Marshall and Tom Bottomore (eds.), *Citizenship and Social Class* (London: Pluto, 1992), 1.

[15] Rawls, *Theory of Justice* (1st ed.), 152. The changes to this passage made in Rawls, *Theory of Justice* (rev. ed.), 132, seem to us to make Rawls's argument less clear.

approach to the evaluation of undemocratic and illiberal policies adopted in societies which are not liberal democracies. Such policies can be justified if they are to everybody's advantage, which is mainly a question of economic welfare, and if they prepare the way for the development of a society in which justice as fairness then prioritizes basic liberties over the pursuit of economic welfare.

We cannot go into recent international political attempts to militantly impose what are claimed to be liberal-democratic values, but it is necessary to clarify an important point. In *A Theory of Justice*, liberal-democratic societies are straightforwardly analyzed as national polities, with Rawls spending only little time on international issues. When he turned to these issues in later work, Rawls gravely disappointed many of those most enthusiastic about his work because he did not do as they imagined he would and advocate the cosmopolitan creation of an international basic structure which was an extension, or perhaps better, globalization of the domestic basic structures for which he had argued. His *The Law of Peoples* paid a much greater respect to national self-determination, and presented a much greater consciousness of the difficulties of intervention and in particular the consequences of the use of force, than is consistent with normalized militant imposition of values on other nations, and so advocated a very limited form of international promotion of liberal-democratic values. This is not to say that Rawls would not pass judgments on, nor refuse to assist, even by military action, what he called "burdened societies,"[16] but, in essence, so long as such societies met some minimal conditions which, for our purposes, could be described as satisfying the general conception of justice, Rawls took the position that those societies should be allowed to work out their detailed policies as they saw fit. The point we are trying to make is that Rawls's commitment to the superiority of liberal-democratic society, and concomitant judgments about other societies, did not lead to his advocating thrusting liberal-democratic values down the throats of those other societies. This is also our view.

It is our belief, for which we shall provide evidence in the remainder of this chapter, that assessment on the basis of Rawls's views clearly shows the authoritarian legality of the Hong Kong under Britain rule and the conduct of government under that rule to have been plainly legitimate. Our belief turns on two claims. First, we shall very briefly argue that Hong Kong's economic policy under British rule, though it was

---

[16] Rawls, *Law of Peoples*, 105–12.

deliberately not democratic and involved trade-offs quite unacceptable in a liberal-democratic society such as the UK itself, was legitimate in that it was intended to be to the advantage of all. Second, we shall at greater length argue that the legitimacy of the government that could form policy of this sort lay in respect for the Diceyan rule of law, and in particular the convention that government should be conducted for the public good, including respect for the Chinese familial conception of that good. The formulation of economic policy by a government conducted in this manner made Hong Kong an overwhelmingly legitimate political society.

5.3 Hong Kong Economic Policy under British Rule

The postwar Hong Kong economy was, of course, internationally extolled as an exemplar of "neoclassical" market governance.[17] Certain empirical features of this economy undoubtedly supported this view. Postwar Hong Kong had no exchange controls. It was a completely free port. It did not have a public spending deficit even though personal and corporate taxation was extremely low by comparison to the European and North American advanced capitalist economies, even after the tax adjustments made in those economies in the 1980s. There was no direct attempt to equalize wealth through taxation.[18] The legal regulation of business was minimal on a similar comparison to those economies, with the development of environmental law, labor protection law or company and securities

---

[17] Sung Yun-wing, "The Hong Kong Developmental Model and Its Future Evolution: Neoclassical Economics in a Chinese Society," in Y. C. Jao et al. (eds.), *Economic Development in Chinese Societies* (Hong Kong: Hong Kong University Press, 1989), 155.

[18] There was, however, a remarkable system, which was put in place in Hong Kong under British rule from the outset and which continues to this day, to ensure that the government retains a core proprietary interest in virtually all real estate across Hong Kong. The result of this is that Land-Related Public Revenue (LRPR) has remained a key public finance source to a degree not found in any other First World jurisdiction. LRPR has typically provided 20 to 30 percent of gross public revenues in Hong Kong for many decades and this share was once far higher. The effect of this system has been to enhance government finances greatly by, in effect, "taxing" those wealthier Hong Kong residents owning property, which funding has been significantly used for provision of sizeable indirect social welfare, including, notably, the extensive system of rental public housing. For further discussion, see Richard Cullen and Kevin K. S. Tso, "Using Opium as a Public Revenue Source – Not as Easy as It Looks: The British Hong Kong Experience," *British Tax Review* 2 (2012): 226; Richard Cullen, "Land Revenue and the Chinese Dream," Taxation Law Research Programme, Hong Kong University, www.law.hku.hk/aiifl/wp-content/uploads/file/TLRP-TaxComments-No_2.pdf

regulation being vestigial. The government was highly anxious to effect the wishes of business elites and did not indulge in macro-economic planning much beyond pegging the Hong Kong dollar to the US dollar. An authoritative view of the nature of this governance structure was given in the well-known remarks of the former Financial Secretary, Sir Philip Haddon-Cave. Believing that "governments nowadays are anxious to encourage (but frequently inhibit) the development and growth of industry and commerce," Sir Philip described his "attitude to the economy as one of positive non-interventionism," which:

> involves taking the view that, in the great majority of circumstances it is futile and damaging to the growth rate of the economy for attempts to be made to plan the allocation of resources open to the private sector and to frustrate the operation of market forces which, in an open economy, are difficult enough to predict, let alone control.[19]

Positive noninterventionism was, however, a very much more nuanced policy than generally understood.[20] In particular, it was based on very extensive government provision of infrastructure, including public transport, social housing, education, and medical care. It was by no means the case that the economic policy was opposed to considerable government involvement in the economy, but that involvement was very closely circumscribed by an intention, not to expand direct claims on government action to reduce inequality or provide welfare at a level which might be a disincentive to work, but to promote economic growth. As Sir Philip put it:

> Our budgetary and fiscal policies as such have three objectives. The first is to implement government policies and programs which must include, of course, the provision of those services and facilities without which commercial management decisions would be frustrated. The second objective is to ensure that the required revenue is raised as equitably as possible between particular classes and groups of tax payers ... The third objective is to minimize any adverse effects of public expenditure and of the fiscal system on the internal cost/price structure of the economy, on the supply of human effort, on private investment decisions and on the monetary environment.[21]

[19] "Introduction," in David G. Lethbridge (ed.), *The Business Environment in Hong Kong* (Hong Kong: Oxford University Press, 1984), xiv.
[20] The following account is based on Campbell, "Economic Ideology," to which the reader is referred for full referencing.
[21] Haddon-Cave, "Introduction," xv.

The complex and expensive welfare state outcomes experienced in postwar advanced capitalist economies were driven, above all, by the perceived need to create policies aimed at securing democratic electoral success. In Hong Kong, similar, pressured setting of policy priorities was specifically checked by the nondemocratic decision-making mechanisms which applied. It therefore must be said that, by the standards of contemporaneous liberal-democratic societies, Hong Kong economic policy under British rule was in substantial part unacceptable.[22] It could only be defended by an argument that economic growth had to be given a degree of priority that no longer obtained in such societies. And it is, in our opinion, unarguable that such an argument was correct overall. Today's Hong Kong is a highly economically and politically developed, First World society. But it is such only because it continues the success of earlier economic policy under British rule. Hong Kong under British rule was far more wealthy and politically secure than the PRC or most of the rest of East Asia (including Southeast Asia), or indeed the entire Third World. Hong Kong has unarguably stood out as one of the "four little dragons" which were among the greatest successes of postwar economic development.[23]

It is our opinion, which will be merely asserted here, that under British rule, Hong Kong had created such wealth that, had it remained under British rule, with its concomitant political possibilities, it would have been on course to have become essentially a liberal-democratic society based on universal suffrage.[24] If we are right, this would further confirm Rawls's views. But, of course, the handover of Hong Kong to the PRC altered the parameters of Hong Kong's political life. However, Hong Kong under British rule was a legitimate political society. The main plank of this legitimacy was the conduct of government that, though it curtailed democracy, fostered economic success in substantial part by respecting the rule of law.

---

[22] The UK Labour Party was on occasion driven to purport to intervene in Hong Kong domestic affairs for this reason, though it should be said that the reasoning behind purported intervention in the 1970s was itself called into question by subsequent shifts in the prevalent opinion about economic policy in the liberal democracies. Norman Miners, *The Government of Hong Kong* (Hong Kong: Oxford University Press, 1991), 217–19.

[23] Ezra F. Vogel, *The Four Little Dragons* (Cambridge, MA: Harvard University Press, 1991).

[24] In particular, we say nothing about whether UK and US foreign policy would have countenanced the emergence of a liberal democracy in Hong Kong, with its implications for the diplomatic relationship of each of those countries with the PRC.

5.4   Dicey in Hong Kong

5.4.1   Diceyan Constitutionalism

Dicey retained a powerful joint concern about abuses of power arising from unrestrained power in the hands of either rulers or the mass of people within any modern jurisdiction. These views also emphasized the fundamental importance that Dicey placed on the need for balanced judgment of what justice means.

All this thinking, research, and writing by Dicey took place in the midst of brutal nineteenth-century poverty in a UK replete with countless "dark satanic mills." Moreover, the darkest side of the British Empire, during its peak period, included terrible famines both far away, in India, and right within the (then) UK, in Ireland. Despite this reality, the concept of the modern "free and lawful" citizen was still reinforced as a central norm of the common law.

The UK evolved into a functionally secular state, where religious variety was tolerated, with preferment given to the Church of England. Above all it was a state where law, with all its manifest limitations mattered greatly. The basic public policy optimism of nineteenth-century Britain went hand in glove with a capacity to avert one's mind from considering the extensive misery for too long and to retain a belief that liberal progress (as then understood) would ultimately put most of that misery right.

Around 100 years after Victoria came to the throne, George Orwell wrote his 1941 essay, "England Your England" during the German Blitz unleashed on England. It famously begins: "As I write, highly civilized human beings are flying overhead trying to kill me."[25] In the course of the essay, Orwell canvasses the powerful and complex binding forces applying within the highly class-based, UK society. For our purposes, two passages may be quoted with benefit:

> Here one comes upon an all-important English trait: the respect for constitutionalism and legality, the belief in 'the law' as something above the State and above the individual, something which is cruel and stupid, of course, but at any rate incorruptible.
>
> Everyone believes in his heart that the law can be, ought to be, and, on the whole, will be impartially administered. The totalitarian idea that

---

[25] "The Lion and the Unicorn: Socialism and the English Genius," in Peter Davison (ed.), *A Patriot After All: Volume 12 of the Complete Works of George Orwell* (London: Secker & Warburg, 2000), 392.

there is no such thing as law, there is only power, has never taken root. Even the intelligentsia have only accepted it in theory.[26]

Putting aside the contrast between Dicey's faith in "justice" (generally, and within the law) and Orwell's manifest lack of a similar level of confidence, one can see a remarkable continuity in the shared understanding that, while the law stands close to centralized power, it still operates, institutionally, at a very clear distance therefrom. This principal political–legal phenomenon was a product of several centuries of often fractious but continuous, elite–mass interactive experience.

The parliamentary system of government, based on regular elections, which evolved in Britain in the several decades after defeat in the American Revolutionary War, was incorporated into the largely white components of the British Empire including Canada, Australia, and New Zealand from the mid-nineteenth century. This status was not, however, conferred on many other component colonies and territories within the Empire.

Hong Kong thus adopted a form of authoritarian legality governance structurally based on the classical, pre-parliamentary government (partly-authoritarian) model such as applied during the reign of George III (1760–1820). This comprised a strong executive government, headed by the governor; and a legislature known as the Legislative Council (LegCo) with members fully appointed by the governor (this remained the case for almost 150 years). Combined with these two institutions was an independent judiciary.

Incorporated within this formally authoritarian governance structure, however, were powerful governance principles derived from Diceyan constitutionalism. Included within this framework were the independent judicial–legal system and the institutionally separated police force which together applied and enforced the common law and LegCo Ordinances.

In essence, Diceyan constitutionalism brought to British Hong Kong a combination of key principles which shaped the creation and maintenance of a strong, largely constructive and consistent public institutional framework. It also powerfully influenced operational procedures for the officers of these institutions.

Many defects however remained within this scheme. Thus, the Hong Kong governance system during those eras has been portrayed, as, "systematically biased against Chinese and other non-European

---

[26] Ibid., 397.

defendants."[27] Peter Wesley-Smith describes the rule of law as being, throughout this period, "[a British] ideal more dramatically subverted than any other."[28]

The governance system that evolved within Hong Kong was, however, still measurably fair, resilient, and successful. Its enduring merits were more central than its continuing drawbacks and those merits stood up well, comparatively. Hong Kong came to experience an operational governance system which displayed durable institutional integrity.[29]

It is fair to say that this was likely a necessary condition underpinning the success of Hong Kong. It was not, however, a sufficient condition. Proof of this is plain enough: systems based on Diceyan constitutionalism were implanted in a wide range of colonies throughout the British Empire. Few of those British colonies, especially where no natural resources were at hand, experienced the same economic success as Hong Kong.[30]

5.4.2   Chinese Familialism

Around 95 percent of the population of Hong Kong is Chinese.[31] The Chinese have built and maintained the largest, most enduring civilization on the planet. They have created a culture of immense depth and, despite its complexity, a culture that has displayed a set of clear hallmarks over many centuries. Chinese culture has been deeply influenced for over 2,000 years by the seminal writings of the philosopher Confucius (551–479 BC).[32]

---

[27] Christopher Munn, *Anglo-China: Chinese People and British Rule in Hong Kong: 1841–1880* (Richmond: Curzon Press, 2001), 251.

[28] "Book Review: Christopher Munn, *Anglo-China: Chinese People and British Rule in Hong Kong, 1841–1880*," *China Perspective*, www.journals.openedition.org/chinaperspectives/249

[29] Kevin K. S. Tso, "Fundamental Political and Constitutional Norms: Hong Kong and Macau Compared," *Australian Journal of Asian Law* 13(1) (2012): 1.

[30] Singapore, clearly, provides a like example. Once again one finds, there, an advantageous linking of Diceyan constitutionalism and Chinese familialism.

[31] This concept of familialism is rendered both as Chinese familialism and Chinese familism. It is analyzed and defined in Lau Siu-kai, "Chinese Familism in an Urban–Industrial Setting," *Journal of Marriage and the Family* 43 (1981): 977; and *Society and Politics in Hong Kong* (Hong Kong: Chinese University Press, 1991).

[32] For a succinct discussion of Confucianism, see Huston Smith, *The Religions of Man* (New York: Harper & Row, 1964), ch. 4. For discussion of the influence and impact of Confucian thinking on Chinese culture through until modern times, see Wang, Gungwu, *China and the Overseas Chinese* (Singapore: Times Academic Press, 1991); *Renewal: The Chinese State and the New Global History* (Hong Kong: Chinese University Press,

The crucial socioeconomic role of the Chinese family is deeply embedded in Hong Kong.[33] Another historical, abiding concern in Chinese societies is the maintenance of social order. The family rather than the state has been seen and experienced as the most important hedge against chaos.[34]

The central role of the family and the need to fit into one's family structure comprises an actively practiced, fundamental, belief system, which has evolved over many centuries. It is possible to argue that the family is the religion of China, in the sense that it is the fulcrum of a dominant, enduring, venerated belief system.[35]

It is not difficult to see how fundamental concepts, arising from Diceyan constitutionalism, such as the free and lawful citizen whose status was institutionally protected, had remarkable potential to mesh productively with the entrenched, collective-regulating aspects of Chinese familialism in Hong Kong.

5.5   Stress-testing: Authoritarian Legality in British Hong Kong

5.5.1   Introduction

We examine below the very serious stresses applied, over many decades, to the political systems of Hong Kong under British rule and as a special administrative region of China. Our primary aim is to detail the basic relevant facts and to examine how Hong Kong has coped with these stresses and especially how it has recovered afterwards. In the case of key incidents reviewed after 1997, we have also considered pertinent factors which have driven certain protests.

5.5.2   Early Tests

Real pressure on British Hong Kong's stability was experienced during the first decades after the fall of the Qing Dynasty and the establishment

---

Hong Kong, 2013). Further reading identifying fundamental aspects of the Chinese worldview can be found in Simon Leys, *The Burning Forest* (London: Paladin, 1988), 42; Robert E. Allinson, "An Overview of the Chinese Mind," in his (ed.), *Understanding the Chinese Mind* (Hong Kong: Oxford University Press, 1995), 19. See further Michael Harris Bond, *Beyond the Chinese Face* (New York: Oxford University Press, 1991); Han Suyin, *The Crippled Tree* (London: Triad/Panther, 1984).

[33] Lau, *Society and Politics in Hong Kong*, ch 3.
[34] Han Suyin, *Crippled Tree*, 71.
[35] Allinson, "Overview," 19.

of the fledgling, unstable, Republic of China in 1912. On May 30, 1925, Sikh police under British command opened fire on Chinese demonstrators in Shanghai killing around ten and wounding many others. Less than a year later, foreign troops killed another fifty-plus Chinese demonstrators at Shamian Island in Guangzhou.[36]

Following these lethal incidents, China, through a joint Chinese Communist Party (CCP)–Kuomintang (KMT) effort, instigated a strike and boycott directed against British interests, primarily in Guangzhou and Hong Kong. By 1926, the worst of the strike had passed, Hong Kong resumed normal trading, and the economy (and stability) recovered.[37]

5.5.3   Postwar Tests

The first case of serious postwar, political rioting in Hong Kong occurred in 1956, when supporters of the KMT and CCP clashed violently in Tsuen Wan in the New Territories. This was, in essence, a localized, bloody postscript to the Chinese Civil War which had concluded in 1949. There were fifty-nine deaths and much property damage. British military personnel were used to reinforce the Hong Kong police force.[38]

The next serious, postwar riots, from April 1966, are commonly referred to as the "Star Ferry Riots." The dissatisfaction with British rule in Hong Kong at this time was high. There was heightened hostility to the extensive corruption that had grown apace in the 1950s and 1960s.

The "1967 Leftist Riots" were far more serious. They lasted from May to December 1967. This major political disturbance was significantly fueled by the spillover from the early stages of the Cultural Revolution in China. Over fifty people were killed. Initially, Beijing supported the

---

[36] John Mark Carroll, *A Concise History of Hong Kong* (Lanham, MD: Rowman & Littlefield, 2007).

[37] Ibid. See also Anjali Cadambi, "Unions and Students in Hong Kong and Canton Strike – Boycott against British Imperial Rule, 1925–1926," Global Nonviolent Action Database, www.nvdatabase.swarthmore.edu/content/unions-and-students-hong-kong-and-canton -strike-boycott-against-british-imperial-rule-1925-1

[38] Connie Lee Hong-nee, "Society and Policing in Hong Kong: A Study of the 1956 Riot" (master's thesis, University of Hong Kong, 1995), www.hub.hku.hk/bitstream/10722/ 27467/1/FullText.pdf. The author notes that, after the 1956 riot, the police created more military-styled units (for the first time) to deal with large-scale disturbances.

rioters. The Chinese Premier Zhou Enlai was said to have ordered an end to rioting by all leftist groups in late 1967.[39]

Despite these very serious examples of political unrest, most people in Hong Kong remained largely apolitical. The vast majority of the postwar population had migrated or fled the PRC. Many of them saw Hong Kong as a staging post. Their eventual aim was to migrate – or at least see their children migrate – to a range of Western, English-speaking countries. They saw themselves as "sojourners."[40] Another important factor was the rapid economic growth in Hong Kong. Although people often lived in very difficult circumstances, they had entered an economy which was, year after year, growing at a prodigious rate. This reality offered hope.

The creation of the Independent Commission Against Corruption (ICAC) in 1974 proved to be a crucially important initiative of the Hong Kong government. It was instrumental in: (a) reinforcing Hong Kong's adherence to the rule of law; (b) buttressing acceptance of benevolent–authoritarian government; and (c) enhancing social stability. By 1976, major inroads were made in curtailing the massive level of corruption prevailing.

The confluence of these factors noted above produced: (a) a generally stable political climate; (b) government by an elite-influenced civil service; and (c) poor prospects for the growth of party politics.[41]

Moreover, on June 4, 1989, the planning for a "smooth transition" (of sovereign control over Hong Kong from London to Beijing on July 1, 1997) was profoundly disrupted when the PRC government used battle-field weapons to end a massive, long-running demonstration for political reform by thousands of its own citizens in and around Tiananmen Square. This terrible incident swiftly led to what were the largest ever public demonstrations seen in Hong Kong. Over one million people are reported to have marched, first in support of the protesting students, in May 1989, and then in protest, against Beijing, on June 5, 1989.[42] Notwithstanding their massive size, the protests were peaceful and not,

---

[39] Hong Wrong, "Photography, the 1967 Hong Kong Riots," www.hongwrong.com/1967-hkriots; *Wikipedia*, "Hong Kong 167 Leftist Riots," www.en.wikipedia.org/wiki/Hong_Kong_1967_Leftist_riots

[40] Lau, "Chinese Familism"; Lau, *Society and Politics in Hong Kong.*

[41] Sing Ming, *Hong Kong's Tortuous Democratization* (London: Routledge-Curzon, 2004), 143–90.

[42] Bob Beatty, *Democracy, Asian Values and Hong Kong: Evaluating Political Elite Beliefs* (Westport, CT: Praeger, 2003), ch. 1.

in themselves, disruptive of the economic, social, and political order within Hong Kong.

5.6   Stress-testing: Authoritarian Legality in the HKSAR

Our focus here is on several primary, turning-point mass protests: the 2003 massive July 1 march; the 2014 Occupy Central Movement (OCM); and the 2016 Mong Kok riot. It is important, though, to note that there are also several regular, often annual, major protest events which draw medium to very large crowds, including: the June 4 Vigil; the July 1 National Day March; and the New Year's Day March.[43] There have also been more irregular, significant protests related to teaching institutions in Hong Kong.[44]

5.6.1   July 1, 2003 March

In 2003, early in the second term of the first HKSAR government under Chief Executive (C. H. Tung), the government tried to enact new anti-subversion laws under Article 23 of the Basic Law.[45] As this Article 23 project commenced, the severe acute respiratory syndrome (SARS) out-break posed an increasingly lethal threat to Hong Kong.[46]

---

[43] Sonny Lo, *Hong Kong's Indigenous Democracy* (Basingstoke, UK: Palgrave Macmillan, 2015) where, inter alia, these important, embedded, regular mass demonstrations are reviewed.

[44] There was a major successful protest in 2012 against the introduction of changes (seen as pro-China by protesters) to school teaching programs. More recently there have been protests related to Hong Kong University: see, for example: Jerome A. Cohen and Alvin Cheung, "Delay in HKU Appointment of Johannes Chan Makes a Mockery of Beijing's Pledged Support for Rule of Law," *South China Morning Post*, September 25, 2015, www.scmp.com/comment/insight-opinion/article/1861280/delay-hku-appointment-johannes-chan-makes-mockery-beijings; Tony Carty, "What Exactly Does Academic Freedom Mean to Johannes Chan and His Supporters?" *South China Morning Post*, October 7, 2015, www.scmp.com/comment/insight-opinion/article/1864887/what-exactly-does-academic-freedom-mean-johannes-chan-and

[45] Basic Law of the Hong Kong Special Administrative Region of the People's Republic of China (in essence, the HKSAR 'constitution'). See Johannes Chan and C. L. Lim (eds.), *The Law of the Hong Kong Constitution* (Hong Kong: Sweet & Maxwell, 2015). For a review of the significance of Article 23, see Hualing Fu and Richard Cullen, "National Security," ibid., ch. 6.

[46] A comprehensive review of the SARS epidemic can be found in Christine Loh (ed.), *At the Epicentre: Hong Kong and the SARS Outbreak* (Hong Kong: Hong Kong University Press, 2004).

Even while the SARS epidemic remained a serious threat, the government pressed ahead with the highly controversial, Article 23 project. Civil society resentment grew briskly, amplified by significant popular media reflection of this antipathy.[47] The ultimate response was the largest demonstration since the 1989 marches. Over 500,000 people were reported to have rallied and advanced through the center of Hong Kong Island on July 1, 2003, the National Reunification Day Holiday. It was a clearly focused, entirely peaceful protest that dispersed without incident on the same day. Very soon after the march, the government announced that it was dropping the Article 23 proposals.

5.6.2   2014 Occupy Central Movement

The OCM had its origins in a journal article published in January 2013 by Professor Benny Tai from the Faculty of Law at Hong Kong University (HKU). In this article he proposed that residents should plan a civil disobedience occupation of the Central Business District on Hong Kong Island to put pressure on the Hong Kong government and Beijing in the event that the expected 2014 political reform proposals offered only *fake democracy*.[48] The concept of this protest – its purpose and its methodology – aroused significant general interest.

The relevant political reform proposals were specified in a decision of August 31, 2014, delivered by the Standing Committee of the National People's Congress's (NPCSC), which set out a number of requirements which had to be satisfied to allow a graduated step toward a universal suffrage system for the election of the chief executive of Hong Kong in 2017. These stipulations, which included a system for vetting chief executive candidates, meant that it was extremely likely that only broadly pro-establishment candidates would be declared as eligible to stand for election as the chief executive.[49] What was on offer was a plainly attenuated, but measurable first step toward political reform.

---

[47] Ibid. There is a good short reflection, in Loh's book, on the ethics of the "advocacy journalism" which came to play such a significant role in fostering the July 1 march (ibid., ch. 12).

[48] Benny Tai, "The Rationale of Occupy Central Is the Pursuit of Justice," Occupy Central with Love and Peace, August 26, 2014, www.oclphkenglish.wordpress.com/tag/benny-tai

[49] *South China Morning Post*, "NPC Standing Committee Decision on Hong Kong 2017 Election Framework," www.scmp.com/news/hong-kong/article/1582245/full-text-npc-standing-committee-decision-hong-kong-2017-election. Briefly, the NPCSC Decision provided that a Nominating Committee based on the existing, Beijing-friendly Election

Soon after the NPCSC's decision was handed down, the OCM occupations began. In our view, the occupations, which lasted about three months, proceeded on a notably overstated pretext. They were also strikingly disproportionate, immensely disruptive, and lacked coherence in leadership and in purpose. The claimed civil disobedience basis for commencing the occupations was insubstantial. The vast majority in Hong Kong eventually grew weary of the entire project. The main direct achievement that one can see was the raising of political awareness for many supportive participants. In 2015, the supporters of OCM strongly backed the vetoing of the proposed chief executive 2017 election reform package. This vetoing was, however, all but guaranteed by the collective decision-making of the Pan-Democrats (PDs) in LegCo.[50]

The entire OCM project was also remarkable in that it went for so long, involved so many participants, yet the physical harm and property damage suffered were minimal. To have managed this over a period of almost three months is extraordinary.[51] Self-restraint was more displayed than otherwise by all involved, including OCM participants, officials in Beijing and Hong Kong, the police and OCM opponents. This, combined with some effective application of the general law by the judiciary, crucially helped Hong Kong to cope so well with the OCM occupations.

5.6.3   2016 Mong Kok Riot

On Monday evening February 8, 2016 as the lunar new year began, a major political riot, which lasted for ten to twelve hours, erupted in the Mong Kok area of Kowloon.[52] Strong anti-Beijing views plus calls for Hong Kong independence were declared by many protestors. Pavement

Committee would nominate two to three candidates each of whom would require the endorsement of more than 50 percent of the Nominating Committee.

[50] Pan-Democrat is the term most often used to encompass the groups who argue for full universal suffrage to elect the HKSAR Chief Executive and all seats in LegCo. The groups are now numerous. Disagreement among group members is recurrent, but they share a firm resolve to seek democratic political reform. See further, Pro-democracy camp (Hong Kong), https://en.wikipedia.org/wiki/Pro-democracy_camp_(Hong_Kong)

[51] See the positive review by Joseph Wang, "Was Occupy Central a Failure?," Quora, www.quora.com/Was-Occupy-Central-a-failure

[52] Chris Lau, "Timeline and Map: How the Mong Kok Street Hawker Hygiene Clampdown Became a Full-scale Riot," *South China Morning Post*, February 9, 2016, www.scmp.com/news/hong-kong/politics/article/1910858/timeline-and-map-how-mong-kok-street-hawker-hygiene

stones were thrown, fires were lit, and the police were attacked.[53] The police estimated that the active number involved in the riot to be between 400 and 500 persons.[54]

The claimed basis for the protest was to defend the rights of non-licensed street hawkers to sell fish balls during the lunar new year festival.[55] The hawkers themselves seemed to have wanted no part in the protest being conducted on their behalf.[56] Over 120 were injured during the riot with ninety of those being police officers.[57] The rioting was widely condemned.

5.7   Conclusion

Although local issues are prominent, the most significant periods of political unrest in Hong Kong have been powerfully influenced from across the border. The 1967 Leftist Riots were acutely shaped by the start of the Cultural Revolution in China. The 1989 Tiananmen Square protest followed by its bloody suppression led to huge marches in Hong Kong. The July 1, 2003 march was energized by the Hong Kong government's handling of the SARS crisis but, even more so, by the plan to enact new, Beijing-backed national security laws. The OCM occupation was triggered by a decision to protest against the 2014 Decision of the NPCSC on political reform in Hong Kong. The 2016 Mong Kok riot had a strong anti-Beijing separatist–independence impulse at its heart.

In each case, we can see China's influence in igniting political unrest in Hong Kong. However, the China of the immediate postwar era was vastly different economically from the China of recent decades. In 1966, at the time of the Star Ferry Riots, China's annual per-capita GDP was 254 yuan.[58] Between 1978 (the beginning of the Open Door policy following the death of Mao) and 2014, total GDP in China rose from 364 billion

---

[53] Stuart Lau et al., "Mong Kok Riot: How Hong Kong's First Night in the Year of the Monkey Descended into Mayhem," *South China Morning Post*, February 10, 2016, www.scmp.com /news/hong-kong/article/1911341/mong-kok-riot-how-hong-kongs-first-night-year-mon key-descended-mayhem.

[54] Ibid. There was no evidence of any significant, further numbers spontaneously opting to join the violent protest once it began – a striking contrast with the OCM occupations.

[55] Ibid.

[56] Ibid.

[57] Ibid.

[58] China Statistics Press, *China Statistical Yearbook 2001*, www.stats.gov.cn/english/statisti caldata/yearlydata/YB2001e/ml/indexE.htm, section 3.1. (254 yuan was equivalent to about USD103 at that time.)

yuan to 63.6 trillion yuan.[59] Compared to China, Hong Kong's economy dropped from being around 18 percent of the size of China's economy in 1997 to being around 3 percent of that economy by 2014.[60] These GDP figures can give no better than a broad indication but they do this emphatically.

The Economist has reported how the PRC had expanded its middle class by a total of more than 220 million citizens in the period between 2000 and 2016.[61] The Economist also reported that the PRC lifted almost 700 million people out of extreme poverty between 1981 and 2010. In fact China alone was responsible for 75 percent of the total world poverty reduction over this period.[62] According to a 2013 Pew Survey of Global Attitudes, 85 percent of Chinese citizens were "very satisfied" with their country's direction compared to 31 percent of US citizens.[63] These figures underpin our provisional view of the basic legitimacy of the authoritarian legality established within the PRC over the past four decades.

The China which had such a deep influence on the 1967 Leftist Riots was a bitterly impoverished nation riven by an appalling level of deadly internal political conflict. The nation which PD (and localist) opponents confront today is an immensely stronger one-party state run by the CCP.

While the CCP continues to engage in serious abuses of power as documented elsewhere in this volume, it has also led the extraordinary, positive side of China's economic transformation. Within four decades,

[59] Chinability, "GDP Growth in China: 1952–2015," www.chinability.com/GDP.htm
[60] Timothy B. Lee, "Hong Kong Used to be 18 Percent of China's GDP. Now It's 3 Percent," Vox China, September 28, 2014, www.vox.com/2014/9/28/6857567/hong-kong-used-to-be-18-percent-of-chinas-gdp-now-its-3-percent
[61] "225 Million Reasons for China's Leaders to Worry," The Economist, July 9, 2016, www .economist.com/news/leaders/21701760-communist-party-tied-its-fortunes-mass-afflu ence-may-now-threaten-its-survival-225m?cid1=cust/ednew/n/bl/n/2016077n/owned/ n/n/nwl/n/n/AP/n. As the title of this article indicates, The Economist curiously believes that the dominant effect of this unprecedented achievement is to have placed the continuity of CCP leadership in some increased peril.
[62] "Towards the End of Poverty," The Economist, June 1, 2013, www.economist.com/news/ leaders/21578665-nearly-1-billion-people-have-been-taken-out-extreme-poverty-20-years-world-should-aim. The World Bank puts the figure lifted out of poverty in China at over 800 million. The World Bank, China Overview, www.worldbank.org/en/country/ china/overview
[63] "What's Gone Wrong with Democracy," The Economist, March 1, 2014, www .economist.com/news/essays/21596796-democracy-was-most-successful-political-idea -20th-century-why-has-it-run-trouble-and-what-can-be-do. The Pew Research Center is a Washington-based "fact tank" which, inter alia, conducts well-regarded international polling.

China has risen from being vastly impoverished to become one of the world's two superpowers.[64] This, in turn, has energized a new superpower rivalry. Driven primarily by analysis and claims made by the United States, this encounter is increasingly being characterized as a "new cold war."[65] Concerns have been robustly expressed in Beijing about the scope for the United States, especially, to provide support for those legislators within Hong Kong who may wish to challenge China.[66]

The growing, negative impact of social media on operational politics is now a matter of record across developed democracies and nondemocratic jurisdictions. The damaging aspects of its influence are arguably worst in transitional and developing democracies.[67] This negative view is dominant in Beijing.[68]

With the passing of time, further views on the OCM occupations have emerged. Some critics now feel that what came to be known as the "Umbrella Revolution/Movement" took over from the OCM once the occupations began, with adverse consequences.[69] Other commentators see a mainly polarizing legacy and yet others, a political-deadening legacy.[70]

---

[64] Pew Research Center, *The United States and China: The Image of the Globe's Two Superpowers*, July 18, 2013, www.pewglobal.org/2013/07/18/united-states-and-china-the -image-of-the-globes-two-superpowers

[65] Julian Borger and Lily Kuo, "US–China Tensions Soar as 'New Cold War' Heats up," *The Guardian*, October 16, 2018, www.theguardian.com/world/2018/oct/16/us-china-new-cold-war-tensions

[66] Ernest Kao and Tony Cheung, "Chinese Government Rebukes US over Comments on Hong Kong Legislators-Elect," *South China Morning Post*, November 17, 2016, www .scmp.com/news/hong-kong/politics/article/2046914/chinese-government-rebukes-us-over-comments-hong-kong. See also Christine Loh, "Hong Kong's Role in the Trade *War* Should Be to Explain How Far China Has Come" *South China Morning Post*, November 13, 2018, www.scmp.com/comment/insight-opinion/hong-kong/article/ 2172812/hong-kongs-role-trade-war-should-be-explain-world

[67] See, e.g., "Does Social Media Threaten Democracy?," *The Economist*, November 4, 2017, www.economist.com/leaders/2017/11/04/do-social-media-threaten-democracy; Angela Phillips, "Social Media Is Changing the Face of Politics, and It's Not Good News," *The Conversation*, February 9, 2016, www.theconversation.com/social-media-is-changing-the-face-of-politics-and-its-not-good-news-54266; Gordon Hull, "Why Social Media May Not Be So Good for Democracy," *The Conversation*, November 6, 2017 https://theconversation.com/why-social-media-may-not-be-so-good-for-democracy -86285

[68] Philip P. Pan, "The Land That Failed to Fail," *New York Times*, November 18, 2018, www .nytimes.com/interactive/2018/11/18/world/asia/china-rules.html

[69] Wang, "Was Occupy Central a Failure?"

[70] Sonny Lo, "Electoral Reform Hinges on Principles," *China Daily*, July 31, 2016, www .chinadailyasia.com/opinion/2016-07/31/content_15470808.html; Tim Black, "Hong Kong:

Hong Kong has recovered strikingly well and with a sense of continuing positive, hard-working purpose from a significant number of severe tests arising from political protests over the last fifty years. We argue that any primary account of this particular form of societal resilience under pressure must refer to the way in which two of the pivotal foundations of Hong Kong society, Diceyan constitutionalism and Chinese familialism, have worked together so effectively for around 175 years. Diceyan constitutionalism stresses a continuing, shared understanding of the essential, socially beneficial nature of law. Chinese familialism prioritizes inter alia hard work; deep respect for education, obligations within the wider, molecular family; thrift; and impulse control.

It is fair to say that, had the British remained in control Hong Kong for an extra decade, without London having its hands tied by agreement with Beijing, the growing demand by the 1990s for major democratic reform in Hong Kong during British rule would have been (confirmed by Rawls's reasoning) most difficult to resist. This, however, was not how the geopolitical reality unfolded. The Sino-British Joint Declaration on Hong Kong, signed in 1984, makes it very clear that Hong Kong is to be part of the PRC from July 1, 1997, under the *one country, two systems* formula.

Based on: a decisive understanding that stability is always founded on ultimate control; the PRC experience with Hong Kong's continuing level of political disputation; and the possible onset of a new "cold war" between the United States and China, Beijing is now more than ever wedded to allowing only gradual, durably regulated reform in the HKSAR.

For much of the broad PD movement, the political reform that has been offered by Beijing is no more than *fake democracy*. For the more radical members of this movement, the CCP remains, first and always, a repository of supreme and autocratic power. Self-perpetuation continues to be the fundamental core value of the CCP. This tersely abbreviated standpoint credits the CCP with little if any governance legitimacy.

We argue, however, that the one-party system, as it has matured over the last four decades, has established a prima facie legitimacy in compliance with the Rawlsian analysis set out in Section 5.2. The economic development in China across this period has stressed, in accordance with the difference principle, the provision of *primary goods* to the widest

How the Occupy Brand Is Killing Politics," *Spiked*, December 11, 2014, www.spiked-online.com/newsite/article/hong-kong-how-the-occupy-brand-is-killing-politics

spectrum of a vast population – for the benefit of all. India, which is the world's largest functioning democracy, provides a manifestly higher degree of formal liberties than does the PRC yet it, equally, manifestly does a far worse job of providing primary goods to a similarly huge population. In 1950, India and China had an almost 1:1 parity in terms of total GDP. By 2016, Indian total GDP was around 20 percent of Chinese GDP.[71]

It is clear that Hong Kong will have to come to terms, eventually, with the task of making the very best of its special status within China, under the one country, two systems formula. Hong Kong has, overall, remained a stable and flourishing place. It has, though, struggled to move beyond one bitter standoff after another with each attempt at political structure reform.

In our view, the outright rejection of the 2014 NPCSC reform proposal was a cardinal political reform error on the part of the PD movement. It was bad for Hong Kong and it was bad for China. It vetoed the opportunity for Hong Kong to move forward to an enhanced level of democratic participation, from which platform, further reforms would have been within easier reach. It denied the opportunity for Beijing to experiment, in Hong Kong, with a limited form of still significant democratic participation – at an elevated executive level – which could have served as a pilot model for possible adoption within other parts of the PRC. The 2014 reform proposal should have been accepted under clearly articulated, civilized protest.

As Hong Kong undergoes the necessary process of building a difficult, widely based, durable consensus that Hong Kong is a special but fundamentally included part of China, it likely will face continuing polarized, political disputation over the next decade, at least, which may turn violent. One reason for this is that the one-party system run by the CCP looks set, based on a rational analysis, to endure for several more decades at a minimum. Political change within China may unfold in response to expressions of the popular will but that change is most likely to be managed from above, by Beijing.

What this review strongly indicates is that Hong Kong, collectively, has retained a deeply rooted capacity to abide significant mass protesting

---

[71] Ankit Bhardwaj, "What Is the Comparative Picture of Economic Growth of India and China since 1950?," Quora, www.quora.com/What-is-the-comparative-picture-of-economic-growth-of-India-and-China-since-1950; *World Economic Outlook*, "List of Countries by Projected GDP," May 6, 2018, www.statisticstimes.com/economy/countries-by-projected-gdp.php

better than almost anywhere else. This proven capacity to regain its equilibrium, based on widely shared social–political norms, does not guarantee that there cannot be a more grave breakdown of social stability in Hong Kong, arising from further polarized confrontations. If this happens, however, it will be a break from the pattern of the past, which has demonstrated a recurring and powerful understanding – across the political divide – of the mutual value of retained stability.

6

The Clash of Legal Cultures

Hong Kong Efforts to Maintain the Liberal Rule of Law vs. Beijing's Hardline Authoritarian Legality

MICHAEL C. DAVIS

Hong Kong poses an awkward case for this book's theme. Technically, it is a case of authoritarian legality as defined in the opening chapters, since it is not a democracy. But the guarantees in the Sino-British Joint Declaration and the Basic Law have effectively maintained Hong Kong as an open society and have until recently largely held back the sorts of official interference normally expected under an authoritarian regime. Does recent increased Beijing interference in Hong Kong now call this into question? There are a number of ways to assess this. As Jacques deLisle notes, one may locate a given regime on a spectrum from a relatively liberal rule-of-law system to a more repressive rule-by-law paradigm.[1] In the Hong Kong context, the opposite ends of that spectrum are directly in confrontation across the two systems. As deLisle notes, Hong Kong, when not interfered with by the sovereign power, is on the extreme liberal end of the spectrum; China, is on the opposite end, often with low regard for legality or at best with a rule-by-law paradigm. As this writer noted in his 1990 book, this seemed bound to produce a clash of legal cultures.[2]

A second avenue to interrogate Hong Kong's legal culture is to look at the historical legacy of the rule of law within its legal system. Richard Cullen and David Campbell in this book (Chapter 5) wonderfully lay out the evolution of what they describe as the Diceyan tradition of the rule of law in Hong Kong. As they note, this classic British tradition, which holds in the simplest narration that nobody, whatever their station, is above the law and everyone is subject to the law applied in the ordinary manner by

---

[1] Chapter 1 in this volume.
[2] Michael C. Davis, *Constitutional Confrontation in Hong Kong* (London: Macmillan Press, 1990).

the ordinary courts, is deeply rooted in Hong Kong. Yet a third way to interrogate such notion of legality is to view it in its constitutional and political context as a dynamic process, asking what is at stake and why people care enough to mobilize in its defense.

To better interrogate the recent politics of constitutionalism in Hong Kong this latter approach will be taken here. Accepting the rich foundation so amply described by Cullen and Campbell, this chapter will analyze what has been going on in Hong Kong and why activists and their supporters have felt justified in taking such extreme measures, including launching a civil disobedience campaign in support of democracy, but ultimately in defense of Hong Kong's rule-of-law tradition. The aim here is more bottom-up, considering the perspectives of those who have taken public actions to defend the rule of law. In doing so I will consider: first, the political context of the Hong Kong debate, being the perceived mainland interference driving Hong Kong's popular protests; second, the legal narrative regarding commitments made in the Sino-British Joint Declaration (Joint Declaration) and the Hong Kong Basic Law (Basic Law); third, the threat to Hong Kong core values embodied in a series of Beijing-issued reports, decisions, and interpretations; fourth, the anemic Hong Kong government response to these conditions embodied in various government consultations and policy decisions; and, fifth, a conclusion explaining why these developments have bred a radical response.

While these various interfaces between Hong Kong and the mainland are generally discussed on the mainland side in economic developmental terms and on the Hong Kong side in political rule-of-law and open society terms, it is important to keep in mind that these distinctions also shape profoundly different senses of identity on the opposing sides of the Hong Kong border. While a variety of institutional arrangements allow these two communities to survive and project forward, it needs to be appreciated that deep-seated identities are at stake along all these interfaces. While the battles are inevitably over the fulfillment of Basic Law commitments in a rule-of-law-sensitive process, the passions that drive these battles may run more deeply than the mere mechanics of the rule of law. Politicians and political reformers ignore such deep-seated identity politics at their peril.

6.1   The Political Context of the Hong Kong Debate

The "one country, two systems" model was always fundamentally about returning Hong Kong to Chinese sovereign control but doing so in a way that protected Hong Kong from the intrusion of the mainland system. It was widely understood that the mainland system of expedient political control, or at its best "rule by law," is deeply at odds with the rule-of-law system and open society established in Hong Kong. It was further understood that the Hong Kong economy, then already producing one of the highest per-capita incomes in the world, was deeply reliant on the rule of law and the associated human rights protections. It was hoped that the confidence the Hong Kong system inspired would contribute measurably to economic investment and development on the mainland. Very early in the negotiation and transition process, Deng Xiaoping went to great pains to urge investors to "put their hearts at ease."[3] After the Joint Declaration was signed, Chinese officials took the agreement, and later the Basic Law, to foreign capitals to encourage foreign confidence in the agreement and urge foreign governments to treat Hong Kong distinctly in their economic and trade relations. Such Hong Kong and foreign confidence and distinctive foreign official treatment has always depended on fulfillment of the commitments made in the Joint Declaration and the Basic Law.

Such confidence in the "one country, two systems" model, however, has not evolved in a vacuum. Reliance on the Beijing promises has always interacted with the evolution of the mainland system itself. The rapid economic development on the mainland, in which Hong Kong has long been a major investor, has been a positive factor in sustaining confidence in Hong Kong. At the same time, the lack of political reform and the continuing weak commitment to developing the rule of law, has kept in place the very concerns that had originally justified the "one country, two systems" model. In the early 1980s, with Deng Xiaoping's reforms in full throttle, there was great hope in Hong Kong that the huge gap between Hong Kong and the mainland would eventually close, with the mainland moving closer to the rule of law and open society model established in Hong Kong.[4] Early mainland economic reforms such as decollectivizing the economy, expanded private ownership of property, liberalizing the market, privatization, joint venture investments, reforms of the legal system, educational expansion, and legal institutional and educational development all encouraged massive Hong Kong investment in the mainland and much greater confidence in the destiny of one country two systems.

---

[3] Steve Tsang, *A Modern History of Hong Kong: 1841–1997* (London: I.B. Tauris, 2007), 215–25.
[4] Ibid.

Mainland economic reforms have unfortunately not been fully matched with the anticipated political and legal reforms. While the gap between the economic development level of the mainland and Hong Kong has closed considerably, especially with respect to the economic conditions in major mainland cities, the gap in the two legal systems, as well as associated human rights and open society protections, has not closed,[5] leaving the original justifications for the two systems model well in place. This gap has encouraged deep concern in Hong Kong and has driven the many popular protests aimed at full implementation of the Hong Kong commitments.

Increasing mainland intervention in Hong Kong has met growing resistance, as Hong Kong people fear both their way of life and their identity is under threat.[6] Rather than increased integration between the two systems, the threat perception has led to a growing identity gap between Hong Kong and the mainland.[7] Hong Kong people have come more and more to understand and appreciate the core values and the distinctiveness of their vibrant rule-of-law-based society.[8] This has in recent years driven frustrated calls for independence. At the same time, mainland officials and local pro-Beijing elites, perceiving Hong Kong to drift further from the mainland, have pushed for tighter mainland control and greater interference to impose a national identity on Hong Kong. This interference has been markedly self-defeating, driving more popular resistance in Hong Kong, and causing the identify gap to widen.[9]

These developments combine to shine an unfavorable light on the evolving mainland system, often reported on and analyzed more carefully in Hong Kong than under the controlled press on the mainland. There is a widespread perception that the current Chinese President, Xi Jinping, has rolled back, rather than expanded, the moderate reforms of

[5] A comparison between the chapters by Hualing Fu and Michael Dowdle, and Eva Pils with that by Cullen and Campbell easily bears out this gap (see Chapters 2, 3, and 5 in this volume).

[6] Michael C. Davis, "Hongkong Umbrella Movement and Beijing's Failure to Honor the Basic Law," *E-International Relations* (October 29, 2014), www.e-ir.info/2014/10/29/the-umbrella-movement-and-beijings-failure-to-respect-the-hong-kong-basic-law

[7] Marte Philipp Kaeding, "The Rise of 'Localism' in Hong Kong," *Journal of Democracy* 28 (1) (2017): 157.

[8] Carole J. Petersen, "From British Colony to Special Administrative Region of China: Embracing Human Rights in Hong Kong," in Randall Peerenboom, Carole J. Petersen, and Albert H. Y. Chen (eds.), *Human Rights in Asia: A Comparative Legal Study of Twelve Asian Jurisdictions, France and the USA* (Abingdon, UK: Routledge, 2006), 224–64.

[9] Michael C. Davis, "The Basic Law, Universal Suffrage and the Rule of Law in Hong Kong," *Hastings International and Comparative Law Review* 38(2) (2016): 275.

the past.[10] His campaign against corruption has seen increased political interference in the mainland economy. For Hong Kong investors, investment in mainland companies or stocks requires a strong dose of political analysis beyond the usual business calculations. With the many state-owned enterprises that dominate the Chinese economy under party control there is difficulty in assessing what business model applies.[11] Will the massive corporate debt be bailed out by the government? In the face of such political interference what strategies should Hong Kong companies pursue on the mainland? More directly relevant to Hong Kong's development, what role should mainland companies play in Hong Kong? The interface between Hong Kong and the mainland has seen increased problems across all sectors.[12]

Beyond commercial and financial considerations, what dangers does this mixed official and private economic system portend for the rule of law and associated rights? As the mainland government, along with economic development, encounters an increasingly affluent and socially diverse mainland population anxieties appear to have increased for the ruling communist party. This has produced a tendency by nervous party leaders to roll back liberalizing reforms and increase controls over public debate, with respect to the Internet, the state-run media, educational institutions, and domestic and foreign associations – all of this producing an even greater clash with the open society in Hong Kong. Increased efforts to impose constraints on Hong Kong, have produced greater contestation. This clash in legal and political cultures even moved the PRC National People's Congress (NPC) to pass a national security law that for the first time explicitly mentions the obligations of Hong Kong and Macau to maintain national security.[13] Such law was not added to

---

[10] Willy Wo-Lap Lam, *Chinese Politics in the Era of Xi Jinping: Renaissance, Reform or Retrogression* (Abingdon, UK: Routledge, 2015).

[11] Wendy Wu, "How the Communist Party Controls China's State-Owned Industrial Titans," *South China Morning Post*, June 17, 2017, www.scmp.com/news/china/economy/article/2098755/how-communist-party-controls-chinas-state-owned-industrial-titans; Andrew Sheng, "Chinese State-Owned Enterprises at Crossroads," *ejinsights*, June 29, 2016, www.ejinsight.com/20160629-chinese-state-owned-enterprises-crossroads

[12] Ernest Kao, "Hong Kong's Freedom Score Down Due to Beijing's Influence: US-Based Report," *South China Morning Post*, February 2, 2017 (reporting on Hong Kong's reduced score in Freedom in the World 2017), www.scmp.com/news/hong-kong/education-community/article/2067449/us-based-report-says-hong-kongs-freedom-score

[13] National Security Law of the People's Republic of China, n.d. www.chinalawtranslate.com/2015nsl/?lang=en

Annex III of the Basic Law, which would have made it a legal requirement.

Prominent developments on the mainland that have concerned Hong Kong have included the frequent arrests of mainland lawyers who defend human rights, the arrest of mainland feminists that were protesting sexual harassment, a new law to strictly regulate foreign NGOs, including those from Hong Kong, on the mainland, increasing crackdowns on ethnic minorities, and the enactment of extremely regressive mainland laws to regulate the Internet.[14] The arrest of mainland human rights defenders has deeply concerned lawyers in Hong Kong and has met with official objections by the Hong Kong Bar Association.[15] These developments clash with legal rights and practices in Hong Kong.

Some mainland practices have not stopped at the border. As discussed in the following sections, the most elaborate mainland intervention in Hong Kong was the June 2014 White Paper on "one country, two systems," which envisioned a deeply curtailed autonomy for Hong Kong.[16] The saving grace regarding the White Paper was its weak legal status, much like the frequent mainland or pro-Beijing speeches in Hong Kong. While such State Council policy document clearly signals a retreat from the more magnanimous "put your hearts at ease" approach of the 1980s, the practicality of its full implementation, barring a rollup of the Hong Kong model, is in doubt. Frequent mainland lectures on Hong Kong failings tend to attract a similarly muted response. The frequent mainland claim that Hong Kong has no separation of powers, being generally understood as an attack on the well-established institution of constitutional judicial review in Hong Kong, goes directly to the rule of law.[17] Fortunately, this claim, which makes no sense under the common law system, is routinely

---

[14] See Chapters 3 and 4 in this volume.

[15] Fanny W. Y. Fung and Minnie Chan, "Hong Kong Barristers Join 'Deep Concern' at Arrest of Mainland Lawyers: Mainland Rights Activists and Legal Professionals Are Being Detained under Beijing Crackdown," *South China Morning Post*, July 19, 2015, www.scmp.com/news/ hong-kong/law-crime/article/1841205/hong-kong-barristers-join-deep-concern-arrest-mainland

[16] Information Office of the State Council, *The Practice of the "One Country, Two Systems" Policy in the Hong Kong Special Administrative Region*, White Paper, June 10, 2014.

[17] In a recent speech, the former chairman of the NPC Standing Committee, Zhang Dejiang, while announcing Beijing's intention to assert further control over Hong Kong, showed an appalling lack of understanding of Hong Kong's common law system in rejecting the notion of separation of powers – considering that the implementation of the Basic Law since the handover has been chiefly through the exercise of such power by the common law courts. Stuart Lau, "Chinese State Leader Zhang Dejiang Announces Beijing's Plans to Tighten Grip on Hong Kong," *South China Morning Post*, May 27, 2017, www.scmp.com/

ignored.[18] The arrest in Hong Kong of a local bookseller and later a prominent mainland businessman attracted greater concern about the integrity of the Hong Kong system.[19] The mainland Public Security Bureau making arrests in Hong Kong would be a direct violation of the Basic Law. The bookseller was later released and returned to Hong Kong, but the businessman is still missing. The 2019 government proposal to enact an extradition law that would see Hongkongers and visitors routinely sent to the mainland for trial, which met with massive protests in Hong Kong, caused even greater concern in this area.[20]

In an academic conference at Peking University in the late fall of 2014, I was struck by the wide gap in perception between elites in Hong Kong and the mainland. There appears to be a perception that Hong Kong people are insufficiently appreciative of the many privileges they are afforded. I lay this directly at the feet of the pro-Beijing establishment in Hong Kong. Whether driven by patriotism toward the mainland or mere self-preservation, these pro-Beijing elites have not appreciated the importance of guarding Hong Kong's autonomy. Many of these pro-establishment figures with elite Western education likely understand the importance of Hong Kong's high degree of autonomy under the "one country, two systems" model. They should also understand the importance of the rule of law and basic freedoms in Hong Kong. Yet, the practice over the first twenty years since the handover has been for these elites to frequently lecture Hong Kong on mainland requirements and not the other way around. No one expects local Hong Kong elites to be endlessly confrontational to the mainland government but there clearly is a need to find their voice to explain what Hong Kong's concerns are. There is a need to help their mainland counterparts to better understand the fundamentals of the rule of law in Hong Kong and the implications for that posed by mainland interference.

news/hong-kong/politics/article/2095923/chinese-state-leader-zhang-dejiang-details-beijings-plans

[18] Michael C. Davis, "Separation of Powers Is Already a Fact of Life in Hong Kong," *South China Morning Post*, September 18, 2015, www.scmp.com/comment/insight-opinion/article/1859296/separation-powers-already-fact-life-hong-kong

[19] Ilaria Maria Sala, "In Hong Kong Book Industry 'Everybody Is Scared'," *The Guardian*, December 28, 2016, www.theguardian.com/books/2016/dec/28/in-hong-kongs-book-industry-everybody-is-scared

[20] Michael C. Davis and Victoria Tinbor Hui, "Will China Crush the Protests in Hong Kong? Why Beijing Doesn't Need to Send in Troops," *Foreign Affairs*, August 5, 2019, www.foreignaffairs.com/articles/china/2019-08-05/will-china-crush-protests-hong-kong

6.2   The Legal Narrative

Hong Kong shares a characteristic common to most rule-of-law-based societies in that most debates over human rights and political reform are couched in constitutional language grounded in the rule of law. Basic Law guarantees have been a nearly daily topic in the courts, the political arena, and the media. The foundation documents for these guarantees, the Joint Declaration and the Basic Law, offer some rather clear commitments that have yet to be fully realized.[21] Political combatants on both sides of the political spectrum make frequent reference to these guarantees and adherence to most of them has generally enabled China to claim that it has met its obligations, though increased interference has made that claim problematic. In two critical areas, the finality and independence of the local courts and the pace of political reform, performance has come up especially short. Both of these areas are deeply connected to the rule of law and have had profound implications for the current political conflict in Hong Kong.

The Joint Declaration, an international treaty signed and fully registered with the United Nations in 1984, set the stage for decades of political reform debates to follow. In the face of dire conditions in post-Cultural-Revolution China, it guaranteed a liberal program, stipulating the content of the future basic law to include a "high degree of autonomy," "Hong Kong people ruling Hong Kong," a legislature "chosen by elections," a chief executive to be chosen by "elections or consultations held locally," continued maintenance of the common law system, with independent and final courts, and a liberal list of sixteen human rights, including eight related to freedom of expression. The human rights guarantees were backed up further through continuation of the international human rights covenants and relevant labor conventions, as applied to Hong Kong. These guarantees were all elaborated at length in both the declaration and the first annex thereto, leaving little doubt as to a substantial commitment to a liberal constitutional system. The commitments made, taken collectively, would make little sense otherwise.

As noted above, investors and Hong Kong people more generally were encouraged to "put their hearts at ease."[22] These guarantees were to last

---

[21] Joint Declaration of the Government of the United Kingdom of Great Britain and Northern Ireland and the Government of the People's Republic of China on the Question of Hong Kong, 1984, www.mtholyoke.edu/~cngai/jointdeclaration.htm; Basic Law of the Hong Kong Special Administrative Region of the People's Republic of China, 1990, www.basiclaw.gov.hk/en/basiclawtext

[22] Tsang, *Modern History of Hong Kong.*

for fifty years and Deng Xiaoping would hint that there was a great possibility of extension beyond fifty years.[23] Article 7 of the Joint Declaration, made clear that both governments were to implement all provisions of the agreement to which they were bound, leaving no question that the agreement would only be fulfilled when the fifty years after the handover had passed. This, by any reasonable interpretation would discredit any claim, such as Chinese diplomats raised in 2014, that the agreement was fulfilled upon the handover.[24]

The Basic Law, enacted in 1990 after an elaborate consultation process, contains nearly all of the content stipulated in the Joint Declaration. On democratic reform it went further than the language of the Joint Declaration by promising the ultimate aim is election of the chief executive by "universal suffrage upon nomination by a broadly representative nominating committee."[25] The two deficiencies, as noted above, respecting the independence and finality of the courts and the pace of democratic development, set the stage for a battle over the rule of law that persist until this day. The retention of the final power of interpretation in the Standing Committee of the National People's Congress (NPCSC) has effectively meant that the commitment to universal suffrage remains unfulfilled, as the Standing Committee has interpreted the Basic Law to require it to initially approve political reform which it generally has been reluctant to do.[26] At the same time, the vesting of such overriding power in the Standing Committee has meant that the Court of Final Appeal in Hong Kong has the possibility of being overturned by the NPCSC at the prodding of the Hong Kong government, a prodding more likely in politically sensitive cases.[27] Alvin Y. H. Cheung argues Hong Kong

---

[23] Huang Jin, "Interaction and Integration between the Legal System of Hong Kong, Macao and Mainland China 50 Years After Their Return to Mainland China," *Yearbook of Private International Law* 8 (2006): 105.

[24] Gordon Crovitz, "China 'Voids' Hong Kong Rights: Beijing Abrogates 1984 Treaty It Signed with Britain to Guarantee the City's Autonomy," *Wall Street Journal*, December 15, 2014, www.wsj.com/articles/gordon-crovitz-china-voids-hong-kong-rights-1418601004

[25] Basic Law, Art. 45.

[26] Ibid., Art. 158. The Standing Committee has exercised this power several times over political reform but has only intervened three times over cases before the courts, once on invitation from the government, as noted below, once on referral from the Court of Final Appeal in the Congo case, and once on a matter pending in the lower court over oath taking.

[27] This precedent was established soon after the handover in the Court of Final Appeal (CFA) decision respecting the right of abode in Hong Kong. An NPC Standing Committee decision effectively overruled the CFA – though the decision remained final

may be moving further toward an authoritarian rule-of-law system where the rule of law functions normally in commercial cases but less so in politically sensitive cases.[28] This dual deficiency has left the rule of law under threat both as to the interpretation of the Basic Law language and as to the process by which these interpretations are rendered.

Without the promised democratic reform to achieve universal suffrage the chief executive in Hong Kong is chosen by an Election Committee, now of about 1200 members.[29] The Election Committee is itself chosen by a collection of around 240,000 functional sector voters, supplemented by seats chosen by representative officials in political bodies. The resultant mix has consistently produced an Election Committee where about 80 percent of its members come from the establishment or pro-Beijing camp. The result is that Beijing officials often signal and effectively campaign behind the scenes for the candidate they favor in a system where elected officials may be very beholden to Beijing. The Legislative Council suffers a similar fate, with half of the seventy legislative seats being chosen by functional constituencies that heavily favor the pro-Beijing and establishment camps. This, combined with the pro-Beijing camp's ability to garner a minority of directly elected seats, ensures that the Legislative Council nearly always supports the government's position. The pan-democratic legislators who consistently garner 55 to 60 percent of the popular vote in legislative elections remain a minority in the legislator,[30] only able to veto matters that require a super majority of two-thirds of the vote – as they did the 2015 Beijing friendly proposal for political reform.

This circumstance has placed a premium on the political reform promised in Articles 45 and 68 of the Basic Law. Article 45 promises

as to the parties – upon a request by the Hong Kong government. This occurred despite the fact that the CFA had refused referral and there being no provision in the Basic Law for referral over the head of the CFA. *Ng Ka Ling v. Director of Immigration* [1999] 1 HKLRD 315, 318–19 (CFA); *The Interpretation by the Standing Committee of the National People's Congress of Articles 22(4) and 24(2)(3) of the Basic Law of the Hong Kong Special Administrative Region of the People's Republic of China* (Adopted at the Tenth Session of the Standing Committee of the Ninth National People's Congress on 26 June 1999), www.chinadaily.com.cn/china/2007-05/31/content_884547.htm

28 Cheung characterizes this authoritarian model as a "dual state." Alvin Y. H. Cheung, "Beijing Is Weakening Hong Kong's Rule of Law: How Far Will It Go?," *China File*, May 9, 2017, www.chinafile.com/reporting-opinion/viewpoint/beijing-weakening-hong-kongs-rule-of-law-how-far-will-it-go

29 Basic Law, Annex I.

30 Michael C. Davis, "The Basic Law and Democratization in Hong Kong," *Loyola International Law Review* 3 (2006): 165.

the "ultimate aim" is the selection of the chief executive by "universal suffrage upon nomination by a broadly representative nominating committee in accordance with democratic procedures." A similar provision promises universal suffrage in the election of the Legislative Council. To implement the former, the Basic Law requires the approval of the NPCSC. For the latter, the Basic Law language only required approval of the local chief executive and the Legislative Council and reporting to the NPCSC "for the record." In 2004, the NPCSC effectively amended the latter requirement by imposing a five-step process that begins with the NPCSC approval, in effect blocking any independent local initiative to institute democratic reform for the Legislative Council.[31] In 2007, the NPCSC issued a decision indicating that it would be permissible to institute universal suffrage for the chief executive election in 2017 and, if that is done, for the Legislative Council in 2020.[32] In this decision it was suggested that the required Nominating Committee "may be formed with reference to the Election Committee." This set the stage for the political battles that were to follow in 2014, as there was great suspicion that Beijing would ultimately only approve a "universal suffrage" where it could vet the candidates with a heavily pro-Beijing-constituted nominating committee. As discussed below, this suspicion ultimately proved true. Such a degraded notion of universal suffrage not only blocks democratic reform but also makes mincemeat out of Basic Law guarantees, posing a fundamental threat to the rule of law. When basic rights guarantees in the Basic Law have no normally expected meaning, being flexibly interpreted as Beijing prefers, it is no longer the rule of law.

In considering Beijing's actions, it is important to bear in mind that the commitments in both the Joint Declaration and the Basic Law are further backed up by international human rights treaty obligations. As noted above, both the International Covenant for Civil and Political Rights (ICCPR) and the International Covenant for Economic, Social and Cultural Rights (ICESCR) are incorporated in the Joint Declaration, which further stipulates their inclusion in the Basic Law. Basic Law

---

[31] Standing Committee of the National People's Congress, *The Interpretation of Article 7 of Annex I and Article III of Annex II to the Basic Law of the Hong Kong Special Administrative Region of the People's Republic of China*, April 6, 2004, s. 3.

[32] *Decision Relating to the Method for Selecting the Chief Executive of the Hong Kong Special Administrative Region and for Forming the Legislative Council of the Hong Kong Special Administrative Region in the Year 2012 and on Issues Relating to Universal Suffrage* (the 2007 NPCSC Decision), para. 9, www.basiclaw.gov.hk/en/materials/doc/2007_12_29_e .pdf

Article 39 dutifully incorporates those two treaties and, as interpreted by
the Hong Kong courts, renders any laws violating Hong Kong's obligations under the ICCPR effectively a Basic Law violation. The ICCPR is
further applied locally through the Hong Kong Bill of Rights
Ordinance,[33] rendering the ICCPR as the Hong Kong Bill of Rights
both on a constitutional and statutory level.

Article 25 of the ICCPR was a central point of contention in the 2014
debates over political reform respecting popular election of the chief
executive. The Article provides in relevant part that, "Every Citizen
shall have the right and opportunity . . . (b) to vote and to be elected at
genuine periodic elections . . . with universal and equal suffrage . . .
[reflecting] the free expression of the will of the voters."[34] The vetted
election Beijing was proposing in 2014 was widely thought to violate this
language, posing a rule-of-law question about compliance with
a fundamental guarantee in the Basic Law. Some pro-Beijing politicians
have sought to invoke a British reservation, included when Britain
originally acceded to the treaty. Britain at that time reserved application
of Article 25 as to the election of the Hong Kong Legislative Council. The
Human Rights Committee, when evaluating Hong Kong's reports under
the ICCPR has rejected continued application of that reservation, noting
that the local Basic Law now provides for democratic reform in
Hong Kong. In any event, the British reservation makes no reference to
the election of the chief executive, as no such post existed at the time.[35]

Beyond the question of compliance, foot-dragging over the promised
democratic reforms in Hong Kong has left the territory with a seemingly
permanent lopsided political system of minority government.[36] This has
produced a government that is more beholden to Beijing for its grip on
power than it is on the Hong Kong people. Chief executives who lose
Beijing's favor may find themselves encouraged to resign or not run for
a second term, as happened to both the first and the third chief executive.
This reality has further produced a government that is little inclined to
defend Hong Kong's autonomy in critical constitutional respects. The

[33] Hong Kong Bill of Rights Ordinance, Cap. 383 (BORO), www.hklii.org/hk/legis/en/ord/383
[34] International Covenant on Civil and Political Rights, 1966 (ICCPR), www.treaties.un.org/doc/publication/unts/volume%20999/volume-999-i-14668-english.pdf
[35] See British Institute of International and Comparative Law, *Legal Issues Relating to Democratic Participation in Hong Kong*, Scoping Report, 2014, para. 36, www.biicl.org/documents/1866_hong_kong_legal_issues_scoping_paper_final.pdf?showdocument=1
[36] Davis, "Basic Law and Democratization," 165.

chief executives have shown little inclination to even offer a voice openly explaining Hong Kong's core value concerns to the central government. Most significant among such core values is the rule of law. Rather, there is an inclination for chief executives and other pro-Beijing politicians favored with appointment to mainland committees and advisory bodies to lecture Hong Kong on Beijing's requirements.

This is where democracy and the rule of law intersect. It has not been lost on Hong Kong people that maintaining Hong Kong's autonomy is intimately connected to the maintenance of the rule of law and associated human rights. With the mainland lacking the rule of law there is little chance that politicians primarily beholden to Beijing will be willing to defend Hong Kong from arbitrary decisions or mainland interference to advance expedient mainland concerns. It is in this sense that popular protests over democratic reform are in part protests over the rule of law, as democracy is viewed as instrumental to maintaining autonomy and the rule of law. The aim is to have in place a Hong Kong government that will defend Hong Kong's autonomy and represent Hong Kong's concerns. One may doubt that the popular expectation is for a government that is excessively confrontational toward the central government. Rather, one expects the pragmatic Hong Kong voter would simply expect to have a government that can find its voice to represent Hong Kong interests, explain core values, and guard autonomy.

6.3 The Beijing White Paper and Other Political Decisions

It was in the face of these commitments and public expectations that Beijing launched its campaign to rein in Hong Kong in 2014. Beginning with the White Paper, Beijing launched a series of efforts to rein in what it seemingly viewed as excessive expectations in Hong Kong. The June 2014 White Paper on "One Country, Two Systems" offered the most comprehensive attack since the handover on Hong Kong's assertive rule-of-law-based system.[37] Defenders of Hong Kong's rule of law were accused of having a "lopsided and confused view" of "one country, two systems." The old adage that Hongkongers "put their hearts at ease" seemed to be replaced with the implied slogan "Beijing is the boss." Targeting the heart of Hong Kong's distinctive system, the White Paper emphasized that a "high degree of autonomy" is not "full autonomy."

---

[37] Information Office of the State Council, *"One Country, Two Systems"* report.

This latter claim raised direct and substantial implications for the rule of law, especially as to the security of the Basic Law. The White Paper stressed that the NPCSC could interpret or amend the Basic Law as it prefers. The NPCSC was said to have "comprehensive jurisdiction" over Hong Kong and the power of "supervision" over Hong Kong legislative acts. Such concept of "supervision" bears direct relation to practice in the mainland legal system regarding the NPC Standing Committee's powers to supervise the enforcement of the constitution and the Supreme People's Court.[38] The standing committees of local people's congresses have traditionally exercised a similar power of supervision over local people's courts.[39] The document went much further, characterizing Hong Kong judges as "administrative" or "governing" officials, a characterization that drew direct objection by the Hong Kong Bar Association and by the current and previous chief justices. Perplexing provisions emphasized that the NPCSC was the guardian of the Hong Kong rule of law and that judges were to be patriots bound to guard national security. Given that the whole Hong Kong model is based in some sense on the lack of the rule of law on the mainland, assigning such rule-of-law-guarding role to the NPCSC would inspire little confidence. Since some Hong Kong judges are foreign nationals, their ability to be patriots is also in doubt.

The White Paper shook the very foundation of the Hong Kong legal system by seeming to diminish the role of the international treaty commitments in the Joint Declaration. The twelve articles of the Joint Declaration were quoted verbatim in the White Paper, where they were identified as twelve PRC principles "based solely on the authorization" of the central government. This reflects Beijing's concern that characterizing its obligations to Hong Kong as international ones may encourage outside criticism or interference. Hong Kong people, who in the 1980s had felt very insecure about the commitments of the Beijing government, had accepted these commitments because of their connection with China's international treaty obligations in the Joint Declaration. Further concern arose when Chinese diplomats in Britain represented that the Joint Declaration no longer applied, that it had been fulfilled and was now void after the handover.[40]

Being primarily focused on the legal system, the White Paper said very little about the promised democratic development. It merely emphasized

---

[38] PRC Constitution, art. 67(1) and (6).
[39] Ibid., art. 104.
[40] Crovitz, "China 'Voids' Hong Kong Rights."

that the chief executive "must be a person who loves the country and Hong Kong." This seemingly innocuous phrase is viewed in Hong Kong as an admonition that the chief executive cannot be a member of the pan-democratic camp. Predicting the outcome of the consultation over democratic reform, the White Paper emphasized that the Election Committee that now elects the chief executive is "an expression of equal representation and broad representativeness." In its 2014 decision on electoral reform, the NPCSC would require that the model for electing the Election Committee be used in nearly identical form to elect the Nominating Committee.[41] This aimed to put in place a system of nomination that would assure only pro-Beijing candidates could be nominated and put before the voters. This form of vetted nomination was in fact the model adopted by the August 2014 NPCSC decision, leading eventually to a veto of the proposal by the Legislative Council.[42]

6.4   The Anemic Hong Kong Government Response

The State Council White Paper and various NPCSC decisions were not the whole story regarding Hong Kong's autonomy and the related rule of law. If it is appreciated that the thirst for democracy in Hong Kong is in part driven by concerns for autonomy and its role in guarding Hong Kong's distinct rule of law, then the passivity of the Hong Kong government regarding these matters is a central concern. Throughout the debates over democratic reform, the Hong Kong government has failed to find its voice to emphasize the concerns raised by Hong Kong people. Quite the contrary, it has continually served to amplify mainland concerns.

This was most evident in the 2014 Hong Kong government's Consultation Report regarding the proposed democratic reform.[43] In

---

[41] Standing Committee of the National People's Congress, *The Decision of the Standing Committee of the National People's Congress on Issues Relating to the Selection of the Chief Executive of the Hong Kong Special Administrative Region by Universal Suffrage and on the Method for Forming the Legislative Council of the Hong Kong Special Administrative Region in the Year 2016* (the 2014 NPCSC Decision), August 31, 2014, www.2017.gov.hk /filemanager/template/en/doc/20140831b.pdf

[42] Michael C. Davis, "The Basic Law, Universal Suffrage and the Rule of Law in Hong Kong," *Hastings International and Comparative Law Review* 38(2) (2016): 275.

[43] Hong Kong Government, *Report by the Chief Executive of the Hong Kong Special Administrative Region to the Standing Committee of the National People's Congress on whether there is a need to amend the methods for selecting the Chief Executive of the Hong Kong Special Administrative Region in 2017 and for forming the Legislative Council*

spite of massive public expressions of concern about the direction democratic reform was headed,[44] the Consultation report essentially echoed the mainland view, reporting for example: "mainstream opinion" favors exclusive power to nominate chief executive candidates in the Nomination Committee; the "community generally agrees" the chief executive should "love the country and love Hong Kong"; "relatively more views" agree the Nominating Committee composition should be like the Election Committee; "quite a number of views" hold that candidates must obtain the support of a "certain proportion" (code for 50 percent) of the Nominating Committee to show "cross-sector support"; and of the "two major views" one favors limiting the nominees to two or three "to ensure the solemnity of the election." The consultation report concedes that a number of groups and members of the public "express divergent views."[45] There was no mention of the 800,000 voters doing so in civic referendum conducted by the Occupy Central organization. And the report indicated that it was "generally agreed" to ignore reform of the Legislative Council, though massive protests had demanded such reform for a couple of decades.

Ultimately, the NPCSC decision fully endorsed this report and imposed the limits noted: that the Nominating Committee "shall be made in accordance with the number of members, composition and formation method" of the Election Committee, and that it "shall nominate two to three candidates" by 50 percent vote.[46] These limitations assured that any nominee would be from the pro-Beijing camp since the Election Committee selected under its established criteria had long been overwhelmingly from that camp. The Hong Kong government then held a second consultation that was boycotted by the pan-democratic camp. Both in this second consultation and in the earlier one, all proposals for compromise were uniformly rejected, leading to the impression in Hong Kong that Beijing was fully calling the shots throughout the consultation process.[47] On this basis, the bill that was put forth by the

of the Hong Kong Special Administrative Region in 2016, 2014, www.2017.gov.hk/en/liberal/related.html; Hong Kong Government, *Report on the Public Consultation on the Methods of Selecting the Chief Executive in 2017 and for Forming the Legislative Council in 2016*, 2014, www.2017.gov.hk/filemanager/template/en/doc/report/consultation_report.pdf

[44] Nearly 800,000 people had expressed their support for a democratic model in a civic referendum (Davis, "Basic Law," 275).

[45] See Hong Kong consultation reports, 2014 (above, n. 41).

[46] *NPCSC Decision*, 2014.

[47] See Hong Kong Government, *Report on the Recent Community and Political Situation* (2015), www.2017.gov.hk/filemanager/template/en/doc/rcps_report/rcps_report.pdf; Hong Kong

government was blocked by pan-democratic legislators, who barely held enough seats to block a bill requiring a two-thirds approval.[48] Pan-democratic legislators rejected calls to "pocket" the proposed bill, fearing that this legislation would simply lock in an electoral process that would guarantee the pro-establishment camp's lock on the chief executive position. Given the underlying concern with Hong Kong's autonomy and rule of law this was judged unacceptable. To add insult to injury, mainland officials then claimed their decision had won the support and endorsement among the people of Hong Kong.

6.5   Conclusion

After the civil disobedience campaign was launched in Hong Kong in late 2014, Beijing began to argue that activists were undermining the rule of law. On the contrary, a careful look at such situation may lead to the opposite conclusion. Rather, it was the perceived threat to the rule of law that was stimulating such civil disobedience. Civil disobedience to defend the rule of law is not commonly viewed as a threat. Common law judges have long been skeptical of prosecutions of activists engaged in civil disobedience to protect the foundations of the democratic system. Hong Kong has been no exception, as the courts have often either dismissed related charges or have at least been reluctant to impose strict punishment. The rule of law is the core foundation in this regard.

Hong Kong is now at a juncture where a current chief executive, Carrie Lam, is widely seen as reluctant to guard Hong Kong's autonomy. Demands that she defend Hong Kong's autonomy have been the primary concern behind the 2019 protests. And yet mainland officials appear set upon a course to resist Hong Kong's demands for democratic reform and determined to rein in Hong Kong assertiveness. Such increased Beijing interference will surely have the opposite effect of what is intended. Judged by her ability to represent Hong Kong's concerns and reconcile tensions with Beijing Carrie Lam has come up short. There is little sign

Government, *2017: Method for Selecting the Chief Executive by Universal Suffrage* (January 2015), www.2017.gov.hk/en/home

[48] Michael C. Davis, "Beijing Has Failed to Honour Its Promise to Hong Kong," *South China Morning Post*, September 4, 2014, www.scmp.com/comment/insight-opinion/article/1584488/beijing-has-failed-honour-its-promise-hong-kong; Margaret Ng, "Hong Kong's Democracy Dilemma," *New York Times (International edition)*, September 2, 2014, www.nytimes.com/2014/09/03/opinion/hong-kongs-democracy-dilemma.html

that either Beijing or Hong Kong officials appreciate the root cause of popular Hong Kong discontent. The chief executive of Hong Kong could be instrumental in elaborating such root causes, but there has been little sign that such role is understood. Until such understanding is achieved, the rule of law will be at risk and popular protests will persist, as people seek to put in place an elected government that will understand its role in guarding autonomy and, thereby, the rule of law.

Is Singapore an Authoritarian Constitutional Regime? So What If It Is?

KEVIN Y. L. TAN

7.1 Introduction

In 2014, there appeared a fascinating collection of essays in a volume entitled *Constitutions in Authoritarian Regimes* edited by Tom Ginsburg and Alberto Simpser.[1] The main objective of the volume was to try to understand why constitutions matter to authoritarian regimes, given that they are often seen "as meaningless pieces of paper, without function other than to give the illusion of legitimacy to the regime."[2] In his chapter, "Authoritarian Constitutionalism: Some Conceptual Issues,"[3] American legal scholar Mark Tushnet – drawing on recent analytical studies in political science – argues that by defining "authoritarian constitutionalism" as a separate category or variety of constitutionalism, our understanding of constitutionalism might be pluralized and analytically clarified.[4]

Tushnet follows this up with his 2015 article in the *Cornell Law Review*,[5] where he uses an extended case study of Singapore to posit this new category of government. His enterprise stems from his observation that hitherto, "[l]egal scholars and political theorists interested in constitutionalism as a normative concept tend to dichotomize the subject" by drawing the line between "[Western] liberal constitutionalism" and "authoritarianism." In the minds of such scholars, there are thus only two types of regimes – liberal constitutional regimes that have a core

---

[1] Tom Ginsburg and Alberto Simpser (eds.), *Constitutions in Authoritarian Regimes* (New York: Cambridge University Press, 2014).
[2] Ibid., 1.
[3] Mark Tushnet, "Authoritarian Constitutionalism: Some Conceptual Issues," ibid., 36.
[4] Ibid., 37.
[5] Mark Tushnet, "Authoritarian Constitutionalism," *Cornell Law Review* 100 (2015): 391.

commitment to "human rights and self-governance implemented by varying institutional devices"[6] and the rest (all of which are "authoritarian").

This dichotomy, Tushnet argues, is too simplistic to enable us to understand and analyze "hybrid regimes" – those that lie between "liberal constitutionalism" on the one hand and the most extreme cases of "authoritarianism" on the other. There is thus a need to "pluralize" this spectrum of regimes so that we may have greater "analytic clarity."[7] After all, political scientists have long argued that there are distinct types within this category of regimes.[8] A parallel exploration of these hybrid regimes based on "recent literature in political science on hybrid systems" would thus be beneficial, especially for the "normative constitutionalist."[9] It is unclear what Tushnet means when he speaks of "normative constitutionalists," but, presumably, this would refer to scholars who define regime types with reference to some normative conception of what "constitutionalism" means and requires.

In that sense, Tushnet's typology of constitutionalism is based on a normative matrix that juxtaposes two criteria. First, the varying degrees of "liberal freedoms," and, second, "levels of force and fraud in elections." Singapore, says Tushnet, is the archetypal example of an authoritarian constitutional state with its mix of low levels of election force or fraud and its intermediate civil liberties.

In this chapter, I will argue that Tushnet's typology and methodology are problematic for two reasons: first, his starting point, and, second, his analytical framework. I begin by arguing that while interesting, typologies are ultimately limited in helping us understand how constitutionalism works in different societies. Next, assuming that typologies and categorization of constitutions remains a useful tool for analysis, I critically examine Tushnet's axes of analysis, the criteria with which he measures and then categorizes constitutional orders. Finally, I consider his assumptions in his study of Singapore and whether they justifiably give rise to the new category of authoritarian states advanced by him.

---

[6] Ibid., 394.
[7] See also Mark Tushnet, *An Advanced Introduction to Comparative Constitutional Law* (Cheltenham: Edward Elgar, 2014), 115.
[8] See, for example, Alan Siaroff, *Comparing Political Regimes: A Thematic Introduction to Comparative Politics* (Toronto: University of Toronto Press, 2013).
[9] Tushnet, "Authoritarian Constitutionalism," 394.

7.2 Typologies and Normative Ordering:
Do We Need Typologies?

Scholars have long employed categories and typologies as aids in dealing with and analyzing multiple variables when doing comparative study. The field of comparative politics grew out of attempts – largely by American scholars – to understand other political systems and forms of government, especially of states that were considered strategically important to the United States. The field evolved from the study of politics and governance in general, sprinkled with a heavy and healthy dose of constitutional arrangements. As politics became political science, a more scientific approach in such studies was demanded and models and categories were required for organization and comparison. This thus led to the construction of models and ideal types. Naturally, ideal types do not capture the intricacies and nuances of particular political regimes, but they do provide useful frameworks into which states and their political systems might be classified or pigeonholed for the purposes of comparison. Typologies can also be used as models of an idealized state. This was what Aristotle, quite possibly the earliest political typologist, did. In his volume *Politics*, Aristotle categorized types of government into those ruled by "the one," "the few" and "the many," and then by superimposing the various types of government onto the matrix of the "proper" and "improper" behavior by the rulers, he arrived at six possible forms of government: kingship; tyranny; aristocracy; oligarchy; democracy; and mobocracy.[10] This typology was, for Aristotle, a thought exercise in what would be best form of government. Aristotle was not trying to inductively create categories from his observation of what was going on in the real world.

Returning to Tushnet's categorization, one needs to ask: for what purpose does he propose this typology? How is it either necessary or helpful? Tushnet tells us that this is a matter of interest to legal scholars and political scientists who are "interested in constitutionalism as a normative concept." In that case, how does the creation of typologies of this sort provide normative constitutionalists with a better analytical tool? But what do "normative constitutionalists" do? How are normative constitutionalists different from other constitutionalists? Presumably, a normative constitutionalist is one who has a normative idea of what a constitution should look like and what it should do; and for

---

[10] Aristotle, *The Politics*, trans. Benjamin Jowitt (New York: Modern Library, 1943), bk 3, 138–67.

constitutions that check the boxes, they may be categorized as normatively acceptable, and, if they do not, then they are normatively unacceptable. If that is the case, then we need to understand the bases for the
comparativist's normativity. Which norms satisfy and which don't?
Normatively, Tushnet accepts that there exists a divide between states
that are liberal democracies (however defined) and those that are not.
And that the latter category can be intelligibly divided into "constitutionalisms" of different sorts: (a) absolutist constitutionalism; (b) mere
rule-of-law constitutionalism; and (c) authoritarian constitutionalism.

Thus, Tushnet's starting point is that among the world's constitutional
systems, there is a normative constitutional order, at the apex of which
sits liberal-democratic constitutions. All other constitutional orders that
are not liberal democracies nonetheless need to be acknowledged in their
own right and accorded their places in this hierarchy as well. At the top of
that pile comes "authoritarian constitutionalism" and at the bottom,
"absolutist constitutionalism."[11] Beyond the fact that such an analysis is
heavily tinged with a certain sense of superiority and triumphalism, it
does little beyond saying that the color gray is neither white nor black.
Tushnet's enterprise is nothing new. Back in 1964, political scientist Juan
J. Linz used the term "authoritarianism" not only to describe Franco
Spain but also to argue that there existed a regime type that lay between
the dichotomy of liberal democracies and totalitarianism.[12] Linz's categorization served a distinct purpose – to show that "authoritarianism"
was not "totalitarianism," and to extend his analysis of Franco Spain to
the Latin American states where many governments were led by military
strongmen who rose to power in periods of political instability and where
power was strongly centralized. Does Linz's categorization remain relevant today? Writing in the mid-1990s, Linz and Stepan argue that while
the "authoritarian" category proved useful in the 1960s, it became less so
especially as it became apparent that more regimes around the world

---

[11] Interestingly, this exercise is not much different from what happened in the early days of
the modern Olympic Games. At the first games in Athens in 1896, only first-place winners
were acknowledged and crowned with an olive wreath and received a silver medal. There
were no second- or third-place winners. It was only two Olympic games later, at the
American games in St Louis in 1904, that the gold, silver, and bronze medals were
introduced for presentation to the first-, second-, and third-place winners.

[12] See Juan J. Linz, *An Authoritarian Regime: The Case of Spain*, Erik Allardt and
Hrjo Littunen (eds.) (Helsinki: Transactions of the Westermarck Society, 1964), 291;
Juan J. Linz and Alfred Stepan, *Problems of Democratic Transition and Consolidation:
Southern Europe, South America and Post-Communist Europe* (Baltimore: Johns Hopkins
University Press, 1996), 38.

were "authoritarian" than were "totalitarian" and "democratic" combined.[13] This therefore meant that authoritarian regimes were "the modal category of regimes type in the modern world" and the continued adherence to such a limited typology had become an "obstacle" to analysis.[14] Linz's response was to develop a more complex typology, which included two further categories – "post-totalitarianism" and "sultanism" – ranged around four characteristics: pluralism, ideology, mobilization, and leadership.[15] This typology is certainly more sophisticated but adds only marginally to our understanding of how these particular states function.

What purpose does Tushnet's categorization serve? Arguably, such a categorization does not serve much beyond banding countries according to his tripartite typology even if he takes this as his starting point. The problem lies not only in the artificiality of such an exercise, but also with the criteria for determining to which category a particular state belongs. For him, what constitutes "liberal democracy" appears to be self-evident and needs no explanation nor explication, but all else needs to be categorized and tested. Surely, normative constitutionalists cannot only be interested in determining who the winners are in the liberal democracy stakes. That would be tantamount to focusing on the finishing line of a race without any regard to how the race is run. So, what does it mean for a normative constitutionalist to simply declare that Singapore does not belong to the same category of states as the United States or Australia, but neither should it be lumped with states like Brunei and Saudi Arabia? Not much.

7.3 Assessing Tushnet's Axes

What exactly is "authoritarian constitutionalism"? Tushnet argues that a regime practicing this form of constitutionalism has six distinct characteristics. Such a regime: (a) is controlled by a dominant party which makes all relevant public policy decisions and where there is no basis in law to challenge such decisions; (b) does not arrest political opponents arbitrarily, but imposes a variety of sanctions on them such as bankrupting them through libel suits; (c) allows reasonably open discussion and criticism of its policies; (d) operates reasonably free and fair

---

[13] Linz and Stepan, *Problems of Democratic Transition and Consolidation*, 38.
[14] Ibid., 39.
[15] Ibid., 44–5.

elections; (e) is sensitive to public opinion and alters its policies on occasion in response to such views; and (f) may develop mechanisms to ensure that the amount of dissent does not exceed a level it regards as desirable.[16]

This, Tushnet argues, is an ideal type which is based primarily on his observations of the regime in Singapore. He then follows this up with this 2015 *Cornell Law Review* piece in which he further explicates this model. In his 2015 article, Tushnet uses Singapore's experience "to explore the possibility that it exemplifies an as-yet under-examined form of constitutionalism" called "authoritarian constitutionalism." It is *not* an effort to better understand constitutionalism in Singapore, but to tease out elements in its practice that would justify the creation of a new category of states that are "like" Singapore.

I come now to the next problem: Tushnet's comparative matrix. In designing a matrix of variables to be used in analysis and in typology building, regard must be had to the task at hand. What then should normative constitutionalists be interested in? What is the primary task for a normative constitutionalist? Surely the normative constitutionalist must be expected to do more than simply check boxes and categorize constitutions according to some predetermined typology and then count those which are "liberal democracies," "authoritarian constitutions," and "absolutist constitutions." I should like to think that the normative constitutionalist's main task must be to see how *well* a constitutional system *works*, in balancing the rights and obligations of states and their subjects within a particular context rather than categorizing them according to an abstract checklist. If that is the case, then other kinds of "normativities" should be considered relevant.

We must take all these factors into account in the crafting of any comparative project. An overemphasis on any one of them will necessarily distort our analysis. Tushnet's matrix emphasizes just two elements: the extent of liberal freedoms enjoyed by citizens, and elections. Thus, in Tushnet's analysis, whether a polity qualifies as "liberal democracy" depends solely on how well it satisfies these two criteria. But why? Surely "liberal democracy" means a lot more than this. Alas, we get no help from Tushnet, since he does not bother explaining what his definition of "liberal democracy" is anywhere in his article. Indeed, he assumes that this "type" of constitutional order is self-evident and thus known to all and that we should agree that certain states – such as the

---

[16] Tushnet, "Authoritarian Constitutionalism: Some Conceptual Issues," 45.

United States of America, Canada, Great Britain, and the states of Western Europe and possibly Australia and New Zealand – all embody the liberal–democratic ideal and that all other states do not. Quite clearly, that is not the case.

Trevor Allan, in his entry "Liberal Democracy" in the *New Oxford Companion to Law*[17] suggests several criteria which may be helpful: (a) self-government; (b) political equality of citizens; (c) freedom of speech, conscience, association, and privacy; (d) freedom to participate in government and politics; (e) safeguarding of minority views and interests; (f) rule of law; (g) limits on governmental power; and (h) an independent judiciary. This is a much wider and encompassing view of what a liberal democracy is. Thus, if we take all these – and perhaps other – factors into account in designing our research question, we will get a much more variegated matrix than the one which Tushnet has proposed. Gordon Silverstein found Tushnet's two axes to be inadequate and instead proposed a model based on three axes: (a) the degree to which power is limited; (b) the degree or extent of popular consent and legitimacy; and (c) procedures and processes by which law is made and enforced.[18] We can come up with more and more axes to measure "constitutionality," but to what end?

7.4 How Useful Are Typologies?

Of what use are ideal types like "constitutional authoritarianism" for the comparativist? Typologies are certainly useful tools. As extreme examples of a particular type of regularly occurring social phenomena, their exaggerated and sharpened characterizations can help us better understand the phenomena that we are studying. However, they need to be properly constructed, and their construction depends on what research puzzle we seek to solve. Otherwise, they become nothing more than labels that do little more than distinguish distance and "other," without explaining or heightening understanding.

Typologies are useful provided they suit the purposes for which they are constructed. Weber, frustrated by the over-generalization then

---

[17] Trevor Allan, "Liberal Democracy," in Peter Cane and Joanne Conaghan (eds.), *The New Oxford Companion to Law* (Oxford: Oxford University Press, 2008), 731.

[18] Gordon Silverstein, "Singapore's Constitutionalism: A Model, But of What Sort?" *Cornell Law Review* 100 (2015): 1.

prevalent in social analysis, developed the ideal type as a heuristic device and an analytical tool to highlight commonalities that made comparison possible. His concern was that if scholars only looked at differences, commonalities are easily missed, and we are all the poorer in understanding the phenomena under study. A good ideal type should identify sufficient commonalities that could then be used as a basis for falsifying phenomena under investigation. By applying an ideal type to a real situation, we are thus able to identify how closely reality accords with or deviates from the ideal type. The ideal type must thus contain sufficient criteria to enable "similar" polities to be mapped and compared. Significantly, this will enable us to compare the same social phenomena over time, for embedded in Weber's thinking is the assumption that all phenomena are subject to a steady institutional tendency toward one ideal type or another. So, is there such a thing as an ideal classification system? When confronted with this question in relation to political systems, the prominent political scientist Robert Dahl replied:

> Obviously, no. There are thousands of criteria for classifying political systems, Which ones we find most useful will depend on the aspects of politics in which we are most interested. A geographer might distinguish political systems according to the area they occupy, a demographer by the number of persons who are members, a lawyer according to their legal codes.[19]

What then is the starting point for the comparative constitutional law scholar? I suppose the answer must be: "Well, it all depends on exactly what we are interested in learning?" Let me try to answer my own question with a practical example. Let us say that I am interested in understanding the role of religion in shaping constitutional discourse. The logical thing to do is to first identify polities in which constitutional debates over religion have been significant and topical. Having identified these states, the next task must be to find a way to cluster or group these states together so that meaningful comparison is possible. To do this, we may, for example, cluster states with religiously heterogeneous populations together, but make a distinction between larger states and small states since the challenges of constitutional management of diversity are likely to be different. By highlighting areas of commonality, the comparativist is able to capture areas of difference and hopefully explain them. Such an enquiry will illuminate and help explain why similar societies

---

[19] Robert A. Dahl, *Modern Political Analysis* (Englewood Cliffs, NJ: Prentice-Hall, 1976), 71.

may behave differently when confronted with similar constitutional problems. We may be able to understand the role constitutionalism plays in the political culture of that society, or even how and under what circumstances a government may constitutionalize religious issues.

What is certain is that my enquiry will not begin by asking: what type of constitutional regime does a particular polity belong to? The fact that one of the countries I am studying and comparing has a constitutional authoritarian regime is, in the case of this particular enquiry, of no significant relevance. Surely, it cannot be that for the question I want to study, I should only compare states that are classified as constitutional authoritarian. Assuming the problems of characterization and classification are overcome, the determination of typology only serves to organize, categorize, and describe. It tells us nothing about how a given polity uses constitutional rules and principles – or not use or abuse them, for that matter – to deal with problems of governance, rights, and liberties. It says nothing about a state's constitutional culture, nor anything about how different social, economic, and political contexts shape constitutional discourse and development.

7.5   Assessing and Applying Tushnet's Typology

Let us, for a moment, take Tushnet's typology on its own terms, and consider its validity and application in greater depth. For convenience, I have reproduced Tushnet's typological matrix in Table 7.1.[20]

Table 7.1 *Tushnet's typological matrix*

		LEVEL OF FORCE AND FRAUD IN ELECTIONS (OR NO ELECTIONS)			
		Low	Intermediate	High	No Elections
LIBERAL FREEDOMS	Low	Illiberal Democracy or Mere Rule-of-Law Constitutionalism	Semi-Authoritarianism	Authoritarianism	Authoritarianism
	Intermediate	Authoritarian Constitutionalism	[Authoritarian Constitutionalism?]		Mere rule-of-law Constitutionalism
	High	Liberal Democracy			Idealized absolutist monarchy

---

[20] Tushnet, "Authoritarian Constitutionalism," 397.

Based on these variables, Tushnet argues that in a regime where there is either a low or intermediate level of force or fraud in elections, and where an "intermediate" level of freedom is enjoyed by its people, it is a regime which practices authoritarian constitutionalism. From Table 7.1, the only criterion differentiating such a polity from one that practices liberal democracy is the degree of freedoms enjoyed by a state's population. So, what factors does he take into consideration in determining that Singapore has an intermediate rather than a high level of liberal freedoms?

For Tushnet, degrees of liberal freedoms center around two things: freedom of expression[21] and electoral rules.[22] He does not appear to be interested in issues of equality or of religious freedom. In his survey of Singapore's regulation of expression, he highlights the presence of the Internal Security Act (ISA); the Sedition Act; traditional libel laws; internet and press regulations; and the regulation of public space as relevant factors in his assessment. He also cites the alleged lack of judicial independence and "judicial deference" as factors that qualify Singapore as lying on the intermediate scale of liberal freedoms. Let us critically examine each of the examples Tushnet raises in support of his argument.

In the section of his article that assesses Singapore's regulation of expression, Tushnet raises the ISA – which authorizes the executive's detention of persons who are deemed to be a threat to national security – as a factor in limiting the freedom of expression. Interestingly, Tushnet does not consider the mere existence of the legislation in itself to be problematic, presumably because even liberal democracies like the United States also have preventative detention laws in emergency situations.[23] His objection to the legislation lies in the fact that it was abused once in 1987 when twenty-

---

[21] Ibid., 400.

[22] Ibid., 410.

[23] See National Defense Authorization Act for Fiscal Year 2019, s. 1034 (signed August 13, 2018) which permits the American president "to detain belligerents" as well as those who "are part of, or are substantially supporting, al-Qaeda, the Taliban, or associated forces that are engaged in hostilities against the United Sates or its coalition partners" "until the termination of hostilities." See generally, Stephanie Cooper Blum, *The Necessary Evil of Preventive Detention in the War on Terror* (Amherst, NY: Cambria Press, 2008); Halle Ludsin, *Preventive Detention and the Democratic State* (Cambridge, UK: Cambridge University Press, 2016).

two activists and church workers were detained for their alleged involvement in an alleged Marxist conspiracy.[24] So, while like the sword of Damocles it hangs over the heads of Singaporeans, Tushnet did not consider it fatal, for "no more than one abuse in twenty-five or more years is not a terrible record among fully constitutionalist regimes."[25]

The presence of the Sedition Act appears to be another problem. This legislation makes sedition a strict liability offense. Again, Tushnet is less bothered by its existence than by the fact that over the years, it has only been used sparingly, and against persons propagating what might in other jurisdictions be considered "hate speech," which in any case is also banned in liberal democracies.

Tushnet's third example concerns the state of libel law in Singapore, which he states "is rather traditional and has not been substantially modified to take concerns about free expression into more account than the classic common law did."[26] The fact that the local courts have rejected the public figure exception created by the US Supreme Court in *New York Times* v. *Sullivan* (1963) appears to be a sticking point as is the fact that the courts have always awarded damages commensurate with the public reputation of the plaintiffs in defamation suits. This analysis is problematic for several reasons. First, libel law in Singapore is really little different from that of the United Kingdom. The test for defamation was established by the UK House of Lords in the leading case of *Sim* v. *Stretch* back in 1936.[27] Lord Atkin, delivering the leading judgment, proposed the following test: "Would the words tend to lower the plaintiff in the estimation of right-thinking members of society generally?" This remains the test in current use in the courts of the United Kingdom as well as in Singapore. Furthermore, the public figure exception doctrine of *New York Times* v. *Sullivan*[28] was explicitly

---

[24] See Tan Wah Piow, *Smokescreens & Mirrors: Tracing the 'Marxist Conspiracy'* (Singapore: Function 8, 2012); Fr Guillaume Arotcarena, *Priest in Geylang: The Untold Story of the Geylang Catholic Centre* (Singapore: Ethos Books, 2015); Michael D. Barr, "Singapore's Catholic Social Activists: Alleged Marxist Conspirators," in Michael D. Barr and Carl A. Trocki (eds.), *Paths Not Taken: Political Pluralism in Post-War Singapore* (Singapore: NUS Press, 2008), 228.

[25] Tushnet, "Authoritarian Constitutionalism," 401.

[26] Ibid., 402.

[27] *Sim* v. *Stretch* [1936] 2 All ER 1237.

[28] 376 US 254 (1964).

rejected by the UK courts as well as those of other liberal-democratic countries like Australia and New Zealand, as Tushnet has noted.[29] At the same time, the sums of damages awarded by the Singapore courts for public figures correspond to those awarded by the British courts and are in some cases, considerably lower. The disgraced British author and politician Jeffrey Archer was, for example, awarded £500,000 in his defamation suit against the *Daily Star* in 1987; while former Labour MP George Galloway was awarded £150,000 damages in his libel action against the *Daily Telegraph* in 2004.

What Tushnet finds disconcerting is the fact that damage liability "is particularly effective because of its interaction with Singapore's electoral rules, which make people with undischarged bankruptcies ineligible for public office." The implication of this statement is that the government can make use of libel laws to sue and bankrupt their opponents so that they are disqualified from standing for elections. Such an assertion is problematic because no action for defamation would succeed if people abide by the test the courts have used all these decades. In other words, if the government's opponents do not go around making slanderous or libelous statements, no action can possibly be commenced. Furthermore, the disqualification of undischarged bankrupts from standing for elections also exists in countries such as Australia and the United Kingdom.

A fourth problem is the lack of judicial independence in the subordinate courts. Tushnet highlights three examples to hammer home his point. The first is the infamous transfer of Senior District Judge Michael Khoo from the bench to the Attorney-General's Chambers in 1986 shortly after he decided a case in favor of opposition leader J. B. Jeyaretnam. Second, Tushnet raised the case of Christopher Lingle whom he said faced "defamation charges" for accusing the judiciary of being compliant. This is in fact incorrect as Lingle was charged with contempt of court by scandalizing the judiciary. Finally, he cites the case of how Parliament overturned the decision of Singapore's Court of Appeal in *Chng Suan Tze* v. *Minister for Home Affairs* (1989) through legislative intervention (see Chapter 10 in this volume).

While the Michael Khoo transfer from thirty years ago remains a blight on Singapore's legal landscape, it was an exceptional event.

---

[29] Mark Tushnet, "*New York Times v. Sullivan* Around the World," *Alabama Law Review* 66 (2) (2014): 337.

When opposition leader J. B. Jeyaretnam complained in Parliament of executive interference in the judiciary, a commission of inquiry was constituted and it was revealed that the transfer had been ordered by the Chief Justice, acting of his own accord and not as a result of any instruction from any member of the executive.[30] There have been no incidents of such unjustified transfers since, and the higher judiciary is generally protected by security of tenure and remuneration. The case concerning Lingle is neither here nor there since scandalizing the court was then also a common law crime under English law.[31] Finally, there is nothing unusual in Parliament's enacting law to overturn judicial decisions it does not consider desirable (see Chapter 10). The fact that Parliament also attempted to limit the court's jurisdiction raises a separation-of-powers issue in its attempt to curb the court's judicial power and jurisdiction but does not undermine judicial independence.

Tushnet then correctly identifies two factors in which regulation in Singapore is tighter than that of many other states: the use of public spaces especially "for political purposes"[32] and the press. The state's regulation of the Internet is not, however, seen as a major concern. The freedom-of-expression scorecard for Singapore, according to Tushnet is that while it is "clearly not a civil libertarian paradise of free expression" things are not as bad as they seem since "none of the regulations is enforced with a stringency that their terms appear to license."[33] Even then, the "mere existence of regulations with a theoretically broad reach can have troubling effects on the actual practices of freedom of expression."[34]

In his analysis of Singapore's electoral system, Tushnet attributes the ruling People's Action Party's (PAP's) "near total" dominance of the political realm[35] to the Non-Constituency Member of Parliament, the Group Representation Constituency (GRC), and the Nominated Member of Parliament schemes. While these schemes

---

[30] See *Report of the Commission of Inquiry into Allegations of Executive Interference in the Subordinate Courts, 1986*, Cmd. 12 of 1986, presented to Parliament on July 17, 1986 (Singapore: Singapore National Printers, 1986).

[31] In the United Kingdom, the crime of scandalizing the judiciary was only abolished by the Crime and Courts Act 2013. However, it remains part of the law of Singapore under the Administration of Justice (Protection) Act 2016.

[32] Tushnet, "Authoritarian Constitutionalism," 404.

[33] Ibid., 409.

[34] Ibid., 410.

[35] Ibid., 411.

had initially operated in the PAP's favor – especially the GRC
scheme – in the early years of its existence, I have longed argued
that technically things can go either way. If an opposition party is
able to get a foothold in a GRC – as the Workers' Party did in
Aljunied GRC in 2011 – it would be much more difficult to dislodge
them.[36] Moreover, as we saw in 2011, the cost of losing a GRC can
be quite substantial for the ruling party. Its loss of Aljunied GRC –
with its "heavyweight team" – in 2011 saw the political demise of
two cabinet ministers and one senior parliamentary secretary.

PAP dominance in the political space is not merely the result of its
gerrymandering of electoral boundaries, nor of the various institutions it
has established, but also because they have genuinely met most of their
electoral promises. The fact that this single party has been in power
continuously since 1959 seems to trouble most foreign observers.
Regime change through elections appears to be a major factor in determining if genuine democracy is in fact at work. In the case of Singapore,
the only thing stopping it from graduating into Tushnet's league of liberal
democracies is the "authoritarian overtones" that inflict the system:

> Singapore's constitutional system is far from being that of a liberal democracy,
> and it clearly has authoritarian overtones. The use of 'swords of Damocles'
> and the internalization of constraint by some as a result of long-standing and
> well-known instances of coercion of others may allow the government to
> assert control without obvious arbitrary exercise of power. Yet, that point can
> be put another way, perhaps we could describe Singapore's authoritarianism
> as being exercised with a relatively light hand. Rather than electoral fraud,
> there is gentle and completely transparent manipulation of the formal elec-
> toral system. With some difficulty, political opponents can organize reason-
> ably effectively. And of course, while worrying about being forced into
> bankruptcy is not something opposition leaders welcome, neither is it
> much like being concerned, on waking up at home in the morning, that
> one will be spending the evening in prison.[37]

The problem with "authoritarian overtones" is that they exist in all
societies where the government actually has sufficient power to govern.
A discursive analysis of a country's political reality – as performed by
Tushnet – is necessarily hampered by the fact that complex and nuanced
explanations end up beneath the hood of the bare facts. How then can we

---

[36] See Kevin Y. L. Tan, "Constitutional Implications of Singapore's 1991 General Election,"
Singapore Law Review 13 (1992): 13; Kevin Y. L. Tan, "Is Singapore's Electoral System in
Need of Reform," *Commentary* 14 (1997): 109.
[37] Tushnet, "Authoritarian Constitutionalism," 414.

apply Tushnet's analysis to other states we are studying? Moreover, at what point does a constitutional authoritarian state become a liberal democracy or descend into an absolutist constitutional state?

7.6 Conclusion

Calling Singapore an "authoritarian constitutionalist" state is little more than attaching a label to it. It is another way of saying that it is *not* a liberal democracy. But Singapore is not completely authoritarian because there is another category of states that lies beneath it. Exactly what does this kind of categorization tell the comparative constitutionalist about anything other than the fact that those who see themselves in the liberal democracy "club" are not prepared to admit states like Singapore? In recent years, comparative constitutional law scholars have been bitten by the classification bug and have begun identifying numerous forms of "constitutionalisms" in what has come to be known as "adjectival constitutionalism" or "the study of constitutionalisms identified by some modifier."[38] These include: political constitutionalism, judicial constitutionalism, liberal constitutionalism, abusive constitutionalism, illiberal constitutionalism, social-democratic constitutionalism, totalitarian constitutionalism, Islamic constitutionalism, East Asian Constitutionalism, Latin American Constitutionalism, and, now, authoritarian constitutionalism. We now have a "flood of typologies" but how do they help us become better comparativists? Comparative politics scholars have been down this road before – back in the late 1960s and early 1970s – when numerous types of political systems were being "discovered."[39] But they say nothing about how the people of Singapore have to deal with their own realities of living in a multi-ethnic, multi-religious society, wholly dependent on imports for its survival.

---

[38] Mark Tushnet, "Editorial," *International Journal of Constitutional Law* 14(1) (2016): 1.

[39] Some of these, particularly those relevant to democratic systems, are summarized in Arend Lijphart, "Typologies of Democratic Systems," *Comparative Political Studies* 1 (1968): 3. During this time, scholars have "suggested that political systems can be fruitfully classified as autocratic, republican, or totalitarian; as mobilization, theocratic, bureaucratic, or reconciliation systems; as modernizing, totalitarian, traditional, and traditionalistic oligarchies; as Anglo-American, Continental European, pre-industrial or partially industrial, and totalitarian; and as primitive political systems, patrimonial empires, nomad or conquest empires, city-states, feudal systems, centralized historical bureaucratic empires, and modern societies (democratic, autocratic, totalitarian, and 'underdeveloped')" (Dahl, *Modern Political Analysis*, 71).

Ancient Power with Civil Law Foundation

Japan

8

From Signal to Legality

Meiji Japan and Authoritarian Constitutionalism

TOM GINSBURG

Recent years have seen a resurgence in studies that "take authoritarian constitutionalism seriously." We now understand that authoritarian regimes frequently use the form of written constitutions to accomplish certain governance tasks, with great effect. Written constitutions can allow political regimes to coordinate around the basic machinery of government, and to establish institutions that serve to limit government predation.[1] They can motivate regime forces by articulating political goals that have not yet been achieved, as a blueprint. They can also serve as powerful signals of policy intentions, to audiences both domestic and international.

If constitutions can resolve governance problems associated with authoritarian regimes, then we should expect them to be fairly common. After all, regimes that adopt a written constitution tend to be more enduring than those that do not do so.[2] We might also expect that such regimes can benefit from genuine *constitutionalism* of a sort – a set of fundamental rules that limits the behavior of various actors and ties the hands of rulers, not so much vis-à-vis the people as the other elements of the ruling apparatus. That authoritarian regimes have such rules is not surprising; after all, every monarchy has rules of succession, which prevent any individual from undermining the broader intertemporal interests of his or her family. But we typically expect such regimes to rely less on formal rules and more on informal norms.

Authoritarian constitutionalism requires a set of conditions: there must be formal rules, announced in advance, that genuinely constrain

---

[1] See Tom Ginsburg and Alberto Simpser (eds.), *Constitutions in Authoritarian Regimes* (New York: Cambridge University Press, 2014).

[2] Mike Albertus and Victor Menaldo, "The Political Economy of Autocratic Constitutions," ibid., 53–82.

rulers on important issues; these must correspond to some degree to the exercise of actual power in the political system; and the rules must be self-enforcing, in the sense that no powerful actor wishes to overturn them. In other words, all players believe that they are better off *within* the system than outside it. So long as these conditions are met, the rules will be stable.

This chapter examines the *Constitution of the Empire of Japan* (Meiji Constitution) as a kind of authoritarian bargain. It shows that the rules of the Meiji Constitution, complemented by a set of informal rules that channeled the actual exercise of power, served to buttress the regime, and underpinned aspects of modern Japanese development. The Meiji era (1868–1912) dramatically transformed a feudal nation into a great power in little more than three decades, and the Constitution provided a stable basis at least into the 1930s. No subsequent set of reforms anywhere, until the unleashing of capitalism in modern China, can match the Meiji period for ambition, scale, and success. Furthermore, the Meiji experience inspired others in Asia, including Sun Yat-Sen of Republican China and Vietnamese reformers, to wrestle with modern constitutionalism. It is thus worth understanding its institutional underpinnings. While the system did eventually break down, we focus primarily on its period of stability.

The chapter begins by describing the intellectual and historical origins of the Meiji Constitution, originating with the challenge posed by the threat of Western colonialism. It then goes on to explain how the institutional choices served to buttress the particular kind of bureaucratic authoritarianism that has come to dominate modern Japan. We close with some speculative thoughts on how one ought to evaluate authoritarian arrangements, suggesting that the Meiji Constitution ought to be considered an example of a successful one.

8.1 The Context

The Meiji Constitution, along with legal reform more generally, is usually thought of as a part of Japan's rearguard action to protect itself from Western colonialism in the aftermath of the restoration of imperial authority in 1868. In the face of significant threats by Western powers, Japan effected a "revolution from within" that overturned two-and-a-half centuries of Tokugawa rule. Leaders of the Meiji restoration were of course driven by external considerations; but historians have gradually come to emphasize the underlying internal instabilities that had percolated during the latter period of the Tokugawa.[3] We know that Japan's leaders were motivated by a kind of aversive reaction to the Tokugawa system, which was feudal but also had, as all regimes do, a kind of "small-c" constitutional structure. We begin with a brief discussion of the self-enforcing arrangements that served the Tokugawa and institutionalized the long peace.

8.1.1   Tokugawa Precedent

While not relying on a single written constitution-like document (though such documents had been utilized during earlier periods of Japanese history),[4] the long and stable period of Tokugawa rule relied on a set of arrangements that were constitutional in character and self-enforcing in practice. These arrangements include quasi-federal feudalism, in which local lords ruled with some autonomy and were rewarded with status and wealth. The hereditary shōgun, or military leader based in Edo, ruled in practice, but the imperial house continued to reign from Kyoto as a formal matter. This institutionalized division between power and authority is a lingering feature of Japanese political culture.

The feudal relations between the shōgun and daimyō were sustained by the *sankin kōtai* system, in which each daimyō was required to retain a residence in Edo, and to spend as much as half their time there. Their wives and children were to stay there whenever the daimyō were back in their domains, providing a kind of hostage system. This system dated from 1635 and provided a kind of tax on the daimyō's economic base: each ruler had to maintain multiple houses and bear the cost of moving back and forth. This self-enforcing system can be considered quasi-constitutional in that it developed out of a bargain between the center and the subunits, and was in the interests of all in that it provided stability.

Another key feature of the social system was a strict caste structure, with the samurai on top and holders of exclusive privileges to bear swords. Christianity was seen as subversive and was banned, as was extraterritorial travel and contact. In addition, guns, which were available

---

[3] The following draws on Richard Sims, *Japanese Political History Since the Meiji Renovation 1868–2000* (New York: Palgrave, 2001).

[4] Jeffrey P. Mass, *The Kamakura Bakufu: A Study in Documents* (Stanford: Stanford University Press, 1976); Jeffrey P. Mass, *Yoritomo and the Founding of the First Bakufu: The Origins of Dual Government in Japan* (Stanford: Stanford University Press, 1999); Tom Ginsburg, "Constitutionalism: East Asian Antecedents," *Chicago-Kent Law Review* 88 (2012):11.

at the beginning of the period, were phased out. This provided a rough equality of arms and prevented any group from easily displacing the shōgun at the center.

The main internal change over the long peace of the Tokugawa was endogenous and driven by the rise of commercial classes, formally on the bottom of the fourfold feudal social structure. Continuous travel demanded by the *sankin kōtai* system, and political centralization caused by the long peace, as well as expanding religious pilgrimage, led to internal commerce and the thriving of towns. Tokugawa success, from this perspective, bred the conditions for its own demise. When Commodore Perry arrived in 1854, it provoked a crisis that ended with the elimination of the shōgunate in 1868. Western powers demanded unequal treaties that forced Japan to open itself to trade.

If Western pressure provided the context, the proximate cause of the end of the era was a rebellion by the Western regions of Japan, centered around Satsuma and Chōshu. These domains had opposed the Tokugawa at the Battle of Sekigahara in 1600. Once the shōgunate was abolished, young men from these areas went on to become the dominant political figures of the next half-century. After a short war, they fired the shōgun (but left him alive), restored the emperor to authority, and begin reorganizing the regime. It was these characters, known collectively as the Meiji oligarchs, who were the central powerholders and whose interactions were to both produce, and be constrained by, the Meiji Constitution.

8.1.2   Meiji Reforms

8.1.2.1   Early Phase

The Meiji period begins with the establishment of a national government structure, the dismantling of feudal han governments with their replacement by centrally appointed prefectures, and measures to abolish the class system. A good overall statement of goals and conception at the outset of the period can be found in the quasi-constitutional Charter Oath of the Emperor (Charter Oath), promulgated in 1868: this promised to base policy on public opinion, expand administration, and, particularly relevant to the international context, "abolish the uncivilized customs of antiquity and administer justice and impartiality in accordance with universally recognized principles." Thus, law was from the very first instance among the focal points of the restoration, not a surprise given the unequal treaties that formed part of the triggering historical events.

The initial motivation of legal reform was as a signal, to indicate that Japan was in fact heading toward modernity. In addition, the thrust was outward, with the Charter Oath declaring that "knowledge shall be sought throughout the world so as to invigorate the foundations of Imperial Rule."[5] From the very beginning, the Meiji period was designed to be a pragmatic modernization, adopting foreign institutions to strengthen the nation. But the image of a wise emperor and set of oligarchs directing the country's modernization in a master plan understated the intense political battles of the period.[6]

A critical step for the borrowing of legal and constitutional technology was the *Iwakura* mission of 1871–3, which systematically gathered information on particular legal systems from abroad, and to understand how Japan could fit within the system of international law. Prussia's model of a late-developing state had a profound influence on the leaders, and led to a gradual shift during the *Iwakura* mission. A crucial juncture came in an encounter with Bismarck, in which he disabused the Japanese of any faith in international law as a device to protect their interests.[7] Only national strength, founded in strong institutions, guaranteed autonomy, according to Bismarck.[8] The *Iwakura* mission returned home with a more sophisticated view of law and a commitment to realpolitik. It also brought a significant amount of information on constitutional institutions, mostly compiled by Kido Takayoshi during a four-month stay in Washington, DC.

Kido, along with Ōkubo Toshimichi, became major advocates for constitutional government as the essential step to maintain national power. Kido advocated a specifically authoritarian model, as the people were not ready for self-government; instead the emperor should retain absolute authority and "the fundamental law of the state must be

---

[5] Mikiso Hane, *Modern Japan: A Historical Survey* (3rd ed., Boulder: Westview Press, 2001), 75. In practice however, there was a good deal of continuity in certain respects. Public posting of rules in the immediate years after the restoration kept the same rules. Kichisaburo Nakamura, *The Formation of Modern Japan: As Viewed from Legal History* (Honolulu: East West Center Press, 1962), 34. The distinction between samurai and commoners survived until the abolishment of the samurai's exclusive right to wear swords in 1876.

[6] For an account of these domestic politics, see Junji Banno, *Establishment of the Japanese Constitutional System*, trans. J. A. A. Stockwin (London: Routledge, 1992).

[7] Kazuhiro Takii, *The Meiji Constitution: The Japanese Experience of the West and the Shaping of the Modern State*, trans. David Noble (Tokyo: International House of Japan, 2007), 64–9.

[8] Ibid.

'despotic.'"[9] While he recognized that popular will still had to be taken into account, and that "sovereigns do not rule arbitrarily,"[10] he also believed that public opinion did not need formal channels. Instead, he envisioned a harmonious structure in which ruler and ruled each played their roles, in some sense drawing on Confucian tropes. Ōkubo, on the other hand, gave paramount leader Itō Hirobumi a memorandum on the need to establish a government to fit the Japanese nation (*kokutai*) but argued that shared governance was really required – a more progressive vision than that offered by Kido, but one dedicated to the achievement of national greatness.[11] He thought a constitution could "determine the powers of the Emperor and limit the powers of the people."[12] Both Kido and Ōkubo agreed, though, that a stable government required a constitution. Their position advocating domestic regime-building conflicted with a more aggressive group, around Saigo Takamori, that wanted to engage in foreign adventurism rather than consolidation. In the 1870s, the groups engaged in a major debate, ultimately leading to the anti-government Saga rebellion, over whether to invade Korea.

Although most observers emphasize the influence of French and, later, German law on Japanese legal reform during this period, it is important to remember that the Meiji leaders looked initially to Chinese and historical Japanese codes for inspiration, and that Chinese influence was predominant until 1881 when the first phase of legal reforms ended.[13] The first major Code, the *Shinritsu Kōryō*, was substantively adopted from the Chinese Ming and Ch'ing Codes. The initial government structure, based on the *Ritsuryō* system, recalled Japanese adaptation of Chinese institutions from the Taika period. Return to such institutions in the Meiji period reflected in part the ideal of "restoration" of former glory.

The appointment of Etō Shinpei as Minister of Justice in June 1872 was to lead to a series of radical institutional changes. Etō, leader of the militant faction in the government that sought to mimic Western imperialism with an invasion of Korea (and later leader of the Saga rebellion

[9] Ibid., 39.
[10] Ibid.
[11] Hui Zhao, "The Foundation of Meiji Constitutionalism (1868–1890s)", manuscript (2014).
[12] George M. Beckmann, *The Making of the Meiji Constitution: The Oligarchs and the Constitutional Development of Japan* (Lawrence, MA: University of Kansas Press, 1957), 112.
[13] Paul Heng-Chao Ch'en, *The Formation of the Early Meiji Legal Order* (Oxford: Oxford University Press, 1981).

against the new government), clearly saw formal legalism as crucial to maintaining national strength.[14] Etō was also a centralizer, trying to take away jurisdiction from the local governments and centralize it in the Ministry of Justice responsible for the courts.[15] In keeping with the notion of legal institutions as embodying "universally recognized principles," the judiciary was established as a separate branch of government under the supervision of the Ministry of Justice.[16] Professionals in the Ministry would issue advice to judges of the courts when faced with questions of interpretation or application of law.[17]

The Minister of Justice was the presiding judge of the highest court, so separation of powers was incomplete in this early phase. Only in 1875 was the Great Court of Judicature established as the highest judicial authority.[18] In 1877 qualifications for judges and prosecutors were issued and executive officials barred from serving concurrently as judges.[19] Thus, we see in this early period the first steps, if still tentative, toward establishment of autonomous legal institutions.

The trend toward democratization – symbolically captured in the Charter Oath, and seeing institutional manifestation in the Movement for Civil Rights beginning in 1873 – flourished briefly in efforts to create a diet, but also led to a suppressive backlash against criticism. This period also saw illiberal legislation, such as the libel law of 1875, used to suppress popular movements demanding even greater participation.[20] The repressive tendency was to emerge with much greater vigor after the Taishō democracy period, but the seeds were already sown in the early Meiji era. And, critically, there was a meeting of minds among the major figures in

---

[14] Hiyoshi Sonoda, *Etō Shimpei Den* (Tokyo: Taikōdō, 1968).

[15] Even this formal shift did not change the fact that actual establishment of prefectural courts under national administration was slow, leaving the prefectural authorities in control even after the abolishment of the han.

[16] The Shihō Shokumu Teisei [Justice staff regulations], September 1872.

[17] See discussion of these in Nobuhiko Kasumi, "Criminal Trials in the Early Meiji Era – With Particular Reference to the Ukagai/Shirei System," in Daniel Foote (ed.), *Law in Japan: A Turning Point* (Seattle: University of Washington Press, 2003).

[18] Much of the modern judicial structure can be traced back to the Chōshu leader Kido Takayoshi, who secured the establishment of a supreme court at the same time the Genro-in was established in 1875. An initial proposal that the Genro have formal power to review legislation was rejected at Kido's insistence.

[19] Takkaki Hattori, "The Legal Profession in Japan: Its Historical Development and Present State," in Arthur T. von Mehren (ed.), *Law in Japan: The Legal Order in a Changing Society* (Cambridge, MA: Harvard University Press, 1963).

[20] Ryosuke Ishii (ed.), *Japanese Legislation in the Meiji Era*, trans. William Chamblis (Tokyo: Pan-Pacific Press, 1958), 16; Nakamura, *Formation of Modern Japan*, 51.

the era to structure a council of elders that could serve as a legislative body. Members of this group, the *genrō-in*, formed the political leadership for some time to come.

Pressures for constitutionalism came primarily from within the elite, as factions maneuvered against each other. For example, Itagaki Taisuke and his allies from Tosa argued for the importance of public opinion (by which they initially meant samurai such as themselves), in part to prevent domination by the Satsuma-Chōshu samurai.[21] They sent the so-called Tosa memorial to the throne in 1874 arguing for representative government.

This first phase of reform closed with the Imperial Rescript of 1881.[22] Faced with growing calls for more rapid democratic reform and having fought off internal challenges to central authority including the Satsuma rebellion of 1877, the rescript called for public order and announced the formation of a National Assembly by 1890. From then on, legal reforms became more coherent, less piecemeal and more centered on the nascent institutions that had emerged in the early Meiji years. The first phase was a chaotic one, but involved important steps toward securing the formal structure of a modern legal system so as to be free from the humiliation of extraterritorial jurisdiction. This was all in keeping with a view of the world order as one of Darwinian competition; law would help advance state power and autonomy. And a constitutional basis was essential for Japan's further institutional development as a modern nation.

8.1.2.2   The Second Phase (1881–1898)

This phase marks increased institutionalization of the legal and government system. The centerpiece of this period was the adoption of the Meiji Constitution in 1889, establishing the legal infrastructure for the modern state. Most observers describe the very idea of the Meiji Constitution – not one of the demands of the civil rights movement – as an effort to consolidate the position of the Imperial House and governmental interests before rising democratic pressures could be brought to bear.[23] In this sense, it seems the embodiment of an authoritarian legality: a set of rules that organized the state, preempted and channeled opposition, and symbolized modernity all in one fell swoop.

---

[21] Marius B. Jansen, "The Meiji State: 1868–1912," in James Crowley (ed.), *Modern East Asia: Essays in Interpretation* (New York: Harcourt and Brace, 1970), 109.

[22] Reprinted in Ishii, *Japanese Legislation in the Meiji Era*, 720.

[23] Nakamura, *Formation of Modern Japan*, 59.

It also, critically, served to constitute the basis for competition among the oligarchs themselves.[24]

The actual drafting was carried out by Itō Hirobumi and his associates on behalf of the emperor without much external discussion. Itō took a study tour to Europe in 1882 and was heavily influenced by the authoritarian Prussian model. He encountered German legal scholars of the historical school, including Rudolph von Gneist, who were skeptical of Japan's efforts to draft a constitution, because of their emphasis on an organic connection between laws and local political conditions, and the coevolution of law and society. Gneist urged gradualism: Japan should wait until its institutions were sufficiently developed to have a constitution. Itō also encountered general skepticism about parliamentary government, in keeping with the contemporary scene in newly unified Germany. This led him to become somewhat worried about his ability to accomplish his mission.[25]

Itō's spirits improved, however, with his visit to Austria to meet the legal scholar Lorenz von Stein.[26] Stein's theories focused on a balance among the monarch, the legislature, and the executive branch, and, in particular, he warned of the dangers of dominance by the first two. National stability required, most of all, administrative autonomy and a bureaucracy able to act on its own accord. These views shaped Itō's view of the constitution of Japan, writ large, and soon after his return to Japan he began the crucial tasks of building a bureaucracy and developing a constitutional structure for insulation of the emperor. This included selective appointment of peers in anticipation of an upper house.[27] In short, Itō came to understand a constitution as a device, not only to signal legalism, but to ward off democratic pressures and insulate the government.

The promulgation of the Meiji Constitution in 1889 was sudden and preceded by no public discussion, having been produced exclusively by the emperor and his advisers, and framed as a gift from the emperor to the people.[28] Influenced by the Prussian Constitution, the

---

[24] J. Mark Ramseyer and Frances Rosenbluth, *The Politics of Oligarchy* (New York: Cambridge University Press, 1998).

[25] Takii, *Meiji Constitution*, 81–3.

[26] Ibid., 84–6.

[27] Ramseyer and Rosenbluth, *Politics of Oligarchy*, 32.

[28] See Herbert Bix, *Hirohito and the Making of Modern Japan* (New York: HarperCollins, 2000); Beckmann, *Making of the Meiji Constitution*; W. G. Beasley, *The Rise of Modern Japan* (New York: St. Martin's Press, 1990); Banno, *Establishment of the Japanese Constitutional System*.

Meiji Constitution seemed to embody the spirit of *wakon yōsai* ("Japanese spirit, Western technology") in the sense that Western institutional forms were checked by retention of imperial prerogative. The precise relation between the two was complex and subject to much internal controversy in Japan over subsequent decades, particularly on the issue of whether or not the emperor was an organ of the state or its very embodiment.[29] Advocates of the theory that the emperor was an organ allowed some room for popular sovereignty; those who thought the emperor was the very embodiment of the Japanese state viewed the constitutional order as flowing from imperial power, which could implicitly retract it at will.

The Meiji Constitution set the structure for government for the next fifty years. Viewing the Meiji Constitution from the vantage point of today, it seems illiberal, but by the standards of 1889, it was viewed as something of a progressive development, at least when compared with Tokugawa institutions.[30] Perhaps thinking of the retention of the emperor as the locus of sovereignty, Oliver Wendell Holmes praised it for embodying Japanese values in a Western form.[31]

8.2 The Structure of the Meiji Constitution

8.2.1 Government Structure

The Meiji Constitution was designed to head off rising demands for popular involvement in government. This affected its institutional design as an authoritarian document. At the center of the system was the emperor, sovereign and the embodiment of the state. There was a good deal of ambiguity in practice about the extent of the imperial prerogative, which was very large on paper. Clearly, though, the emperor was the formal center of the system.

The Constitution also created an Imperial Diet as a legislative assembly, and this provided greater formal transparency in the legislative process, even if the *genrō* continued to exercise extensive power. The

---

[29] Bix, *Hirohito and the Making of Modern Japan*, 77–80.
[30] In particular it is noteworthy that contemporary English constitutional lawyers did not recommend adoption of their own form of cabinet government for Japan. Kenzo Takayanagi, "A Century of Innovation: The Development of Japanese Law 1868–1961," in von Mehren (ed.), *Japan*, 9.
[31] Takii, *Meiji Constitution*, 134–5.

Diet was bicameral, with a House of Representatives elected on the basis of a limited franchise, and a House of Peers, appointed by the emperor. (In practice, this allowed the oligarchs to construct a veto gate for legislation.) The Cabinet was responsible to the emperor, and in practice frequently headed by the oligarchs Yamagata Aritōmo and Itō Hirobumi. These two were rivals, whose competition within the party system prevented either from completely dominating.[32] The Privy Council, the successor to the pre-constitutional *Genrō-in,* was a crucial institution. Although only mentioned in a single article of the Constitution, Article 56, its powers were amorphous and broad. The members were to deliberate on matters of state when the emperor consulted with them, and in practice this meant that they could consider just about any matter they wished. This institution allowed for the *genrō* to have a formal position in government, even when they were out of power, and in practice, they greatly influenced the use of the imperial name by the Cabinet.

The legislative domain was not unlimited, particularly because the use of imperial edicts limited it. Though spending was supposed to be centered on the House of Representatives, the Cabinet had the power to raise funds through imperial order when the Diet was not in session and public safety required it. Indeed, imperial orders provided a powerful quasi-legislative device. In practice, these were drafted by government but subject to the advice of the Privy Council. The "democratic" institutions were thus constrained by the oligarchic ones. With power balanced between the formal Montesqueieuean institutions of government and the Privy Council that spoke for the emperor, there were channels for competition and for checks and balances within the authoritarian regime.

Constitutional amendment was limited too, and the document, like its 1946 successor to date, was never amended. Amendment required a two-thirds majority in both houses, but could only be initiated by imperial order. No legislatively approved amendment was to be allowed to the Imperial Household Law, insulating the core elements of the autocracy from change. Thus, the Meiji Constitution provided a good deal of stability.

The court system had been gradually upgraded and reformed even before the adoption of the text, as the justice system's lack of autonomy had been one of the key justifications for the unequal treaties. Courts were declared to be independent in the Meiji Constitution. They did not, however, have the power of constitutional control, which in any case was fairly rare among

[32] Ramseyer and Rosenbluth, *Politics of Oligarchy.*

world constitutions in that era. By imperial order, the Privy Council was allowed to comment in statutory disputes related to the Constitution.

The 1884 Rules on Appointment of Judges and the 1886 Court Organization Act established an examination requirement for judges and prosecutors, and insulated judges from being fired at will. Reappointment of existing judges and prosecutors was not required, so the movement toward a professional judiciary was not fully articulated, but by the mid-1880s the direction seemed clear.

The judicial system was reformed by organic law in 1890, after the passage of the Constitution. The law was in fact drafted by a German judge, Otto Rudorff, and drew on the German *Gerichtsverfassungsgesestz* (Court Organization Law) of 1878, in which bureaucratic appointment by the Ministry of Justice replaced earlier discretionary models of reappointment.[33] This German law specified detailed protections for judicial independence, with appointment for life and procedural protections against salary reduction, involuntary transfer, and dismissal. It thus provided a model for judicial autonomy within an authoritarian regime.

8.2.2   The Rule of Law

An important test of the new reforms came in a famous incident in 1891 when a policeman attempted to kill the Russian crown prince at Ōtsu. Ordinarily, attempted murder was punishable only by life in prison, but the government sought the death penalty, by analogy to offenses against the Japanese imperial household. Resisting this pressure, the courts demonstrated independence under the leadership of Supreme Court Justice Kojima Iken, and established the principle of judicial independence in the Japanese context.[34] This ruling became a wellspring for the traditions of institutional autonomy and freedom from pressures, which remain the hallmark of the Japanese judiciary. It is instructive that judicial independence was maintained to a greater extent in wartime Japan than in Nazi Germany.[35] Whatever else their faults, the Japanese

---

[33] Kenneth Ledford, "Career Advancement, Professional Discipline, and Judicial Independence: Judges in the German Empire as the Model Judiciary in East Asia," paper presented at the Third East Asia Law and Society Conference, KoGuan Law School, Shanghai Jiaotong University, Shanghai, 2013.

[34] Ramseyer and Rosenbluth, *Politics of Oligarchy*, 77.

[35] Takayanagi, "Century of Innovation," 12; see generally Ingo Müller, *Hitler's Justice: The Courts of the Third Reich*, trans. Deborah Lucas Schneider (Cambridge, MA: Harvard University Press, 1990).

judges are generally seen as being free from corruption so prevalent elsewhere in the region.[36]

This account is not universally accepted. Ramseyer and Rosenbluth, in their provocative revisionist account of imperial Japan, argue that in fact the judges were subject to pressures from the oligarchs.[37] They note that Kojima was prosecuted shortly thereafter for gambling, and that he retired shortly thereafter for mysterious reasons. They also point to evidence that many judges were removed, through early retirements, from the bench in the late 1890s.

Ramseyer and Rosenbluth's interpretation, however, is not fully convincing. Kojima won his trial for gambling, and two other judges were able to successfully refuse transfer orders, belying expected outcomes of a system of crude punishment.[38] There is also a tension in Ramseyer and Rosenbluth's overall story, which focuses on the inability of the Meiji oligarchs to act collectively, and the idea that the oligarchs *were* able to act collectively to discipline judges. To be sure, many judges were retired in the late 1890s, but as Ramseyer and Rosenbluth recount, there were good reasons to do so from the point of view of ensuring judicial quality. The judges in question, too, were essentially bought off to leave their courts rather than summarily fired in violation of the law. This illustrates rather than undermines the idea of the semiautonomous nature of the judiciary and the institutionalization of the legal system: had the political principals been better able to influence the judges, we would not see the retirees leave with such a share of the "surplus."[39]

A final point about the Ōtsu incident is that Japanese judges *themselves* have interpreted it as a sign of their institutional autonomy. This could, of course, be ideological obfuscation, but the counter-image of judges acting in accordance with the political preferences of the political parties does not seem to comport with judges' own understanding of their role. While Ramseyer's evidence in other work of career punishment for postwar Japanese judges in "right-tail" cases is convincing, the impact of this fact on ordinary cases is likely to be minimal.[40] Judges

---

[36] Hattori notes that "there is not a single recorded instance of judicial corruption" ("Legal Profession in Japan," 122); see also John Haley, *The Spirit of Japanese Law* (Athens: University of Georgia Press, 1998).

[37] Ramseyer and Rosenbluth, *Politics of Oligarchy*, 77–8.

[38] Ibid.

[39] Indeed, Ramseyer and Rosenbluth concede that judicial autonomy was greater than that of bureaucrats (ibid., 169–70).

[40] J. Mark Ramseyer and Eric Rasmusen, *Measuring Judicial Independence* (Chicago: University of Chicago Press, 1993).

stayed away from high-profile cases, and this laid the groundwork for genuine autonomy in the lesser realms of ordinary law, including contract enforcement and protection of property rights.

The story of the development of judicial autonomy in Japan is really a remarkable one in comparative terms. Before Etō's reforms of 1872, the notion of a distinct branch of government for judicial affairs seemed, to use the most appropriate term, foreign. Within two-and-a-half decades, a profession had been created and judges had developed enough sense of professional autonomy to resist executive pressure from an authoritarian government. Although the initial motivation for creating a judiciary may have largely been symbolic, designed to satisfy foreigners that Japanese justice was not barbaric, it led to genuine institutional autonomy rather quickly.

In addition, this institutional change had important effects on the development of the law. Takayanagi notes that Meiji-era judges played an active part in introducing Western norms into Japanese law.[41] Particularly whenever a clear answer was not to be found, the judges would utilize the (pre-Meiji) notion of "judicial reason" to find that particular Western norms ought to be adopted as logical rules. This adaptation played an important role in transforming the normative basis of Japanese law.[42]

Bureaucratic insulation was another subcomponent of Meiji success. Here it must be emphasized that the modern civil service builds on elements of the ancient tradition of Confucian meritocracy that had been the basis of East Asian state for thousands of years. The possibility of joining the bureaucracy was, in theory, a great equalizer in the Chinese system of governance, and so participation through selection provided one outlet in an otherwise rigid social order. Once selected, loyalties were to the emperor and state rather than society. In the modern era, the idea of a professional bureaucracy, composed of high-quality individuals selected through competitive methods, plays a similar role. Japan's feudal order lacked such a mechanism but after the Meiji restoration, professionalization came rapidly, with a civil service system being instituted by 1887.

---

[41] Takayanagi, "Century of Innovation"; Ishii, *Japanese Legislation in the Meiji Era*, 53.

[42] Foreigners also played a role here. In 1887, there was a proposal to allow foreign nationals as judges and prosecutors in cases involving foreign nationals. This was rejected. Of course, foreign training had been sought by lawyers and judges, so the adoption of Western rules was hardly surprising. Hattori discusses the 1875 Libel Law as an example of this ("Legal Profession in Japan," 19).

8.2.3   Balance of Power

The history of the Meiji Constitution is one of competition among institutions, each of which was too weak to dominate the system. Rather than representing unconstrained and autocratic imperial rule, it instead reflected the interests of an authoritarian set of oligarchs, whose interests involved both cooperation and competition. Some of the oligarchs, including Ōkubo and Itō, formed political parties; others such as Yamagata developed a power base in the military, which they ensured remained insulated from civilian control. Critically, the emperor was commander-in-chief and responsible for military appointments, preventing the civilian institutions that eventually emerged from ever asserting effective control over the military. The Constitution made neither of them dominant, but its vague formulae did serve to limit the emergence of stable popular government as well as pure military rule for several decades.

By the end of World War I, massive social and economic change had led to pressures for more democratic forms of government. Japan was now a great power, having been on the right side of the Great War and having defeated China, Russia, and Korea in its imperial expansion. Social changes associated with industrialization and rising levels of education also generated pressure for the expansion of parliament, and the formation of governments centered around political parties. The nascent system of party governments had proven unstable, which was in part the result of the electoral law that institutionalized the single-nontransferable vote in multi-member districts. This system tends to emphasize intra-party competition, and became entrenched even though political actors might have done better under other rules. Particularly after the assassination of Prime Minister Hara Takashi in 1921, political instability was the norm. This instability, to be sure, also resulted from genuine divisions in society, with rising communist agitation.

This period, known as the era of Taishō democracy, ultimately reflected a failure of the system to adjust to new demands; the limited constitutional space for democratic government doomed the attempts to institutionalize democracy.[43] To be sure, Taishō democracy had profound institutional legacies, including experience with parliamentary institutions, experiments with a jury system, and universal manhood suffrage that served as touchstones for later developments. But in

---

[43] Robert Scalapino, *Democracy and the Party Movement in Pre-War Japan: The Failure of the First Attempt* (Berkeley: University of California Press, 1953).

the short term it was not to last. The economic crisis of the 1930s put pressure on many governments around the world, and in Japan it led to increasing adventurism by an unchecked military, culminating in a coup in 1936. The rest, as they say, is history. While the Constitution remained formally in force, the main elements of the balance of power deteriorated. One can, however, sustain the argument that the Constitution endured for at least forty-seven years over several periods of political change.

8.3   Analysis and Conclusion

The leading strategic interpretation of the Meiji Constitution, that of Ramseyer and Rosenbluth, finds that it was ineffective in sustaining coop-eration among the oligarchs. They argue that the Constitution was insuffi-ciently adaptive over time to allow for more stable political institutions, and to constrain the military.[44] This, however, is a harsh view, especially in light of subsequent scholarship on the general fragility of constitutional arrangements. At forty-seven years, the Meiji Constitution endured more than two-and-a-half times as long as the average constitution, and three times longer than the average authoritarian constitution.[45] Instead of considering the failures of the document, we should consider how the effective channeling of public power set the basis for phenomenal eco-nomic performance and political stability. By setting a framework for governance of the state, independent of the oligarchs' interest, the docu-ment helped to make modern Japan work.

Several elements deserve mention. In constructing a constitutional structure, the oligarchs set up a vague system in which none of them could dominate, but in which they were collectively insulated from popular rule. This system depended on who could best speak in the name of a pliant emperor, and this describes what Japan had in the three emperors who ruled under the Meiji Constitution. The various intra-governmental relationships under the Meiji Constitution were not completely specified, and much depended on the decisions announced in the emperor's name. The ambiguity resulted from the lack of pres-sure to specify institutional roles, as well as the agreement of all to place the emperor in a paramount role. Ambiguity was a central feature, but

---

[44] Ramseyer and Rosenbluth, *Politics of Oligarchy*, 165.
[45] Zachary Elkins, Tom Ginsburg, and James Melton, *The Endurance of National Constitutions* (New York: Cambridge University Press, 2009).

this does not mean that it was ineffective – vagueness allowed adjustment of the system over time, to accommodate both oligarchy and democracy.

Constitutional monarchy is an interesting and underexplored form for comparative constitutionalism. The logic is that representatives of the people govern most of the time, but in a monarch they enjoy a unifying symbol. In some cases, the monarch can serve to intervene from time to time to keep society from going off track, or to resolve a political crisis. Such was the role many ascribed to Thailand's King Bhumibhol Aulyadej during his long reign.[46]

Ramseyer and Rosenbluth suggest that the vagueness of the Meiji Constitution bears some of the blame for the eventual disaster of military rule. To be sure, there was a good deal of truth in the fact that civilian control could never be completely ensured under the constitution's dictates. But to blame the structure is to ignore contingency, in particular, the possibility that the imperial institution would have actually exercised a modicum of effort in steering the ship during the frequent moments of gridlock. Had the Japanese constitutional monarchy developed like that of Thailand, there may have been a true arbiter at the center of the system.

Very little evidence exists about the role of the various emperors in the disastrous policies that were launched in their name.[47] But had one of them spoken up firmly at any one point, there would be little their advisers could do but follow. To be sure, the "organ theory" of imperial power, which viewed the emperor's powers as limited to those roles outlined in the Constitution, may have stood in the way. But the formal institutions clearly mandated deference to the emperors. In practice, the emperors reigned without ruling, as the Imperial House had done under Tokugawa. In this sense the "restoration" was simply a change in who governed in the emperor's name.

The ultimate demise of the Constitution came with Japan's total defeat in war and the decision by the Supreme Commander of the Allied Powers to order a replacement. There has been much historical discussion of the role, or lack thereof, of Hirohito in the decision to go to war. Famously, three months before Pearl Harbor, the young emperor took the

---

[46] Paul Handley, *The King Never Smiles* (New Haven: Yale University Press, 2006); Tom Ginsburg, "Constitutional Afterlife: The Continuing Impact of Thailand's Post-Political Constitution," *International Journal of Constitutional Law* 7(1) (2009): 83.

[47] But see Bix, *Hirohito and the Making of Modern Japan* (ascribing a good deal of responsibility to Hirohito).

opportunity to recite a pacifist poem written by his grandfather Meiji.[48] Some believe that this was his last-minute effort to head off the chain of events, initiated and pushed by low-level bureaucrats, that led to Pearl Harbor. However, his majesty did not clarify what he meant, and the proverbial train left the station. Surely a stronger emperor would have been able to mediate between the civilian and military factions.

Constitutional vagueness is a useful drafting technique when forces cannot agree on an outcome.[49] In the case of the Meiji Constitution, the relatively narrow group of people who did the drafting suggests that the vagueness was born not of a bargaining problem, but out of the need to head off nascent demands for genuine popular government. Vagueness and ruling in the name of the emperor were the solutions to this problem, but they engendered another, unanticipated problem: power struggles among competing centers of power that allowed, eventually, the military to take over. However, to treat this as a kind of failure is to ignore the very real achievements that it facilitated: the long period of stable growth, with significant social and economic change, and the retention of genuine independence from European colonialism. There were also the various institutional experiments of the Taishō period, which laid the groundwork for postwar democracy in some ways. Furthermore, while there were plenty of repressive institutions, including the feared military police,[50] nothing approached the depths of the German regime during the comparable period.

One can imagine an alternative history of Meiji that would look very much like the gradual evolution of genuine parliamentarism in many European constitutional monarchies like Sweden and Norway, in which rising social forces bargained with the king to obtain more and more power. The Japanese military was a spoiler to this story, but then again the gradualist European evolution did not take place in the middle of the Great Depression, with global fascism on the rise, and in a context of

---

[48] Eri Hotta, *Japan 1941: Countdown to Infamy* (New York: Penguin Random House, 2013). The poem in question read:

> The seas of the four directions –
> all are born of one womb:
> why, then, do the wind and waves rise in discord?

[49] Tom Ginsburg and Rosalind Dixon, "Deciding Not to Decide: Deferral in Constitutional Design," *International Journal of Constitutional Law* 9 (2012): 636.

[50] Raymond Lamont-Brown, *Kempetai: Japan's Feared Military Police* (Stroud, UK: Sutton Publishing, 1998).

colonial encirclement; rather it took place before the Great War under very different environmental conditions.

As an authoritarian constitution, the Meiji document had profound influence on Chinese constitutional thought. Here the synthesis of Western constitutional form with more traditional notions of elitism had resonance. The idea of an elite group that made decisions, advised by the people but in no way constrained by them, fitted squarely into the Chinese thought of the time, and was reflected in Sun Yat-Sen's theoretical synthesis that informed the five-power constitution in Republican China. The idea of tutelage for the people while they moved through stages of development, as a means of generating national power, was the dominant constitutional idea for many decades.

The Meiji Constitution also remains relevant to understanding contemporary Japan. Although the postwar constitution would seem to mark a very sharp break, given its very different context and drafting history, in fact its scope was very similar to that of the Meiji Constitution, in terms of topics covered and structure.[51] In addition, the revisionist wing of the Liberal Democratic Party, which has long sought to engage in constitutional revision, looks back to certain aspects of the Meiji document as desirable, particularly the emphasis on duties over rights, and the centrality of the imperial institution as a unifying force. While no one argues for reinstating the document, the powerful forces seeking to restore Japan's glory and independence view the period of militant nationalism as a touchstone. One might call it a form of Meiji nostalgia looking back to an era in which Japan was tough, independent, and rooted in its own (invented) traditions.

At the end of the day the Meiji Constitution must be understood in the context of its time. It was an authoritarian constitution that because of its division of power created a self-enforcing equilibrium among the major political actors. The military, ultimately, broke through the constraints, but even this fact depended on pliant emperors. The bottom line is that the Meiji Constitution, with its vague system of competing power centers, endured for forty-plus years, limiting any one group from dominating for much of that time.

What does this tell us about authoritarian constitutionalism in general? First of all, it reminds us that constitutions can contribute to the stability of an authoritarian regime, as the Meiji Constitution did for the

---

[51] Zachary Elkins, Tom Ginsburg, and James Melton, "Baghdad, Tokyo, Kabul: Constitution-making in Occupied States," *William and Mary Law Review* 49 (2008): 1139–78.

first decades after its adoption. The document's functions were to coordinate the elites and to co-opt political forces that might otherwise hinder the government's program of rapid state-led modernization. The cooptation took place both through the creation of parliament to serve as a locus for popular movements, as well as the Privy Council, both of which exercised a good deal of power but also served as a forum for leading oligarchs to have a voice, even when they were out of formal power. As time went on and the oligarchs faded from the scene, the parliament became more important than the Privy Council, during the brief period of Taisho democracy.

The vagueness of the document was both a blessing and curse, allowing for competing forces to work around the focal point of the emperor, without any one of them dominating. This factor, however, meant that the individual character of the emperor was something of a wild card, as was the ability of the competing oligarchs to work in productive tension and keep a particular balance. Agency factors, then, had as much to do with the constitution's survival as did the particular structures within it. With global pressures from rising fascism and Western colonialism, and a rogue military willing to create the conditions for its own takeover, the demise of the Meiji Constitution was perhaps overdetermined. But its legacy remains relevant even today.

Emerging Case

Vietnam

Vietnamese Deliberative Authoritarianism and Legality

DO HAI HA AND PIP NICHOLSON

9.1 Introduction

More than thirty years have lapsed since the Communist Party of Vietnam (CPV, or the party) initiated its 1986 economic reforms, *Đổi mới*.[1] Although the principal focus was economic, *Đổi mới* has also generated remarkable legal reform. Unlike the pre-*Đổi mới* period when the Vietnamese economy and society were regulated primarily by party policy, administrative fiat, and moral principles,[2] the CPV now commits to the construction of a "socialist law-based state" (*nhà nước pháp quyền xã hội chủ nghĩa*), in which law is "characterized" as the primary governance mechanism,[3] predicated on substantial legislative change[4] and sustained legal institutional reform.[5] These reforms reside

---

[1] *Đổi mới*, literally "renovation," endorsed two crucial changes, namely: (1) transition to a more market-based economy; and (2) opening of the economy to international trade and foreign investment. See generally Adam Fforde and Stefan de Vylder, *From Plan to Market: The Economic Transition in Vietnam* (Boulder, CO: Westview Press, 1996); Pietro P. Masina, *Vietnam's Development Strategies* (London: Routledge, 2006).

[2] Nguyen Nhu Phat, "The Role of Law during the Formation of a Market-Driven Mechanism in Vietnam," in John Gillespie (ed.), *Commercial Legal Development in Vietnam: Vietnamese and Foreign Commentaries* (Singapore: Butterworths Asia, 1997), 400–2; John Gillespie, "Concepts of Law in Vietnam: Transforming Statist Socialism," in Randall Peerenboom (ed.), *Asian Discourses of Rule of Law: Theories and Implementation of Rule of Law in Twelve Asian Countries, France and the US* (New York: Routledge Curzon, 2004), 145–7.

[3] CPV, *Nghị quyết 08-NQ/HNTW Hội nghị lần thứ tám Ban chấp hành Trung ương Đảng khoá VII* [Resolution No. 08-NQ/HNTW of the 8th Plenum of the 7th Party Central Committee], 1995, Part One.

[4] A search of *Thư viện Pháp luật*, https://thuvienphapluat.vn, a widely used legal database in Vietnam, reveals 404 statutes adopted between 1987 and 2018.

[5] Pip Nicholson and Pham Lan Phuong, "Roots and Routes: Adapting the Soviet-Inspired Vietnamese Court and Procuracy System," in Hualing Fu et al. (eds.), *Socialist Law in*

228 DO HAI HA AND PIP NICHOLSON

alongside a resilient and powerful party-state which we contend continues to operate as a deliberative authoritarian socialist state, albeit one in dialogue with a range of actors.

We suggest the legal reform dynamics (ideas and actors) in post-*Đổi mới* Vietnam reflect what Baogang He and Mark Warren characterize as "authoritarian deliberation and its associated ideal-type regime as deliberative authoritarianism."[6] In a study, which takes China as its focus, He and Warren contend the party-state manages a community dialogue to "manufacture consent."[7] In the abstract, this framing of contests between reformers (some of whom are activists) and the party-state creates a deliberative space which, in theory, has the potential to transform authoritarianism.[8]

In this chapter, we focus on the contests about the meaning of legality in Vietnam. More particularly, we explore Vietnamese legality by asking to what extent law is used instrumentally or has been transformed to produce a normative conception of justice reflecting Western liberal rule of law principles. We do this in three ways. First, we offer a brief history of the adoption of socialist legality, and other relevant socialist principles and practices, in Vietnam and how these have been transformed after *Đổi mới*. This offers insights into the continuity and change of the CPV's legal instrumentalism (Section 9.2).

Second, in Section 9.3, we explore whether party instrumentalism has ceded its authority to law and its legal institutions. We therefore examine two critical sites contributing to the construction of Vietnamese legality. We first summarize the secondary literature on recent Vietnamese constitutional debates to conclude that the contested space afforded by deliberative authoritarianism produced sophisticated legal reform strategies in legal activists (those seeking fundamental reform) that are being continuously refined. As well as shaping "legality" reform dynamics, these contests have entrenched ambiguities in

Socialist East Asia (Cambridge, UK: Cambridge University Press, 2018), 238–52; Pip Nicholson, "Renovating Courts: The Role of Courts in Contemporary Vietnam," in Jiunn-Rong Yeh and Wen-Chen Chang (eds.), *Asian Courts in Context* (Cambridge, UK: Cambridge University Press, 2016), 528–65; Brian J. Quinn, "Vietnam's Continuing Legal Reforms: Gaining Control Over the Courts," *Asian-Pacific Law & Policy Journal* 4 (2003): 432–68.

[6] Baogang He and Mark E. Warren, "Authoritarian Deliberation: The Deliberative Turn in Chinese Political Development," *Perspectives in Politics* 9 (2011): 269.

[7] Ibid., 281.

[8] Ibid., 271; Pip Nicholson, "Vietnamese Constitutionalism: The Reform Possibilities," *Asian Journal of Comparative Law* 11 (2016): 199.

the Vietnamese legal system that can, in turn, incrementally shape a more transparent and accountable Vietnamese legality, while not dismantling CPV instrumentalism.

We then shift our analysis from the contests about doctrinal and institutional architecture to explore how criminal defense lawyers use law and legal institutions to argue for reform within the CPV-proclaimed system of individual rights (Section 9.4). This is a second testing of the ways in which party legal instrumentalism is challenged, albeit at the grassroots level. Our focus on public law, its legal institutions, criminal procedure and its relevance to the protection of individual rights, as illustrated by a lawyer's advocacy concerning wrongful convictions in Vietnam, supports a thesis that while instrumentalism is being reshaped and challenged, it remains a potent force constraining rights-based liberal notions of legality.

He and Warren's analytical framework assists to place the legality-focused reform dynamics in the context of broader party-state deliberations about political power. It also reveals the ways in which different actors can engage and be constrained by the party-state through its deliberative forums, while illustrating how law itself can be used to provoke a widening of the deliberative space.

This publication notes that legality can fall between democratic rule of law and lawless autocracy.[9] We argue there is an emerging thin rule by law in Vietnam, that affords limited challenge of the party-state. This deliberative space lacks clear rules. As a result, legal reformers risk arbitrary sanction.[10] Further, it is not yet clear that legal challenge of the party-state is more effective than working political channels when seeking to reform legal instrumentalism. Assessing the comparative efficacy of political and legal strategies targeting law reform is beyond this chapter.

A question remains. Why would the CPV embark on legal reform at all? He and Warren convincingly argue that deliberative authoritarianism is fundamentally interested in regime legitimacy, and therefore, dialogue with stakeholders which, in turn, affords regime renewal. We note that studies focusing on Vietnam have revealed that legal reform was

---

[9] See Chapter 1 in this volume.

[10] Benedict J. Tria Kerkvliet, "Government Repression and Toleration of Dissidents in Contemporary Vietnam," in Jonathan D. London (ed.), *Politics in Contemporary Vietnam: Party, State, and Authority Relations* (London: Palgrave Macmillan, 2014), 129. Kerkvliet argues there are certain activist attributes that protect against government prosecution.

primarily undertaken to realize party-mandated objectives, such as facilitating the shift toward a socialist-oriented market economy, fostering Vietnam's integration into the global economy, strengthening party paramountcy and enhancing party-state legitimacy through governance reform.[11] We do not focus on motivations for reform in the balance of this brief chapter. We map the contests about legality concerning public law and legal institutions and criminal defense work by lawyers, to protect individual rights in the context of wrongful convictions, to better understand contemporary Vietnamese legality.

In short, we argue that despite the continued subordination of legality to party control, the post-*Đổi mới* era has witnessed a selective and escalating tension about the extent to which the party-state can rely on instrumentalism. This has created an ambiguous space with an elastic concept of law serving to constrain state power and afford reform-focused debates. This space, however, remains limited with porous boundaries that are largely subject to party discretion. Party-dominated deliberation about legal reform preserves the party-state's control. The uncertainty of consequences for those seeking to use the law to censure the party-state limits their activities.

9.2 Vietnamese Legality and Legal Instrumentalism (1945–2018)

Vietnam declared independence from France in 1945. The evolution of Vietnamese legality since then can be roughly divided into two periods. Between 1945 and 1985, the preexisting colonial legality was gradually displaced, while a socialist legal order evolved which was increasingly entrenched in northern Vietnam and, from 1975, across the country. Subsequent to the introduction of *Đổi mới* in 1986, this socialist legal order has been reshaped to shift from an exclusively instrumental use of law.

This brief chapter does not include a longer view of Vietnamese history. We note, however, that socialist morality selectively built on

---

[11] See Fu et al. (eds.), *Socialist Law in Socialist East Asia*; John Gillespie and Pip Nicholson (eds.), *Law and Development and the Global Discourses of Legal Transfers* (New York: Cambridge University Press, 2012); Martin Gainsborough, *Vietnam: Rethinking the State* (New York: Zed Books, 2010); Stephanie Balme and Mark Sidel (eds.), *Vietnam's New Order: International Perspectives on the State and Reform in Vietnam* (Basingstoke: Palgrave Macmillan, 2006); John Gillespie and Pip Nicholson (eds.), *Asian Socialism and Legal Change: The Dynamics of Vietnamese and Chinese Reform* (Canberra: ANU Press, 2005).

Confucian values, which were a potent moral force in precolonial Vietnam,[12] to bolster CPV leadership (see below).[13]

9.2.1   A Socialist Legal Order (1945–1985)

France's attempt to regain colonial power in Indochina and the Western allies' determination to stop the spread of communism resulted in a thirty-year war (1945–75). This military conflict substantially disrupted nation building, including construction of law and legality by the Democratic Republic of Vietnam (DRVN). Following the conclusion of the Geneva Peace Accords in 1954, Vietnam was split into two rival states and war continued. The DRVN controlled the north and the USA and its allies supported the Republic of Vietnam (RVN) in the south. Vietnam was reunified after the collapse of the southern regime in 1975.[14]

Between 1954 and 1975, the RVN retained the French colonial system, adapted to wartime conditions, and propped up by the USA-led allies.[15] The DRVN, under CPV leadership, adopted the Soviet development model. The northern communist state replaced the preexisting legal order with a socialist model from the 1950s.[16] This socialist legal order was exported south soon after the RVN collapsed in 1975.[17] The unified

---

[12] Nguyễn Ngọc Huy and Tạ Văn Tài, *The Lê Code: Law in Traditional Vietnam* (Athens, OH: Ohio University Press, 1987), 18; David G. Marr, *Vietnamese Tradition on Trial* (Berkeley: University of California Press, 1981), 60; John Gillespie, *Transplanting Commercial Law Reform: Developing a "Rule of Law" in Vietnam* (Aldershot, UK: Ashgate, 2006), 41–3.

[13] Shaun Kingsley Malarney, "Culture, Virtue, and Political Transformation in Contemporary Northern Viet Nam," *Journal of Asian Studies* 56 (1997): 907–9; Margaret Kohn and Keally McBride, *Political Theories of Decolonization: Postcolonialism and the Problem of Foundations* (Oxford: Oxford University Press, 2011), 61–8. The dynamic between Confucian morality, imperial and colonial laws is beyond this chapter. See Milton Osborne, *The French Presence in Cochinchina and Cambodia* (Ithaca, NY: Cornell University Press, 1969); Marr, *Vietnamese Tradition on Trial*; Gillespie, *Transplanting Commercial Law Reform*; Pip Nicholson, *Borrowing Court Systems: The Experience of Socialist Vietnam* (Leiden: Nijhoff, 2007).

[14] See Melanie Beresford, *Vietnam: Politics, Economics, and Society* (London: Pinter, 1988), 17–52.

[15] Vincent Sherry, "The Evolution of the Legal System of the Republic of Vietnam," PhD diss., University of Southern Mississippi, 1973; Gillespie, *Transplanting Commercial Law Reform*, 53.

[16] Bernard Fall, *The Viet Minh Regime: Government and Administration in the Democratic Republic of Vietnam* (Connecticut: Greenwood Press, 1956); Nicholson, *Borrowing Court Systems*, 1.

[17] Nicholson, "Renovating Courts," 529–530.

state, the Socialist Republic of Vietnam (SRVN), committed to construct socialism nationally. Thus, the colonial legacy was largely marginalized nationally from the mid-1970s. There is arguably a different understanding of legality in the North and South of Vietnam today.[18] This difference is not taken up here, but it roots in divergent colonial histories is suggested as a possible explanation.

9.2.2 Borrowing Soviet Legality

The DRVN's adoption of a socialist legal order was marked by the promulgation of a Soviet-style constitution in 1959 and the introduction of Soviet-style courts and procuracies in 1960.[19] Underpinning these constitutional and institutional reforms was the Soviet doctrine of "socialist legality" (*pháp chế xã hội chủ nghĩa*), which was introduced at the 1960 CPV Congress.[20] While requiring strict legal compliance by state agencies, economic and social organizations, public officials, and citizens,[21] socialist legality differs fundamentally from liberal legality in that it reflects a class-based, instrumental conception of law inspired by Marxism–Leninism.[22] Socialist jurists argue that law is a reflection of the "will of the ruling class" (*ý chí của giai cấp thống trị*) and their control

---

[18] Pip Nicholson and Minh Duong, "Legitimacy and the Vietnamese Economic Courts," in Andrew Harding and Pip Nicholson (eds.), *New Courts in Asia* (London: Routledge, 2010), 31–55.

[19] Pham Van Bach and Vu Dinh Hoe, "The Three Successive Constitutions of Vietnam," *International Review of Contemporary Law* 1 (1984): 105–18; William J. Duiker, "The Constitutional System of the Socialist Republic of Vietnam," in Lawrence W. Beer (ed.), *Constitutional Systems in Late Twentieth Century Asia* (Seattle: University of Washington Press, 1992), 331–62; Mark Sidel, *The Constitution of Vietnam: A Contextual Analysis* (Cambridge, UK: Cambridge University Press, 2009), 45–65; Nicholson, *Borrowing Court Systems*.

[20] CPV, *Nghị quyết Đại hội đại biểu toàn quốc lần thứ ba* [Resolution of the 3rd National Party Congress], 1960, Part IV.6.

[21] Hoàng Quốc Việt, "Xây dựng pháp chế xã hội chủ nghĩa và giáo dục moi người tôn trọng pháp luật" [Developing Socialist Legality and Educating People to Respect the Law], *Tạp chí Cộng sản* [Communist Review], 9 (1963) reproduced in Viện khoa học pháp lý, *Xây dựng hệ thống pháp luật và nền tư pháp nhân dân dưới sự lãnh đạo của Đảng* [Constructing the Legal and Judicial Systems of the People under Party Leadership] (Hanoi: Nhà xuất bản Tư pháp, 2005), 71; Gordon B. Smith, "Development of Socialist Legality," in F. J. M. Feldbrugge and William B. Simon (eds.), *Perspectives on Soviet Law for the 1980s* (The Hague: Nijhoff, 1982), 80–91.

[22] Pham Duy Nghia and Do Hai Ha, "The Soviet Legacy and Its Impact on Contemporary Vietnam," in Fu et al. (eds.), *Socialist Law in Socialist East Asia*, 104.

over the means of production.[23] Viewed in this light, the main function of socialist law is to serve the interest and dictatorship of the working class.[24]

Socialist legality, therefore, upholds party leadership and state power rather than confining their powers and protecting citizens' rights.[25] By emphasizing the class-based and instrumental nature of law it denies the existence of natural law, and subordinates individual rights to collective interests.[26] Rejecting the Western notion of the paramountcy of law, socialist jurisprudence maintains that law is not higher than, but derives from the state.[27] And, as party leadership is deemed essential for proletarian dictatorship, socialist law operates as a tool to realize party policy.[28] Consequently, law was by and large subservient to and replaceable by party policy and administrative edict in pre-*Đổi mới* Vietnam.[29]

Democratic centralism was another socialist principle borrowed from the Soviet Union: first set out in the CPV Statute of 1960 and noted in the 1959 DRVN Constitution.[30] Put briefly, the doctrine requires that party members unquestionably comply with party directives, once settled.[31] Before settling policy, party members can debate issues.[32] While in 2011 changes to the Party Statute allowed debate to be referred up within party

---

[23] Lê Minh Tâm, "Bản chất, đặc trưng, vai trò các kiểu và hình thức pháp luật" [Nature, Characteristics, Role and Types, and Forms of Law], in Lê Minh Tâm (ed.), *Giáo trình Lý luận nhà nước và pháp luật* [Textbook on Theory of State and Law] (Hanoi: Nhà xuất bản Công an nhân dân, 2003), 61–5.

[24] Hoàng, "Xây dựng pháp chế xã hội chủ nghĩa và giáo dục moi người tôn trọng pháp luật," 67–71; Lê Duẩn, *Cách mạng xã hội chủ nghĩa tại Việt Nam. Tập I* [Socialist Revolution in Vietnam, vol. I] (Hanoi: Nhà Xuất bản Sự thật, 1980), 633–4.

[25] Gillespie, "Concepts of Law in Vietnam," 143.

[26] Lê, "Bản chất, đặc trưng, vai trò các kiểu và hình thức pháp luật," 61; V. Gsovski, "The Soviet Concept of Law," *Fordham Law Review* 7 (1938): 2–3.

[27] Lê, "Bản chất, đặc trưng, vai trò các kiểu và hình thức pháp luật," 68–9.

[28] Lê, *Cách mạng xã hội chủ nghĩa tại Việt Nam. Tập I*, 637; Hoàng Quốc Việt, "Tăng cường pháp chế trong sự hoạt động kinh tế của các cơ quan, xí nghiệp nhà nước" [Reinforcing Legality in Economic Activities of State Bodies and Enterprises], *Tạp chí Cộng sản* [Communist Review], 6 (1962) reproduced in Viện khoa học pháp lý [Institute of Legal Science], *Xây dựng hệ thống pháp luật và nền tư pháp nhân dân dưới sự lãnh đạo của Đảng* [Constructing the Legal and Judicial Systems of the People under Party Leadership] (Hanoi: Nhà xuất bản Tư pháp, 2005), 61–2.

[29] Nguyen, "Role of Law," 400–2; Gillespie, "Concepts of Law in Vietnam," 147.

[30] Statute of the Vietnam Workers Party 1960, Preamble and art. 10; see also Nicholson and Pham, "Roots and Routes," 228–9.

[31] Statute of the Vietnam Workers Party 1960, Preamble and art. 10; see also Statute of the CPV 1976, Preamble and art. 10; Statute of the CPV 2011, Preamble and art. 9.

[32] Nicholson and Pham, "Roots and Routes," 228–9.

organizations, ultimately the embargo on debate once policy (or legal reform debates, for example) is settled remains.[33]

The 1959 DRVN Constitution adopted a Soviet-style structure of powers which upheld unity, rather than separation, of state powers.[34] As a result, legal institutions, including courts and procuracies, are inferior to the National Assembly (NA).[35] Further, socialist courts generally have no power to "check" other branches of state power, for example by way of constitutional or administrative review.

Vietnamese legality in the high socialist era was also shaped by the doctrine of "revolutionary morality" (*đạo đức cách mạng*), which emphasized the importance of party rule through moral example and edict.[36] The doctrine reflected selective use of neo-Confucian moral principles in order to validate party leadership and the newly imported Marxist-Leninist ideology.[37] Neo-Confucianism agrees with Marxism–Leninism in many important respects, including the notion of law as a means to uphold social order and the prioritization of public needs over individual interests.[38]

Revolutionary morality enabled ethical values to penetrate jurisprudence. Hồ Chí Minh, for example, said that: "Unless imbued with the proletariat morality [and] the benevolent virtue of morality, legal officials cannot effectively discharge the tasks of lawmaking and implementation."[39] In the same vein, it was contended by a former DRVN minister of justice that "there was no distinction between law and ethics as well as between legalism and virtue-rule," and that "'ethics was the root of law.'"[40]

The Maoist theory of "mass line" (*đường lối quần chúng*) also left its imprint on pre-Đổi mới legal practice.[41] Party-state officials were regularly called to apply the method of "mass mobilization" (*dân*

---

[33] Ibid., 229.

[34] DRVN Constitution 1959, art. 4.

[35] Ibid., arts. 104, 108.

[36] John Gillespie, "Understanding Legality in Vietnam," in Balme and Sidel (eds.), *Vietnam's New Order*, 142–3.

[37] Ibid.; Malarney, "Culture, Virtue, and Political Transformation," 907–9; Kohn and McBride, *Political Theories of Decolonization*, 61–8.

[38] Gillespie, "Understanding Legality in Vietnam," 142.

[39] Cited in Bùi Thị Ngọc Mai, "Một số vấn đề của tư tưởng Hồ Chí Minh về pháp luật" [Some Issues of Hồ Chí Minh Thought on Law], *Tạp chí Tổ chức Nhà nước* [*Journal of State Organization*], 7 (2009): 17.

[40] Vũ Đình Hoè, *Pháp quyền nhân nghĩa Hồ Chí Minh* [Hồ Chí Minh's Benevolent and Righteous Rule of Law] (Hanoi: Nhà xuất bản văn hoá-thông tin and Trung tâm Văn hoá ngôn ngữ Đông Tây, 2001), 327–36.

[41] Gillespie, "Concepts of Law in Vietnam," 49.

vận) in bureaucratic and legal work.[42] While prioritizing the goal of the party-state, this method recognizes the necessity for compromise between individual and collective interests and emphasizes the use of explanations and propaganda.[43] Hence, while affirming party paramountcy, "mass mobilization" concurrently fosters compromising, flexible and outcome-oriented solutions to legal problems.[44]

To conclude, imported Marxist–Leninist and Maoist thinking and its conflation with neo-Confucianism in pre-*Đổi mới* socialist Vietnam resulted in a legal order fundamentally different from liberal legality. In this system, law was a mere political instrument with limited capacity to constrain party-state power and protect individual rights. Nor did it have capacity to guide people in the conduct of their affairs. Rather, law was secondary to and replaceable by Party policy, administrative commands, and moral precepts.

9.2.3   Conceiving a "Socialist Law-based State" (1986)

As noted above, the quick expansion of market relations and the increasing opening of the economy to global markets after *Đổi mới* pressed the CPV to review its legal order.[45] Following discussion in the late 1980s,[46] the party officially introduced the doctrine of "law-based state" (*nhà nước pháp quyền*) in 1994,[47] an adapted version of the Russian doctrine of *pravovoe gosudarstvo* revived in the USSR during the perestroika era.[48] The new doctrine was constitutionalized in 2001 and was reconfigured as "socialist law-based state."[49] Since then, it has gradually replaced "socialist legality" as the core doctrinal foundation of the Vietnamese legality.

---

[42] Hoàng Quốc Việt, "Về sự lãnh đạo của Đảng đối với Viện kiểm sát nhân dân" [Speech: Party Leadership over People's Procuracies], Procuracies' Conference, Hanoi, October 1966, reproduced in *Kiểm sát* [Procuracy], May 20, 2015, http://tapchikiemsat.org.vn/ArtDetails.aspx?id=5756#.Va7mJOiqqko; Văn Thị Thanh Mai, "Học tập và làm theo phong cách quần chúng của Chủ tịch Hồ Chí Minh" [Study and Follow President Hồ Chí Minh's Mass Style], *Tạp chí Cộng sản Điện tử* [Communist Review Online], November 25, 2013, www.tapchicongsan.org.vn/Home/PrintStory.aspx?distribution=24656&print=true

[43] Do Hai Ha, "Strike Settlement in Transitional Vietnam and the Persistence of Socialist and Marxist–Leninist Influences," in Fu et al. (eds.), *Socialist Law in Socialist East Asia*, 303–4.

[44] Ibid.

[45] Gillespie, "Concepts of Law in Vietnam," 147.

[46] Đỗ Mười, "Bài phát biểu tại Hội nghị Tư pháp năm 1989" [Speech delivered at the 1989 Judicial Conference], reproduced in Viện khoa học pháp lý, *Xây dựng hệ thống pháp luật và nền tư pháp nhân dân dưới sự lãnh đạo của Đảng* [Constructing the Legal and Judicial Systems of the People under Party Leadership] (Hanoi: Nhà xuất bản Tư pháp, 2005), 154.

[47] CPV, *Báo cáo chính trị tại Hội nghị đại biểu toàn quốc giữa nhiệm kỳ khoá VII* [Political Report at the Mid-Term National Party Congress of the 7th Tenure], 1994, Part One I.2.

[48] Gillespie, "Concepts of Law in Vietnam," 147.

[49] SRVN Constitution (Revised) 2001, art. 2.

Policy and scholarly discourse suggest that "socialist law-based state" diverges from "socialist legality" in many respects. First, the new doctrine places less emphasis on the class-based conception of state and law.[50] Additionally, law is posited as the principal instrument to manage economic and social affairs in "socialist law-based state."[51] Although this continues to reflect the instrumental conception of law embedded in "socialist legality," it concurrently indicates the party-state's commitment to at least a thin version of the rule by law rather than party resolution, administrative edict, and ethical principles.

Third, "socialist law-based state" declares "the supreme role of law in society."[52] While "socialist legality" focuses exclusively on the observance of state laws, the new doctrine suggests the party-state's commitment to be bound by law.[53] In addition, it implicitly endorses a separation between the CPV and the state.[54] In particular, the new doctrine suggests that the party focus on policy formulation while the main function of the state is translating party policy into law.[55]

Moreover, in affirming the unity of state power "socialist law-based state" simultaneously advocates legal instrumentalism and limited "checks and balances" between state bodies.[56] Finally, and more recently, "socialist law-based state" promises to protect human rights.[57]

---

[50] Gillespie, "Concepts of Law in Vietnam," 149; Pham and Do, "Soviet Legacy and Its Impact on Contemporary Vietnam," 124.

[51] CPV, Nghị quyết 08-NQ/HNTW, Part One.

[52] CPV Organization Commission, Xây dựng nhà nước pháp quyền xã hội chủ nghĩa của dân, do dân, vì dân [Constructing the Socialist Law-Based State of the People, for the People, by the People], 2018, www.xaydungdang.org.vn/Home/vankientulieu/2018/12111/Tai-lieu-boi-duong-thi-va-huong-dan-bao-ve-de-an.aspx, 18–19.

[53] Nicholson, Borrowing Court Systems, 244.

[54] Gillespie, "Concepts of Law in Vietnam," 149–53; Bui Hai Thiem, "Deconstructing the 'Socialist' Rule of Law in Vietnam: The Changing Discourse on Human Rights in Vietnam's Constitutional Reform Process," Contemporary Southeast Asia 36 (2014): 81–2.

[55] Nhị Lê, "Đổi mới và tiếp tục giải quyết những vấn đề đặt ra, không ngừng hoàn thiện phương thức lãnh đạo trong điều kiện Đảng cầm quyền hiện nay" [Renovating, Continuously Addressing Remaining Issues of [and] Perfecting the Methods of Party Leadership in the One-Party System], Tạp chí Cộng sản Điện tử [Communist Review Online], December 7, 2015, www.tapchicongsan.org.vn/Home/Nghiencuu-Traodoi/2015/36547/Doi-moi-va-tiep-tuc-giai-quyet-nhung-van-de-dat-ra.aspx; Gillespie, "Concepts of Law in Vietnam," 151.

[56] CPV, Cương lĩnh xây dựng đất nước trong thời kỳ quá độ lên chủ nghĩa xã hội (bổ sung, phát triển năm 2011) [Political Program for National Construction in the Transitional Period to Socialism (Revised in 2011)], 2011, Part IV.

[57] Ibid.; CPV Organization Commission, Xây dựng nhà nước pháp quyền xã hội chủ nghĩa của dân, do dân, vì dân, Part I.2.3.

To sum up, "socialist law-based state" implies significant doctrinal change for post-*Đổi mới* law and legality. By alleviating the class rhetoric, it opens space for selective borrowings of Western rule-of-law ideas and principles. In addition, it has enhanced the role of law in state governance and created the possibility of using law to constrain party-state power and enforce human rights. While socialist legality has been reframed, democratic centralism remains as a potent principle and practice to enable ongoing instrumentalist conceptions of legal practice.[58]

9.2.4   Ambiguities and Contests within a Socialist Law-based State

The "law-based state" doctrine, however, contains critical ambiguities and tensions. To a large extent, these ambiguities and tensions stem from attempts to retain most of the key aspects of pre-*Đổi mới* legality and reconcile them with new ideas eclectically borrowed from liberal legality. The class-based conception of law retains a place in "socialist law-based state" and has significant implications. Party theorists still invoke this conception to reject liberal political–legal principles.[59] Significantly, class rhetoric upholds party paramountcy[60] rather than the supremacy of law. CPV leadership remains a core feature of the "socialist law-based state."[61]

[58] Nicholson and Pham, "Roots and Routes," 224–54.

[59] See, e.g., Hoàng Chí Bảo, "'Tam quyền phân lập' không phải sự lựa chọn mô hình tổ chức nhà nước của Việt Nam" ["Separation of Powers" Is Not the Choice for Vietnamese State Organization], *Tạp chí Quốc phòng toàn dân* [*Journal of All-People's National Defense*], September 11, 2017, http://tapchiqptd.vn/vi/phong-chong-dbhb-tu-dien-bien-tu-chuyen-hoa/tam-quyen-phan-lap-khong-phai-la-su-lua-chon-mo-hinh-to-chuc-nha-nuoc-cua-viet-nam/10566.html; Nguyễn Xuân Yêm, "Phòng, chống khuynh hướng 'phi chính trị hoá lực lượng vũ trang' ở nước ta hiện nay" [Prevention of [and] Fighting against the Current Tendency of "Depoliticization of the Armed Forces" in Our Country], *Công an nhân dân* [People's Police], December 27, 2016, http://cand.com.vn/Hoat-dong-LL-CAND/Phong-chong-khuynh-huong-phi-chinh-tri-hoa-luc-luong-vu-trang-o-nuoc-ta-hien-nay-422849; Trương Minh Tuấn, "Bản chất chính trị của quân đội nhân dân Việt Nam" [The Political Nature of the Vietnamese People's Army], *VOV*, March 18, 2013, https://vov.vn/chinh-tri /ban-chat-chinh-tri-cua-quan-doi-nhan-dan-viet-nam-252225.vov

[60] SRVN Constitution 2013, art. 4.1. See also Lê Hữu Nghĩa, "Sự lãnh đạo của Đảng đối với nhà nước pháp quyền" [Party Leadership over the Law-Based State], *Tạp chí Cộng sản online* [Communist Review Online], January 18, 2007, www.tapchicongsan.org.vn /Home/Xay-dung-nha-nuoc-phap-quyen/2007/1665/Su-lanh-dao-cua-dang-doi-voi-nha-nuoc-phap-quyen.aspx

[61] See, e.g., CPV, *Báo cáo chính trị tại Đại hội đại biểu toàn quốc lần thứ mười hai* [Political Report at the 12th National Party Congress], 2016, Part XIV; CPV Organization Commission, *Xây dựng nhà nước pháp quyền xã hội chủ nghĩa của dân, do dân, vì dân*, 20–1.

Concurrently, party policy is integral to the spirit of the law which directs lawmaking and implementation.[62] These are inconsistent with the CPV's commitment to rule by law, let alone the promise to confine its power within legal boundaries. The endurance of the class-based notion also reinforces the inferiority of individual interests, which contradicts the emergent emphasis on human right protection. As shown in Section 9.3, individual rights remain statist, largely conditional, and subordinate to collective interests, as earlier purported by "socialist legality."

Furthermore, despite the rule-by-law promise, the CPV continues to rely heavily on moral leadership and mass mobilization. It is repeatedly noted by the party and its leaders that the socialist law-based state also gives weight to "education [and] promotion of socialist morality."[63] Nguyễn Phú Trọng, the current General Secretary, has also stressed that the law-based state has to "combine the power of law with the power of the masses."[64] Thus, the CPV continues frequently to utilize political–moral campaigns.[65]

Moreover, although the party has allowed state agencies to have greater autonomy in discharging their functions,[66] the party–state division has never been clearly defined. State agencies still – albeit less often – have to take operational directives from party organizations, especially in important matters.[67] Further, the penetration of party organizations into

---

[62] Nguyễn Minh Đoan, *Giáo trình Lý luận về Nhà nước và Pháp luật* [Textbook on Theory of State and Law] (Hanoi: Nhà Xuất bản Chính trị Quốc gia, 2010), 298–301.

[63] CPV, *Nghị quyết 08-NQ/HNTW*, Part One. See also, eg, CPV, *Nghị quyết 04-NQ/TW Hội nghị lần thứ ba Ban chấp hành Trung ương Đảng khoá X* [Resolution No. 04-NQ/TW of the 3rd Plenum of the 10th Party Central Committee], 2006; CPV, *Nghị quyết 04-NQ/TW Hội nghị lần thứ tư Ban chấp hành Trung ương Đảng khoá XII* [Resolution No. 04-NQ/TW of the 4th Plenum of the 12th Party Central Committee], 2016; Nguyễn Phú Trọng, *Phát huy dân chủ, tiếp tục xây dựng nhà nước pháp quyền xã hội chủ nghĩa của nhân dân, do nhân dân vì nhân dân* [Promoting Democracy [and] Continuing to Construct the Socialist Law-Based State of the People, for the People, by the People] (Hanoi: Nhà Xuất bản Chính trị Quốc gia – Sự thật, 2011), 87–8.

[64] Nguyễn, *Phát huy dân chủ, tiếp tục xây dựng nhà nước pháp quyền xã hội chủ nghĩa của nhân dân, do nhân dân vì nhân dân*, 87. See also CPV, *Nghị quyết 25-NQ/TW Hội nghị lần thứ bảy Ban chấp hành Trung ương Đảng khoá XI* [Resolution No. 25-NQ/TW of the 7th Plenum of the 11th Party Central Committee], 2013.

[65] See, e.g., CPV, *Nghị quyết 25-NQ/TW*; CPV, *Nghị quyết 04-NQ/TW*, 2016. See also Bui, "Deconstructing the 'Socialist' Rule of Law in Vietnam," 80.

[66] Dang Phong and Melanie Beresford, *Authority Relations and Economic Decision-Making in Vietnam: An Historical Perspective* (Copenhagen: NIAS, 1998), 85; Jonathan D. London, "Politics in Contemporary Vietnam," in London (ed.), *Politics in Contemporary Vietnam*, 1.

[67] Jonathan D. London, "Vietnam and the Making of Market Leninism," *Pacific Review* 22 (2009): 378–9.

the state apparatus,[68] the *nomenklatura* system[69] and the continuation of democratic centralism, have rendered the party-state largely inseparable.

Significantly, the party has made several attempts to reinforce its control over the state since 2011. It has reestablished functional bodies, the Commission of Economic Affairs and Commission of Internal Affairs for example, to strengthen party supervision over state economic and judicial agencies.[70] The CPV has also taken over the Steering Committee of Anti-Corruption from the government and tightened its direct control over the armed forces.[71] More recently, it has experimented with merging certain state institutions and leadership positions with their party counterparts.[72] As a result, the party-state division purported by "socialist law-based state" is modest, ill-defined, and unstable.

Finally, though endorsing a limited form of checks on power, "socialist law-based state" offers no concrete mechanisms to realize its conceptual development from socialist legality. Legal and other state institutions continue to operate in accordance with Marxist–Leninist organizational principles, including party leadership, democratic centralism, and unity of power.[73] As we will demonstrate below, this leaves several critical questions unanswered, including how checks on power can be reconciled with longstanding Marxist–Leninist principles.

Arguably, the foregoing ambiguities and tensions substantially impede the "socialist law-based state" doctrine from delivering on its rhetorical promises. Nonetheless, ambiguities are also a strategic asset for reformers and activists, exploited where possible.

9.3   Constitutional Debate and Vietnamese Legality

The greatest public deliberative moment in recent Vietnamese legal reform history was the constitutional debate of 2012–13. While the

---

[68] Ibid.
[69] Ibid. The *nomenklatura* system guarantees that leadership positions in state institutions be occupied by party members.
[70] Pham and Do, "The Soviet Legacy and Its Impact on Contemporary Vietnam," 120.
[71] Ibid.; Bui Hai Thiem, "Vietnam's Constitutional Politics in Focus: Investigating the Arenas of the Rule of Law and Human Rights," in Marco Bünte and Björn Dressel (eds.), *Politics and Constitutions in Southeast Asia* (Abingdon, UK: Routledge, 2016), 213.
[72] CPV, *Nghị quyết 18-NQ/TW Hội nghị lần thứ sáu Ban Chấp hành Trung ương Đảng khoá XII* [Resolution No. 18-NQ/TW of the 6th Plenum of the 12th Party Central Committee], 2017.
[73] Pip Nicholson and Do Hai Ha, "Vietnam," in David Law, Alex Schwartz, and Holning Lau (eds.), *The Oxford Handbook of Constitutional Law in Asia* (Oxford University Press, forthcoming 2021).

debates of 1992 and 2001 were substantial and arguably serve as examples of deliberative authoritarianism,[74] the party-state proclaimed that the 2012 debates had "no taboo."[75] This allowed scholars, building on earlier activism and a tradition of scholarly engagement with reform issues, to debate the proposed changes.[76] This also continued the more open, albeit elite, dialogic mode of the CPV, when compared with China.[77]

Calls were made for fundamental reform by many. A group of seventy-two intellectuals launched a public petition, Petition 72, calling for: a multiparty state; free elections; separation of powers and constitutional review; security of land tenure; removal of a proposed requirement that the military be loyal to the CPV; and locating the basis of constitutional power in popular referenda, rather than party-led review.[78] Very few of these ambitions were fully realized, although reforms were enacted: recognizing that the constitution is made by and serves to protect Vietnamese people (rather than the socialist motherland (Preamble, Article 2(2)); instituting mutual control and supervision between leading agencies (national, assembly, judiciary, and procuracy: Articles 2(3), 107(1)) with the National Assembly remaining the key institution to which the courts and procuracies account (Articles 69 and 70(2)); the recognition of human rights (chapter 2); introducing a National Assembly referendum power (Article 70(15)); vesting judicial power in the courts (Article 102(1)); and the requirements for party members to be bound by law (Article 4(3)).[79] The latter change fell short of demanding that the party itself to be bound by law.

There were many actors in the debate calling for fundamental thick, rule of law reforms.[80] Vo identified four activist groups: progressive politicians;

[74] Mark Sidel, "Analytical Models for Understanding Constitutions and Constitutional Dialogues in Socialist Transitional States: Re-Interpreting Constitutional Dialogues in Vietnam," *Singapore Journal of International and Comparative Law* 6 (2002): 42–89.
[75] Bui Ngoc Son and Pip Nicholson, "Activism and Popular Constitutionalism in Contemporary Vietnam," *Law and Social Enquiry* 42 (2017): 689.
[76] Ibid., 685–8; see also Kerkvliet, "Government Repression and Toleration of Dissidents in Contemporary Vietnam," 102.
[77] Hualing Fu and Jason Buhi, "Diverging Trends in Socialist Constitutionalism," in Fu et al. (eds.), *Socialist Law in Socialist East Asia*, 143–7.
[78] Bui Ngoc Son, "Petition 72: The Struggle for Constitutional Reforms in Vietnam," *I·CONnect*, March 28, 2013, www.iconnectblog.com/2013/03/petition-72-the-struggle-for-constitutional-reforms-in-vietnam
[79] SRVN Constitution 2013.
[80] See Vo Tri Hao, "Integrating the Principle of Separation of Power into the Constitution Amendment 2013 within the 'Keeping Face' Cultural Context," paper presented at conference "Constitutional Debate in Vietnam," National University of Singapore,

members of the intelligentsia; dissidents; and blue capitalists.[81] Vo identified a group, including conservative politicians and members of the police force and military, as "defending" the status quo.[82] The constitutional debate arguably remained a site in which intellectual elites, whether located within universities or retired from the government and/or the CPV, engaged.[83] Petition 72 was the most explicit constitutional challenge to the party-state.[84]

This elite, but profound activism epitomized by Petition 72, debated the very fundamentals of the legal bases of the Vietnamese party-state and its institutions. Petition 72 sought the reforms, outlined above, integral to a thick rule of law. They demanded that the party, all its institutions, and its membership, be bound by law.[85] More particularly, they sought that the constitution be generated by a National Assembly, entrenched through constitutional referenda and subject to judicial review. Its adoption would have fractured the continuing relevance of democratic centralism and the socialist law-based state. The petition was the ultimate challenge to an instrumentalist view of law.

Given the realism of those seeking profound legal reform, activists also strategically introduced ambiguities into the reformist discourse in the hope of realizing greater future reform, even where they were stymied in 2013.[86] There are various examples of new terms in the Constitution, which are, and will continue to be, defined incrementally. One example is the introduction of an undefined concept, "judicial power," in Article 102. In 2014, Article 2 of the Law on the Organization of People's Courts (2014 LOOPC) offers nine features of judicial power. These are, however, cast generally enabling continuity of party instrumentalism so long as that instrumentalism reflects "justice" which is, in turn, not defined:

March 19–20, 2016) [on file with authors]. Vo notes that the NA reported 26 million people commented on the proposed constitutional reforms (at 12). Likely a generous estimate, allowing each person named on a joint submission to be counted as a single commentator (Bui and Nicholson, "Activism and Popular Constitutionalism," 689–9).

[81] Vo, "Integrating the Principle of Separation of Power," 13–19. Blue capitalists are those located entirely within the private sector affording no opportunity for siphoning value into the state sector or its actors through land deals, low-rate loans, or other forms of noncompetitive advantage.

[82] Ibid., 17.

[83] Bui and Nicholson, "Activism and Popular Constitutionalism," 704–5.

[84] Ibid., 689–9.

[85] Party members today are bound by the 2011 Statute of the CPV.

[86] Vo, "Integrating the Principle of Separation of Power," 3.

> People's courts have the duty to safeguard justice, human rights, citizens'
> rights, the socialist regime, the interests of the State, and the lawful rights
> and interests of organizations and individuals.
>
> Through their activities, courts shall contribute to educating citizens in
> the loyalty to the Fatherland, strict observance of law, respect for rules of
> social conduct and the sense of struggle to prevent and combat crimes and
> other violations.[87]

Standing resolute, in the face of an agenda that would dismantle the
foundations of CPV leadership, the party enabled some ambiguous concessions, many of which require detailed legislative and institutional
change for implementation. Returning to the example of judicial
power, while the 2014 LOOPC legislates courts as responsible for safeguarding justice, judges must do this where they are recruited with party
credentials, tightly supervised, have to meet emulation targets, and can be
sanctioned for falling short of party-state behaviors.[88] This reality fore-
stalls the activists ideal of a thick rule of law protected by an independent
judiciary.

Analyses diverge about the significance of this deliberative moment for
the continuity of Vietnamese socialist legality, particularly party
instrumentalism.[89] Fu and Buhi argue that Vietnamese legality has
both allowed greater reform and has not "hardened" against further
constitutional reform, as has China.[90] Arguably their characterization
enables ongoing reform-based change as anticipated as a possibility by
He and Warren. Bui Ngoc Son argues the Vietnamese Constitution now
functions both as a "traditional, hegemonic socialist constitution" and as
a vehicle of constitutionalism.[91] Nicholson and Bui have argued there is
now a form of popular constitutionalism, albeit led by an elite.[92] Read
together these accounts highlight conflict between the reform trajectory
of the CPV and Vietnamese activists, but they also recognize an incremental shift away from the inscrutability of socialist legality.

While the trajectory for reform will be debated, the Vietnamese
Constitution remains socialist, as it includes: proclaimed socialist

---

[87] SRVN Constitution 2013, art. 102(1).

[88] Pip Nicholson and Nguyen Hung Quang, "Independence, Impartiality and Integrity of
the Judiciary in Vietnam," in H. P. Lee (ed.), *Asia Pacific Judiciaries*, ed. (Cambridge, UK:
Cambridge University Press, 2017), 372–93.

[89] Fu and Buhi, "Diverging Trends in Socialist Constitutionalism," 143–7.

[90] Ibid., 163.

[91] Bui Ngoc Son, "Constitutional Dualism: Socialism and Constitutionalism in
Contemporary Vietnam," in Fu et al. (eds.), *Socialist Law in Socialist East Asia*, 165–6.

[92] Bui and Nicholson, "Activism and Popular Constitutionalism."

objectives; Leninist power structures – built on the basis of party leadership, unity of state power, and democratic centralism; and a statist, conditional approach to citizens' rights.[93] As constitutional principles are not self-executable, many important civil–political rights, such as freedom of association and the right to demonstrate, remain largely ineffective with no implementing laws.[94] Where laws are being introduced to protect features of a nascent new legality, such as protection of judicial power and human rights, they butt up against ingrained and continuing institutional practices, and the continuing instrumentalism explained in Section 9.2.[95]

9.4   Lawyer Activism and Vietnamese Legality: Challenging Wrongful Convictions

9.4.1   Vietnamese Criminal Procedure and the Problem of Wrongful Convictions

Vietnam has a Soviet-style investigatory system of criminal procedure that prioritizes the discovery of crimes and protection of collective and state interests.[96] The Vietnamese Soviet-inspired procuracy exercises two functions: acting as both prosecutor and supervisor of judicial, including police and court, activities.[97] Procuracies have widely used their supervisory power to steward criminal judgments, influencing both trial procedure and determination.[98] While reforms ostensibly challenge the procuracy as

---

[93]   Bui, "Vietnam's Constitutional Politics in Focus: Investigating the Arenas of the Rule of Law and Human Rights"; Fu and Buhi, "Diverging Trends in Socialist Constitutionalism"; Nicholson and Do, "Vietnam."

[94]   Bui, "Vietnam's Constitutional Politics in Focus," 211–22; Nicholson and Do, "Vietnam," 15–16; Vu Cong Giao and Kien Tran, "Constitutional Debate and Development on Human Rights in Vietnam," *Asian Journal of Comparative Law* 11 (2016): 235–62.

[95]   Nicholson and Nguyen, "Independence, Impartiality and Integrity"; Vu and Kien, "Constitutional Debate and Development."

[96]   See CPC 1988, art. 1; CPC 2003, art. 1; CPC 2015, art. 2 prescribing the objective of criminal procedure. The CPC 2015 has softened this priority by adding "protecting justice [and] human rights" to this objective (art. 2). See also Nicholson and Pham, "Roots and Routes," 224–54. For Soviet influence on Vietnamese criminal procedure, see Tim Lindsey and Pip Nicholson, *Drugs Law and Legal Practice in Southeast Asia* (Oxford: Hart, 2016); see also Peter H. Solomon, "Post-Soviet Criminal Justice: The Persistence of Distorted Neo-Inquisitorialism," *Theoretical Criminology* 19 (2015): 159–62 for a brief account of Soviet-style criminal procedure.

[97]   SRVN Constitution 2013, art. 107(1); CPC 2015, arts. 20, 40–43.

[98]   Lindsey and Nicholson, *Drugs Law and Legal Practice*, 250–1; Nicholson and Pham, "Roots and Routes," 247–8.

dominating trials, judgments (particularly in serious or sensitive cases) are subject to influence and/or negotiation with the procuracy.[99]

A major characteristic of this system is the enormous and discretionary police powers. This is demonstrated in the common saying by Vietnamese legal officers: "*án tại hồ sơ*," suggesting that judges decide cases in accordance with the case files (*hồ sơ vụ án*) developed by investigators (police).[100] While technically the procuracy is supposed to supervise the investigation phase,[101] this responsibility is reportedly not discharged effectively.[102] Additionally, procedural safeguards for defendants' rights are weak – as exemplified by: the inferior position of lawyers; the inadequate recognition of the right to silence and the right to counsel; and the absence of effective mechanisms to prevent torture.[103] Defense counsel have limited access to defendants and case files, and a limited role in the collection of evidence.[104] This has left the police with substantially unchecked power and wide discretions with regard to evidence, including its inclusion, exclusion, or manipulation.[105] The courts are given the power to return files to clarify evidential issues, a power which has been unchecked, and is alleged to have been abused.[106]

---

[99] Lindsey and Nicholson, *Drugs Law and Legal Practice*, 250–1; Nicholson and Pham, "Roots and Routes," 247–9.

[100] Huy Anh, "Toà bị "ép" xử ... theo hồ sơ?" [Courts Are "Forced" to Decide ... in Accordance with Case Files?], *Pháp luật Việt Nam*, October 28, 2014, http://baophapluat.vn/thoi-su/toa-bi-ep-xu-theo-ho-so-200042.html; Lindsey and Nicholson, *Drugs Law and Legal Practice*, 255–6. Interviews with Lawyers L3–L19, L21, and Lawyers–Former Judges LJ1–LJ2 strongly confirm this practice. See also interviews with Judges J1–J3, People's Assessors PA1–PA3, and Procurators P1–P2 demonstrating the practice to varying degrees.

[101] CPC 2015, arts. 20, 40–43.

[102] NA Standing Committee, *Báo cáo số 870/BC-UBTVQH13* [Report 870/BC-UBTVQH13], 2015, 13–15; interviews with Judge J2, Lawyers L11, L14, and Lawyers–Former Judges LJ1–LJ2.

[103] Interviews with Judges J1 and J3, Lawyers L3, L4, L7, L9–L11, L13–L17, L19, Lawyer–Former Judge LJ2, People's Assessor PA1–PA4, and Procurator P2; UNDP, *Report on the Right to Counsel in Criminal Law and Practice in Vietnam* (Hanoi: UNDP, 2012), 35–80. See also generally CPC 1988, CPC 2003, and CPC 2015. The police, for example, are not obliged to give a *Miranda*-style warning, and permit private meetings between defendants and their lawyers. And lawyers are participants, equal in status to their clients (Lindsey and Nicholson, *Drugs Law and Legal Practice*, 252–3).

[104] Interviews with Investigator I, Judge J4, Lawyers L1–L4, L7, L9–L11, L13–L17, L19, Lawyer–Former Judge LJ2, People' Assessors PA1–PA2, and Procurator P1; UNDP, *Report*, 35–80.

[105] Lindsey and Nicholson, *Drugs Law and Legal Practice*, 250–1.

[106] Interviews with Judges J3–J4, Lawyers L1, L3, L9–L11, L14, L19, Lawyer–Former Judge LJ2, and People's Assessors PA2–PA3; Lindsey and Nicholson, *Drugs Law and Legal Practice*, 250–1; NA Standing Committee, *Báo cáo số 870/BC-UBTVQH13*, 9.

Courts, therefore, largely feature as an instrument of the party-state in criminal cases. This is evident in the prevalence of formalistic trials that offer limited opportunities for contestation of evidence and legal argument.[107] Significantly, courts often hesitate to act against investigation bodies and procuracies,[108] due to the powerful position of the police in the party-state[109] and subordination to procuratorial supervision, despite reforms.[110] In addition, there is a well-established practice of cooperation between the three institutions.[111] This practice has roots in Marxist–Leninist political–legal principles, including party supremacy, democratic centralism, unity of power, and socialist legality, which promote cooperation between state bodies.[112] Further, courts, procuracies, and investigation bodies have a shared responsibility to discover crime and protect the public and state interests.[113] Therefore, when a court finds the indictment of the procuracy unconvincing, the court often returns the case file to the procuracy for supplementary investigation rather than declaring the defendant innocent.[114]

Defense counsel have a limited role in this Soviet-style criminal justice system. They have faced substantial difficulties in communicating with their clients, accessing case files, participating in the activities of investigation bodies and in submitting evidence on their own initiative.[115] The 2015 Criminal Procedure Code (CPC), which came

[107] Interviews with Judges J1–J3, Lawyers L3–L19, L21, Lawyers–Former Judges LJ1–LJ2, People's Assessors PA1–PA3, and Procurators P1–P2; Lindsey and Nicholson, *Drugs Law and Legal Practice*, 255–8.

[108] Interviews with Judge J3, Lawyers L3, L5, L11, L14, Lawyer–Former Judge LJ2, and People's Assessors PA1–PA3; Nicholson and Pham, "Roots and Routes," 236–237, 247–8. Nicholson and Pham also note that courts have become increasingly independent from procuracies.

[109] Interviews with Lawyers L11, L14.

[110] Interview with Lawyer L14; Nicholson and Pham, "Roots and Routes," 224–4.

[111] Lindsey and Nicholson, *Drugs Law and Legal Practice*, 250–2; Nicholson and Pham, "Roots and Routes," 252–4.

[112] See Nicholson and Pham, "Roots and Routes," 224–4 for discussion of the impact of democratic centralism and socialist legality on court–procuracy relations.

[113] See CPC 2015, arts. 2, 6.

[114] Interviews with Judge J3, Lawyers L3, L11, L14, Lawyer–Former Judge LJ2, and People's Assessor PA2; Lindsey and Nicholson, *Drugs Law and Legal Practice*, 250–1.

[115] Interviews with Investigator I, Judge J4, Lawyers L1–L4, L7, L9–L11, L13–L17, L19, Lawyer–Former Judge LJ2, People' Assessors PA1–PA2, and Procurator P1; UNDP, *Report*, 35–40; Lindsey and Nicholson, *Drugs Law and Legal Practice*, 239–42.

into effect in January 2018, aimed to reduce these difficulties,[116] but its impact remains to be seen. Formalistic trials substantially prevent lawyers from contesting the evidence and the position of the procuracy at trials.[117] In part, these problems have stemmed from legal short-comings, like inadequate recognition of the right to counsel; cumber-some and opaque procedures; lawyers' limited power to collect evidence and their inferiority to investigators, procurators, and judges; and the absence of the presumption of innocence (at least until 2017).[118] The implementation of developments in criminal procedures has also been weak due to: political control over criminal justice institutions; the discretionary and relatively unchecked power of legal institutions; incapable legal officers; corruption and manipulation of law; lack of independence and professionalism by lawyers; and unfamiliarity with new laws.[119]

Vietnamese criminal procedure, therefore, reflects a high degree of accusatorial bias, uncontrolled and arbitrary power, and weak protection of due process. Unsurprisingly, wrongful convictions have been and remain a major problem of the Vietnamese criminal justice system. Vietnamese criminal lawyers widely comment on these challenges.[120] The problem of wrongful conviction has also been reported extensively in state-controlled newspapers[121] and acknowledged in party-state documents.[122]

[116] Supreme People's Procuracy, *Tờ trình 23/TTr-VKSTC-V8 về ·dự án Bộ luật tố tụng hình sự (sửa đổ i)* [Submission Paper No. 23/TTr-VKSTC-V8 regarding the Revised Criminal Procedure Bill], 2014, 10–12; see also CPC 2015, chs. V, VI.

[117] Interviews with Judge J4, Lawyers L3–L19, L21, Lawyers–Former Judges LJ1–LJ2, and People's Assessors PA1–PA2.

[118] Lindsey and Nicholson, *Drugs Law and Legal Practice*, 199–299; UNDP, *Report*, 35–80. See also generally CPC 1988; CPC 2003; and CPC 2015.

[119] Interviews with Judges J1–J4, Lawyers L1–L21, Lawyers–Former Judges LJ1–LJ2, People's Assessors PA1–PA4, and Procurators P1–P2; Lindsey and Nicholson, *Drugs Law and Legal Practice*, 199–299; UNDP, *Report*, 27–98.

[120] Interviews with Lawyers L1, L3–L21.

[121] For example, the online version of *Thanh Niên* – a popular Vietnamese newspaper – contains 340 articles from February 3, 2012 to January 29, 2019 having the keyword "*oan sai*" (wrongful conviction). See Thanh Niên, "Từ khoá: oan sai" [Keyword: Wrongful Conviction], https://thanhnien.vn/tin-tuc/oan-sai.html

[122] CPV, *Nghị quyết 08-NQ/TW về ·một số nhiệm vụ trong tâm công tác tư pháp trong thời gian tới* [Resolution No. 08-NQ/TW on Major Tasks of the Judicial Work in the Forthcoming Period], 2002 ['Resolution 08-NQ/TW']; CPV, *Nghị quyết 49-NQ/TW về · chiến lược cải cách tư pháp đến năm 2020* [Resolution No. 49-NQ/TW on Strategies for Judicial Reforms until 2020], 2005 ['Resolution 49-NQ/TW']; NA Standing Committee, *Báo cáo số 870/BC-UBTVQH13*.

9.4.2   Judicial Reforms and Their Impact on Criminal Defense Lawyers

Along with the introduction of the doctrine of "law-based state," the CPV has initiated incremental reforms of its legal institutions, including reviving legal education and professionalism,[123] establishing administrative and economic courts, and narrowing the procuracy's functions, in the early years of *Đổi mới*.[124] Subsequently, the party set out clearer and more comprehensive reform strategies – namely, "judicial reforms" (*cải cách tư pháp*) – in Resolution 08-NQ/TW in 2002 and Resolutions 48-NQ/TW[125] and 49-NQ/TW in 2005.

In brief, judicial reforms have targeted the competence of legal institutions, including courts, procuracies, and investigation bodies.[126] This consists of increasing legal professionalism, enhancing the judicial role in guiding legal procedure, and utilizing technologies in judicial work.[127] Judicial reforms also aim to improve the transparency, accountability, and accessibility of the courts and other legal institutions,[128] as exemplified by the recent publication of judgments.[129] The CPV has, however, never demonstrated an intention to relax its control over courts (as well as other legal institutions).[130] Rather, it has aimed to develop a self-managed court system.[131]

Judicial reforms have, however, had considerable impact on the work of criminal defense lawyers. First, they have fostered the development of

---

[123] Pip Nicholson and Do Hai Ha, "Vietnam: From Cadres to a 'Managed' Profession," in Richard L. Abel et al. (eds.), *Lawyers in 21st-Century Societies* (Oxford: Hart, 2020), 855–73.

[124] Nicholson and Pham, "Roots and Routes," 224–54; see also Sidel, *Constitution of Vietnam*.

[125] CPV, *Nghị quyết 48-NQ/TW về ʾchiến lược xây dựng và hoàn thiện hệ thống pháp luật Việt Nam đến năm 2010, định hướng đến năm 2020* [Resolution No. 48-NQ/TW on Strategies for Development and Improvement of the Vietnamese Legal System up to 2010 and Vision up to 2020], 2005 ['Resolution 48-NQ/TW'].

[126] Resolution 08-NQ/TW; Resolution 49-NQ/TW. See also Nicholson and Pham, "Roots and Routes," 224–54; Nicholson, "Renovating Courts," 528–65.

[127] Resolution 08-NQ/TW; Resolution 49-NQ/TW. See also Nicholson, "Renovating Courts," 528–65; Pip Nicholson, "Vietnamese Courts: Contemporary Interactions between Party-State and Law," in Balme and Sidel (eds.), *Vietnam's New Order*, 178–97.

[128] Resolution 08-NQ/TW; Resolution 49-NQ/TW.

[129] See Supreme People's Court, *Trang thông tin điện tử công bố bản án, quyết định của Toà án* [Website for Publication of Court Judgments and Decisions], congbobanan .toaan.gov.vn

[130] Resolution 08-NQ/TW, Part II.A.1; Resolution 49-NQ/TW Part I.2.1. See also Nicholson, "Renovating Courts," 528–65.

[131] Ibid.

the legal profession generally. The 2006 Law on Lawyers and its 2012 successor relaxed requirements regarding admission to bar associations and incorporation of legal businesses.[132] These changes have contributed to a remarkable growth in the number of lawyers in recent decades.[133] The 2006 Law on Lawyers also established a stronger basis and more autonomy for lawyers' associations, including the Vietnam Bar Federation (VBF) founded in 2009.[134] Although these associations are tightly controlled by the party-state, they have served as a sanctioned channel for dialogue between lawyers and the party-state.[135] In fact, the VBF was an influential voice in the 2015 criminal procedure reforms.[136]

Judicial reforms have also specifically targeted the criminal justice system, including the problem of wrongful convictions.[137] Resolution 48-NQ/TW recommended the following:

> [To undertake] bold reforms of judicial proceedings with a view to [enhancing their] democracy, equality, publicity, transparency [and] sufficiency while [concurrently] guaranteeing the efficiency of and people's supervision over judicial activities; [and] to ensure the quality of debates at trials, regard the result of such debates as important grounds for court decisions [and] consider this the key step to improve the quality of judicial activities.[138]

Resolution 49-NQ/TW specifically refers to the role of lawyers in court proceedings, suggesting that the party-state "perfect mechanisms for the effective role of lawyers in debates at trials while simultaneously clearly setting out their responsibilities."[139] As a result, at least aspirationally, and while remaining subordinate to party control,[140] lawyers have been ceded a greater role in criminal proceedings. More particularly, incremental reforms of criminal procedure in 2003 and 2015 have expanded defendants' right to access a lawyer and the rights of defense counsel to access their

---

[132] Nicholson and Do, "Vietnam: From Cadres to a 'Managed' Profession," 858.
[133] Ibid.
[134] Ibid. See also Mark Sidel, *Law and Society in Vietnam* (Cambridge, UK: Cambridge University Press, 2008), 166–194.
[135] Pip Nicholson, "Access to Justice in Vietnam: State Supply–Private Distrust," in John Gillespie and Albert Chen (eds.), *Legal Reforms in China and Vietnam: A Comparison of Asian Communist Regimes* (New York: Routledge, 2010), 188–216; Nicholson and Do, "Vietnam: From Cadres to a 'Managed' Profession," 867–9.
[136] Nicholson and Do, "Vietnam: From Cadres to a 'Managed' Profession," 867.
[137] Resolution 08-NQ/TW; Resolution 48-NQ/TW; Resolution 49-NQ/TW.
[138] Resolution 48-NQ/TW, Part II.1.5.
[139] Resolution 49-NQ/TW, Part II.2.3.
[140] Ibid. Lawyers remain considered institutions supplementary to courts, procuracies, and investigations bodies.

clients and case files, participate in interrogation and other investigation activities, including the collection of evidence.[141] Procedural reforms have also enabled lawyers to debate procurators at trials, albeit they remain inferior to criminal justice officers.[142] Considerable evidence demonstrates the weak enforcement of these reforms, at least until recently.[143] Nevertheless, judicial reforms have created a greater space for criminal lawyers to negotiate with the party-state in individual cases as well as when debating criminal justice reforms.[144]

9.4.3   The Activism of Lawyers and Wrongful Convictions

Lawyers have been activist on the issue of wrongful conviction since the failing was acknowledged by party documents. In 2004, a group of eight lawyers in Hanoi initiated a project, For-Justice (*Vì Công lý*), which aimed to collect and communicate concerns of lawyers to the party-state in cases involving serious errors made by criminal justice bodies.[145] The project received support from several legal practitioners, scholars, and retired officials, including a former chief justice of the Supreme People's Court.[146] The Hanoi Bar Association, however, condemned these activities as unlawful and requested the group to cease their activities.[147] The Bar president publicly warned that lawyers participating in this project risked disciplinary action, including removal from the bar roll.[148]

The For-Justice group were involved in a number of cases.[149] In a famous case, the "cashew farm case" (*vụ án vườn điều*), lawyer Trần

---

[141] See CPC 2003 particularly chs. IV, V, X; CPC 2015, particularly chs. V, VI, XI; cf. CPC 1988 particularly chs. 3, 4, 9.

[142] See CPC 2003, ch. XXI; CPC 2015, ch. XXI(V); cf. CPC 1988, ch. 20. Lindsey and Nicholson, *Drugs Law and Legal Practice*, 252–3.

[143] Interviews with Investigator I, Judges J1, J3–J4, Lawyers L2, L6–L14, L16–L21, Lawyer–Former Judge LJ2, and People's Assessors PA1–PA3. See also Lindsey and Nicholson, *Drugs Law and Legal Practice*, 252–53; UNDP, *Report*, 35–80.

[144] Sidel, *Law and Society in Vietnam*, 166–94; Nicholson, "Access to Justice in Vietnam," 188–216.

[145] Anh Thư, "Việc ra đời nhóm sáng kiến 'Vì công lý' có vi phạm pháp luật?" [Is the Emergence of the "For-Justice" Initiative Group Unlawful?], *VnExpress*, May 7, 2004, https://vnexpress.net/phap-luat/viec-ra-doi-nhom-sang-kien-vi-cong-ly-co-vi-pham-phap-luat-2005157.html

[146] Ibid.; Interviews with Lawyers L11, L14, L20.

[147] Sidel, *Law and Society in Vietnam*, 188; Anh, "Việc ra đời nhóm sáng kiến 'Vì công lý' có vi phạm pháp luật?"

[148] Anh, "Việc ra đời nhóm sáng kiến 'Vì công lý' có vi phạm pháp luật?"

[149] Interviews with Lawyers L11, L14, L20.

Vũ Hải – the leader of the group – and two colleagues succeeded in clearing seven people from being wrongfully convicted of murder.[150] Despite this, the group soon had to reduce their activities owing to pressure from the Hanoi Bar and other difficulties, including lack of resources, procedural impediments, and resistance from criminal justice authorities.[151] The lawyers involved in the cashew farm case, for example, faced strong pressure, threats of disciplinary action, and prosecution.[152]

The activism of lawyers was then picked up in individual cases, albeit with rare success.[153] In general, lawyers' efforts to overturn wrongful convictions were largely disregarded by criminal justice authorities.[154] During this time, lawyers became increasingly vocal about impediments to their defense work in the state media and other sanctioned channels.[155]

From 2013, bolder advocacy, particularly after the case of Nguyễn Thanh Chấn, commenced.[156] Whether this is a legacy of constitutional reformism needs separate investigation, but it is possible. Chấn was sentenced to life imprisonment for murder and robbery.[157] Subsequently, his family obtained evidence showing that he was innocent and that the crime had been committed by another, forcing the court to review the case and eventually clear him of all charges.[158] Chấn had by this stage spent ten years in prison.[159] The case was extensively reported

[150] Ibid. See also *VnExpress*, "Vụ án vườn điều" [Cashew Farm Case], accessed February 3, 2019, https://vnexpress.net/vu-an-vuon-dieu/topic-11750.html containing twenty-six articles reporting this case from June 26, 2001 to November 4, 2014.

[151] Interview with Lawyer L20.

[152] Interviews with Lawyers L11, L15; Phan Thương, "Luật sư Trần Vũ Hải kể hành trình giải oan Huỳnh Văn Nén" [Lawyer Trần Vũ Hải Described the Road to Clear Huỳnh Văn Nén's Criminal Charges], *Thanh Niên*, December 2, 2015, https://thanhnien.vn/thoi-su/luat-su-tran-vu-hai-ke-hanh-trinh-giai-oan-huynh-van-nen-641217.html

[153] Interviews with Lawyers L11, L14, L15, L19, and Lawyer–Former Judge LJ2.

[154] Ibid.

[155] See, e.g., Hoàng Khuê, "Những 'rào cản' với luật sư trong tố tụng" [Impediments to Lawyers in Court Proceedings], *VnExpress*, October 8, 2009, https://vnexpress.net/phap-luat/nhung-rao-can-voi-luat-su-trong-to-tung-2146351.html; Đức Minh and Thanh Tú, "Nâng cao vị thế luật sư" [Improving Lawyers' Position], *Pháp luật TPHCM*, July 8, 2011, http://plo.vn/plo/nang-cao-vi-the-luat-su-bai-2-vat-va-chuyen-bao-chua-117873.html

[156] Media reports on this case are voluminous. *VnExpress* alone has ninety-one articles between November 4, 2013 and June 27, 2017 in this regard. See *VnExpress*, "Vụ Nguyễn Thanh Chấn kêu oan" [Nguyễn Thanh Chấn Claims Innocent], accessed February 3, 2019, https://vnexpress.net/topic/vu-nguyen-thanh-chan-keu-oan-17509-p1

[157] Ibid.

[158] Ibid.

[159] Ibid.

in popular newspapers.[160] Journalists recounted, in painstaking detail, the devastating physical, psychological, and economic suffering of Chấn and his family.[161] They also proved the failure of criminal justice authorities, including using extortion and torture, manipulating evidence, cover-ups, and ignoring legal advocates.[162] The case triggered strong criticism and distrust of the criminal justice system from the public, as well as party-state actors, including the NA.[163]

Many lawyers utilized Chấn's case to push for redress of wrongs in other cases. Huỳnh Văn Nén, for example, was serving a life sentence for murder and robbery.[164] While Chấn was in the spotlight, Nén's lawyers and family actively lobbied NA delegates, organized a press conference, and shared the details of his case on Facebook.[165] In another example, Hàn Đức Long, a prisoner on death row accused of murder and rape, had his lawyer send complaints to central party-state organizations.[166] His lawyers argued in newspapers, on Facebook, and blogged that he was innocent.[167] In both cases, lawyers succeeded in drawing support from the public and the central party-state and pressed the authorities to overturn wrongful decisions. This support also enabled lawyers to successfully negotiate for extraordinarily high compensation for Chấn and Nén,[168] setting precedents for the reversal of wrong court decisions and compensation.

---

[160] These newspapers include *VnExpress, Thanh Niên, Tuổi Trẻ, Dân Trí*, to name a few.

[161] See *VnExpress*, "Vụ Nguyễn Thanh Chấn kêu oan."

[162] Ibid.

[163] Ibid.

[164] See Thanh Niên, "Từ khoá: Huỳnh Văn Nén" [Keyword: Huỳnh Văn Nén], accessed February 3, 2019, https://thanhnien.vn/tin-tuc/huynh-van-nen.html containing sixty-six articles relative to this case from November 3, 2014 to September 14, 2018.

[165] Interviews with Lawyers L11 and L20; Phan, "Luật sư Trần Vũ Hải kể hành trình giải oan Huỳnh Văn Nén." See also Nguyễn Thận's Facebook site, https://www.facebook.com /nthan1908, for hundreds of posts on this case in 2014–17. Mr. Thận spent seventeen years to assist Huỳnh Văn Nén and his family.

[166] See Ngô Ngọc Trai, "Án oan Hàn Đức Long" [The Case of Wrongfully Convicted Hàn Đức Long], https://ngongoctrai.com/danh-muc/an-oan-han-duc-long containing a series of twenty-seven memoirs chronicling how Lawyer Ngô Ngọc Trai assisted his client, Hàn Đức Long.

[167] Ibid. See also Ngô Ngọc Trai's Facebook site, www.facebook.com/ngongoctrai.ngo, for hundreds of posts regarding Long's case in 2014–16. Many of these posts were to share Trai's commentaries in domestic and international newspapers.

[168] Chấn, and Nén were compensated VND7.2 and VND10 billion (roughly USD311,000 and USD432,000) respectively. Before their cases, wrongfully convicted people were usually compensated up to approximately VND1 billion (USD 43,200). Interview with Lawyer–Former Judge LJ2.

As a result of the cases of Nguyễn Thanh Chấn, Huỳnh Văn Nén, and Hàn Đức Long, wrongful convictions are now an issue that attracts a lot of public attention in state and social media.[169] In addition, the problem has received greater attention from the central authorities, especially the NA. NA delegates have periodically spoken out about particular cases allegedly involving wrongful conviction and advocated for reforms to the criminal justice system.[170] In 2014, the NA established a taskforce to investigate "wrongful convictions" and in 2015 spent a day-long plenary session discussing the issue.[171] These developments have enabled lawyers to communicate their concerns about wrongful conviction more effectively.

Lawyers now regularly utilize the press, social networks, and central party-state communication channels to pressure criminal justice authorities.[172] The outcomes of these strategies are various and remain modest.[173] Yet, criminal lawyers suggest that they are now more successful in challenging wrongful decisions than in the past.[174] Individual lawyers and their organizations, including the VBF, have also employed similar strategies to press for systemic change.[175] Lawyer advocacy contributed to the 2015 reforms of the CPC, including: recognition of the right to silence; reduction of procedural impediments for the participation of defense counsel in investigation; and the compulsory use of video recording in interrogation.[176] While these reforms may take a while to be fully implemented, they signal changes to the assumed instrumentalism of the criminal justice system.

[169] Interviews with Lawyers L6 and L14, and Lawyer–Former Judge LJ 2. See also, e.g., Thanh Niên, "Từ khoá: oan sai."

[170] See, eg, NA Standing Committee, *Báo cáo 870/BC-UBTVQH13*; Nguyễn Hưng, "Đại biểu Quốc hội đề nghị làm rõ việc ép cung ông Chấn" [NA Delegate Request to Verify the Extortion of Mr. Chấn], *VnExpress*, November 8, 2013, https://vnexpress.net/thoi-su/dai-bieu-quoc-hoi-de-nghi-lam-ro-viec-ep-cung-ong-chan-2907153.html

[171] NA Office, *Thông cáo 13 Kỳ họp thứ 9, Quốc hội khoá XIII* [Notice No. 13 of the 9th Session of the 13th Tenure of the National Assembly] http://quochoi.vn/hoatdongcua quochoi/cackyhopquochoi/quochoikhoaXIII/kyhopthuchin/Pages/thong-cao.aspx? ItemID=29626; NA Standing Committee, *Báo cáo 870/BC-UBTVQH13*.

[172] Interviews with Lawyers L6–L21. See also Thanh Niên, "Từ khoá: oan sai" for numerous examples.

[173] Interviews with Lawyers L6–L21.

[174] Interviews with Lawyers L6, L9, L11, L14, L16–L17, L20–L21, and Lawyer–Former Judge LJ2.

[175] Interviews with Lawyers L4, L20–L21, and Lawyer–Former Judge LJ2; Nicholson and Do, "Vietnam: From Cadres to a 'Managed' Profession," 867–9. See also, e.g., *VnExpress*, "Quyền im lặng" [Right to Silence], https://vnexpress.net/topic/quyen-im-lang-21140 for several examples.

[176] Interview with Lawyer–Former Judge LJ2; Nicholson and Do, "Vietnam: From Cadres to a 'Managed' Profession," 867. See also *VnExpress*, "Quyền im lặng."

While affording more contestation by criminal lawyers, the party-state continues to control the emergent deliberative space. Interviews with lawyers and journalists suggest that state-sponsored newspapers have been directed to maintain moderate coverage of wrongful conviction issues.[177] Admission of errors is seen to enhance the legitimacy and performance of the CPV and its courts, but the CPV is worried that extensive coverage may be counterproductive.[178] The party-led NA is also constrained in its comments. This was illustrated vividly by the robust political attack recently initiated by the Ministry of Public Security against delegate Lưu Bình Nhưỡng following his criticism of police investigators.[179] Further, the party-state has targeted newly emergent groups of activist lawyers, such as "Defense Counsel" (*Hội đồng Bào chữa*), "Serving Justice" (*Phục vụ Công lý*), and the "Nine Lawyers' Channel" (*Kênh 9 Luật sư*), which aim to assist wrongfully convicted persons and other vulnerable people.[180] Because of party-state targeting, these groups have recently retreated.[181]

In short, constitutional and criminal justice reforms have opened a greater space for communication and negotiation between criminal lawyers and the party-state. Arguably, the party-state's acknowledgment of wrongful conviction and its promise of an increased role for lawyers in trials have provided advocates with a shield behind which they can be activist. As already seen, such contestation and negotiations have not only occurred in the courtroom. Dialogue between criminal lawyers and the party-state has also taken place in other state-controlled channels, such as: complaints and petitions submitted to party-state organizations; parliamentary forums; lawyers' organizations; and state-sponsored and social media.

9.5 Ambiguous Legality

The "socialist law-based state" promises a greater reliance on law. The possibility of using law to constrain arbitrary power and enforce human

---

[177] Interviews with Lawyer L14, Lawyer–Former Judge LJ2, and Reporter R.

[178] Ibid.

[179] "Đảng ủy Công an Trung ương kiến nghị Đảng đoàn Quốc hội xem xét sự việc của đại biểu Lưu Bình Nhưỡng" [The Central Party Committee of the Police Suggest that the NA's Party Group Consider the Incident of Delegate Lưu Bình Nhưỡng], *An ninh Thủ đô*, November 7, 2018, https://anninhthudo.vn/chinh-tri-xa-hoi/dang-uy-cong-an-trung-uong-kien-nghi-dang-doan-quoc-hoi-xem-xet-su-viec-cua-dai-bieu-luu-binh-nhuong/789071.antd

[180] Interviews with Lawyers L9–L10, L12–L15, L17–L21. See also Nicholson and Do, "Vietnam: From Cadres to a 'Managed' Profession," 872–3.

[181] Interviews with Lawyers L9–L10, L12–L15, L17–L21.

rights is also increasing. However, the persistence of the class-based and instrumental conception of law signifies a weak normative commitment to legality by the party-state.

Notwithstanding this, post-*Đổi mới* law reforms have produced a narrow, albeit porous, space that activists and reformists periodically exploit to advance aspects of the rule of law. The Vietnamese deliberative authoritarian state has both allowed debate and been shaped by debates. Further, contemporary lawyers strategically use legality to advance reformist discourse. Protesting wrongful conviction and constitutional debate are instances of this. Arguably, this reflects a nascent commitment by the party-state to restraining the arbitrary power of its agencies and protecting citizens' rights, particularly when this is not a threat to, but rather a positive feature of party supremacy and political stability. The boundaries and ultimate trajectory of this space have, however, never been clearly defined. Rather, they are changeable and tightened at the discretion of the party-state, particularly when it perceives a threat to regime survival.

Appendix: List of Interviews

Interviewee	Date	Location
Investigator I	May 23, 2012	Ho Chi Minh City
	May 29, 2012	
Judge J1	May 27, 2012	Ho Chi Minh City
Judge J2	May 27, 2012	Ho Chi Minh City
	June 5, 2012	
Judge J3	August 15, 2012	Ho Chi Minh City
Judge J4	August 16, 2012	Ho Chi Minh City
Lawyer L1	June 5, 2012	Ho Chi Minh City
Lawyer L2	June 8, 2012	Ho Chi Minh City
Lawyer L3	August 16, 2012	Ho Chi Minh City
Lawyer L4	August 17, 2012	Ho Chi Minh City
Lawyer L5	August 27, 2012	Ho Chi Minh City
Lawyer L6	October 4, 2018	Ho Chi Minh City
Lawyer L7	October 8, 2018	Ho Chi Minh City
Lawyer L8	October 9, 2018	Ho Chi Minh City
Lawyer L9	October 9, 2018	Ho Chi Minh City
Lawyer L10	October 10, 2018	Ho Chi Minh City
Lawyer L11	October 12, 2018	Ho Chi Minh City
	October 13, 2018	
Lawyer L12	October 16, 2018	Ho Chi Minh City
Lawyer L13	October 18, 2018	Ho Chi Minh City
Lawyer L14	October 19, 2018	Ho Chi Minh City
	October 27, 2018	
Lawyer L15	October 21, 2018	Ho Chi Minh City
Lawyer L16	October 24, 2018	Ho Chi Minh City
Lawyer L17	October 24, 2018	Ho Chi Minh City
Lawyer L18	October 31, 2018	Ho Chi Minh City
Lawyer L19	October 31, 2018	Ho Chi Minh City
Lawyer L20	November 1, 2018	Hanoi
	November 3, 2018	
Lawyer L21	November 2, 2018	Hanoi
Lawyer–Former Judge LJ 1	May 25, 2012	Ho Chi Minh City
Lawyer–Former Judge LJ 2	October 20, 2018	Dong Nai

(*cont.*)

(*cont.*)

Interviewee	Date	Location
People's Assessor PA1	August 10, 2012	Ho Chi Minh City
People's Assessor PA2	August 13, 2012	Binh Duong
People's Assessor PA3	August 14, 2012	Ho Chi Minh City
People's Assessor PA4	August 20, 2012	Ho Chi Minh City
Procurator P1	May 26, 2012	Ho Chi Minh City
Procurator P2	June 4, 2012	Ho Chi Minh City
Reporter R	October 12, 2018	Ho Chi Minh City

PART III

Authoritarian Legality in Transition

Authoritarian-Era Foundations for
the Transition to Democracy

Preserving Constitutionalism by Changing the Constitution

A Revisit and Defense of the *Chng Suan Tze* Period

JIANLIN CHEN

10.1 Introduction

When confronted in the late 1980s with a judicial decision in *Chng Suan Tze* v. *Minister for Home Affairs*[1] that sought to expand the scope of judicial review over the executive's power to detain individuals without trial, the Singapore government rapidly enacted statutory and constitutional amendments that specifically overturned that judicial decision ("*Chng Suan Tze* episode"). The *Chng Suan Tze* episode is perhaps the most iconic, notorious, and universally examined episode in scholarly discussion regarding the rule of law in Singapore. The episode is perceived as epitomizing the ruling regime's approach to governance, and has been roundly criticized by numerous scholars and commentators.

This chapter revisits the *Chng Suan Tze* episode and argues that the criticisms levied on the reactions of the Singapore government are misplaced. As compared to sanctions against judges and direct interferences with the judiciary by other authoritarian regimes in response to adverse judicial outcomes, the utilization of statutory and constitutional amendments to negate objectionable judicial decisions poses the least harm to the integrity and independence of the judicial institution. More fundamentally, the otherwise legitimate objections to authoritarianism should not distract from the fact that political mobilization to effect statutory and constitutional amendments is precisely the proper action that political actors should undertake in a liberal democracy that duly respects

[1] *Chng Suan Tze* v. *Minister for Home Affairs* [1988] 2 SLR(R) 525.

constitutionalism/rule of law. This chapter argues that whether in terms of maintaining the best possible authoritarian rule from the perspective of the authoritarian regime, or facilitating the eventual transition to the ideal of liberal-democratic constitutionalism, the *Chng Suan Tze* episode should be quietly celebrated.

This chapter is organized into six sections: Section 10.2 presents the *Chng Suan Tze* episode; Section 10.3 presents the scholarly criticisms and responses to the episode; Section 10.4 explains how the bulk of existing literature on the *Chng Suan Tze* episode failed to take proper account of how the authoritarian regime is inevitably motivated by self-preservation, and that it is unrealistic and unhelpful to expect the authoritarian regime to remain uninvolved during the perceived judicial weakening of its control. Section 10.5 presents the normative defense of the *Chng Suan Tze* episode. Section 10.6 concludes.

10.2   The Episode

A copious amount of ink has been spilled on the *Chng Suan Tze* episode, whether in the academic literature or the popular press. This is not surprising, since the *Chng Suan Tze* episode easily captures scholarly and public imagination with its combination of all the notorious features of Singapore governance – detention without trial under the Internal Security Act (ISA), overzealous government suppression of social actions and civil society, and the political dominance facilitating constitutional amendment at will. A brief outline here will suffice, given that extensive analysis on both the underlying activities and the legal issues have been amply provided by other scholars.[2]

The incident was officially kicked off by Operation Spectrum in mid-1987, whereby pursuant to the ISA, the Internal Security Department of the Ministry of Home Affairs arrested twenty-two individuals over their involvement in a "Marxist conspiracy to subvert and destabilize the country to establish a Marxist state."[3] The factual basis of this allegation

---

[2] See Li-ann Thio, "Lex Rex or Rex Lex? Competing Conceptions of the Rule of Law in Singapore," *UCLA Pacific Basin Law Journal* 20(1) (2002): 1, 58–63; Jack Tsen-Ta Lee, "Shall the Twain Never Meet? Competing Narratives and Discourses of the Rule of Law in Singapore," *Singapore Journal of Legal Studies* (2012): 289, 307–13; Jothie Rajah, *Authoritarian Rule of Law: Legislation, Discourse and Legitimacy in Singapore* (Cambridge: Cambridge University Press, 2012), 205–12 and 226–39.
[3] *Chng Suan Tze* v. *Minister for Home Affairs*, 530.

is suspect, to say the least, and commentators have typically opined that the detained individuals were at best engaging in social activism inspired by Catholic liberation theology.[4] Four of the arrested persons, Chng Suan Tze, Kevin de Souza, Teo Soh Lung, and Wong Souk Yee, sought judicial review of their detention, culminating in the landmark Court of Appeal decision *Chng Suan Tze* v. *Minister for Home Affairs* in December 1988.[5]

The Court of Appeal reversed the lower court dismissal of the appellants' habeas corpus application. The Court's ratio is a narrow technical point. The detention order was essentially quashed as invalid because it was signed by the Permanent Secretary to the Minister for Home Affairs rather than by the Minister for Home Affairs himself as required by the ISA.[6] This sufficed to justify the Court's order for the release of the appellants. Nonetheless, the Court went on to deliver a lengthy *obiter dictum* as to the reviewability of the exercise of discretion under the ISA. The Court expressly rejected the subjective test applied in the 1971 Singapore High Court case of *Lee Mau Seng* v. *Minister for Home Affairs*[7] that excluded judicial inquiry into whether there were sufficient grounds to justify the detention orders or even whether the executive acted in bad faith. Rather, the Court of Appeal, having extensively reviewed case law developments in the United Kingdom and other commonwealth jurisdictions, chose to adopt the objective test whereby for the ISA, there would be judicial review on the grounds of "illegality, irrationality or procedural impropriety."[8] It was telling that the Court of Appeal buttressed this jurisprudential move not only with common law doctrinal reasoning, but with the broader rule of law principle that "[a]ll power has legal limits and the rule of law demands that the courts should be able to examine the exercise of discretionary power," and thus "the notion of a subjective or unfettered discretion is contrary to the rule of law."[9]

---

[4] See e.g. Mark Tushnet, "Authoritarian Constitutionalism," *Cornell Law Review* 100(2) (2015): 391, 400; Rajah, *Authoritarian Rule of Law*, 226–41; Lee, "Competing Narratives," 307.

[5] *Chng Suan Tze* v. *Minister for Home Affairs*.

[6] The rationale is that only the minister can provide admissible evidence that the president is satisfied that the detention order is warranted. *Chng Suan Tze* v. *Minister for Home Affairs*, 537–42.

[7] *Lee Mau Seng* v. *Minister for Home Affairs* [1971–3] SLR(R) 135.

[8] *Chng Suan Tze* v. *Minister for Home Affairs*, 558–64.

[9] Ibid., 553.

The *Chng Suan Tze* decision did not prevent the redetention of the appellants, and indeed after they were released on the afternoon of the decision, they enjoyed a good five minutes of "freedom" before being sent back to the detention center upon presentation of a duly signed detention order.[10] It is also worth noting that judicial review on the grounds of "illegality, irrationality or procedural impropriety" still presents a very high threshold for applicants,[11] especially with the continued rejection of proportionality review in Singapore.[12] Nonetheless, the Singapore Parliament passed legislative amendments to the ISA to specifically reverse the *Chng Suan Tze* decision and reinstate the subjective test.[13] At the same time, a constitutional amendment was also enacted in 1989 to expressly confer on Parliament the power to legislatively determine the scope of judicial review for national security legislations, and to exempt such legislations from challenge under the constitutional right of equality and right against retrospective criminal sanctions.[14] The exemption from the constitutional prohibitions of retrospective criminal sanctions is particularly salient and ensured the legislative amendments to the ISA were applicable to the new detention orders served on the day of the *Chng Suan Tze* decision.

One of the original appellants, Teo Soh Lung, launched a fresh judicial challenge on the new detention orders in court, but was unsuccessful in the High Court and in the Court of Appeal, which duly applied the amended ISA and Constitution.[15] Notably, the High Court rejected the notion that the Parliament's powers to amend the Constitution were somehow inherently and implicitly limited by the prohibition against changing the "basic structure of the Constitution," and held that Parliament can make constitutional amendments with the stipulated two-thirds majority except where expressly prohibited in the case of

[10] *Teo Soh Lung* v. *Minister of Home Affairs* [1989] 1 SLR(R) 461, HC, 465.

[11] For a critical discussion about the application of this doctrine in Singapore courts, see Daniel Tan, "An Analysis of Substantive Review in Singapore Administrative Law," *Singapore Academy Law Journal* 25 (2013): 296, 298–301, and 308–9.

[12] Jolene Lin, "Administrative Law in Singapore," in Clauspeter Hill and Jochen Hoerth (eds.), *Administrative Law and Practice from South to East Asia* (Singapore: Konrad Adenauer Stiftung, 2008), 47–79, 66; Jack Tsen-Ta Lee, "According to the Spirit and Not to the Letter: Proportionality and the Singapore Constitution," *Vienna Journal on International Constitutional Law* 8 (2014): 276, 283–7.

[13] Four new provisions – sections 8A, 8B, 8C, and 8D – are added to the ISA. See *Teo Soh Lung* v. *Minister of Home Affairs* [1989], 465–7.

[14] Constitution of the Republic of Singapore (Amendment) Act 1989 (Act 1 of 1989).

[15] *Teo Soh Lung* v. *Minister of Home Affairs* [1989]; *Teo Soh Lung* v. *Minister of Home Affairs* [1990] 1 SLR(R) 347, CA.

surrender of sovereignty.[16] This essentially gave free rein to the ruling People's Action Party (PAP), given how it has always secured no less than 90 percent of parliamentary seats since Singapore's independence, even during the "watershed" electoral defeat in 2011.[17]

10.3   The Critique

The *Chng Suan Tze* episode has received widespread criticism from scholars locally and abroad, not least because the *Chng Suan Tze* decision itself has been frequently lauded as an example of the judiciary recognizing that the role of the court is to uphold the rule of law by reining in subjective or unfettered discretion by the government. Prominent constitutional scholar Li-ann Thio gave a glowing appraisal of the *Chng Suan Tze* decision as a "well-reasoned and principled judgment" and a "high water mark of judicial review."[18] This is typically echoed by other academics,[19] and, rather interestingly, by successive chief justices when giving public speeches about upholding the rule of law in Singapore.[20]

---

[16] Constitution of the Republic of Singapore (Amendment) Act 1989 (Act 1 of 1989), arts. 5 and 8.

[17] Elvin Ong and Mou Hui Tim, "Singapore's 2011 General Elections and Beyond: Beating the PAP at Its Own Game," *Asian Survey* 54(4) (2014): 749, 750–1; Stephan Ortmann, *Politics and Change in Singapore and Hong Kong: Containing Contention* (New York: Routledge, 2010), 32.

[18] Li-ann Thio, "Beyond the 'Four Walls' in an Age of Transnational Judicial Conversations: Civil Liberties, Rights Theories and Constitutional Adjudication in Malaysia and Singapore," *Columbia Journal of Asian Law* 19(2) (2006): 428, 451.

[19] See e.g. Po-Jen Yap, "Transnational Constitutionalism in the United States: Toward a Worldwide Use of Interpretive Modes of Comparative Reasoning," *University of San Francisco Law Review* 39 (2005): 999, 1039: "In vindicating the rule of law in Singapore, Chief Justice Wee appealed to transnational principles to justify the epistemological transplant into local soil. Although this decision was subsequently reversed by a constitutional amendment truncating judicial review in national security cases, *Chng Suan Tze* had laid down a groundbreaking legal precedent in Singapore for the universalist approach to adjudication to take root"; Rajah, *Authoritarian Rule of Law*, 210–11: "The [*Chng Suan Tze* litigation] showed a momentary promise of Singapore's Bench and Bar coming together to protect basic rights … The Court's words hold the promise of a collaborative legal complex mobilization, of judges uniting with lawyers to assert the 'rule of law' in the face of 'rule by law' state practices." Chan Sek Keong, one of the judges in *Chng Suan Tze* and who subsequently became chief justice, continued this appreciation about the danger of arbitrary power in subsequent decisions. Lee, "According to the Spirit," 290–1.

[20] Chan Sek Keong, "Judicial Review – From Angst to Empathy," *Singapore Academy of Law Journal* 22 (2010): 469, 472; Sundaresh Menon, "The Rule of Law: The Path to Exceptionalism," *Singapore Academy of Law Journal* 28 (2016): 413, 421–2.

10.3.1   Assault on Rule of Law

Such accolades inevitably aggravate the dismay over the subsequent reversal and the court's subdued response. The primary thrust of the critique is that the *Chng Suan Tze* episode demonstrates the absence of rule of law in Singapore. Lynette Chua considered the episode as telling evidence of "weak" judicial review in Singapore.[21] Victor Ramraj utilized the incident to highlight the difficulty courts faced in upholding constitutionalism.[22] Li-ann Thio argues that the incident contributes to the curtailing of "an 'adventurous' spirit and judicial creativity in constitutional construction" and the resulting "deferentialism to state authorities"[23] and in a separate piece of writing noted the constitutional amendment meant that "[e]ffectively, where the making of such 'special Powers [against Subversion and Emergency Powers]' laws is concerned, the Constitution is not supreme, Parliament is."[24] Jothie Rajah echoed Thio's negative characterization of *Chng Suan Tze*[25] before arguing the episode as an "effective imposition of silence [on the advocacy for the 'rule of law' by the legal profession]."[26]

Other commentators continued this line of attack with emphasis on the broader chilling effect on the judiciary. Tey Tsun Hang regarded the incident as "an overt exercise of executive control over the judiciary"[27] and argued that the ministerial statement made during the constitutional amendment "foreshadowed a marked shift in judicial reasoning and

[21] Lynette J. Chua, "Pragmatic Resistance, Law, and Social Movements in Authoritarian States: The Case of Gay Collective Action in Singapore," *Law and Society Review* 46(4) (2012): 713, 716: "Judicial review is weak; the PAP-dominated Parliament has swiftly passed constitutional and legislative amendments to overrule a court ruling that it may review executive decisions on preventive detention."
[22] Victor V. Ramraj, "Constitutional Tipping Points: Sustainable Constitutionalism in Theory and Practice," *Transnational Legal Theory* 1(2) (2010): 191, 202–4.
[23] Thio, "Transnational Judicial Conversations," 517.
[24] Thio, "Lex Rex," 59
[25] Rajah cites Thio's work when writing that the "decision has been described as conceiving of 'law' as entirely within Parliament's hands and denying the role of the courts in policing, so to speak, the content of 'law' – thereby rendering irrelevant the status of the *Constitution* as the legal text that sets substantive standards" (*Authoritarian Rule of Law*, 212).
[26] Ibid.
[27] Tey's characterization of "executive" as the primary actor of the incident seems at odds with his recognition that the "control" was effected through constitutional and legislative amendments. Tsun Hang Tey, "Judicial Internalising of Singapore's Supreme Political Ideology," *Hong Kong Law Journal* 40 (1995): 293, 299 and 300. Cf. Ross Worthington, *Governance in Singapore* (London: RoutledgeCurzon, 2003): "(T)he political executive is so autonomous that it makes the laws, not the parliament" (104).

attitudes, towards an excessive deference to the government, and its supreme political ideology."[28] Po Jen Yap observed that "the judiciary was equally shaken [as with the case of Malaysia judges being impeached and removed on trumped-up charges in 1988]" by the incident.[29]

Mark Tushnet represents the minority of scholars who are relatively sympathetic to the Singapore regime. He considers it as "authoritarian constitutionalism" (not the "abusive constitutionalism" of Hungary and Venezuela where duly enacted constitutional amendments threaten civil liberties) or "mere rule-of-law constitutionalism" (where the legal system satisfies the core requirements of publicity, prospectively, and generality, but little more in terms of political and individual freedom),[30] and argues this is due to the ruling regime's normative commitment to constitutionalism.[31] Nonetheless, even Tushnet considered the *Chng Suan Tze* episode as an example of "mere rule-of-law."[32]

10.3.2 Mere "Legislative Overruling"

It is also worth noting a related but distinct line of critique by Li-ann Thio and a few other scholars: namely, to downplay the constitutional element in the reversal, and frame the *Chng Suan Tze* episode as the legislature prevailing over the judiciary. In a 2006 piece, Thio bemoaned the "legislative overruling" of the *Chng Suan Tze* decision.[33] While she did indicate somewhere later in the article that overturning the judgment was achieved through "constitutional and statutory amendments,"[34] the relevant subheading was "Legislative Overruling of 'Activist' Decision," and categorized the overruling as "A clamp down ... swiftly ensued through legislative action."[35]

Indeed, Thio has consistently characterized the incident as "legislative overruling." In a 1997 article, she stated its introduction that the article would "consider how the Court of Appeal decision of *Chng* was

[28] Tey, "Judicial Internalising," 299–301.
[29] Po Jen Yap, "Constitutional Fig Leaves in Asia," *Washington International Law Journal* 25 (2016): 421, 422.
[30] Tushnet, "Authoritarian Constitutionalism," 448–50.
[31] Ibid., 451–60.
[32] Ibid., 419: "But, in a mere rule-of-law state, the government can fill the gap once it is brought to its attention, as indeed happened in Singapore: Parliament responded to the *Chng* decision by amending the relevant statute to make it clear that the test was a purely subjective one."
[33] Thio, "Transnational Judicial Conversations," 451.
[34] Ibid., 454.
[35] Ibid., 451.

legislatively overruled,"[36] with the subheading "Curbing *Chng*: Judicial Self Restraint versus Legislatively Imposed Restraints."[37] Again, it was only in the middle of the text where she noted that "the decision of *Chng* sufficiently discomfited Parliament for it to precipitate the legislative overruling of the case through constitutional and statutory amendments," and even then the qualifier of "legislative overruling" is reemphasized when stating that constitutional amendments were involved.[38] Such framing/labelling is understandable, given the central thrust of the piece about how the Constitution should be taken seriously by courts to safeguard citizens' fundamental liberties,[39] especially in light of the limitations of common law rights vis-à-vis constitutional rights in terms of amendment threshold (i.e. common law rights can be abridged by ordinary legislation and apply to the executive branch and not the legislature).[40] Nonetheless, the significance of the fact that the *Chng Suan Tze* decision was overruled via a duly enacted constitutional amendment was nowhere discussed in the piece.[41] Given Thio's preferred choice of framing, it is not surprising that where the episode was mentioned for a quick point, only "legislative overruling" was used without any mention of the involvement of constitutional amendment.[42]

A similar approach was undertaken by Seow Hon Tan, where she utilized the *Chng Suan Tze* incident as the flagship example of how judicial review is being whittled down by ouster clauses, and observed how the *Chng Suan Tze* decision had been "legislatively overrule[d]" by the amendment to the ISA but without mentioning the accompanying constitutional amendment that was designed to secure the constitutionality of the amendment to the ISA.[43]

---

[36] Li-ann Thio, "Trends in Constitutional Interpretation: Oppugning Ong, Awakening Arumugam?" *Singapore Journal of Legal Studies* (1997): 240.

[37] Ibid., 241.

[38] Ibid., 243.

[39] Ibid., 285–90.

[40] Ibid., 258–9.

[41] Cf. Silverstein, who observes that the courts' hands are tied, given the lack of constitutional space – especially given the ease of constitutional amendments – for an expansion of judicial role. Gordon Silverstein, "Globalization and the Rule of Law: 'A Machine that Runs of Itself.'" *International Journal of Constitutional Law* 1 (2003): 427, 442–3.

[42] See e.g. Li-ann Thio, "Implementing Human Rights in ASEAN Countries: Promises to Keep and Miles to Go Before I Sleep," *Yale Human Rights and Development Law Journal* 2 (1999): 1, 35 n. 113: "The government showed its displeasure with the decision in *Chng* by legislatively overruling it within a month."

[43] Seow Hon Tan, "The Constitution as 'Comforter' – An Assessment of the Safeguards in Singapore's Constitutional System," *Singapore Law Review* 16 (1995): 104, 136–7.

10.3.3 Neutral/Supportive

There are some scholars who sought to present the *Chng Suan Tze* episode in a more sympathetic or nuanced perspective. For example, while Chin Leng Lim recognized that the *Chng Suan Tze* episode is an "exceptional situation" resulting from a "hard case," he defended the existence of separation of powers in Singapore and argued that the episode should be assessed holistically rather than on one incident, especially since the government did not resort to constitutional or statutory amendments a decade later when confronted with another significant judicial loss.[44]

More common are scholars who argue from a realist perspective that the *Chng Suan Tze* episode is understandable and arguably excused, given the political realities of Singapore. Gordon Silverstein recognizes that the overruling of the *Chng Suan Tze* decision was achieved by the government through "[c]arefully and precisely following their constitutional rules,"[45] and observes that the reason why the Singapore courts did not manage to reach the third step of the "economic engagement-rule-of-law process" (i.e. legal doctrine developed by the judiciary to assure economic goals spill over to govern cases in the political and social realms) was due to the limited "constitutional space" the judiciary enjoys in the context where constitutional amendments can easily be secured under the existing amendment rules and the political reality of the one-party dominant state.[46] He also noted that there is "no discernible internal political demand for an expanding judicial role."[47]

---

[44] C. L. Lim, "The *Singapore Constitution and Its* Critics," *Denning Law Journal* 17(1) (2005): 63, 99–100. Lim further argues that the constitutional dimension – in the broad sense as to the institutional function under the constitutional order – of the cases should be acknowledged, and that persistent conflict between the judiciary and the other branches of government is not ideal (101–3).

[45] Silverstein, "Globalization," 439–40.

[46] Ibid., 442–3. Under the economic engagement-rule-of-law model, step one is for judges to establish judicial power in a nonthreatening context. Step two is to develop broad readings of key constitutional provisions (ibid., 437). See also Gordon Silverstein, "Singapore's Constitutionalism: A Model, But of What Sort?" *Cornell Law Review* 100 (2015): 1, 15–16.

[47] Silverstein, "Globalization," 443. This may be contrasted with the situation in Pakistan. Leveraging on the mounting social and political discontent over deteriorating living conditions arising from economic liberalization policies and government mishaps in handling a major earthquake, the then Chief Justice Iftikhar Chaudhry expanded judicial power that defied General Pervez Musharraf's military authoritarian regime and which ultimately contributed to the regime's demise (Shoaib A. Ghias, "Miscarriage of Chief Justice: Judicial Power and the Legal Complex in Pakistan under Musharraf," *Law & Social Inquiry* 35 (2010): 991–1001).

10.4   The Key Issue: Dealing with Authoritarian
Political Dominance

Gordon Silverstein is not alone in recognizing how any assessment of the Singapore judiciary's performance (or of any judiciary for that matter) must be sensitive toward the underlying political context. For example, Po Jen Yap recognizes that judges are constrained by political realities, and can only exercise token judicial review in Singapore.[48] He argued that the employment of "constitutional fig leaves" by courts – such as the use of formalism to limit judicial intervention or the employment of symbolic review to effectively give leeway to the politically dominant executive branch[49] – have "an important function by preserving judicial legitimacy" when the political realities do not permit more activist or robust judicial intervention.[50]

Similarly, Victor Ramraj explained his concept of a "tipping point," which includes factors such as:

> (1) popular dissatisfaction with the status quo and an awareness of the possibility that legal constitutionalism holds; (2) a strong legal infrastructure in terms of both the training of key "legally-trained personnel" in a society and their ability to engage constructively with the government; and (3) an alternative set of legal and political norms that are minimally threatening to the political elite.[51]

He suggests that it might not be normatively desirable to move toward legal constitutionalism if the "tipping point" has not been reached.[52]

---

[48] Yap, "Constitutional Fig Leaves" 438–40:

> Singapore and Malaysia have a semi-permanent form of government in power, and where a dominant, disciplined political party or coalition is in control, the less space domestic courts have to operate. Where legislative and executive power is consolidated in a single party or coalition, the dominant government can display its displeasure more easily by eliminating judicial review or even ousting the judges themselves. Constitutional review does not operate in a political vacuum; where judges are significantly constrained by the actions of other political actors, judicial review of state action becomes merely an exercise in tokenism.

[49] Ibid., 424–40.

[50] Ibid., 445. Cf. Worthington, *Governance in Singapore*, 124: discussing "the intellectual games which some judges are forced to play in order to meet the political outcomes required of the executive; not according to executive instruction, but according to convention and political culture."

[51] Ramraj, "Tipping Points," 214–19.

[52] Ibid., 218. Marie Seong-Hak Kim made a similar point in the context of Korea. She argued that under the political realities of the Yusin authoritarian regime, judges understandably sought to merely ensure minimum due process of law as prescribed in the constitution

More broadly, there is a strand of literature grounded in political science and/or a realist conception of law and which argues that while the judicial branch can play an important role in shaping political discourse and the underlying political dynamic, it risks losing its legitimacy if it overextends itself and triggers insurmountable political backlash.[53]

This ambivalent or even mild endorsement of judicial submission by scholars can be contrasted with the work of those who argue the opposite. Tan Seow Hon argues that where a constitution can be easily amended, as in the case of Singapore, a possible solution is the Kesavananda Basic Features doctrine that posits "the only way to amend a Basic Feature [such as the secular character of the Constitution and the neutrality of the government toward religion in Singapore] is to set up a Constituent Assembly and establish a new grundnorm."[54] Similarly, Tey Hsun Hang argues that, given its overwhelming political dominance, the role of the judiciary is more crucial in Singapore's political context compared to other nations.[55]

Both approaches are not necessarily irreconcilable or inconsistent with each other. Advocating for more judicial intervention in an otherwise politically domineering legislature and executive branch can be seen as pushing for a first-best solution in achieving an ideal – if admittedly rather idealistic – governance framework with appropriate checks and balances and separation of powers. The more circumspect recognition of the political constraints on judicial activism does not repudiate the normative desirability of such an ideal, but is either a descriptive account of the imperfect realities of circumstances, or a mild argument in favor of

without substantively challenging the oppressive provisions. She further argued that their actions have resulted in the positive outcome of preserving the basic framework of legality that would "prove essential to ushering liberal democracy" later ("Travails of Judges: Courts and Constitutional Authoritarianism in South Korea," *American Journal of Comparative Law* 63 (2015): 606–7).

[53] See e.g. Tom Ginsburg and Tamir Moustafa (eds.), *Rule by Law: The Politics of Courts in Authoritarian Regimes* (New York: Cambridge University Press, 2008), 1–22. For a concise review of the relevant literature, see Tamir Moustafa, "Law and Courts in Authoritarian Regimes," *Annual Review of Law and Social Science* 10 (2014): 281, 283–93.
[54] Tan, "Constitution as 'Comforter,'" 116–17. There is a similar suggestion by H. P. Lee in the context of Australia, where he is receptive to the notion that duly enacted constitutional amendments by the parliament to remove certain judicial powers may be invalidated ("Judges and Constitutional Government," *Lawasia Journal* (2000–1): 30, 34–5. Cf., Yap, "Constitutional Fig Leaves": discussing the political turmoil underpinning the development of the Basic Feature doctrine, and observing that the Indian judges "were convinced that if they did not intervene, all vestiges of democracy in India would eventually be removed" (440–5).
[55] Tey, "Judicial Internalising," 298.

a second-best solution, especially in light of the greater detriment when the judiciary prematurely pursues the first-best solution.

More crucially for the purpose of this chapter, both approaches focused on the actions that could or should be taken by the judiciary, but without concerted inquiry as to what the authoritarian regime should do when confronted with attempts by the judiciary to enhance judicial review or otherwise expand the judicial check on the government. As illustrated in the *Chng Suan Tze* episode, where there is near-universal condemnation of the ruling regime's explicit reversal of the *Chng Suan Tze* decision, the implicit normative prescriptions for the authoritarian regime is that the regime should have simply acceded to the judicial expansion of checks. Similar critiques and assumptions underpinned scholarly assessments on the electoral changes and institutional innovations undertaken by the PAP in responses to electoral defeat.[56]

This is perfectly understandable, since authoritarianism is almost unanimously considered by scholars as normatively undesirable in a governance regime. There is at best, very modest defense for authoritarian rule as a temporary measure given dire socioeconomic conditions. For example, Randall Peerenboom alluded to the importance of social norms and state of economic development in calibrating the appropriate rule of law and/or democratic reform in developing countries.[57] Mark Tushnet recognized that Singapore "authoritarian constitutionalism" may be necessary to preserve ethnic and religious harmony as claimed by the Singapore government, notwithstanding the skepticism about the underlying motivation of political self-preservation.[58]

However, it is undesirable to translate normative objections of authoritarian rule into ready dismissal of the authoritarian regime's motivation of self-preservation. First, it is premised on an unrealistic assumption: by arguing that the authoritarian regime should have simply acceded to any potential weakening of their grip on power is to deny the authoritarian nature of the regime. This denial renders hollow and counterproductive any normative prescriptions on what the authoritarian regime should do.

---

[56] These measures include creation of Group Representation Constituencies (GRCs), the Elected Presidency, the Non-Constituency Members of Parliament (MPs), and Nominated MPs (Ortmann, *Containing Contention*, 73–5); Garry Rodan, "Singapore 'Exceptionalism'? Authoritarian Rule and State Transformation," in Joseph Wong and Edward Friedman (eds.), *Political Transitions in Dominant Party Systems: Learning to Lose* (London: Routledge, 2008), 240–1; Thio, "Lex Rex," 45–53.

[57] Randall Peerenboom, "Law and Development of Constitutional Democracy in China: Problem or Paradigm?" *Columbia Journal of Asian Law* 19(1) (2005): 185, 229–34.

[58] Tushnet, "Authoritarian Constitutionalism," 414–15.

If the authoritarian regime does not have an inherent motivation for authoritarian rule, then it would not be an authoritarian regime, and all the subsequent governance flaws relating to authoritarian rule would not have materialized. On the reverse side, the authoritarian regime would steadfastly and categorically reject those prescriptions, given the premise is to dilute their authoritarian rule.

Second, the dismissal prevents a more circumspect analysis regarding the relative normative desirability of the responses undertaken by the authoritarian regime to challenges of its power. As will be elaborated in Section 10.5, authoritarian regimes around the globe have adopted a variety of measures to deal with disagreeable judicial decisions, ranging from sanctions of the individual judges and dissolution of the entire court, to direct reversal via constitutional and legislative amendments. While it is undeniable that all such measures are normatively undesirable from the perspective of developing a robust constitutionalism, rule of law, and/or liberal democracy, they are also clearly not equal in terms of detriments. Careful assessment of the measures' relative strengths and weakness is critical to advancing our understanding of authoritarian governance regimes.

Next, this chapter will argue that, under the more realistic premise of the authoritarian regime seeking to perpetuate its control and respond to perceived challenges of its hegemony, the measures undertaken by the PAP during the *Chng Suan Tze* episode were the best possible response (i.e. the least harmful manner to maintain authoritarian rule).

10.5 What Should an Authoritarian Regime Do (Besides Not Being Authoritarian)? Changing the Constitution to Preserve Constitutionalism

In the *Chng Suan Tze* episode, the PAP took full advantage of its overwhelming parliamentary majority and the relatively easy constitutional amendment procedures in Singapore to effect rapid constitutional and legislative amendments and specifically reverse judicial decisions perceived by the PAP as objectionable. This chapter is fully sympathetic to the detrimental curtailing of a more robust judicial review approach developed by the Court of Appeal, and does not support the substance of those constitutional and legislative amendments. However, this chapter does argue that those actions were the best response one can expect from a ruling regime preserving its authoritarian rule.

First, other available alternatives that can be and have been employed by the authoritarian regime are much worse for the judges and the judiciary. Ran Hirschl described various political backlashes around the world in response to unsolicited judicial intervention in the political sphere: notably, interference in a court's composition in terms of appointment, removal, or even the dissolution in Argentina, Ecuador, Hungary, Kazakhstan, Pakistani, Russia, Trinidad and Tobago, Venezuela, and Zimbabwe.[59] Victor Ramraj noted the scenario in Malaysia where five judges who issued an adverse ruling against the government were suspended and eventually removed.[60] More recently, the independence of the Polish judiciary has been systematically dismantled by the elected autocratic governments through a combination of personal and institutional changes.[61] It is without a doubt that when compared to the previous scenarios, the adverse personal consequences to judges in the *Chng Suan Tze* decision were minimal.

The detriment to the judiciary as an institution was also much more muted in the *Chng Suan Tze* episode. It is undeniable that the judiciary understood the constitutional and legislative amendments represented a direct rebuke from the ruling regime; however, this cannot be compared to direct intervention on the personnel and institution of the judiciary. In the latter scenario, the direct personal and institutional costs drove the stakes prohibitively high for a judicial miscalculation of the authoritarian regime's tolerance. In contrast, while commentators have observed how the *Chng Suan Tze* episode had a broader, chilling effect on judges in subsequent decisions involving judicial review of state actions,[62] the judges in Singapore could take some solace that a judicial decision objected to by the regime would not trigger a negative reaction or direct hostility against the judges or the institution of the judiciary. Thus, Singapore judges would be more likely to push the envelope of substantive judicial review, even if just modestly, moving forward upon subtle shifts in sociopolitical conditions.[63]

---

[59] Ran Hirschl, "The New Constitutionalism and the Judicialization of Pure Politics Worldwide," *Fordham Law Review* 75(2) (2006): 721, 747–51.

[60] Ramraj, "Tipping Points," 201.

[61] Kriszta Kovács and Kim Lane Scheppele, "The Fragility of an Independent Judiciary: Lessons from Hungary and Poland – And the European Union," *Communist and Post-Communist Studies* 51 (2018): 194–8; Tomasz Tadeusz Koncewicz, "The Capture of the Polish Constitutional Tribunal and Beyond: Of Institution(s), Fidelities and the Rule of Law" *Review of Central and East European Law* 43 (2018): 120–3.

[62] Tey, "Judicial Internalising," 299–301; Yap, "Constitutional Fig Leaves," 422.

[63] See Lin, "Administrative Law in Singapore," 48–9, discussing how:

Indeed, the 2015 case of *Tan Seet Eng* v. *Attorney General*[64] that similarly involved the power of detention without trial is instructive of this dynamic. The appellant in that case had sought judicial review of his detention under the Criminal Law (Temporary Provisions) Act.[65] The Court of Appeal decided in favor of the appellant, holding that the minister "must state all the grounds relied on as justifying the detention so that the exercise of his power can be *properly understood and assessed*" (emphasis added) and that the courts will "closely scrutinize the grounds" of detention to ensure the minister was acting within the scope of power conferred by the legislature.[66] Having examined the legislative history and statutory provisions and concluded that the power of detention under the statute relates only to serious criminal activities that affected Singapore, the court quashed the detention order on the grounds that criminal activities stated in the detention order were neither serious enough nor involve Singapore.[67] The appellant was released and detained a week later with a new detention order that complied with the requirements set out by the court in *Tan Seet Eng*. More significantly, there was no legislative and constitutional overruling of the decision this time around, with the law minister taking pains to make a public statement with regards to how the government respects the Court of Appeal decisions.[68] Commentators in Singapore cheered the *Tan Seet Eng* decision as the contemporary successor of the much-lauded *Chng Suan Tze* decision.[69] Admittedly, it is impossible to assess with certainty whether the Court of Appeal would have adopted a more deferential approach in *Tan Seet Eng* had the Singapore government employed more aggressive/

> the judiciary today appears to be gradually shifting away from this earlier approach [of significant deference to the executive branch] ... towards a more critical application of common law principles and the creation of a distinctive body of administrative law that reflects the realities of government decision-making in Singapore and the role of the law, in promoting effective and efficient public administration, while protecting the rights and liberties of individuals against the State.

[64] *Tan Seet Eng* v. *Attorney-General* [2015] SGCA 59.

[65] Criminal law (Temporary Provisions) Act (Cap. 67, 2000 Rev. Ed.).

[66] *Tan Seet Eng* v. *Attorney-General*, 829.

[67] Ibid., 830–5.

[68] *TODAY*, "New Detention Order Issued against Dan Tan," December 5, 2005, www .todayonline.com/singapore/new-detention-order-issued-against-dan-tan

[69] See e.g. Jason Lee and Bin Hong Ng, "All Powers Have Their Limits: A Guide to Rationalising the Legality of Government Actions," *Singapore Law Watch Commentary* 1 (2016): 4; Cavin Liang and Lijing Tham, "Fair Play and Match Fixing: A Dialogue on *Tan Seet Eng* v. *Attorney-General*," *Singapore Law Gazette*, April 2016. www .v1.lawgazette.com.sg/2016–04/1544.htm

intrusive responses in the *Chng Suan Tze* episode. Nonetheless, that the *Tan Seet Eng* decision itself openly – and proudly – acknowledged the precedent force of the *Chng Suan Tze* decision arguably owed much to how the surgical rebuttal by the ruling regime twenty-five years ago had left the integrity of the core judicial principle of the *Chng Suan Tze* decision (and the institution of the judiciary) intact.

More fundamentally, the responses of the ruling regime in the *Chng Suan Tze* episode are prima facie the same measures that a government and/or political party in a liberal democracy should have adopted under the same circumstances. When confronted with an adverse judicial outcome, the proper response of a liberal democracy should be to muster political support to amend the statutory/constitutional language and resolve any ambiguity that "facilitated" the adverse judicial interpretation. Where the judicial decision is premised on constitutional interpretation, the government or party could seek to amend the constitution such that the actual supermajority democratic will of the people is given effect to. The last thing that these political actors *should* do, even if they often do it anyway, is to readily and wantonly impugn the personal integrity and political motivation of the judges deciding the cases.[70] Such criticisms can provide immediate political benefit to the political actors in terms of galvanizing their support bases. However, the direct assault on the judiciary distracts from the true goal of democracy (namely, to persuade and convince the rest of the polity on the merits of policy/law) and unduly undermine public confidence in the judiciary.[71] Constitutional amendments may be abusively employed by an aspiring authoritarian actor to undermine democracy,

---

[70] James L. Gibson, "The Legitimacy of the U.S. Supreme Court in a Polarized Polity," *Journal of Empirical Legal Studies* 4(3) (2007): 507, 508–9; Or Bassok, "The Israeli Supreme Court's Mythical Image – A Death of a Thousand Sound Bites," *Michigan State International Law Review* 23 (2014): 39, 76–90.

[71] Nicholson P. Stephen and Thomas G. Hansford, "Partisans in Robes: Party Cues and Public Acceptance of Supreme Court Decisions," *American Journal of Political Science* 58 (3) (2014): 620, 620–3. See Bassok, "Israeli Supreme Court," 47–68 and 97–105, discussing how the entrance of a commercial television channel in Israel dramatically altered the previous media portrayal of the Israeli Supreme Court as an impartial institution that decides cases based on legal expertise to a prevailing depiction of judges being motivated by ideology and partisan politics in adjudication, and arguing that this shift in media portrayal is at least partly responsible for the sharp decline in public support for the Israeli Supreme Court. Vanessa Baird and Amy Gangl, "Shattering the Myth of Legality: The Impact of the Media's Framing of Supreme Court Procedures on Perceptions of Fairness," *Political Psychology* 27(4) (2006): 597, 606–7: "(O)ur findings also suggest that if the media were consistently to portray the Court as a site of political bargaining and

especially in jurisdictions where the constitution is relatively easy to amend.[72] Nonetheless, the fault arguably lies with the design of the constitution and the authoritarian motivation of the actor,[73] rather than the mechanism of constitutional amendments.

This renders the *Chng Suan Tze* episode of particular normative significance once transition is taken into account. As a model of governing framework, the consensus is the ideal of liberal-democratic constitutionalism or "thick" rule of law. An authoritarian regime – whether ruled by a despotic dictator or governed under an elaborate "rule by law" regime – is clearly undesirable. The key question is: How does transition occur from an authoritarian regime to the ideal liberal democratic constitutionalism? Democratization (or democracy) and rule of law do not necessarily go hand in hand. There remain many democratic regimes, whether established, recent, or emerging ones, whose legal systems fall far short of the rule of law, with all the consequential corruption, governance failure, and societal costs.[74]

This is unsurprising, given the difference in the process by which democratization and rule of law is ushered.[75] The building up of rule of law or even a professional legal system for a rule by law regime requires both substantial and sustained investment in law-related human capital, and cultivated acceptance by the ruling party and the underlying society of adhering to law as the primary means of governance.[76] On the other hand, democratization of an authoritarian regime may be triggered by

---

compromise, we might expect a decline in public support for the institution over time ... Indeed, given that the Court relies on its persuasive power to be effective, our analyses suggest that media reports over time could directly affect the effectiveness and ultimately the power of the Court."

[72] David Landau, "Abusive Constitutionalism," *UC Davis Law Review* 47 (2013): 195–9.

[73] For a discussion of how "tiered constitutionalism" (i.e. the amendment threshold of certain more integral constitutional provisions are made more difficult to change as compared to the bulk of the constitution) may serve to reduce (although not necessarily prevent) the occurrences of antidemocratic constitutional changes in severe conditions of democratic fragility, see Rosalind Dixon and David Landau. "Tiered Constitutional Design," *George Washington Law Review* 86 (2018): 503–10.

[74] Peerenboom, "Problem or Paradigm?," 202–9: examples include Guatemala, Kenya, Papua New Guinea, the Philippines, and Thailand.

[75] Cf. Maciej Kisilowski, "The Middlemen: The Legal Profession, the Rule of Law, and Authoritarian Regimes," *Law and Social Inquiry* 40(3) (2015): 700: "The popularity of the rule-of-law-without-democracy idea has been growing among legal and political commentators, partly because of the meager success of more ambitious attempts at political liberalization."

[76] Ronald J. Daniels and Michael Trebilcock, "The Political Economy of Rule of Law Reform in Developing Countries," *Michigan Journal of International Law* 26 (2015): 99, 107–9;

performance failure (e.g. sudden deterioration of economic conditions) that demolishes the popular support of the regime, or internal political struggle that weakened the original power base.[77] Of course, sustainable transition to democracy is by no means easy or straightforward. Reversion to authoritarianism after democratization is not uncommon (e.g. Russia, Egypt), and underscores the importance of social, cultural, and economic conditions in maintaining the democratic order.[78] Nonetheless, even in such scenarios, there was at least a period where the "authoritarian" nature of the regime was dismantled and replaced by some form of democratic process. Such temporary respites are largely absence for "constitutionalism" (or "rule of law" in the thin sense).

Thus, the central takeaway of this chapter is that criticism should be levied against the proper target. The ruling regime did the right thing in the *Chng Suan Tze* episode, which simply reflects the nature of regimes. Making this distinction, admittedly subtle in the middle of the understandable outrage at the adverse outcome, is crucial for allowing us to confront the real issue: namely, to effect regime change. This is certainly a harder and more difficult issue, since it entails effecting a widespread opinion change among the polity as to the support and perceived desirability of the regime. The population must be persuaded that economic development and material well-being are not worth the suppression of political freedom and individual liberty, or that there are underlying social ills and corruption censored by the state-controlled media environment.[79] That these arguments do not gain widespread traction among the population, at least as reflected in electoral results, may

Stephen McCarthy and Kheang Un, "The Evolution of Rule of Law in Cambodia," *Democratization* 24(1) (2015): 1, 2–5; Peerenboom, "Problem or Paradigm?," 230–3.

[77] Gilbert Achar, *The People Want: A Radical Exploration of the Arab Uprising* (Berkeley: University of California Press, 2013), 148–55; Karim Mezran and Eric Knecht, "Actors and Factors in Libya's Revolution," in Justin Frosini and Francesco Biagi (eds.), *Political and Constitutional Transitions in North Africa: Actors and Factors* (New York: Routledge, 2015), 85–92. Cf. Jack F. Matlock, *Autopsy on an Empire: The American Ambassador's Account of the Collapse of the Soviet Union* (New York: Random House, 1995), 694: observing how entrenched political systems across history persisted for significant durations despite unambiguous problems in their economic and social institutions.

[78] Karrie J. Koesel, *Religion and Authoritarianism: Cooperation, Conflict, and the Consequences* (New York: Cambridge University Press, 2014), 36–42 and 144–7; Nathan J. Brown, "Egypt: A Constitutional Court in an Unconstitutional Setting," in Frosini and Biagi (eds.), *Political and Constitutional Transitions*, 46–7.

[79] See e.g. Kenneth Paul Tan, "Choosing What to Remember in Neoliberal Singapore: The Singapore Story, State Censorship and State-Sponsored Nostalgia," *Asian Studies Review* 40 (2016): 236–43; Terence Chong, "'Back Regions' and 'Dark Secrets' in Singapore: The Politics of Censorship and Liberalisation," *Space & Polity* 14 (2010): 243–8.

arguably be attributed in part to all the illiberal measures typically employed by authoritarian regimes (e.g. favorable electoral laws, curtailing free speech and civil liberties, conflating party with state, suppressing opposition).[80] This should be highlighted and criticized. However, constitutional and legislative amendments to reverse adverse judicial decisions are symptoms and not the causes of authoritarian rule, and are certainly not among those illiberal and undesirable measures.

10.6 Conclusion

Constitutionalism and legality are ultimately processes whose outcomes are beholden by the nature of the regime. The outcome of the much-vilified *Chng Suan Tze* episode is bad, with the budding emergence of judicial check ruthlessly thwarted. However, fault lies not in the process itself. Failure to recognize this distinction may yield a marginal benefit in the assault on the overall legitimacy of the authoritarian regime. Yet, that comes at the dear price of sacrificing the governance toolkit of law that is arduous to acquire, and which is crucial to sustain any regime, democratic or otherwise.

---

[80] Ortmann, *Containing Contention*, 73–5; William Case, *Politics in Southeast Asia: Democracy or Less* (Richmond, UK: Curzon Press, 2002), 90–5; Li-ann Thio, "The Right to Political Participation in Singapore: Tailor-Marking a Westminster-Modelled Constitution to Fit the Imperatives of 'Asian' Democracy," *Singapore Journal of International and Comparative Law* 6 (2002): 181.

Angels Are in the Details

Voting System, Poll Workers, and Election Administration Integrity in Taiwan

YEN-TU SU

11.1 Introduction

Taiwan is widely considered a success story of democratization through elections.[1] It experienced its third presidential and first parliamentary party turnover in 2016. The first modern elections in Taiwan date back to 1935 when Taiwan was under Japanese colonial rule. Before Taiwan held its first comprehensive parliamentary elections in 1991–2, voters in Taiwan already had over four decades worth of voting experience for local offices and subsequently a few parliamentary seats under the authoritarian rule of the KMT regime. Elections held before the KMT's first presidential loss in 2000 exemplify authoritarian legality in action. But even the most elementary assumptions of electoral integrity – that the elections are not rigged by those who manage the voting process – were not achieved overnight and should not be taken for granted. From the 1950s to 1970s, the KMT regime attempted to rig several elections. The last proven case of ballot stuffing occurred in 1992. Nevertheless, the election administration in Taiwan has managed to gain significant trust

The author would like to thank Erik Mobrand, Weitseng Chen, Hualing Fu, Jacques deLisle, and Nathan Batto for their comments and suggestions. The author would also like to thank the Department of Electoral Affairs, Central Election Commission of Taiwan for providing valuable information, and Tzung-en Hsieh for his research assistance.

[1] See e.g. Shelley Rigger, *Politics in Taiwan: Voting for Democracy* (New York: Routledge, 1999); Andreas Schedler, "The Contingent Power of Authoritarian Elections," in Staffan Lindberg (ed.), *Democratization by Elections: A New Mode of Transition* (Baltimore, MD: Johns Hopkins University Press, 2009); Steven Levitsky and Lucan A. Way, *Competitive Authoritarianism: Hybrid Regimes After the Cold War* (New York: Cambridge University Press, 2010).

among voters and foreign election observers since the 1980s. What had prevented the KMT regime from stealing more elections during its heyday, and facilitating Taiwan's transition to democracy under the long-existing voting rules? And what does that tell us about the actual workings of authoritarian legality in general and in the electoral arena in particular? This chapter seeks to answer these questions.

The existing literature views the integrity of election administration in authoritarian states mainly as a function of what the authoritarian rulers do. Rigging elections is but one among many strategies listed on the menu of electoral manipulation, and whether to do so is usually considered by and large the authoritarian rulers' call. The decision of a given electoral authoritarian regime is, in turn, influenced by a myriad of factors, including the regime's ideological commitment to liberal democracy, geopolitics, the strength of civil society, the dynamics of political competition, and the costs and benefits of manipulation.[2] While offering important insights on the different trajectories toward democratization or authoritarian entrenchment, the regime-based theories are unable to adequately explain the rise and fall of vote rigging in Taiwan. After all, an authoritarian regime is not an "it," but a "they," and its agents do not always act in unison.

Crucially, the institutional design of the voting process shapes the incentives and disincentives for those who administer the votes. To deter vote rigging by agents of the state, the existing literature recommends thoughtful design of an election management body (EMB), domestic and international election monitoring, free speech and free media, and a functioning criminal justice system against election fraud.[3] With the exception of domestic election monitoring, however, these often-discussed institutional factors

---

[2] See e.g. Andreas Schedler, "The Menu of Manipulation," *Journal of Democracy* 13 (2002): 36; Fabrice Lehoucq, "Electoral Fraud: Causes, Types, and Consequences," *Annual Review of Political Science* 6 (2003): 233; Andreas Schedler (ed.), *Electoral Authoritarianism: The Dynamics of Unfree Competition* (Boulder, CO: Lynne Rienner, 2006); Andreas Schedler, "Authoritarianism's Last Line of Defense," *Journal of Democracy* 21 (2010): 69; Beatriz Magaloni, "The Game of Electoral Fraud and the Ousting of Authoritarian Rule," *American Journal of Political Science* 54 (2010): 751; Levitsky and Way, *Competitive Authoritarianism*; Sarah Birch, *Electoral Malpractice* (New York: Oxford University Press, 2011); Alberto Simpser, *Why Governments and Parties Manipulate Elections: Theory, Practice, and Implications* (New York: Cambridge University Press, 2013).

[3] See e.g. Daniel Calingaert, "Election Rigging and How to Fight It," *Journal of Democracy* 17 (2006): 138; Jonathan Hartlyn, Jennifer McCoy, and Thomas M. Mustillo, "Electoral Governance Matters: Explaining the Quality of Elections in Contemporary Latin America," *Comparative Political Studies* 41 (2008): 73; Judith Green Kelley, *Monitoring Democracy: When International Election Observation Works, and Why It Often Fails* (Princeton, NJ: Princeton University Press, 2012); Pippa Norris, Richard W. Frank, and

appear to have made limited contributions to the eradication of vote rigging in Taiwan. To the extent that the angels of election administration integrity live in the institutional details, the case of Taiwan invites us to rediscover where they live.

This chapter argues that two underappreciated voting arrangements – (1) on-site ballot counting after polls are closed, and (2) the selection of government employees, schoolteachers, and those recruited by competing candidates as poll workers – play critical roles in improving and safeguarding election administration integrity in Taiwan. In addition to facilitating the detection of anomalies, these measures also prevent those in power from stealing elections at the last minute. The salutary effects of these two voting arrangements, however, cannot be fully explained in such functional terms as transparency in ballot counting and checks and balances among poll workers representing competing camps. To begin with, on-site ballot counting has arguably become a ritualized electoral practice in Taiwan.[4] The whole process has long been carefully scripted to ensure that each ballot would be duly counted before vigilant voters. The standardized ballot-counting procedures have been repeatedly practiced in all types of elections, including those run by schoolchildren. As such, the ritual may have helped to cultivate a sense of solemnity in the voters and poll workers with regard to ballot counting. Although the opposition and some public intellectuals in Taiwan once viewed the selection of civil servants and schoolteachers as poll managers with suspicion, these public sector employees have, over time, proven themselves to be dutiful and trustworthy in administering votes. Their heavy presence at polling stations further helped to quell the conspiracy theories that elections were rigged against the KMT presidential candidates in 2000 and 2004, because the public sectors used to be strongholds of the KMT. In short, both the vigilant voters and the street-level poll workers have played their part to protect elections from being rigged in Taiwan. They are the unsung heroes that make the labor-intensive voting system work.

As opposed to being measures founded solely on the goodwill or hypocrisy of the KMT regime, these two features of the voting system

Ferran Martínez i Coma (eds.), *Advancing Electoral Integrity* (New York: Oxford University Press, 2014); Patrick Merloe, "Election Monitoring vs. Disinformation," *Journal of Democracy* 26 (2015): 79.

[4] For the conception of elections as rituals, see generally Mark W. Brewin, *Celebrating Democracy: The Mass-Mediated Ritual of Election Day* (New York: Peter Lang, 2008); Graeme Orr, *Ritual and Rhythm in Electoral Systems: A Comparative Legal Account* (New York: Routledge, 2016).

are vestiges of historical contingencies. Were it not for those enlightened local bureaucrats of the early 1950s who designed the voting rules around the electoral experiences in Taiwan (as opposed to those in Republican China), voters in Taiwan might not have the opportunity to monitor ballot counting at nearby polling stations. Were it not for the growing opposition in the 1950s, the KMT regime might not have shared the power of appointing poll supervisors with its competitors in the 1960s. To the extent that authoritarian elections in Taiwan were not rigged as a matter in general, this achievement of authoritarian legality was thanks in no small part to human struggles within and over election law. Moreover, the use of the paper-ballot voting system was by no means a sure thing in Taiwan. Had the KMT regime, during its heyday, heeded the advice of certain progressive commentators and "modernized" the voting system (by replacing paper ballots with automated voting machines), there probably would not be much to say about the cultural influence of ballot counting as a meaningful ritual in and of itself, nor would the selection of the poll workforce have mattered very much to the integrity of election administration in Taiwan. But with the benefit of hindsight, we now know that election administration integrity can be strengthened not only by creating and applying incentive-based safeguards against election fraud, but also by choosing upstanding individuals to manage a transparent and ritualized voting system.

The remaining of this chapter is organized as follows. Section 11.2 examines the different perceptions and the changing state of election administration integrity during Taiwan's authoritarian period. It also reviews the existing theories about vote rigging in order to set the stage for further historical–institutional inquiry in the case of Taiwan. Section 11.3 traces the development of on-site ballot counting in Taiwan. It argues that this ritualized procedure not only empowers vigilant voter to monitor elections, but also encourages a culture that respects the sanctity of votes. Section 11.4 examines the evolution of poll worker selection rules in Taiwan. It explores both the short-term and long-term effects of these rules on the actual administration of elections and public perception thereof. Section 11.5 concludes the case study of Taiwan with several general lessons for the study of authoritarian legality. It suggests that greater attention should be paid to the complexity of the authoritarian regime, the differences made by small changes in institutional design, and those front-line individuals who implement the rule of law.

11.2   The Curious Appearance and Disappearance of Election
Rigging in Taiwan

Taiwan is a young democracy with a long history of elections. The first
two modern elections in Taiwan were held in 1935 and 1939 under
Japanese colonial rule. Although the Taiwanese people were grossly
underrepresented in the city/county councils under the stringent suffrage
limitation and the biased electoral rules, they had learned, and remembered long after the Japanese left Taiwan, the taste of orderly elections.[5]
After taking over Taiwan in 1945 and before losing China to the com-
munists in 1949, the Republic of China (ROC) held several popular
elections in Taiwan for borough chiefs, county/town council members,
and the Taiwan delegation to the two national bodies established under
the 1947 ROC Constitution – the 1st National Assembly and Legislative
Yuan. However, this transition period is most remembered for the tragic
February 28 Incident of 1947. The subsequent massacre (including that
of many Taiwanese elites) not only erased any hope of liberation and
democratic self-governance, but also cast a long shadow of fear over the
authoritarian elections held in Taiwan thereafter.[6]

The KMT regime, which fled from China to Taiwan in 1949–50, was
a pioneer of electoral authoritarianism. After all, having some sort of
electoral mandate appeared crucial to the regime's standing and survival
as a member of the free world during the Cold War era. But given that
Taiwan was regarded merely as a province and a temporary base for the

[5] On the local elections held by the Japanese colonial government in Taiwan, see Ming-
Tong Chen and Jih-wen Lin, "Tai wan di fang syuan jyu de ci yuan yu guo jia she huei guan
si jhuan bian" [The Origins of the Local Elections and the Transformation of the State–
Society Relations in Taiwan], in Ming-Tong Chen and Yong-Nian Jheng (eds.), *Liang an ji
ceng syuan jyu yu jheng jhih she huei bian cian* [The Local Elections and the Political and
Social Change in Both Sides of the Taiwan Strait] (Taipei: Yue Dan Press, 1998), 23–69;
Rou-lan Chen, "Tai wan chu cih di fang syuan jyu: Rih ben jhih min jheng fu de jhih du
sing cao zuo" [First Local Election of Taiwan: An Analysis of Institutional Manipulation of
Japanese Colonial Government], *Taiwan Historical Research* 22 (2015): 139. On the
nostalgia for the reasonably well-ordered local elections held under Japanese rule, see Yu-
De Ren, *Siang sia za gen: Jhong guo guo min dang yu tai wan di fang jheng jhih de fa jhan
1949-1960* [Taking Root: The KMT and the Development of Local Politics in Taiwan from
1949 to 1960] (Taipei: Dao Xiang Press, 2008), 386–7.
[6] On the lasting influence of the February 28 Incident, see Naiteh Wu, "Transition without
Justice, or Justice without History: Transitional Justice in Taiwan," *Taiwan Journal of
Democracy* 1 (2005): 77; Tsui-Lien Chen, *Bai nian jhuei ciou: Tai wan min jhu yun dong de
gu shih, volume1: Zih jhih de meng siang* [A Century's Quest: The Story of the Democratic
Movement in Taiwan, vol. I: The Dream of Autonomy] (Taipei: Acropolis Press, 2013),
282–302.

ROC to launch its reclamation of mainland China, the KMT's first two decades of exile only saw local elections held under martial law. From 1950 to 1991, the KMT held roughly eighty-one cycles of local elections, which comprised the bulk of authoritarian elections in Taiwan. The KMT had dominated these local elections by cultivating and collaborating with the clientelist networks known as local factions (*difang paixi*). However, some non-KMT political actors (later known and self-identified as *dangwai*, i.e. people outside the KMT) also managed to gain footholds in certain local elections.[7]

With time it became increasingly clear that the KMT regime could legitimately represent neither China nor Taiwan, and by the early 1970s, even some KMT-affiliated intellectuals called for immediate democratization of the ROC government.[8] Propelled in part by the growing crisis in legitimacy, the regime began to hold in 1969 parliamentary elections for a handful of "supplemental representatives" to the 1st National Assembly and Legislative Yuan, the terms of which were indefinitely extended to signify the KMT regime as the representative government of the whole China. In the following two decades, ten more cycles of the limited parliamentary elections were held. These elections were limited in the sense that they would not alter the KMT's grasp over the two parliament houses because the so-called old thieves (*laozei*) – tenured/senior representatives who could hold their seats indefinitely without being periodically reelected – firmly controlled the parliamentary majorities on behalf of the authoritarian regime.[9] By 1988, one year after the 38-year-old martial law was lifted and the year when President Chiang Ching-Kuo died, 91 percent of the National Assembly seats and 76 percent of the Legislative Yuan seats were still occupied by these old thieves.[10] Their entrenchment, which was originally rationalized as a temporary measure

---

[7] On the local elections held under KMT authoritarian rule, see e.g. Rigger, *Politics in Taiwan*; J. Bruce Jacobs, *Local Politics in Rural Taiwan under Dictatorship and Democracy* (Norwalk, CT: East Bridge, 2008); Erik Mobrand, "South Korean Democracy in Light of Taiwan," in Kate Xiao Zhou, Shelley Rigger, and Lynn T. White III (eds.), *Democratization in China, Korea and Southeast Asia?: Local and National Perspectives* (New York: Routledge, 2014), 19–35.

[8] See Naiteh Wu, *Bai nian jhuei ciou: Tai wan min jhu yun dong de gu shih*, volume 2: *Zih you de cuo bai* [A Century's Quest: The Story of the Democratic Movement in Taiwan, vol. II: The Setback of Freedom] (Taipei: Acropolis Press, 2013), 244–64.

[9] See Jiunn-rong Yeh, "The Cult of Fatung: Representational Manipulation and Reconstruction in Taiwan," in Graham Hassall and Cheryl Saunders (eds.), *The People's Representatives: Electoral Systems in the Asia-Pacific Region* (Sydney: Allen & Unwin, 1997), 23–37.

[10] Rigger, *Politics in Taiwan*, 63.

in a time of national emergency, had become exhibit A of how undemocratic the KMT regime was.

In the wake of the March 1990 Wild Lily Student Movement, a massive student sit-in that demanded immediate and comprehensive democratic reform, the Grand Justices (later known as the Taiwan Constitutional Court) ordered the termination of the infamous "Ten-Thousand-Year Parliaments" (*wannian guohui*) in its landmark ruling Judicial Yuan Interpretation No. 261 (1990). Subsequently, the people of Taiwan elected the ROC's 2nd National Assembly and Legislative Yuan in 1991 and 1992 respectively, and all parliamentary seats in Taiwan were thereafter subject to periodic elections. In 1996, Taiwan witnessed the first direct presidential election in its history. Lee Teng-hui, the first Taiwanese leader of the KMT, won the election with 54 percent of the vote. Although the KMT successfully remained in power throughout the 1990s, the presidency changed hands in 2000. As such, Taiwan could be regarded as a fledgling electoral democracy from as early as 1991.[11]

Elections held under the KMT's authoritarian rule (1945–91) were certainly not as free and fair as those held in a liberal democracy. Vote buying was a chronic disease in Taiwan, and the KMT regime used to persecute political opponents and ban new political parties.[12] Still, in view of the KMT's rationale for holding elections, it would not be a stretch to say that these authoritarian elections were by and large genuine insofar as the administration of the voting process is concerned. Elections were invaluable to the KMT regime. In addition to enhancing regime legitimacy, moderating political opposition, and providing feedback information, holding elections helped the émigré regime settle down and take root in Taiwan by enabling the KMT to co-opt local elites, build party networks, and, perhaps most importantly, obtain the much-needed American support in the early 1950s.[13] Rigging elections would have sharply undercut the utility of holding elections in the first place,

---

[11] Schedler, "Contingent Power," 303.

[12] On the vote buying in Taiwan, see e.g. Frederic Charles Schaffer (ed.), *Elections for Sale: The Causes and Consequences of Vote Buying* (Boulder, CO: Lynne Rienner, 2007). On the persecution of political dissents under KMT authoritarian rule, see e.g. Sheena Chestnut Greitens, *Dictators and Their Secret Police: Coercive Institutions and State Violence* (New York: Cambridge University Press, 2016), 179–210.

[13] On the functions of authoritarian elections in general, see e.g. Chia-Lung Lin, "Paths to Democracy: Taiwan in Comparative Perspective," PhD diss., Yale University, 1998; Jennifer Gandhi and Ellen Lust-Okar, "Elections under Authoritarianism," *Annual Review of Political Science* 12 (2009): 403; Mark Tushnet, "Authoritarian Constitutionalism," *Cornell Law Review* 100 (2014): 391.

and might even put the survival of the precarious regime in jeopardy. Besides, all of the elections held prior to 1991 were limited in scope, and the single-non-transferable vote (SNTV) used for legislative elections operated in the KMT's favor.[14] Given its resources, monopoly on violence, and control of media, the KMT was able to win (or buy) lots of elections during its height of power. Therefore, there was arguably no urgent need for the KMT to use a riskier method of electoral manipulation for the sake of retaining power.

However, in the eyes of many locals (especially those who opposed KMT authoritarian regime), the KMT was not only a frequent buyer of votes, but also a habitual thief of votes. Rumors of vote rigging by the KMT were heard of as early as 1950.[15] In the wake of the 1957 local elections, the integrity of election administration evolved into a major issue of the day. Before it was banned by the KMT regime in 1960, the iconic liberal magazine *Free China* (*Ziyou Zhongguo*) ran a series of articles vividly describing how the KMT used "security measures (*ancyuan cuoshih*)" such as violating voting secrecy and inducing power outages during ballot counting, to manipulate the votes.[16] In the 1950s to 1970s, several *dangwai* candidates brought suits to challenge the validity of elections. With the exception of a few minor elections involving narrow margins, though, the courts did not bother to order recounts of the contested votes.[17]

Rampant vote rigging allegedly took place in 1975, when the *dangwai* guru Kuo Yu-hsin (郭雨新) ran and lost his bid for a seat in the Legislative Yuan.[18] Kuo contested the election in court to no avail, since the high court dismissed the vote-rigging allegations as hearsay and saw no need to recount the votes or review the voter rolls. Kuo was represented by Yao Jia-wen (姚嘉文) and Lin Yi-shiung (林義雄), two

[14] On the Effects of the SNTV system in Taiwan, see Jih-Wen Lin, "Democratization under One-Party Dominance: Explaining Taiwan," *Issues and Studies* 35 (1999): 1.

[15] See Ren, *Siang sia za gen [Taking Root]*, 275.

[16] See e.g. Hua-Yuan Syue, *Zih you jhong guo yu min jhu sian jheng: 1950 nian dai tai wan sih siang shih de yi ge kao cha* [The Free China Fortnightly and Constitutional Democracy: A Study of Taiwan Intellectual History in the 1950s] (Taipei: Dao Xiang Press, 1996), 327–39; Linda Chao and Ramon H. Myers, "How Elections Promoted Democracy in Taiwan under Martial Law," *China Quarterly* 162 (2000): 387.

[17] See Chang-Cyuan Siang, *Tai wan di fang syuan jyu jhih fen si yu jian tao* [On the Local Elections in Taiwan] (Taipei: Commercial Press, 1971), 217–29.

[18] See Huei-Ling Hu, *Bai nian jhuei ciou: Tai wan min jhu yun dong de gu shih, volume 3: Min jhu de lang chao* [A Century's Quest: The Story of the Democratic Movement in Taiwan, vol. III: The Wave of Democracy] (Taipei: Acropolis Press, 2013), 64–71.

then-rising lawyers well regarded in opposition circles. Yao and Lin later wrote and published a book documenting the electoral injustice Kuo suffered in his final campaign.[19] A year later, they collaborated to publicize another similar experience of their client Huang Ma (黃蔴), who ran and lost the election for county magistrate of Yunlin in 1977.[20] Both of these two books were widely circulated at that time even though they were banned by the KMT regime.

The brewing public suspicion of election rigging by the KMT later led to the Zhongli Incident of 1977, which is often considered a watershed event that marked the beginning of the decline of the KMT's authoritarian rule.[21] The Incident concerned an election protest following the dramatic magistrate election in Taoyuan. Hsu Hsin-liang (許信良), an independent candidate who was a former rising star in the KMT prior to his expulsion from the party, ultimately won a resounding victory against the KMT's nominee. Taking seriously the risk of election rigging, Hsu's campaign urged voters to keep an eye on election day voting irregularities. Many voters did so, and when word spread that a head poll manager was suspected of tampering ballots, tens of thousands took their anger to the streets. The protest ended in the burning of a police station and two deaths. While the very suspect of election malpractice that led to the protest was not prosecuted for lack of evidence, an eyewitness was convicted of insulting poll workers. However, ballot stuffing at another polling station during the same election was proven in another court case.[22]

The popular perception of the KMT as an election cheater was confirmed once again in 1992, when the first full election of the Legislative Yuan was held at the end of the year. Huang Hsin-chieh (黃信介), then a former chairperson of the Democratic Progressive Party (DPP), ran a legendary race in the Hualien district. On election night, Huang was about to lose the election – by a razor-thin margin of sixty-two votes – to Wei Mu-cun (魏木村), the then-Mayor of Hualien City and a candidate affiliated to the KMT. Tipped off that the election had been rigged,

---

[19] See Yi-shiung Lin and Jia-wen Yao, *Hu luo ping yang* [When the Tiger Fell] (Taipei: Published by Authors, 1977).

[20] See Jia-wen Yao and Yi-shiung Lin, *Gu keng ye tan* [A Night Tale about Gukeng] (Taipei: Published by Authors, 1978).

[21] See Thomas B. Gold, *State and Society in the Taiwan Miracle* (New York: ME Sharpe, 1986).

[22] For a detailed narrative of the Zhongli Incident, see Jheng-Jie Lin and Fu-Jhong Chang, *Syuan jyu wan suei* [Viva Elections] (Taipei: Published by Authors, 1978).

Huang's campaign negotiated a partial recount under the supervision of district prosecutors. During the recount, prosecutors uncovered clear evidence of ballot stuffing, as there were about 730 "ghost ballots" found in 12 out of 54 polling stations of the Hualien City. Several poll managers later confessed that they stuffed the ballots for Wei, who later became the only KMT politician sentenced for election rigging.[23]

It is difficult to tell whether these anecdotes should be regarded as exceptions to the rule or merely the tip of an iceberg. But the looming presence of real, attempted, or alleged vote rigging under the KMT's watch invites us to rethink the calculus of election rigging. In the literature on electoral malpractice, one prevailing school of thought holds that due to the risk and expense of manipulating elections, vote rigging tends to be used by weak electoral authoritarian regimes as a last resort.[24] However, most of the election fraud actually or allegedly perpetrated by the KMT regime does not look like a strategy of last resort used by a weak regime facing imminent defeat. Another school of thought views excessive and blatant electoral manipulation as a message of power that aims to influence political actors' behaviors in ways beneficial to the manipulators.[25] This theory, however, explains the vote buying better than the vote rigging of the KMT regime, as one cannot help but wonder what post-election considerations could ever justify the grave risks and costs associated with the latter.

That the KMT engaged in seemingly unnecessary vote rigging while trying to win elections can be understood as a symptom of the collective action problem inherent to the electoral authoritarian regime. Even with its Leninist party structure and its enormous party-state apparatus, the authoritarian KMT regime was not a unitary actor but a complex system composed of multiple members.[26] In this conception, each member had

---

[23] For an analysis of the Hualien case, see Chin-Shou Wang, *Tai wan de sih fa du li gai ge yu guo min dang shih cong jhu yi de beng kuei* [Judicial Independence Reform and the Breakdown of the Kuomintang Clientelism in Taiwan], *Taiwan Political Science Review* 10 (2006): 129.

[24] See e.g. Mark R. Thompson and Philipp Kuntz, "After Defeat: When Do Rulers Steal Elections?," in Andreas Schedler (ed.), *Electoral Authoritarianism: The Dynamics of Unfree Competition* (Boulder, CO: Lynne Rienner, 2006), 113–28; Birch, *Electoral Malpractice*, 61; Sarah Birch, "The Electoral Tango: The Evolution of Electoral Integrity in Competitive Authoritarian Regimes," Max Weber Lecture Series No. 2016/02, European University Institute, www.cadmus.eui.eu/bitstream/handle/1814/40331/MWP_LS_2016_02.pdf?sequence=1, 8–9.

[25] See Simpser, *Why Governments and Parties Manipulate Elections*.

[26] For the basic ideas about systemic analysis, see Adrian Vermeule, *The System of the Constitution* (New York: Oxford University Press, 2011).

her own self-interests that did not necessarily align with the regime's interests. Under pressure from the top to "deliver votes" or "win elections," local captains or certain segments of the KMT (such as its secret police) had much to gain by rigging votes if they were able to get away with it, even if doing so was bad for the regime as a whole. In other words, while it makes sense to assume that the KMT would hold honest elections out of self-interest, it does not follow that the regime could easily solve the collective action problem with authoritarian command and control.

In any event, election administration fraud has rarely surfaced in Taiwan after the Zhongli Incident of 1977, albeit the 1992 Hualien incident being an exception to the norm. During the late period of the KMT's authoritarian rule in the 1980s and Taiwan's democratic transition in the 1990s, many people were still deeply suspicious of the KMT as a rehabilitated vote rigger. But among the general public and election observers, there was growing confidence in the integrity of election administration.[27] What precipitated this change? Driven by socioeconomic development and the increasing isolation of the KMT regime in the international arena, it appears that the increasing demand for actual democracy was one important background factor.[28] A more immediate factor was the Zhongli Incident itself. By raising the public's awareness of how elections might get rigged, the Zhongli Incident may have led to heightened public scrutiny of election administration in the subsequent years and thus increased the deterrence of fraud detection. Simultaneously, the KMT may also have learned that the cost of repressing post-election protest could outweigh the benefits of vote rigging.[29] But what did the KMT do to prevent its members from crossing the line? The collective action problem that led to vote-rigging incidences in the earlier periods had to be addressed. External monitoring of elections would have helped, but it was also a measure that might have given the

---

[27] In the first Taiwan Social Change Survey (TSCS) conducted in 1984–5, respondents were asked to identify how they participated in the electoral process: 13.3 percent of the respondents reported that they would occasionally question and criticize the competence and attitude of workers in election administration, while 62.6 percent of the respondents never did so. See Ming-Tong Chen and Fo Hu, "Tai wan di cyu min jhong de syuan jyu can yu sing wei" [Electoral Participation in Taiwan], in Guo-Shu Yang and Hai-Yuan (eds.), *Bian cian jhong de tai wan she huei II* – [Taiwanese Society in Transition II] (Taipei: Institute of Ethnology, Academia Sinica, 1988), 407–9.

[28] See Levitsky and Way, *Competitive Authoritarianism*, 309–18.

[29] Jhan Bi-shia (詹碧霞), a veteran KMT staffer, reported in her memoir that the KMT ceased to engage in systemic vote rigging after the Zhongli Incident (Bi-Sia Jhan, *Mai piao chan huei lu* [The Confession of a Vote Buyer] (Taipei: Business Weekly, 1999), 126).

regime bad publicity should misdeeds be detected. What else could the KMT do?

Voting reform offers one solution, and Wakabayashi Masahiro (若林 正丈), a leading historian of postwar politics in Taiwan, credits the 1980 enactment of the Elections and Recalls Act During the Period of National Mobilization for the Suppression of the Communist Rebellion (動員戡 亂時期公職人員選舉罷免法) (Elections Act) for making the much-needed improvements in election administration.[30] As the first-ever statute governing the electoral process for all kinds of elected offices in Taiwan, the long-overdue Elections Act was part of the political reform propelled by the USA's derecognition of the ROC government in 1979. That the Elections Act was enacted following the Zhongli Incident of 1977, the manipulative postponement of parliamentary elections in 1978, and the Formosa Incident of 1979 (a pro-democracy demonstration that resulted in the jailing of many *dangwai* activists who later formed the DPP), suggests that the Elections Act was part of a progressive move in the "electoral tango" scenario, a typical development in competitive authoritarian regimes whereby conditions of electoral integrity deterio-rated before getting improved.[31] However, it remains debatable whether, how, and to what extent the substance of the legislation made the ballot boxes any safer than before. The political opposition and public intellec-tuals at that time heavily criticized the legislation on grounds that it merely codified preexisting regulations without making significant changes to the electoral and voting systems.[32] One major reform accom-plished by the Elections Act was the creation of a new Central Election Commission (中央選舉委員會; CEC). But before 2000, the CEC was, for the most part, headed by the Minister of the Interior, and its status as an independent agency was not fully secured until the enactment of the Organic Law of the Central Election Commission (中央選舉委員會組 織法) in 2009.[33] The Elections Act of 1980 also added a few rules

---

[30] See Wakabayashi Masahiro, *Jhan hou tai wan jheng jhih shih: Jhong hua min guo tai wan hua de li cheng* – [The "Republic of China" and the Politics of Taiwanization: The Changing Identity of Taiwan in Postwar East Asia], trans. Yu-Ru Hong and Pei-Fong Chen (Taipei: National Taiwan University Press, 2014), 176.

[31] See Birch, "Electoral Tango."

[32] See e.g. The 80s Press, *Syuan jyu li fa shih mo ji* [On the Birth of the Elections Act] (Taipei: The 80s Press, 1980).

[33] During the 1980s, some foreign election observers raised concerns over the independence and impartiality of the CEC; see e.g. Committee on Foreign Affairs of the US House of Representatives, *Elections in Taiwan: Report of a Staff Study Mission to Taiwan, December 1–9, 1988* (Washington, DC: US Government Printing Office, 1988), 18–19.

concerning campaign regulation, poll worker selection, election litigations, and the criminal investigations of election-related crimes. The
causal link between these marginal reform measures and the disappearance of vote rigging in Taiwan has yet to be examined.

To the extent that the Elections Act of 1980 may be characterized
as old wine in new wineskins, Taiwan may be said to have achieved
some progress in its election administration integrity since the 1980s
without significant changes in its voting rules. This is no surprise
given that the old voting system in Taiwan has some desirable
features that were instrumental for cultivating integrity in street-
level election administration in the long run. Had the voting system
in Taiwan not evolved in the way that it did, Taiwan might have had
a very different history of elections and democracy to tell. The next
two sections explore and assess two understudied features of the old
voting system in Taiwan: on-site ballot counting and poll worker
selection.

11.3   On-Site Ballot Counting as an Electoral Ritual

Thanks in no small part to the effective household registration system
first established by the Japanese colonial government, elections in Taiwan
have been able to avoid certain forms of election fraud with relative ease.
For instance, voter registration is far less of a problem in Taiwan because
voter rolls are generated directly from the household registration
database.[34] Voter identification is also a nonissue in Taiwan, because
voters simply cannot vote without first presenting their national ID cards
issued by the household registration offices. However, elections may still
be rigged by other means, and much is dependent on the institutional
design of how votes are cast and counted. Voting in Taiwan is executed
by Australian paper ballot (i.e. uniform paper ballots printed and distributed by the government), and votes are manually counted at each
polling station immediately after the poll is closed. This combination is
arguably the simplest and most widely used voting and results management system around the world, and it has been practiced in Taiwan for

---

[34] The author would like to thank Nathan Batto for raising this point. It should be noted,
however, that a citizen's household registration does not necessarily match his or her real
residence, and there are "ghost voters" who knowingly falsify their household registration
for the sole purpose of influencing elections in specific localities. This type of voter fraud
is one of the most common election-related criminal offenses prosecuted and punished in
Taiwan.

more than seven decades.[35] Such a mundane practice arguably has profound yet underappreciated influences on the state of election administration integrity in Taiwan.

There are many ways to count votes, and we may refer to the one used in Taiwan as "on-site balloting counting" for the sake of simplicity. To be specific, this decentralized method of managing electoral results at ground-level entails three institutional choices: (1) timing: ballots are counted immediately after the poll is closed as opposed to sometime later; (2) place: ballots are first counted at each polling station as opposed to some other centralized counting centers; (3) manner: ballots are manually counted by poll workers, as opposed to being counted by or with the help of machines. Compared to the alternatives, Taiwan's low-tech and labor-intensive system scores very high in terms of timeliness and transparency. However, these valuable benefits may come at the expense of higher administrative costs, the inconvenience of election monitoring, and inevitable human errors.[36] Still, the trade-offs make sense in Taiwan's context, especially when Taiwan was under the KMT's authoritarian rule. To be sure, votes could still be rigged at remote polling stations controlled by the KMT, and the practice could not prevent votes from being rigged (or perceived as being rigged) through the use of dramatic measures such as sudden power outages during the vote counting. But there is arguably no better way for the electoral authoritarian regime to showcase its commitment to democracy than by counting votes immediately after the poll is closed and in front of the suspicious crowds, one ballot at a time. Under this arrangement, the *dangwai* candidates learned to mobilize their supporters to operate precinct-level election monitoring, which in turn made it increasingly difficult for the KMT to rig elections at the last minute without making a scene.

---

[35] Government-issued paper ballots were also used in the first few local elections before 1950, but voting back then was performed by writing the candidate's name on the blank ballot. On-site counting was first introduced in 1946. In the two elections held by the Japanese colonial government, ballots were counted at local counting centers rather than polling stations.

[36] See ACE Electoral Knowledge Network, *The ACE Encyclopaedia: Results Management Systems*, 3rd rev., 2013 ed., www.aceproject.org/ace-en/pdf/vc/view; ACE Electoral Knowledge Network, *Timing of Counting Votes*, www.aceproject.org/electoral-advice /archive/questions/replies; Helen Catt et al., "Electoral Management Design," International Institute for Democracy and Electoral Assistance 2014, www.idea.int /sites/default/files/publications/electoral-management-design-2014.pdf

This practice of on-site ballot counting is usually taken for granted in Taiwan because it came into existence in as early as 1946, when the KMT regime held its first ground-level local elections.[37] However, this was not the way votes were counted in the first two parliamentary elections held in the whole of the ROC in 1947 and 1948. According to the election law at that time, all the ballot boxes of a given district had to be transported to the local elections authority upon closing of the polls, and the votes were counted by the authority after it had received all the ballot boxes. This centralized vote-counting procedure, unlike Taiwan's experience under Japanese rule, was replete with fraud.[38] Under the leadership of K. C. Wu (吳國楨), a Princeton-educated KMT elite with the backing of the US government, the bureaucrats of the Taiwan provincial government had to decide between the approach of postwar Taiwan and ROC when making rules for local elections in the early 1950s. The task of election rulemaking was left primarily in the hands of Yang Jhao-jia (楊肇嘉) and Siang Chang-cyuan (項昌權), who served as the chief and deputy-chief of the Civil Affairs Department of Taiwan Provincial Government at that time. Yang was a Taiwanese elite who played a critical role in the campaign for autonomous elections in the 1930s when Taiwan was still under the Japanese colonial rule.[39] Siang was a French-educated main-lander who came to Taiwan with the KMT regime and later became a political science professor at National Chengchi University.[40] Both individuals knew very clearly what was at stake, and they opted for on-site ballot counting to better safeguard the integrity of election administration.[41] Their decision has since become a cornerstone for all following elections in Taiwan.

---

[37] See Taiwan Provincial Governor's Office (臺灣省行政長官公署), *Tai wan sheng ge sian shih cun li jhang syuan jyu ban fa* [Rules on Borough Chiefs Elections in Taiwan Province], 1946, art. 15.

[38] See Siang, *Tai wan di fang syuan jyu jhih fen si yu jian tao* [On the Local Elections in Taiwan], 36.

[39] See Chen, *Bai nian jhuei ciou* [A Century's Quest], 182–8.

[40] See Vivianne Yan-Ching Weng, "*Heng jhu si dian yi li dong yong: Chu tan jhih nan shan sia de sian jheng sih wei*" [Exploring the Use of Western Canons in the East: On the Constitutional Thoughts of the Jhih nan Shan School], in Wan-Ying Yang (ed.), *Chuan cheng yu chuang sin: Jheng da jheng jhih syue si yu tai wan jheng jhih syue de fa jhan* [Tradition and Innovation: The Department of Political Science at the NCCU and the development of political science in Taiwan] (Taipei: National Chengchi University Press, 2016), 67–102.

[41] See e.g. Taiwan Provincial Government, *Tai wan sheng ge sian shih yi huei yi yuan syuan jyu ba mian guei cheng* [Elections and Recalls Regulations for the Members of the County/Town Councils in the Taiwan Province], 1950, art. 18. See also Jhao-jia Yang, *Yang jhao*

To the credit of subsequent election administrators, including those who served under the KMT's authoritarian rule, Taiwan soon developed a scrupulous standard operating procedure for on-site ballot counting on election day.[42] With years of testing and refinement, the core procedure of on-site ballot counting in Taiwan presently involves the following steps:[43] Poll manager A picks up a ballot from the ballot box and unfolds the ballot for the inspection of poll manager B, who does so in the presence of at least two poll supervisors representing the competing candidates. After taking the ballot from poll manager A and consulting with the poll supervisors who have closely examined the ballot, poll manager B declares the result of the counting with a loud voice and holds up the ballot using both hands for the audience to see. Upon hearing the counting judgment of poll manager B, poll manager C, who stands in front of a large tabulation chart displayed on a wall (or a blackboard), recites the judgment and marks the vote on the chart. Poll manager B then hands over the counted ballot to poll manager D, who is responsible for sorting the ballots so counted. The whole procedure is meticulously designed to minimize counting errors and suspicions of wrongdoings. And when poll workers follow this deliberate procedure and count votes one by one and step by step, they have to do so diligently in order to earn the trust of vigilant voters. In this regard, one may argue that on-site ballot counting in Taiwan is no longer a mundane task of electoral mechanics per se, but has been transformed into a ritual that honors every sacred vote. With countless replays performed and watched at all polling stations around the country after every election, the ritualized on-site ballot counting has become one of the most remarkable features of Taiwan's electoral process. Moreover, the ritual is carefully scripted to a solemn rhythm. Being fairly easy to learn, the procedure is extensively practiced at all levels of student elections in Taiwan. As such, the ritual has profoundly shaped citizens' expectations of how votes ought to be counted in Taiwan.

---

jia huei yi lu [The Memoir of Yang Jhao-jia] (Taipei: San Min Press, 2004), 374–76; Siang, *Tai wan di fang syuan jyu jhih fen si yu jian tao* [On the Local Elections in Taiwan], 40.

[42] See e.g. Central Election Commission, *Di shih sih ren zong tong fu zong tong ji di jiou jie li fa wei yuan syuan jyu tou kai piao suo gong zuo ren yuan shou ce* [Poll Worker Handbook for the 14th Presidential and the 9th Legislative Elections] (Taipei: Central Election Commission, 2015), 23.

[43] After the poll closes and prior to the counting process, the polling stations are closed temporarily for the poll workers to seal the ballot boxes, count the unused ballots, and make preparations for the ballot-counting procedure.

That on-site ballot counting in Taiwan may be seen as a well-established electoral ritual offers a powerful explanation as to why the practice may have played a prominent role in the long-term progress of election administration integrity in Taiwan. By raising the visibility and significance of ballot counting in popular culture, the ritual may have helped to create and sustain a strong cultural norm against vote rigging. Even though vote rigging was rarely punished during the authoritarian period in Taiwan, the norm was arguably observed owing to the cultural influences that the solemn ritual had on those who participated in the ballot-counting process. Although there have been calls to upgrade the precinct-level voting system in Taiwan to reduce costs and improve accuracy, the general public and the CEC are in no hurry to automatize the ballot-counting process in the foreseeable future. Viewing the existing practice as a meaningful ritual also helps to explain the entrenchment of such a practice in a country that is proud of its advanced IT industry.

11.4   The Selection Effects of the Poll Worker Recruitment

It is poll workers who perform the ritual of ballot counting, and who are responsible for running the polling stations on election day. Two types of poll workers exist in Taiwan: First, poll managers are in charge of administering the entire precinct-level voting system from end to end. Their jobs include, among other things, checking and sealing ballot boxes, checking in voters, issuing ballots, maintaining order, counting votes, and writing final reports of the poll. Second, poll supervisors take coresponsibility with the poll managers by overseeing the whole voting (and vote-counting) process and reporting irregularities and/or violations of law that occur in the polling station. Minimally, each polling station is required to have four poll managers (including one head manager) and two poll supervisors (including one head supervisor). Accordingly, nationwide elections in Taiwan require a large quantity of manpower. For instance, in the first limited (supplemental) parliamentary elections (for members of the Legislative Yuan) in 1969, some 51,000 poll workers operated a total of 6,149 polling stations for an electorate of about 6.69 million people.[44] By 2004, the sixth parliamentary elections,

---

[44] Syuan jyu zong shih wu suo [Chief Executive Office of Elections], *Dong yuan kan luan shih ci zih you di cyu jhong yang gong jhih ren yuan zeng syuan bu syuan jyu shih lu* [Records of the Supplemental Parliamentary Elections During the Period of National Mobilization for the Suppression of the Communist Rebellion] (Taipei: Chief Executive Office of Elections, 1970), 5(1): 10.

which were held for an electorate of 16.56 million people, required 13,930 polling stations and 162,782 poll workers.[45]

The election laws and regulations in Taiwan only stipulate some basic guidelines for the selection and training of poll workers, and the local election commissions are accorded the discretion to recruit, train, and assign poll workers for national and local elections alike. Initially an administrative convention developed under colonial/authoritarian rule and subsequently a guideline stipulated by election law, a large number of poll workers in Taiwan (especially in the case of poll managers) have been recruited from the civil service, government employees, and schoolteachers. This defining feature of the poll workforce has profound influence on the state and public perception of election administration integrity in Taiwan, because the poll workers' vocations may well affect how they administer the voting process on election day.

Elections in authoritarian regimes are often run by nonvoluntary poll workers coming from the public sector. This common practice is largely shaped by a historical contingency. When elections were first held under the authoritarian rule, the voting process was tightly controlled by the authoritarian regime with little help from civil society, which was still too weak to deliver enough volunteers of good standing to handle the large-scale elections. Meanwhile, the public viewed the poll workers with suspicion because it was distinctly possible that the authoritarian regimes might use the handpicked poll workers to rig elections.[46] When suspicions of election rigging by "puppet" poll workers ran high and threatened the legitimacy of the electoral authoritarian regime, the regime would acquiesce to the opposition's demands and restore public confidence in its election administration by opening up the poll worker selection process. This scenario recounts Taiwan's first change in poll worker selection in 1960, when the KMT regime accepted the opposition's proposal for reform and revised local elections regulations to allow candidates to take part in the recruitment of poll supervisors (but not poll managers).[47] By introducing checks and balances within the poll workers

[45] The Central Election Commission, *Di liou jie li fa wei yuan syuan jyu shih lu* [Records of the Elections for the Sixth Legislative Yuan] (Taipei: Central Election Commission, 2005), 77 and 181.

[46] See e.g. International IDEA, "Electoral Management During Transition: Challenges And Opportunities," International IDEA August 2012 Policy Paper, www.idea.int/sites/default/files/publications/electoral-management-during-transition.pdf, 14.

[47] See Taiwan Provincial Government, *Tai wan sheng sian shih gong jhih ren yuan syuan jyu ba mian jian cha wei yuan huei zu jhih guei cheng* [Organization Rules for the County/City Elections and Recalls Supervision Committees], 1960, art. 8.

298 YEN-TU SU

of the same polling station, the selection of candidate-recommended poll supervisors may have, to a certain extent, improved the integrity of Taiwan's election administration after the 1960s. One prominent witness of this change was Henry Kao (Kao Yu-shu; 高玉樹), a renowned *dangwai* politician who ran for mayor of Taipei City four times during the 1950 and 1960s.[48] Following some dubious power outages during ballot counting, Kao lost his reelection in 1957, and he dropped out of the mayoral race in 1960 on the grounds that he was not permitted to recommend poll supervisors to ensure electoral integrity at polling stations. However, Kao ran and won the mayoral race again in 1964. Thanks to the voting reform on poll worker recruitment, his subsequent campaign managed to place some 500 poll supervisors in two-thirds of the polling stations. These poll supervisors were equipped with flashlights and were even instructed to drink less water so as to avoid using the toilets.[49] No election irregularities were detected in this election, and Kao defeated the KMT's incumbent by a comfortable margin.

Although poll supervisors recruited by non-KMT candidates may have done a great service in keeping elections honest, their availability was often limited during the authoritarian period. In the 1960s and 1970s, candidates could only recommend (1) local elders/civic leaders, (2) government and education workers, (3) elected local representatives (allowed in 1960–3 only), and (4) college students (allowed only after 1977) to serve as poll supervisors.[50] Such qualifications no longer remain since the enactment of the Elections Act in 1980, but poll supervisors must still be certified by local election commissions. In addition, the opportunity to recommend poll supervisors has to be shared equally among all candidates for elections held at the same time. As such, poll supervisors recommended by non-KMT candidates often could serve in some but not all of the polling stations. In the 1964 Taipei mayoral election, Kao was able to organize a larger army of poll supervisors only because he allied with fellow mayoral candidate Lee Chien-sheng (李建生), who entered the race solely for the purpose of helping Kao

[48] See Edwin A. Winckler, "Roles linking State and Society," in *The Anthropology of Taiwanese Society*, ed. Emily M. Ahern and Hill Gates (Stanford: Stanford University Press, 1981), 71.

[49] Jhong-Sheng Lin, *Gao yu shu huei yi lu: Yu shu lin fong bu bu gao* [The Memoir of Kao Yu-shu] (Taipei: Avan Guard, 2007), 131.

[50] See Taiwan Provincial Government, *Tai wan sheng sian shih gong jhih ren yuan syuan jyu ba mian jian cha wei yuan huei zu jhih guei cheng* [Organization Rules for the County/ City Elections and Recalls Supervision Committees], 1960/1963/1967/1971/1977, arts. 8–9.

deter possible vote rigging on the KMT's part.[51] The Committee on Foreign Affairs of the US House of Representatives sent a staff delegation to study the 1986 parliamentary elections in Taiwan, and the delegation reported that there were fewer candidate-recommended poll supervisors than they thought. Rather, many poll supervisors at that time were recruited by the local election commissions as required by the Elections Act. The staff delegation thereby surmised that "opposition candidates did not in fact have major concerns about election fraud during the voting per se, or were simply unable to mobilize sufficient poll watchers."[52]

In any event, the polling stations in Taiwan are primarily operated by the poll managers, whose selection is entirely in the hands of local election commissions. When the Elections Act of 1980 was under consideration, some *dangwai* legislators had sought but failed to exclude government and public school employees from serving as poll managers.[53] Although the Elections Act did not require poll managers to possess particular qualifications, the practice of recruiting poll managers from public sector employees has expanded since the early 1980s. Between 1983 and 1991, the Enforcement Rules of the Elections Act (動員戡亂時期公職人員選舉罷免法施行細則) had even required that (1) all poll managers be recruited from government and education workers ("the public-sector-only rule,") and (2) those who work in the government and education sectors must accept the poll worker assignments ("the mandatory rule").[54] The public-sector-only rule was relaxed somewhat in 1991, but the mandatory rule remains effective and has become a statutory rule since 2003.[55] As revised in 2007, the current Elections Act requires that, in each and every polling station, the head manager, the head supervisor, and the majority of poll managers all be selected from active government and education workers.[56]

---

[51] See Lin, *Gao yu shu huei yi lu* [The Memoir of Kao Yu-shu], 131.

[52] Committee on Foreign Affairs of the US House of Representatives, *Elections in Taiwan*, 31.

[53] See The 80s Press, *Syuan jyu li fa shih mo ji* [On the Birth of the Elections Act], 225 and 311.

[54] Ministry of the Interior, *Dong yuan kan luan shih ci gong jhih ren yuan syuan jyu ba mian fa shih sing si ze* [The Enforcement Rules of the Elections and Recalls Act During the Period of National Mobilization for the Suppression of the Communist Rebellion], 1983, art. 65.

[55] Enforcement Rules of the Elections Act of 1991, art. 65; Elections Act of 2003, art. 58.

[56] Elections Act of 2007, arts. 58 and 59.

Since the late period of the KMT's authoritarian rule, Taiwan's poll workforce has been bureaucratized to an even greater extent. The selection policy was originally mandated by the KMT regime notwithstanding the objections of the *dangwai* opposition. But after the DPP was founded in 1986, the opposition essentially went along with its implementation and made little effort to change its course – even in the aftermath of the 1992 Hualien vote-rigging incident. The opposition's muted resistance to the selection of poll managers from the public sector during the 1980s and 1990s reflected the growing public confidence in the integrity of the ground-level election administration. Rather than arousing suspicion of election meddling, the fact that the great majority of poll workers in Taiwan come from the government and the education sector has become an asset for building trust in the electoral process. When the KMT lost the presidential elections in 2000 and 2004, many DPP supporters who used to question the integrity of poll workers were among the first to defend them against vote-rigging allegations made by the conspiracy theorists. Unsurprisingly, when the Elections Act was revised in 2007 to entrench the practice of recruiting poll workers from the ranks of schoolteachers and government employees, the legislation sailed through with bipartisan support.

Heavy reliance on government employees and schoolteachers to administer the voting (and vote-counting) process at the precinct level in Taiwan makes much sense because they have the capacity to be good poll workers. To begin with, these individuals can be relied upon to timeously show up for work on election day. Trained to accomplish things by the book throughout their professional lives, these employees can easily abide by the poll worker instructions. Furthermore, such employees tend to be law-abiding, possess risk-averse mindsets, and are highly invested in their professions, which make it far less likely for these individuals to commit crimes to rig the elections. Although many civil servants and schoolteachers during the authoritarian era joined the KMT or preferred to vote for the KMT, that connection alone did not render them puppets of the authoritarian regime. On the contrary, the proven vote rigging during the 1977 election for Taoyuan's county magistrate was first exposed thanks to a report made by a government employee, who served as one of the poll managers at the vote-rigging station.[57] Moreover, few persons are motivated to assume the demanding, modestly paid, and thankless job of a poll worker, and the government

---

[57] See Lin and Chang, *Syuan jyu wan suei* [Viva Elections], 305–6.

employees and schoolteachers are no exception. Nevertheless, the mandatory rule requires these designated poll workers to answer the call, and they have proved that they can carry out this task with professionalism.

During the 1980 legislative deliberation of the Elections Act, a tenured KMT representative suggested that, with the passing of the Act, local elections authorities should stop selecting those who work for the KMT and/or its affiliated organizations to serve as poll workers.[58] To the extent that some KMT party officials had opportunities to serve as poll workers and rig elections for their comrades in the foregoing era, the public-sector-only rule that governed poll manager selection from 1983 to 1991 may be regarded as a measure of reform aimed at reducing the risk of vote rigging. It appears that the KMT regime saw in this measure not only a way to secure the supply of poll workforce, but also a means to enhance electoral integrity. The trade-off made much sense for the KMT, since the occasional vote rigging in the previous era had contributed more harm than good to the electoral authoritarian regime as a whole. It did not take too long, either, for the opposition and the general public in Taiwan to realize that poll worker selection could impact the integrity of election administration. The henhouse is much safer, after all, if it is guarded not by foxes but by dogs.[59]

11.5   Conclusion

Students of electoral authoritarianism often regard Taiwan as a positive example of why an authoritarian regime is willing to hold and abide by honest elections. However, many Taiwanese citizens believe that the KMT regime was adept at rigging votes, especially during the 1950s to 1970s. This chapter reconciles the discrepancy between these two views by noting how the collective action problem may explain the occasional vote rigging during the early authoritarian elections organized by the KMT regime. Since the 1980s, the election administration in Taiwan has gradually gained the trust of the general public and election observers. However, the enactment of the Elections Act in 1980 was not the only factor contributing to the actual and perceived progress in election administration integrity that began in the late authoritarian period. This chapter highlights and explores how ritualized on-site ballot

---

[58] See The 80s Press, *Syuan jyu li fa shih mo ji* [On the Birth of the Elections Act], 245.
[59] For the idea of selection effects, see generally Vermeule, *System of the Constitution*, 101–33.

counting and the development of poll worker selection rules contributed to administrative integrity in the street-level voting process in Taiwan.

The secrets behind Taiwan's achievement in election administration integrity further invite us to rethink the larger undertaking of taming and transforming an authoritarian regime with the rule of law. This chapter suggests that even a seemingly mundane achievement such as protecting votes from being rigged may require the hard work of many people and cannot be sustained solely on the authoritarian rulers' good will. The micro-institutional design of a voting system greatly affects whether and how elections are vulnerable to last-minute vote rigging by agents of an authoritarian ruler. It certainly helps that the polling stations are staffed with conscientious public servants rather than those who answer only to the authoritarian party-state. Furthermore, it helps to elevate the mundane business of ballot counting into a solemn ritual, which, in turn, makes it possible to constrain the electoral authoritarian regime through cultural norms. While echoing a common theme of this edited volume that strong state capacity serves as an important building block for the development of authoritarian legality in Asia, this chapter emphasizes the contributions made by institutional design, cultural norms, and those street-level bureaucrats who can be empowered, and relied on, to follow and enforce the rule of law.

There is no guarantee that the strengthening of election administration integrity will hasten the downfall of an electoral authoritarian regime. To the contrary, one may argue that better election administration plays to the hands of the electoral authoritarian regime, which can hold on to power with or without resorting to the various means of electoral manipulation other than rigging votes. But, as illustrated by the case of Taiwan, enhancing and ensuring the administrative integrity of authoritarian elections may make it more likely that when the time has come for democratization, the regime change will occur through peaceful elections as usual.

Student Activism and Authoritarian Legality Transition in Taiwan

WEITSENG CHEN

12.1 Introduction

The Kuomintang (KMT) party ruled Taiwan throughout the authoritarian era (1945–87) and the short period of democratization that followed (1987–96) until it lost the presidential election in 2000.[1] From its inception, this one-party state embraced democracy and the rule of law, albeit through an autochthonous expression of these ideals. As such, Taiwan provides useful insight into the operation of authoritarian legality and a state's transition into liberal democracy. Although Taiwan's transformation is multifaceted at various societal levels, this chapter only focuses on Taiwan's student activism to shed light on the conditions of Taiwan's transition. Such a study may provide useful guidance for understanding similar developments in other jurisdictions.

Leaders of authoritarian states view the law as instruments for preserving power, stability, and the status quo. It is therefore no surprise that authoritarian politicians commonly employ the law for means contrary to promoting democracy.[2] Such an instrumental commitment to law is ordinarily subject to the rulers' political will, which should be distinguished from a normative commitment to law where even the rulers are

The author would like to gratefully recognize the fellowship and research support by Seoul National University Faculty of Law and the Center for Asian Legal Studies of National University of Singapore Faculty of Law, and thank Muhammad Nurshazny Bin Ramlan for very helpful research assistance.
[1] Scholars generally are of the view that Taiwan's democratization completed in 1996 when the first direct presidential election took place through universal suffrage.
[2] See e.g. William P. Alford, "Exporting 'The Pursuit of Happiness,'" *Harvard Law Review* 113 (2000): 1677.

subject to the law.[3] Taiwan, among several other countries, exemplifies how an authoritarian regime can experience transition from an instrumental to a normative commitment to law. What remains to be examined are the explanations for such a transition. To this end, this chapter studies the signals, potential mechanisms, and lingering effects of the authoritarian legality transition by honing in on one of the most significant transitional phenomena in Taiwan: student movements.

Between 2014 and 2015, three massive waves of student movements took place in three Asian jurisdictions that had previously experienced legal reforms during their nondemocratic eras. First, the Sunflower Movement in Taiwan resulted in the suspension of the Legislative Yuan for almost one month. Protesting students (along with nonstudent participants) occupied the congressional building in response to a controversial trade agreement with the People's Republic of China (China). In Hong Kong, the Occupy Central movement saw protestors gather on an unprecedented scale to call for electoral system reforms. Subsequently, the Students Emergency Action for Liberal Democracy (SEALDs) in Japan organized the nation's largest demonstration in the last fifty years outside the National Diet building, protesting against the Legislation for Peace and Security on grounds that it was unconstitutional. Significantly, all three movements share two strikingly similar features: first, the concerted involvement of constitutional law scholars; and, second, the use of legal concepts within the major slogans that fueled the movement. Whereas the events in Japan and Hong Kong are addressed by other authors in this volume, this chapter argues that Taiwan's student activism and its focus on constitutional rights are key to understanding the dynamics and determinants of Taiwan's transition away from authoritarian legality.

Ahead of its counterparts in Hong Kong and Japan, Taiwanese student activism that called for legal and democratic reforms emerged as early as in the 1980s and played a crucial role in the country's democratization. In fact, student activism continues to shape Taiwan's direction through nongovernmental organizations (NGOs), think tanks, and other sociopolitical groups. Activists from the 1980s continue the legacy by participating in these organizations and assisting the new generation of student activists to promote their cause. As such, the scope of this chapter moves

---

[3] Mark Tushnet, "Authoritarian Constitutionalism," *Cornell Law Review* 100 (2015): 391; Tom Ginsburg, "Constitutionalism: East Asian Antecedents," *Chicago-Kent Law Review* 88 (2012): 11; Gretchen Helmke and Frances Rosenbluth, "Regimes and the Rule of Law: Judicial Independence in Comparative Perspective," *Annual Review of Political Science* 12 (2009): 345.

beyond student activism within campus and also includes broader multi-generational student activism outside the campus that has facilitated the transformation of authoritarian legality in Taiwanese society.

The rest of this chapter comprises four parts. Section 12.2 discusses authoritarian legality generally in pre-democratic Taiwan. Section 12.3 examines student activism through the lens of authoritarian legality transition. Section 12.4 evaluates Taiwan's student activism from a broader perspective, including its role and impact on the rule of law, democracy, and post-transitional politics. Section 12.5 concludes.

12.2   Legality Engineering in Authoritarian Regimes

Authoritarian legality refers to how authoritarian rulers utilize the law to streamline the bureaucratic system, institutionalize policies and political competition, and bolster the economy and their own legitimacy. This process of legalization is similar to what literature about the rule of law discusses in the context of authoritarian states. However, this chapter prefers the comparably neutral conception of "legality" or "legalization" in lieu of the expression "rule of law," which has multifaceted connotations.[4] In contrast, the concept of "legality" is contextual and path-dependent without having to follow idealist notions. For instance, when using "legality" or "legalization," one might refer to past conceptions of injustice rather than current notions of justice.[5] Additionally, "legality" is not apolitical. Rather, it can be political even in democratic regimes, since political elites may define "legality" by reference to political processes and thereby oppress those who fall outside their categorization of legal rights.[6]

Notably, the authoritarian state's instrumental commitment to law is very different from a normative commitment. An instrumental commitment to law is subject to the ruler's strategic interests, which may be inconsistent or vary from time to time. In comparison, a normative

---

[4] For a discussion, see Michael J. Trebilcock and Ronald J. Daniels, *Rule of Law Reform and Development: Charting the Fragile Path of Progress* (Northampton, MA: Edward Elgar, 2009), 16–29; Randall Peerenboom, *China's Long March toward Rule of Law* (New York: Cambridge University Press, 2002).

[5] Ruti Teitel, "Transitional Jurisprudence: The Role of Law in Political Transformation," *Yale Law Journal* 106 (1997): 2009; Alford, "Exporting 'The Pursuit of Happiness.'"

[6] See e.g. David Kennedy, "Some Caution about Property Rights as a Recipe for Economic Development," *Accounting, Economics, and Law* 1 (2011): 1; Frank K. Upham, "The Illusory Promise of the Rule of Law," in Andras Sajo (ed.), *Human Rights with Modesty: The Problem of Universalism* (Boston, MA: Nijhoff, 2004), 279–313.

commitment to law helps to 'institutionalize' legal uncertainty, in at least two ways. First, it minimalizes legal uncertainty through the legalization of policies and orders. Second, and perhaps more importantly, it subjects all interests to equal and fair uncertainties. Under this approach, powerful groups that would not otherwise be compelled to accept undesirable legal outcomes under an authoritarian regime would nonetheless be subject to legal outcomes even if the law undermines their interests. No one can intervene and everyone must subject their interests to such uncertainties.[7]

In addition, the scope and magnitude of legality granted by the authoritarian states vary. An authoritarian state may carve out a fraction of legal rights (e.g. voting rights, or rights to freedom of speech and assembly) so as to preserve stability while maintaining a strong commitment to the other aspects of the law in a normative manner.[8] This is particularly true with regards to economy-related matters in developmental states. For instance, the East Asian Tiger nations commonly employ this form of 'legality engineering' for the purpose of attracting foreign investment and managing economy-related matters.[9] Yet, authoritarian regimes could ultimately still control the legislative process, influence judicial decision, and/or amend laws that obstruct the objectives of the authoritarian regime.

However, it is not easy for an authoritarian regime to undertake legality engineering and optimize the portfolio of varying levels of commitment to law. Variations in market conditions and size of territory may be the key determinants. For instance, compared to the East Asian Tiger states that have perfected this approach in light of economic achievements during their authoritarian years, China has greater difficulty in emulating this approach. When a myriad of state-owned enterprises (SOEs) rely on the party's political guarantee rather than developing their own competitive advantage, the complexity of risk and revenue portfolios confronting these firms make the process of subordinating market players to a standardized legal regime extremely challenging.

---

[7] Adam Przeworski, "Some Problems in the Study of the Transition to Democracy," in Guillermo O'Donnell and Philippe C. Schmitter (eds.), *Transitions from Authoritarian Rule: Comparative Perspectives* (Baltimore, MD: Johns Hopkins University Press, 2013), 58.

[8] Weitseng Chen, "Twins of Opposites: Why China Will Not Follow Taiwan's Model of Rule of Law Transition toward Democracy," *American Journal of Comparative Law* 66 (2018): 481.

[9] See e.g. Weitseng Chen, "Arbitrage for Property Rights: How Foreign Investors Create Substitutes for Property Institutions in China," *Washington International Law Journal* 24 (2015): 47; Yuhua Wang, *Tying the Autocrat's Hand: The Rise of the Rule of Law in China* (New York: Cambridge University Press, 2015), 154–5.

Consequently, a mix of standardized legal regimes, flexible party orders, informal rules, and extralegal measures would be considered the more effective method of regulation.

Furthermore, with respect to matters regarding politically sensitive rights, it is unrealistic to expect authoritarian rulers to submit themselves to laws that would constrain their power and challenge their legitimacy even though legalization would gradually provide a useful mechanism to discipline government officials. Rather, what is more common is that authoritarian rulers wield the law to enhance their legitimacy and justify the violation of political rights.[10] The state often converts a political issue into a legal one by asking courts either to adjudicate in its favor or defuse the tension through a lengthy procedure.[11] Taiwan's Constitutional Court (formerly, the Grand Justice Council) operated in this way during the authoritarian era. In its Interpretation No. 31 (1954), the Court defended the authoritarian KMT by justifying the KMT's suspension of nationwide legislative elections, thereby freezing the liberal part of Taiwan's constitution, ironically, via a constitutional approach.[12] Similar examples in other jurisdictions have been well documented.[13]

---

[10] For example, authoritarian regimes may benefit from delegating controversial and divisive political questions into the courts. To be fair, however, this phenomenon is also familiar in democratic settings. Tamir Moustafa, "Law and Courts in Authoritarian Regimes," *Annual Review of Law and Social Science* 10 (2014): 286; George I. Lovell, *Legislative Deferrals: Statutory Ambiguity, Judicial Power, and American Democracy* (New York: Cambridge University Press, 2003); Mark A. Graber, "The Nonmajoritarian Difficulty: Legislative Deference to the Judiciary," *Studies in American Political Development* 7(1) (1993): 35.

[11] For a general and comparative discussion about this phenomenon, see e.g. Ran Hirschl, "The Judicialization of Mega-Politics and the Rise of Political Courts," *Annual Review of Political Science* 11 (2008): 93; Juan, J. Linz, "Crisis, Breakdown, and Reequilibration," in Juan J. Linz and Alfred Stepan (eds.), *The Breakdown of Democratic Regimes* (Baltimore, MD: Johns Hopkins University Press, 1978), 17.

[12] For a further discussion, see Kevin Tan et al., *Constitutionalism in Asia: Cases and Materials* (Oxford: Hart, 2014); Jiunn-Rong Yeh and Wen-Chen Chang, "The Emergence of East Asia Constitutionalism," *American Journal of Comparative Law* 59 (2011): 805; Sean Coony, "The Effects of Rule of Law Principles in Taiwan," in Randall Peerenboom (ed.), *Asian Discourse of Rule of Law: Theories and Implementation of Rule of Law in Twelve Asian Countries, France and the U.S.* (New York: RoutledgeCurzon, 2004).

[13] See e.g. Tom Ginsburg, *Judicial Review in New Democracies: Constitutional Courts in Asian Cases* (Cambridge: Cambridge University Press, 2003); Clark B. Lombardi, "The Constitution as Agreement to Agree: The Social and Political Foundations (and Effects) of the 1971 Egyptian Constitution," in Denis J. Galligan and Mila Versteeg (eds.), *Social and Political Foundations Effects of Constitutions* (Cambridge: Cambridge University Press 2013), 398–425; Anil Kalhan, "'Gray Zone' Constitutionalism and the Dilemma of Judicial Independence in Pakistan," *Vanderbilt Journal of Transnational Law* 46 (2013): 1.

Ultimately, legalization serves to organize and thus prolong the authoritarian party's hold on power because the maintenance of authoritarian regimes depends on more than just the unrestrained and arbitrary use of power.[14] Authoritarian regimes increasingly adopt institutions that are commonly associated with liberal democracy.[15] In the same way a state may harness new and emerging technologies to bolster its strength and status, it can also employ innovative legal and institutional designs to solidify its regime. As such, despite the rule of law being a hope-inducing mechanism in the comparative democracy literature, the correlation and causation between legality and democracy is arguably ambivalent.[16] While Taiwan demonstrates that the rule of law heralds, and is dependent on, democratic institutions, Hong Kong does not. Further examples of rule by law (if not the rule of law) without democracy can be found in history, such as the Soviet Union or Nazi Germany.

The bottom line is that the transition of authoritarian legality is highly context-dependent, although literature has offered some general observations. For example, the frequency of protests often bears a curvilinear relationship with political openness. Protests are less likely to occur if claimants are permitted to fully voice their concerns within an open and functional political system or, conversely, if claimants are completely suppressed in a repressive polity.[17] In contrast, protests often occur frequently when claimants lack sufficiently open channels to voice their grievances but can nonetheless benefit from a limited space of tolerance by a polity – such is the case in most Asian authoritarian states that embrace the idea of authoritarian legality. However, this inherent defect of authoritarian legality is usually offset by the fact that, in Asia, legality is usually promoted by strong states that ultimately have a high degree of control and influence over their respective societies. In comparison, the rule of law took root in Europe when the monarchies of European states

---

[14] Jason Brownlee, *Authoritarianism in an Age of Democratization* (Cambridge: Cambridge University Press 2007), 202; Ellen Lust, "Competitive Clientelism in the Middle East," *Journal of Democracy* 20 (2009): 122.

[15] See Brownlee, *Authoritarianism*, 25–7; Larry Diamond, "Thinking about Hybrid Regimes," *Journal of Democracy* 13 (2002): 21.

[16] Jacques deLisle, "Law and Democracy in China: A Complex Relationship," in Kate Xiao Zhou, Shelley Rigger, and Lynn T. White III (eds.), *Democratization in China, Korea, and Southeast Asia? Local and National Perspectives* (New York: Routledge, 2014), 126.

[17] Charles Tilly, *From Mobilization to Revolution* (Reading, MA: Addison-Wesley, 1978); Charles Tilly, *Popular Contention in Great Britain* (Cambridge, MA: Harvard University Press, 1995).

STUDENT ACTIVISM AND AUTHORITARIAN LEGALITY 309

were weak in the face of the Catholic churches.[18] Similar paradoxes exist in other sociopolitical dimensions. For example, as demonstrated in many Asian countries including Taiwan, the authoritarian elites' commitment to political reforms appear to be the decisive precondition to the transformation of authoritarian legality, but a strong authoritarian regime may also effectively marginalize any judicial and legal institutions, if necessary, for the sake of regime survival.

Considering these inherent limits for any potential transition away from authoritarian legality, one may have to broaden the scope of the potential determinants for such a transition from endogenous factors within authoritarian legality to exogenous factors beyond the authoritarian rulers' calculation. Student activism in Taiwan is one of these factors.

12.3 Student Activism and Authoritarian Legality Transition

Taiwan's student activism emerged in the late 1980s and developed in parallel with the country's democratization and transformation of authoritarian legality in the following years. From the first large-scale movement – the Wild Lily Movement (1990) that led to several waves of constitutional reforms – to the latest Sunflower Movement (2014) that led to indefinite suspension of the Cross-Strait Service Trade Agreement (CSSTA) with China, student activism in Taiwan has almost three decades of history. To be precise, the beginnings of student activism can be traced back to an earlier period when students participated in social reforms in a less outspoken manner.

12.3.1 A Tradition of Student Activism in Taiwan

During the 1960s and 1970s, a variety of student societies dedicated to social service emerged in most universities. Although most of these societies were led by faculty members and were financially sponsored by the universities, the focus of these societies varied. For example, while some societies dedicated themselves to social services for less privileged groups, such as the fishing or the agricultural villages, other societies served the interests of youths in localities or high schools where university students had affiliations (e.g. the alumni society of a high school would provide higher education consultation services for prospective

---

[18] Francis Fukuyama, *The Origins of Political Order* (New York: Farrar, Straus and Giroux, 2011); Richard Pipes, *Property and Freedom* (New York: Vintage, 1999).

candidates back at their hometowns). At the national level, for example, the China Youth Anti-Communist National Salvation Corps was created in 1952, and aimed to provide basic organizational and military training to youths. Subsequently, guided by the government, its objectives shifted to the provision of community building and recreational services to young students, and the promotion of student participation in community and social services. In this way, the authoritarian government organized and made the best use of young talent for the creation of a social safety net and for economic modernization.

Furthermore, the KMT recruited elite college students from a cluster of student societies dedicated to extracurricular studies of the social sciences. For instance, one common name shared by these societies across universities (as well as some elite high schools) was the "Society for Studying Dr. Sun Yet-Sen's Thoughts." Dissatisfied with the regular curriculum centered on practical subjects such as computer science and electronic engineering, some students organized academic societies to plug the academic gap. By organizing reading groups under the guidance of their seniors and faculty members, members of these student associations were able to study socialism, sociology, and political philosophy. Most of these societies were monitored by the KMT in a noninterventionist manner, such as through the engagement of faculty members. Some student association members were also affiliated with the KMT's party units within the universities as a result of the KMT's efforts to recruit university talent. One case in point is the Association of Mainland China Studies at the National Taiwan University (NTU). Closely affiliated with the KMT during the authoritarian era, NTU served as an important channel through which the KMT recruited talented students.

In the 1980s, along with burgeoning economic growth and increasing rights consciousness among the public, the political climate on university campuses gradually began to change. Following in the footsteps of the social service-oriented student societies, the student societies dedicated to social science studies developed their own approaches to participating in social and community services. Some of these methods included publications in university newspapers, off-campus fieldwork, and summer camps promoting awareness of social, economic, and political issues. Consequently, students were made aware of the social injustices suffered by the general populace as they sought to increase engagement with the public. Inspired by liberal and/or leftist views learned during their extracurricular humanities education, students from these societies became the driving force of anti-government student activism in the late 1980s and 1990s. For example, the Association of Mainland China Studies at NTU, once closely connected with the KMT through its leaders and faculty advisers, eventually became a main base for liberal-minded students advocating for democratic reforms and regime change. Many cabinet members, legislators, and city mayors of the current ruling party – the Democratic Progressive Party (DPP) – spent their formative college years at this student association.

During the critical juncture of Taiwan's democratic transition in the late 1980s, divergent strands of student activism converged, resulting in a rich repertoire of collective action in the following years.[19] In 1990, a few months after the Tiananmen Student Movements in Beijing across the Taiwan Strait, the Wild Lily Movement took place in Taipei. Approximately 6,000 students occupied the Chiang Kai-Shek Memorial Hall for a week and required the KMT government to: first, abolish the "Temporary Provisions Effective During the Period of National Mobilization for Suppression of the Communist Rebellion," effectively freezing the Constitution at the time (e.g. legislative elections were suspended indefinitely); second, abolish the National Assembly on the grounds that it was a Leninist constitutional organization in the same vein as the National People' Congress in China, which sought to achieve the socialist idea of democratic concentration;[20] third, organize a national consultation meeting to discuss constitutional issues; and, fourth, formulate a timeline for political and constitutional reforms. When faced with the unprecedented scale of student protests, the KMT President Lee Teng-Hui accepted the students' proposals in their entirety.[21] As it turned out, the Wild Lily Movement was a milestone in Taiwan's process of constitutionalization and democratization that led to several constitutional amendments in the next few years.

---

[19] Generally, the period of 1980 and 1987 (when the Martial Law was suspended) saw a sharp increase in frequencies of protests from 175 in 1983 to 1,172 in 1988, with the average size of protests increasing from 73 people to 267 people. All incidents of large-scale protests with over 5,000 participants prior to democratization took place during this period too. Hsin-Huang Michael Hsiao, "The Rise of Social Movements and Civil Protests," in Tun-Jen Cheng and Stephan Haggard (eds.), *Political Change in Taiwan* (Boulder, CO: Lynne Rienner, 1992), 57–72.

[20] Li Hung-Hsi, "Fe guomindahui, ci qi shi ye" [It Is about Time to Abolish the National Assembly], *New Century Think Tank Forum* 10 (2000): 32–6, www.taiwanncf.org.tw /ttforum/10/10-12.pdf

[21] As it was revealed later, President Lee Teng-Hui accepted students' proposals partly because he wanted to have a greater leverage over the opposition to carry out his own reform agenda and to distance himself from the conservative power within the KMT.

In the next two decades, student participation in social and political reforms became the norm. Two waves of massive protests led by scholars and students between 1991 and 1992 brought an end to the legal regime that legitimized the KMT's control over freedom of speech. This legal regime comprised Article 100(II) of the Criminal Law and two special laws – the Act for the Control and Punishment of Rebellion (1949) and the Act for Prosecuting Communist Spies (1950). Both made capital punishment mandatory for individuals who "prepared or conspired to" overthrow the government even in the absence of any concrete action. Enraged by the KMT's arrest of members of a reading group who were studying a banned book about Taiwan's history, approximately 1,000 students occupied the Taipei Main Station, calling for the release of the arrested individuals and for the abolishment of the legal regime. Although the protest was violently suppressed within a few days, the ensuing violence against the students and professors precipitated a burst of public anger across Taiwan's academic circles. Shortly after, public sentiment gave rise to another round of protests on a much larger scale, which involved students and scholars from all major universities and law schools across the country. Overwhelmed by the unrest, the KMT allowed the Legislative Yuan to abolish the two special laws and acquitted the arrested persons shortly thereafter, thus setting a precedent for the developments in the following two decades.

However, the KMT's compromise did not reduce the momentum of groups calling for the end of legal regimes restraining the freedom of speech. Eventually, the KMT abolished Article 100(II) in 1992, the final pillar of the legal regime responsible for the White Terror era that had endured for nearly fifty years. The KMT's willingness to end governmental control on speech only encouraged student activism on all fronts.[22] Generally, the student movements continued in a relatively low-profile manner, with the agendas of these movements becoming increasingly diversified. Students volunteered in NGOs, social organizations, think tanks, and political parties to engage in social and political reforms. Thus, student activism became one of the major forces that incrementally compelled the authoritarian state to honor its promise of the rule of law and democracy.

One may wonder why the tradition of student activism existed in pre-democratic Taiwan in the first place. Two factors account for this tradition. The first is a cultural factor. Since the colonization of

[22] Wang Tay-Sheng, *Guoli Taiwan daxue falv xuen yuanshi 1928-2002* [The History of National Taiwan University College of Law 1928-2002], (Taiwan: National Taiwan University, 2002), 106.

Taiwan by Japan (between the years of 1895 to 1945), legal professionals and social elites (e.g. medical doctors) in Taiwan cultivated and preserved a tradition of activism.[23] Legal historians observe how vigorously Taiwanese citizens resorted to law to defend their property and contractual rights at the time.[24] As early as the 1920s, local elites had started to discuss political issues in the context of constitutionalism, commonly citing the 1889 Meiji Constitution, which applied to Taiwan since the beginning of Japanese rule, to challenge the Japanese colonial government's policies.[25] After all, intellectual criticism against the government has its moral foundation in Confucianism as an alternative form to checks and balances.[26] Similar traditions exist in other authoritarian jurisdictions that share a Confucianist tradition, such as China and Vietnam.[27]

The second factor is associated with the KMT's own political calculation. When the KMT took over Taiwan in 1945, it did not eliminate but in fact chose to tolerate the activist tradition to the extent that it worked in its favor to create and uphold its own legitimacy. Through the preservation of local elections that began during the Japanese rule and the tolerance of local activism (however limited), the KMT was able to distinguish itself as a "free China" in contrast with the communist mainland controlled by its rival, the Chinese Communist Party (CCP). Thanks to the KMT's tolerance of the *dangwai* (literally, "outside the party") activities, student activists enjoyed a limited but lively public forum for engaging in social and political matters. This is no surprise given that the KMT government also encouraged student participation in social services in the party's comfort zone as part of its social modernization and mobilization, which were connected with patriotism and nationalism during the Cold War era.

---

[23] Wang Tay-Sheng, "Riben zhimintongzhizhe de falv zhenya shi yu taiwanren de zhengzhi fankang wenhua" [Japanese Colonial Rulers' Legal Suppression and the Politically Rebellion Culture in Taiwan], *Taiwan Law Review* 116 (2005): 123.

[24] See e.g. Lin Wen-Kai, "Riben chuqi jilong tudi jiufen shijian de falv shehui shi fenxi" [A Study of Legal Social History on the Land Disputes in Keelung during the Early Japanese Colonial Period 1898–1905], *Cheng Kung Journal of History Studies* 48 (2015): 1.

[25] Ibid.

[26] Though it is far from sufficient. For a general discussion, see Fukuyama, *Origins of Political Order*, 132–3.

[27] See Bui Ngoc Son, *Confucian Constitutionalism in East Asia* (New York: Routledge, 2016); Michael Dowdle, "Popular Constitutionalism and the Constitutional Meaning of Charter 08," in Jean-Philippe Beja, et al. (eds.), *Liu Xiaobo, Charter 08, and the Challenges of Political Reform in China* (Hong Kong: Hong Kong University Press: 2012).

Importantly, having a *tradition* of student activism is as important as any particular student movement. In Taiwan, social movements often had an impact when there was an internal power struggle within the KMT. With the benefit of hindsight, the Wild Lily Movement succeeded partly because the then President Lee Teng-hui needed social support in the face of strong political opponents within the party following the death of President Chiang Ching-Kuo. Similarly, the Sunflower Movement succeeded partly because the head of the Legislative Yuan, Wang Jing-Ping, being in the middle of a political fight against the then President Ma Ying-Jeou, found it advantageous to gain the support of students during the occupation. In other words, the success or failure of social movements is primarily affected by political opportunities revealed by the social and economic structures at any given time. However, student activists are unlikely to know of these political opportunities in advance before planning their actions. Only a constant repertoire of activism may exert its impact when there is a chink in the armor of the party's power.

Moreover, the student activists' focus on legal reforms signals a favorable political opportunity under the regime of authoritarian legality.[28] By upholding authoritarian legality, the KMT embraced the idea of the rule of law and democratic values, albeit with their own definitions of those expressions. Accordingly, instead of invoking outright confrontation and making threats against the authoritarian regime, student activists in Taiwan have chosen to frame their concerns in rational terms of legal injustice and to advocate their agenda by resorting to legal principles or constitutional rights under a legal framework that the KMT had explicitly promised. In this regard, student activism has exerted a crucial impetus for the authoritarian legality transition by creating and expanding public discourse about the regime's commitment to legality per se.

As demonstrated by student activism in Taiwan, creating a sustainable public forum for constitutional discourse and deliberation between the state and society is a crucial transitional mechanism. In the context of developing constitutionalism in nondemocratic countries, scholars have emphasized the importance of such constitutional discourse. Michael Dowdle argues that successful constitutionalism is the product of a slow process of constitutional learning and adaptation, a process he coins as "discursive benchmarking."[29] Similarly, Baogang He and Mark

---

[28] Lauren B. Edelman, Gwendolyn Leachman, and Doug McAdam, "On Law, Organizations, and Social Movements," *Annual Review of Law and Social Science* 6 (2010): 653, 664.

[29] Michael Dowdle, "Of Parliaments, Pragmatism, and the Dynamics of Constitutional Development: The Curious Case of China," *New York University Journal of*

Warren suggest that a controlled but genuine deliberation that influences the authoritarian state's decision-making is possible because political elites may use the deliberation to co-opt opposition forces, thereby enhancing the regime's legitimacy.[30] Several other commentators have observed, in various contexts, how citizens in rural China resort to the constitutional text to challenge local injustices, a process that Kevin O'Brien and Lianjiang Li describe as "rightful resistance."[31] Advocates of popular constitutionalism also emphasize the importance of public activism, in both positive and normative senses, for constitutional changes.[32]

One may wonder why student activism remains active in Taiwan even after the successful democratization and authoritarian legality transition. One reason is that a cognitive threat against democracy and the rule of law remains a prevailing public sentiment given the continuing Taiwan–China tensions. Moreover, the divided polity in post-democratization Taiwan has negatively impacted the government's performance, which in turn has resulted in social and economic dissatisfaction. Influenced by patterns of past conflicts and inspired by recorded successes, activists have opted to continue their activist approach by pursuing social and political reforms.[33] Most importantly, thanks to the tradition of student activism developed over the course of nearly thirty years, it is not difficult

International Law and Politics 35 (2002): 1; Keith J. Hand, "Resolving Constitutional Disputes in Contemporary China," University of Pennsylvania East Asia Law Review 7(1) (2011): 51.

[30] Baogang He and Mark E. Warren, "Authoritarian Deliberation: The Deliberative Turn in Chinese Political Development," Perspectives on Politics 9 (2011): 268, 278.

[31] Kevin J. O'Brien, "Rightful Resistance Revisited," Journal of Peasant Studies 40 (2013): 1051; Keith Hand, "Constitutionalizing Wukan: The Value of the Constitution Outside the Courtroom," China Brief 12 (2012), jamestown.org/program/constitutionalizing-wukan-the-value-of-the-constitution-outside-the-courtroom; Kevin J. O'Brien and Lianjiang Li, "Selective Policy Implementation in Rural China," Comparative Politics 31 (1999): 167.

[32] See e.g. Bruce Ackerman, We the People, Volume III: The Civil Rights Revolution (Cambridge, MA: Belknap Press of Harvard University Press, 2014); Mark Tushnet, "Popular Constitutionalism as Political Law," Chicago Kent Law Review 81 (2006): 991; Mark Tushnet, Taking the Constitution Away from the Courts (Princeton, NJ: Princeton University Press, 1999); Larry D. Kramer, The People Themselves: Popular Constitutionalism and Judicial Review (Oxford: Oxford University Press, 2004); Robert C. Post and Reva B. Siegel, "Popular Constitutionalism, Departmentalism, and Judicial Supremacy," California Law Review 92 (2004): 1024.

[33] The public jurisprudence literature discusses how patterns of conflicts may constrain the actors' behavior and influence their choice of legal strategy. See Rogers M. Smith, "Political Jurisprudence, the 'New Institutionalism,' and the Future of Public Law," American Political Science Review 82(1) (1988): 89; Robert W. Gordon, "Critical Legal

for activists to find their audience among the public, especially since some of the social elites and influencers were themselves participants of student activism.[34] Hence, activist groups benefit from economic resources, which only galvanizes the mobilization effort for social and student activism.[35] As this chapter will discuss in Section 12.3.2, a cross-generation collaboration among activists exists in Taiwan, which also continues to facilitate public discourse about legality and student activism itself.

In summary, exercises of "discursive benchmarking" and deliberative interaction require collective action. While an individual citizen may perceive the costs of rightful resistance to be too high to pursue, if each individual believes that other citizens share similar beliefs, a cascade of deliberation and public discourse is more likely to take place.[36] Such collective action may eventually exert an influence on the authoritarian regime's commitment to law.[37] Legality incrementally becomes an indispensable component of the regime's legitimacy, and therefore any illegality in state actions cannot be justified by other once-crucial sources of legitimacy such as economic growth.

12.3.2   Characteristics of Student Movements in Taiwan

The literature concerning social movements focuses on whether they can channel the public expression articulated during movements into the political system, which mechanisms and strategies activists are likely to choose, and what factors account for their choices. Conventional wisdom emphasizes the role of courts as the main mechanism that channels

---

Histories," *Stanford Law Review* 36 (1984): 57; David J. Danelski, "Law from a Political Perspective," *Western Political Quarterly* 36(4) (1983): 548.

[34] See Hsiao-Wei Kuan, "Connecting Gender and Trade: Gender Framing in the Anti-Cross Strait Service Trade Agreement Movement," *Hong Kong Law Journal* 45 (2015): 249; Brian Christopher Jones, "Introduction: The Taiwan Sunflower Movement and Hong Kong Umbrella Movement," in Brian Christopher Jones (ed.), *Law and Politics of the Taiwan Sunflower and Hong Kong Umbrella Movements* (London: Routledge 2017).

[35] Nella Van Dyke, "Crossing Movement Boundaries: Factors That Facilitate Coalition Protest by American College Students, 1930–1990," *Social problems* 50(2) (2003): 240.

[36] Hand, "Resolving Constitutional Disputes," 91.

[37] For a general discussion about collective action and the authoritarian regimes, see Jay Ulfelder, "Contentious Collective Action and the Breakdown of Authoritarian Regimes," *International Political Science Review* 26 (2005): 311; Sidney Tarrow, *Power in Movement: Social Movements and Contentious Politics* (New York: Cambridge University Press, 1998); Charles Tilly, *From Mobilization to Revolution* (Reading, MA: Addison-Wesley, 1978).

public pressure into the political system through judicial review. However, such an approach has limited explanatory power for the transformation of authoritarian legality in pre-democratic Taiwan. There, the public (including student activists) did not assert their views on constitutionalism and legality through the courts. Additionally, Taiwan's courts in the authoritarian era did not have supremacy over other governmental branches. As such, the presumption based on the centrality and supremacy of courts does not hold true in pre-democratic Taiwan, and thus the court-centric theory is largely irrelevant to pre-democratic Taiwan.

An alternative strand in the literature on democratic transition focuses on how respective actors' interests (e.g. the labor class or the bourgeoisie) and their postures in the power structure (e.g. hard-liners or soft-liners) determine the behavior of activists and their choice of strategies to impact the polity.[38] However, it is difficult to impute student activists in pre-democratic Taiwan with specific interests that they were expected to defend and promote. Students fighting for constitutional law reforms might have no legal training or come from families that were in fact beneficiaries of the authoritarian regime. These activists were in all likelihood insensitive to risks and willing to fight battles with a slim chance of winning. In other words, some interest-centric factors (i.e. risk aversion, expectation of success, or posture in the political system) that are crucial to understanding the strategic behavior of political actors appear to be of little predictive value when analyzing the behavior of student activists in Taiwan.[39] Therefore, theorists should look for alternative mechanisms.

To fully comprehend China's constitutional movement, for instance, Keith Hand suggests that the inquiry should shift away from court-based legal disputes and toward the manner in which citizens and the party-state interact, such as patterns of bargaining, consulting, and mediating across wide-ranging disputes.[40] In analyzing the US Tea Party movement and its impact on US constitutionalism, Mark Tushnet focuses on the political party system through which popular expression on constitutional matters are presented, absorbed, or ignored to various degrees, depending on the ways it interacts with

---

[38] See e.g. Juan J. Linz and Alfred Stepan, *Problems of Democratic Transition and Consolidation: Southern Europe, South America, and Post-Communist Europe* (Baltimore, MD: Johns Hopkins University Press, 1996).

[39] This approach is commonly adopted by theorists who analyzed the transitions of East European states in the 1990s. See e.g. Przeworski, "Some Problems," 54–5.

[40] Hand, "Resolving Constitutional Disputes," 76–82.

the party system.[41] Seen in this light, Taiwan's student activists exert their influence on the legal system by their actions on the streets rather than from within the courthouses, and inject popular opinions into the legal system through their interactions with political parties, whether directly or indirectly through social groups intermediaries . This section suggests that such interactions are effective because of three characteristics of student activism in Taiwan.

12.3.2.1   Higher Law-Centric Agenda

During Taiwan's authoritarian era, most student societies studied leftist theories and literature through the lens of growing Taiwanese nationalism at the time, which portrayed the KMT as a minority émigré regime in the same mold as the Japanese colonialists that ruled the Taiwanese majority. Inspired by nationalism and leftist theories, students found democratic value-centric jurisprudence as the perfect vehicle for expressing their reformist agenda. Law, as it turned out, provided a rich vocabulary of injustice, and helped student activists to put normative pressure on the KMT that had already embraced the ideal of legality. Concepts of constitutionalism and the rule of law also served as powerful ideas that defeated KMT's legal instrumentalism, especially in the face of legal constraints created by the KMT. Numerous movements utilized the principle of due process as a weapon against KMT's nontransparent policymaking. Human rights claims were used to air the grievances of convicted political dissidents. Freedom of speech served to weaken the KMT's control over universities and academics. In totality, a strategic focus on higher law principles and constitutionalism served as a strong counterforce against KMT's legal instrumentalism.

More specifically, students sought to amend the relevant laws to achieve their goals of social and political reform. For example, in the 1990s, the social rights movement called for a constitutional amendment to expand the scope of human rights stipulated in the Constitution to afford protection for the less privileged after four decades of rapid economic growth. In defense of academic freedom, students advocated for the amendment of the University Law and contributed to several rounds of revisions beginning in 2002. Furthermore, student activists worked with labor organizations and unions to expedite amendments to the Labor Union Law, the Collective Bargain Law, and the Labor Dispute

[41] Mark Tushnet, "Popular Constitutionalism and Political Organization," *Roger Williams University Law Review* 18 (2013): 1.

Resolution Law in late 2010s. Those working on gender issues called for the amendment of the family and inheritance chapters in the Civil Code. Moreover, participants in the Sunflower Movement demanded not only a specialized law regulating future negotiations between Taiwan and China, but also an amendment of the Constitution to hold the president more accountable to the parliament under Taiwan's semi-presidential system.[42] More recently, student activists engaged in legalizing same-sex marriage, which gave rise to fierce debates, including public protests in the streets of Taipei organized by both supporters and detractors.

There are instrumental, societal, and ideological reasons that account for this higher law-centric approach. As noted, students found that rights talk served as an effective instrument to deliver rhetorical force and exert political clout in Taiwan given that the authoritarian rulers already promised to honor such legal rights.[43] Indeed, it appears that framing grievances in terms of legal injustices has been a far better strategy than framing the same as political issues. By doing the former, student activists have been able to garner greater support by bolstering their moral ground and employing the power of persuasion.[44] Furthermore, thanks to the Japanese colonial legacy, lawyers are highly regarded in Taiwanese society, in contrast to a much less prestigious status accorded to lawyers under the Chinese tradition.[45] Higher law-centric public discourse, together with the support by lawyers, bar associations, and law professors, have collectively boosted the cause of student activism.

Finally, students are more idealistic than political strategists.[46] Students opt for legal rhetoric not just for the sake of effective political mobilization,

[42] See Wang Yuen-Ru et al., "Sunflowers in Blossom: Constitutional Crisis and Constitutional Moment in Taiwan," *Taiwan Law Review* 231 (2014): 260.

[43] Catherine R. Albiston, "Bargaining in the Shadow of Social Institutions: Competing Discourses and Social Change in Workplace Mobilization of Civil Rights," *Law & Society Review* 39 (2005): 11; Anna Maria Marshall, "Injustice Frames, Legality, and the Everyday Construction of Sexual Harassment," *Law & Social Inquiry* 28 (2003): 659.

[44] Edelman, Leachman, and McAdam, *On Law, Organizations, and Social Movements*, 664.

[45] After analyzing the admission rate of law schools and background of law students during Taiwan's authoritarian years, Wang Tay-Sheng demonstrates that mainlander families in Taiwan generally discouraged their children from pursuing legal careers whereas local Taiwanese families tended to do otherwise. Mainlanders refer to persons who came to Taiwan after World War II and account for approximately 14 percent of Taiwan's total population ("Taiwan sifaguan shequn wenhua zhong de zhongguo yinsu: cong qingmo minguo shidai zhongguo zhuisu qi" [The Chinese Element in the Culture of Judicial Officials in Taiwan: Tracing the Legacy from the Qing and Republican Era of China], *Zhengda faxue pinglun* [*Chengchi University Law Review*] 142 (2015): 1, 29–30, 37–8.

[46] For a general discussion on different types of activists, including those who are rational, calculated movement entrepreneurs and those who would relentlessly mobilize people

but because of the inspiration they obtain from constitutional discourse. During the Sunflower Movement, apart from the customary movement flyers, an academic article titled "The Struggle for Law" by German legal theorist Rudolf von Jhering was widely circulated online by the student activists. In that article, von Jhering posits that "[a]ll the law in the world has been obtained by strife. Every principle of law which obtains had first to be wrung by force from those who denied it."[47] Translated by an influential political scientist, Sa Meng-Wu, during the heydays of authoritarianism in Taiwan, the article was later included as the first chapter in a widely read civil code textbook of the most influential private law scholar in Taiwan, former Grand Justice Wang Tze-Chien.[48] For the past thirty years, first-year law students read this inspiring article before they begin to learn the Civil Code.[49] In 2014, one law student publicly testified that he would not have participated in the student movements but for von Jhering's article.[50] A similar sentiment may have been felt by law students of preceding generations.

It appears that the higher law-centric student activism has successfully created momentum for political discourse and continues to maintain a space for political maneuvering in the political arena. A key reason is that the jurisprudential underpinnings of recent student activism complements the DPP's strategy for political mobilization. While the DPP conventionally resorted to nationalism or democratic ideals to mobilize its crowd, many student activists focused on social reforms through legal engineering.

The DPP's power structure explains its tendency to concentrate on political mobilization rather than on legal reforms. During Chen Shui-Bian's presidency between 2000 and 2008, the DPP remained a minority

---

despite frequent failures, see William A. Gamson and David S. Meyer, "Framing Political Opportunity," in Doug McAdam, John D. McCarthy, and Mayer N. Zald (eds.), *Comparative Perspectives on Social Movements: Political Opportunities, Mobilizing Structures, and Cultural Framings* (New York: Cambridge University Press, 1996), 275–90; David S. Meyer "Protest and Political Opportunities," *Annual Review of Sociology* 30 (2004): 139.

[47] This article was expanded into a book later. Rudolph von Jhering, *The Struggle for Law* (Chicago: Callaghan, 1915), 1.

[48] Interestingly, as Wang's publications have been widely used in mainland China, discussions about von Jhering's article can be readily accessed in China too.

[49] Interestingly, the authoritarian KMT did not find this article problematic, probably because Sa Meng-Wu was a KMT member and Wang Tze-Chien was a private law scholar who rarely participated in political activities.

[50] "Yi pian taida falvxi xuesheng de fanxing wen" [A Reflexive Account by a Law Student of a National Taiwan University College of Law], *Apple Daily*, April 22, 2014, www .appledaily.com.tw/realtimenews/article/new/20140422/383778

party of the Legislative Yuan after winning the presidency, much to their surprise.[51] As a result, the Chen administration met constant political challenges from the Legislative Yuan.[52] Accordingly, the DPP did not have the urgency to rectify the institutional weakness of the legal and political systems, but continued its political battles with the KMT on high-profile, politically sensitive topics. For many within the DPP, this was a rational strategy as law-centric reforms would inevitably be boycotted at the KMT-controlled Legislative Yuan. Furthermore, DPP's veteran politicians were good at the populist approach. One DPP student activist opined, "DPP's supporters expected their leader to be a warrior who would fight and slaughter the KMT, instead of an idealist or theorist that challenges such a shared wish."[53] Against this backdrop, the student activists' focus on law-centered reforms and public discourse injected new dynamics into the political arena, filling the gap between political activism and effective governance. In this way, the DPP government was able to align itself with international human rights values and enter into the international community of democratic states.[54]

Another related issue regarding the relationship between student activism and the party system is the practical limit that all student activists share: Where will they go and what can they do after completing their tertiary education? Three common options exist: first, to join a political party; second, to join a nonparty organization; or, third, to end one's brief encounter with political reforms and pursue a different career altogether. Most students adopt the pragmatic third option, with far fewer choosing between the first two. For those who choose to join parties or public interest groups, another challenge ensues – while a political party may welcome student activists as members, such parties may not lend much

[51] President Chen and his colleagues admitted that they did not expect to win the presidency and were not ready to govern the country.
[52] Huang Tsung-Hao, "State–Business Relations of the Chen Shui-Bian Presidency in Taiwan: Minority Government, Personal Network and Financial Reforms," *Taiwan Journal of Democracy* 10(3) (2013); Jacques deLisle, "Democracy and Constitutionalism in China's Shadow: Sunflowers in Taiwan and Umbrellas in Hong Kong," in Brian Christopher Jones (ed.), *Critical Neighbors: The Legal and Political Significance of the Sunflower and Umbrella Movements* (New York: Routledge, 2017).
[53] He Ron-Shin, "Interview with Wong Chang-Liang," in He Ron-Shin (ed.), *Student Movement Generation: From Wild Lily to Sunflower* (Taipei: Reading Times, 2014), 233.
[54] For a discussion about similar phenomena in different jurisdictions, see Sally Engle Merry and Rachel E. Stern, "The Female Inheritance Movement in Hong Kong: Theorizing the Local/Global Interface," *Current Anthropology* 46 (2005): 387; Ellen Lutz and Kathryn Sikkink, "Justice Cascade: The Evolution and Impact of Foreign Human Rights Trials in Latin America," *Chicago Journal of International Law* 2 (2001): 1.

support to the visions and agendas of these student activists. Perhaps such a difficulty may be overcome by permitting the formation of political factions within an existing party, or, more radically, by allowing the establishment of new parties.[55] Unfortunately, both options are challenging for young students to achieve.[56] Nonetheless, as mentioned earlier, some student activists have found their space in political parties and carried out their agendas on social reforms through law.

From a broader perspective, the legal reform-centric agendas of student activists have facilitated the political transition as well. At the end of the day, what matters to the stability of any authoritarian regime is not merely the legitimacy of its domination, but also the presence or absence of preferable alternatives.[57] While gradual liberalization may appear to undermine the authoritarian regime, a complete transformation requires more than that – it requires a viable alternative regime.[58] In its infancy, the opposition movements were characterized by street protests, grassroots mobilization, and physical altercations in congress – alternatives to the KMT's authoritarianism indeed, but wholly unreliable.[59] However, the idealism of student activists and resulting public discourse about legality helped to strengthen the moral ground and viability of alternatives to the authoritarian regime.

12.3.2.2   Institutionalization of Student Activism

In the 1980s and 1990s, student activism was loosely organized. Student leaders of the Wild Lily Movement admitted that their movement was led by a coalition of student groups that did not share coherent core values.[60]

---

[55] See e.g. Tushnet, "Popular Constitutionalism and Political Organization," for a discussion in the context of the Tea Party movement.

[56] Twenty-five years after the Wild Lily Movement, no third political party had successfully emerged despite several attempts. That changed in 2016, when student activists of the Sunflower Movement successfully established a third party for the first time. Riding on the momentum generated by the movement, this new party – the New Power Party – won more than 5 percent of the ballots in the 2016 legislative elections.

[57] Przeworski, "Some Problems," 51–2.

[58] Ibid., 56.

[59] Similarly, in their studies about antiwar protests in the USA during the Vietnam War period, Doug McAdam and Yang Su point out that the movement, with extreme and disruptive tactics (e.g. violence or property damage), successfully set the political agenda but could not determine the resolution of that agenda ("The War at Home: Antiwar Protests and Congressional Voting, 1965 to 1973," *American Sociological Review* 67 (2002): 718); David S. Meyer, "Protest and Political Opportunities," *Annual Review of Sociology* 30 (2004): 138.

[60] He, "Interview with Wong Chang-Liang," 233.

In fact, the student leadership of the movement split at various points and experienced public acrimony. In subsequent years, despite attempts to collaborate, student activist societies remained limited within the campus of each university. Nevertheless, within the campus, activist groups collaborated on a regular basis and gradually institutionalized their activism in various forms. Some examples include cross-association training camps, joint fieldwork, model government bodies, model parliament, student representation at faculty meetings, reading groups, student courts, and student movements. Annual elections for the president of student government that exists in many universities serve as a significant platform to mobilize and organize student activists. At NTU, students from liberal student associations conduct an arduous month-long campaign to support their preferred candidate. It is not uncommon for students to set up a campaign office to accommodate the members of the campaign team and their volunteers.[61] One might say that the scale of the NTU Student Government President campaign is equivalent to that for a mayoral election of the township government.[62]

During Chen Shui-Bian's presidency (2000–8), student activism was empowered in a more institutionalized way. In 2001, the Ministry of Education implemented a special program in elite high schools to provide a specialized social science curriculum for selected gifted students.[63] Furthermore, in 2000, the Ministry initiated a cross-school humanities and social sciences camp for selected high school students. As such, these initiatives have altered the decades-long tradition in Taiwan's education system where the specialized programs for talented students used to be only science-oriented (e.g. math, physics, biology). In addition, most of the faculty members involved are liberal economists, sociologists, or political scientists. Interestingly, many of these faculty members have roots in the first wave of the student movements during the early 1990s, and some were even leaders of the Wild Lily Movement and members of liberal student societies across universities. According to a Sunflower Movement leader, many active members of student movements in the last decade were the students of those student-activist-turned professors.[64]

---

[61] Interviews with the author.
[62] For example, in 2000, the number of enrolled undergraduate students at NTU eligible to vote for the president of NTU Student Government was approximately 15,000. This is equivalent to that in a medium-sized township in Taiwan.
[63] Chien-Kuo High School, "Humanity and Social Science Special Program of Chien-Kuo High School," www.ck.tp.edu.tw/~secoseweb/social.html
[64] He, *Student Movement Generation*, 20.

In other words, student activism has not only trickled down to the high school level in an institutionalized way, but the government appears to endorse, whether intentionally or otherwise, the intergenerational support of student activism. Given that student activism is the product of intellectual enlightenment in a process of learning, one cannot find a more powerful form of institutionalization than in a school-wide, newly designed curriculum. Unsurprisingly, many key members of student movements over the past decade, including the Wild Strawberry Movement, the Sunflower Movement, and several conservation movements (for historical sites and communities) were graduates from the gifted programs in elite high schools or participants in the humanities and social science camps.[65]

Recently, several NGOs, social organizations, and think tanks have also facilitated the gradual institutionalization of student activism. Partly attributable to the collaboration between different generations of student activists, activists of earlier generations have laid a solid foundation for activism to take place outside the campus.[66] As a result, the boundary between student and social movements has been blurred, and students who participate in organizations dedicated to social reforms no longer regard themselves as "students." NGOs have recruited an increasing number of students. For example, the Judicial Reform Foundation, a leading NGO dedicated to legal reforms for more than two decades, has regularly recruited student assistants and provided internships for various legal reform programs that the foundation operates, including conducting surveys about the public's attitude toward the judiciary, evaluating the performance of prosecutors and judges, carrying out field research, and working with scholars and lawyers to draft judicial reform bills. Many other organizations operate in a similar way, focusing on varying issues, such as human rights, gender equality, and labor rights.[67] Interestingly, government agencies have been receptive to, if not reliant on, bills drafted by activist groups.[68] As activists from earlier generations join the public sector, the cross-generational collaboration further blurs the boundary between the state and society. Such a broad base for social activism has also given rise to ad hoc coalitions between activists across public interest groups and professionals on an issue-by-issue basis. Student activists typically organize activist groups in response to

---

[65] Interviews with the author.
[66] He, *Student Movement Generation*, 20, 24–5.
[67] See e.g. Taiwan Think Thank, Judicial Reform Foundations, Taiwan Labor Front, Awakening Foundation, and Taiwan Democracy Watch.
[68] Interviews with the author.

trending cases or issues, dissolving the organization after the issue is no longer current.[69] Such a flexible form of organization creates numerous opportunities for public participation in a liberal polity.

12.3.2.3   Seeking Political Dialogue

The focus of student movements on legal reform avoids provoking aggressive confrontation and instead stimulates public discourse. Persuasion, consistent with democratic values, is usually more effective than threats as far as the social movement outcome is concerned.[70] Even during the Wild Strawberry Movement in 2008 that featured highly political protestations against a Chinese delegation's visit for a cross-strait exchange agreement, the student activists remained focused on the Assembly and Parade Act that was criticized for unconstitutionally limiting the right of assembly.

It takes two to tango; in this regard, the government is often willing to engage in dialogue with the activists to varying degrees of interaction and efficacy. One early case in point is the Wild Lily Movement in 1990. Bringing their petition into the Presidential Office, student leaders met with the then President Lee Teng-Hui, who accepted the petitions and later implemented the requests made in the memoranda.[71] Moreover, negotiations and communications with activists during large-scale protests were also common. For instance, during the Anti-National Parade Movement in 1991, seen by many as a direct challenge to the legitimacy of the ruling nationalist party, KMT moderates continued to communicate with student activists privately even while the hardliners were urging a crackdown.[72] These communications led to the Criminal Law revision in the following months. Significantly, such dialogues are uncommon in student movements worldwide. For example, when the SEALDs protested outside the Japanese Diet, the Abe administration unreservedly refused to engage in any substantive dialogue with the participants. Likewise, barring one fruitless meeting, the Hong Kong government called off its talks with leaders of the Umbrella Movement.[73] It is thus no surprise that the movement eventually fizzled out.

---

[69] He Ron-Shin, "Interview with Chen Wei-Ting," in He (ed.), *Student Movement Generation*, 43–4.
[70] McAdam and Su, "War at Home," 717.
[71] With the benefit of hindsight, President Lee was willing to implement these reforms because he had already intended to pursue them from the onset.
[72] Interviews with author.
[73] "Hong Kong Government Calls off Student Talks," *BBC*, October 9, 2014, www.bbc.com /news/world-asia-china-29554755

Various strands in the literature denote the importance of dialogues between the government and its opponents in promoting constitutional and democratic reforms. Scholars studying the democratic transitions of East European countries such as Poland, Hungary, and the former Yugoslavia during the 1990s refer to such dialogues as the "roundtable talk" approach.[74] In constitutionalism literature, theorists have accorded weight to the public's expression on constitutional matters, particularly during critical moments.[75] Were there no such dialogues, the alternative would be violent repression if the state possesses more than sufficient coercive power to suppress any societal challenge, or mere ignorance if the state is confident about its political legitimacy.[76]

Unlike a democracy where society restrains the government through the electoral mechanism, authoritarian regimes are characterized by rulers who subject themselves to an indirect restraint – their subjective estimations of, among all risk factors, how far they can go without creating social unrest.[77] Viewed in this light, the willingness to engage in dialogue may be seen as a signal of the authoritarian leaders' calculation. Furthermore, one strong indication that an authoritarian regime may be on the brink of an implosion is when groups or key figures within the ruling bloc make a move to seek external support.[78] In this scenario, concessions made to the public engender expectations of further concessions, leading to more protests. As a result, the party-state is forced to adopt a piecemeal approach to maintain its legitimacy on borrowed time. In fact, this was the precise situation during several successful student movements in Taiwan. Thus, it may be said that the transition of authoritarian legality in Taiwan is intertwined with the democratization process.

---

[74] Jon Elster (ed.), *The Roundtable Talks and the Breakdown of Communism* (Chicago: University of Chicago Press, 1996). For a discussion in the context of Taiwan, see Yeh Jiunn-Rong, *Minzhu zhuanxing yu xianfa bianqian* [Democratic Transition and Constitutional Change] (Taiwan: Angle Publishing, 2003), 49–52.

[75] See e.g. Bruce Ackerman, *We the People, Vol. II: Transformations* (Cambridge, MA: Harvard University Press, 2000); Tushnet, "Popular Constitutionalism as Political Law," 996. But see also Yeh and Chang, "Emergence of East Asia Constitutionalism."

[76] Minxin Pei, "The Chinese Political Order: Resilience or Decay?," *Modern China Studies* 21 (2014): 1.

[77] Elster (ed.), *Roundtable Talks*, 3–4.

[78] Przeworski, "Some Problems," 56.

12.4   Path of Transition and Post-Transitional Struggles

Throughout the greater part of Taiwan's authoritarian era, the relative success of Taiwan's authoritarian legality may be attributed to a social contract between the state and the people premised on a performance-centric legitimacy. A pledge of commitment to economic development rather than to the rule of law gave the regime an aura of credibility because the reality of a war-torn economy aligned the interests of the rulers with that of the public. Citizens desired a government that provided basic necessities and addressed collective action problems rather than a government that made abstract commitments (or precommitments) to legality.[79] Moreover, the Taiwanese people's unfamiliarity with the rule of law and democracy under the prevailing Chinese culture may have enhanced this shared direction. As long as people believe, or are made to believe, that revocation of individuals' legal rights is necessary for net social welfare, such governmental acts may be justified.

One example is Taiwan's successful land reform in the early 1950s through the enactment of the 37.5 percent Arable Rent Reduction Act (1951) and the Act to Allocate Lands for Peasants (1953). As a result of these legislative developments, landowners were deprived of 99 percent of their entitlements in exchange for shares in war-torn SOEs as compensation. Although one might have reasonably imagined a resultant uprising of disgruntled landlords, such a revolution did not take place. On the contrary, several influential, well-educated, and wealthy landowners understood the importance of land reforms for the economy, and assisted the government by persuading other landowners to surrender their proprietary entitlements.[80]

However, by the early 1980s, legality had become an importance source of the KMT's legitimacy, a fact which the party took notice of. In particular, the KMT saw legality as a useful instrument for diplomacy. For example, the 1980 Kaohsiung Incident trial concerning several political dissidents was heavily scrutinized by the international community to an extent similar to that of the more recent Bo Xilai trial in China. Similarly, in a published diary entry of former President Lee Teng-hui, a conversation between Lee and the then President Chiang Ching-Kuo

---

[79] For a general discussion, see Kevin Tan, "The Role of Public Law in Developing Asia," *Singapore Journal of Legal Studies* (2004): 265; Tom Ginsburg, "Constitutionalism: East Asian Antecedents," *Chicago-Kent Law Review* 88 (2012): 11, 14–16.

[80] Huang Tian-Tsai and Huang Zhao-Heng, *Guzhenfu rensheng jishi* [Biography of Gu Zhen-Fu] (Taipei: Linking, 2005).

revealed such a mentality when the pair were discussing ways to handle a political scandal involving the death of the American citizen and political dissident Liu Yi-Liang. While in the USA, he was assassinated by a KMT-affiliated gangster. When the dissident's widow sued the Taiwanese government in a US court, Chiang instructed the KMT officials not to settle privately but to abide by the public legal proceedings for the sake of national dignity.[81] Later, in June 1987, a few months before the beginning of Taiwan's democratization, Lee again disclosed a similar sentiment in his diary. To manage the DPP-led protests that resulted in violent conflict, President Chiang insisted that legal proceedings were necessary for maintaining public trust in the government.[82] Thus, compared to the approach of instrumental legality in Taiwan's early years, the 1980s witnessed a gradual change in the KMT's hitherto strategic commitment to law.

Nevertheless, transformation through activism has posed several challenges to legality itself. First, the higher law-centric approach – an approach that might be inevitable in an authoritarian state – is a double-edged sword. Activism under authoritarian rule characteristically uses extralegal approaches in pressurizing rulers to accept a reformistic agenda. Using the higher law-centric strategy, reformists often initiate public discourse by wielding legal and constitutional law principles to combat constraints existing in positive laws passed by the authoritarian regime. "Civil disobedience" was the widely used concept by students and professors supporting the 2014 Sunflower Movement,[83] and the maxim, *lex injusta non est lex* ("unjust law is not law") was also commonly cited by their peers during earlier student movements in the 2000s.[84]

However, a higher law-centric discourse encounters criticism from opponents who argue that it ultimately erodes legality and the supremacy

[81] Academia Historica, *Jiang Jingguo zongtong yu wo – Li Denghui biji yu Li Denghui koushou lishi* [President Chiang Ching-Kuo and Me: The Diary of President Lee Teng-Hui] (Taiwan: Yun-Chen Publishing, 2004): 153.
[82] Ibid., 227.
[83] See e.g. Wen-Chen Chang, "Peaceful But 'Illegal' Assemblies? Comparisons between Taiwan's Constitution and the International Covenant on Civil and Political Rights," *Hong Kong Law Journal* 45 (2015): 295; Jiunn-Rong Yeh, "Marching towards Civic Constitutionalism with Sunflowers," *Hong Kong Law Journal* 45 (2015): 315; Chia-Ming Chen, "Searching for Constitutional Authority in the Sunflower Movement," *Hong Kong Law Journal* 45 (2015): 211.
[84] Lin Shan-Tien, *Shenpan? Lin Shantian tan fa lun zheng* [Trial? Lin Shan-Tien Discusses Law and Politics] (Taiwan: Angle, 2000).

of law. Commenting on Sunflower Movement's occupation of the Legislative Yuan, Yun-Han Chu, a prominent political scientist, criticized the students' actions as rendering Taiwan's democracy "not far from a total failure." Chu observed that "in any normal democratic country, either the law enforcers or the mainstream public opinion, would never allow anyone to illegally invade the parliament in the name of political protest."[85]

Although divergent opinions are nothing new, they underscore a three-decades-long clash in Taiwan between legal formalists and legal realists. On one hand, the legal realists do not presume the autonomy of the legal system and justify populist activism by means of higher law principles or populist constitutionalism. On the other hand, legal formalists emphasize positive laws and doctrines, positing that only a narrower scope of actors (e.g. legal professionals and legislators) are in a proper position to contemplate and change legal doctrines through formal procedures (e.g. legislative process or litigations).[86]

Currently enjoying a stronger backing in Taiwan, the realists' higher law-centric approach for organizing social movements also appears to be a slippery slope to political populism. A populist approach is not intrinsically tied to one party and can be adopted by opposing parties too. Since taking over the reins in May 2016, the Tsai administration and the DPP-controlled Legislative Yuan have faced several rounds of strong protests against the DPP's legislative bills, including those pertaining to same-sex marriage, pension reforms, and labor working hours.[87] Somewhat ironically, following a physical assault during a public protest in 2016 against Ke Chien-Ming, the DPP's party whip from the Legislative Yuan, Ke responded in a tone echoing that of his KMT counterparts earlier: "Taiwan's democracy is moving toward its end."[88] Although circumstances may change with the passage of time, it appears that higher law-

[85] Yun-Han Chu, "How Far Is Taiwan from the Collapse of Democracy?," *Tian Xia Magazine*, April 1, 2014, www.cw.com.tw/article/article.action?id=5057056

[86] The conflict between realists and formalists are by no means unique in Taiwan. For a historical discussion, see Gordon, "Critical Legal Histories."

[87] *The Economist*, "Taiwan Debates Gay Marriage," December 3, 2016, www.economist.com/news/asia/21711096-it-would-be-first-country-asia-legalise-it-taiwan-debates-gay-marriage

[88] Zhou Enyu and Yao Zhiping, "Bei laotun weiou Ke Jianming: Taiwan minzhu zou dao jintou le" [Beaten by Labor Groups Ke Chien Ming: Taiwan's Democracy Is Moving towards the End'], *China Times*, December 2, 2016, www.chinatimes.com/realtimenews/20161202003997-260407

centric activism may paradoxically weaken the supremacy of positive law and the legislative body itself.

A second repercussion of activism-driven transformation is the fueling of divisiveness between an already bipartisan electorate in Taiwan. From the onset, the conflict between legal realists and formalists lies in their political positions rather than legal philosophies, and there is little that can be done to bridge the divide given that political rhetoric carries minimal substantive dialogue. Furthermore, as positive laws are often questioned through constitutional challenges, the regular courts' decisions on ancillary issues rarely resolve disputes (or, worse, create further antagonism). Accordingly, disputes flow into the Constitutional Court, burdening it with politically complex cases, some of which are ill-suited for constitutional adjudication as far as political reconciliation is concerned, or, worse, might unnecessarily politicize the role of the judiciary.[89]

Third, polarized politics often incentivizes the majority party to adopt a majoritarian conception of democracy, which tends to result in the majority's refusal to compromise with the dissenting minority "for the sake of peace."[90] A majoritarian conception of democracy may in fact be a backlash against the higher law-centric activism, which is perceived by the majority party as being counter-majoritarian. For instance, during the 2014 Sunflower Movement, the majority of KMT legislators took only thirty seconds to approve the CSSTA that would profoundly impact Taiwan–China economic and political relationships, an outcome that provoked students to occupy the parliament building. In the face of tyranny of majority, the institutional solution proposed by the opposition in Taiwan is usually a referendum as a way of applying one majoritarian mechanism to overrule another majoritarian one.[91] Thus, the system appears to facilitate a negative feedback loop: activism provokes the

---

[89] For example, during Chen Shui-Bian's presidency (2000–8), legislators of the KMT and the People First Party, after losing constitutional litigation, jointly retaliated against the Constitutional Court by cutting the annual budget of the Court as well as the justices' salaries, travel, and legal research funding. Weitseng Chen and Jimmy Chia-Shin Hsu, "Horizontal Accountability in a Polarised New Democracy: The Case of Post-Democratisation Taiwan," *Australian Journal of Asian Law* 15 (2014): 6.

[90] Brian Christopher Jones and Yen-Tu Su, "Confrontational Contestation and Democratic Compromise: The Sunflower Movement and Its Aftermath," *Hong Kong Law Journal* 45 (2015): 193, 207.

[91] Jimmy Chia-Shin Hsu, "Bringing the Sunflower Movement into Perspective: Rule of Law on a Flawed Political Foundation," conference paper (2018) prepared for ICON-S (International Society of Public Law) annual meeting at the University of Hong Kong (on file with the author).

invocation of a majoritarian conception of democracy, which in turn worsens the state of divisive politics and triggers further activism, which is another form of majoritarian politics (or populism).[92]

Fourth, the obsession with the higher law-centric discourse may lead to insufficient policy implications. Granted, higher law discourse enables rule-of-law concepts to take root in an authoritarian regime and institutionalizes ideas on rights and justice. However, higher law principles, which emphasize procedural accountability and human rights, do not provide sufficiently substantive guidance for policymaking, which typically requires interdisciplinary considerations. It is one thing for activists to undermine dictatorships and authoritarianism by protesting, and quite another to transform activism into democracy and good governance, as demonstrated by the failure of the Arab Spring.[93] Activism will continue to rear its head where the young democratic system is unable to handle tough issues such as those involving nationalism and perceived threats from China. In the face of a complex political and economic climate, legal reforms alone have become unduly laden with expectations and obligations above and beyond that which a normal legal system ought to carry.

Lastly, the pattern of social activism imposes a heavy burden on the judiciary. As higher law-centric activism represents the erosion of the legislative branch's supremacy,[94] the judiciary is expected to play a larger role. This expectation is a common view shared by liberal constitutional law scholars in Taiwan. For example, in response to the outcry arising from the Sunflower movement, Jiunn-Rong Yeh advocates for "civic constitutionalism" and emphasizes how the judiciary needs to be more engaged with civil groups through dialectic interpretations of the law, while leaving room and time for resolution by the political branches.[95] However, Yeh's proposal is only a viable solution if the political branch has the capacity

---

[92] Over years, Taiwan's polarized politics have raised concerns among reformists. A group of well-known bipartisan reformists created a new party in 2007 and called for "the cease of democratic civil war." But this movement faded away after the new party failed to earn any seat in the 2008 parliamentary election. The problem of divided politics in Taiwan is unlikely to fade away anytime soon.

[93] Larry Diamond, "From Activism to Democracy," in Lina Khatib and Ellen Lust (eds.), *Taking to the Streets: The Transformation of Arab Activism* (Baltimore, MD: Johns Hopkins University Press, 2014).

[94] Yeh, "Marching towards Civic Constitutionalism."

[95] Ibid., 14; Jiunn-Rong Yeh, "Presidential Politics and Judicial Facilitation of Political Dialogue between Political Actors in New Asian Democracies: Comparing the South Korean and Taiwanese Experiences," *International Journal of Constitutional Law* 8 (2011): 911.

among divided politics to solve those tough issues, which appear to be little more than political or ideological solutions disguised in legal form.

All in all, the interplay between law and politics is path dependent. Activists do not act and strategize in a vacuum;[96] rather, their interpretation of legal doctrines, expectations of their entitlements, and conceptions of law are largely shaped and constrained by patterns of past conflicts and successes.[97] Taiwan's successful democratization has been characterized by a back-and-forth confrontation and concession and the well-received rights-based claims couched in the language of a "higher" law, self-determination, and popular sovereignty. Going forward, these factors contributing to the authoritarian legality transition will probably continue to shape Taiwan's legal system and its post-democratization politics. Strong activism can improve a state's capacity to improve its governance and performance, but may conversely impose pressure on the state if it fails to respond with satisfactory policy.[98] In Taiwan, it remains to be observed how this young democracy will resolve this dilemma and reap the benefits from its tradition of strong activism.

12.5   Conclusion

Taiwan's transformation from an authoritarian legality is impressive and wide-ranging. It transformed not only the authoritarian rulers' strategic commitment to law, but also the authoritarian regime itself. The process was intertwined with Taiwan's democratization and the subsequent consolidation period. In this regard, Taiwan's story is not one that tells how authoritarian legality may sustain itself, but one that shows how authoritarian legality can eventually fail.

On the one hand, the experience of authoritarian legality in Taiwan resonates with those in other parts of the world. Civic activism and engaged citizens are necessary for the transformation of authoritarian legality, which is part of a broader, perhaps more turbulent, democratization process. That being said, while activist lawyers and law-centric public discourse are crucial catalysts for democratization, other democracy determinants matter too, including per-capita income, wealth

---

[96] Meyer, "Protest and Political Opportunities," 127.

[97] Edelman, Leachman, and McAdam, "On Law, Organizations, and Social Movements," 661; Smith, "Political Jurisprudence, the 'New Institutionalism', and the Future of Public Law," *American Political Science Review* 82 (1988): 89.

[98] Herbert P. Kitschelt "Political Opportunity Structures and Political Protest: Anti-Nuclear Movements in Four Democracies," *British Journal of Political Science* 16 (1986): 57.

distribution,[99] the extent of middle-class dependence on the state,[100] the cultural and religious composition of the populace,[101] media proliferation,[102] country size,[103] and other institutional settings such as the electoral system.[104]

On the other hand, the implications of Taiwan's authoritarian legality transition remain limited in terms of the causation between legality and democratization. One common but wrong presumption about authoritarianism is that it is merely transitional, and the adoption of legality is the usual signal of a transition.[105] On the contrary, authoritarianism can endure, and young democracies may revert to authoritarianism. Democratization may not be the inevitable process that authoritarian regimes go through, regardless of whether or not they embrace the idea of legality.[106] After all, democracy is not the only source of political legitimacy in the history of political systems.[107]

This chapter argues that student activism is one crucial dimension for understanding the dynamics of the authoritarian legality transition in Taiwan. It is higher law-centric, institutionalized, and dialectic, with collaborative efforts across generations within and outside the legal system and the state apparatus. It blurs the boundary between the state and society as well as the one between social and student movements. However, common to many young democracies, this transition mechanism may appear to be a slippery slope to

---

[99] Carles Boix, *Democracy and Redistribution* (New York: Cambridge University Press, 2003); Adam Przeworski and Fernando Limongi, "Modernization: Theories and Facts," *World Politics* 49 (1997): 155.

[100] Seymour Martin Lipset, "On the General Conditions for Democracy," in Stein Ugelvik Larsen (ed.), *The Challenges of Theories on Democracy* (New York: Columbia University Press, 2000), 11; Andrew J. Nathan, "The Puzzle of the Chinese Middle Class," *Journal of Democracy* 27 (2016): 5; Jie Chen and Chunlong Lu, "Democratization and the Middle Class in China: The Middle Class's Attitudes toward Democracy," *Political Research Quarterly* 54 (2011): 705.

[101] Steven Fish, "Islam and Authoritarianism," *World Politics* 55 (2002): 4; Seymour Martin Lipset, "The Social Requisites of Democracy Revisited," *American Sociology Review* 59 (1994): 5.

[102] Jan Teorell, *Determinants of Democratization: Explaining Regime Change in the World 1972-2006* (New York: Cambridge University Press, 2010), 5-6.

[103] Ibid., 50-2; Boix, *Democracy and Redistribution*, 41-4; Robert Dahl and Edward Tufte, *Size and Democracy* (Palo Alto, CA: Stanford University Press, 1973).

[104] Lust, "Competitive Clientelism"; Shelley Rigger, *Politics in Taiwan: Voting for Democracy* (New York: Routledge, 1999), 15.

[105] For a further discussion, see Chen, "Twins of Opposites."

[106] Ibid.

[107] For a further discussion, see Fukuyama, *Origins*.

populism, and thereby paradoxically weaken the function of positive law and the legislative body, especially in the middle of heavily polarized politics.

Taiwan's democratization has been led by liberal-minded lawyers. Similar to their liberal counterparts in the US and Europe, they have formed a coalition with workers, women, environmentalists, and the lesbian and gay communities. While their counterparts in the West have been shaken by a democratic recession and backlash against liberalism, they remain confident about the prospect of liberalism.[108]Moving forward, it remains to be observed how Taiwan, as a young democracy sensitive to international trends and contexts, will deepen the roots of its rule of law and liberal democracy in the middle of the growing tide of discontent toward liberalism and democracy.

---

[108] For a general discussion, see Larry Diamond, "Facing up to the Democratic Recession," *Journal of Democracy* 26 (2015): 141.

Persistence of Authoritarian Legality
after the Transition to Democracy

13

Neoliberal Turn of State Conservatism in Japan

From Bureaucratic to Corporatist Authoritarian Legality

KOICHI NAKANO

This chapter seeks to explore the shifting modes of authoritarian legality in Japan. It shall be pointed out that certain features of authoritarian legality, which I call *state conservatism*, persisted in post-World War II, in spite of the democratization of the regime that followed the US occupation of Japan. In the final stages of the Cold War in the 1980s, the worldwide trends toward a neoliberal transformation of politics, economy, and society affected Japan, and opened a window of opportunity for a fuller commitment to liberal-democratic norms, including the rule of law. It appeared as if the lasting legacies of bureaucratic dominance were finally being challenged and dismantled as part of the spread of the neoliberal paradigm, and it looked set to liberate and empower the people. Although political and administrative reforms were pursued and accomplished in the 1990s, it became increasingly apparent that a new mode of *corporatist authoritarian legality* was merely replacing the earlier *bureaucratic authoritarian legality*. In what follows, we shall first depict the nature of state conservatism and of the bureaucratic authoritarian legality that persisted in the postwar period. Then, we shall proceed to analyze the impact of neoliberal transformation, and how that ironically ushered in a new type of corporatist authoritarian legality in today's Japan.

13.1 State Conservatism and Bureaucratic Authoritarian Legality

As a late-developing country that embarked upon the process of modernization in the nineteenth century under an enormous pressure to "catch up" with the West, the oligarchic rulers of early modern Japan came to form a dominant ideology of government that sought to integrate and

337

mobilize the nation and its resources under a conservative normative order centered around the state – the emperor and his bureaucrats. This is what may be called "state conservatism."[1]

There are two ways in which one can explain the state–society relations prevalent in a regime with state conservatism. First, state conservatism can obviously be understood as a form of conservatism, whose authority draws on the state, and which seeks to subjugate society under a state-centered normative order. To attain this goal, the state education system, with the Imperial University of Tokyo at its apex, trained elite bureaucrats, who were placed in charge to promote material modernization while preserving the normative values and power structures that existed since premodernization.

As a variant of conservative thought, the state-centric character of conservatism in Japan stands in stark contrast to the anti-state and anti-government tenets of the predominant US conservatism that highly values individual freedoms, property rights, and the right to bear arms. This form of conservatism also holds strong attachment to pluralism and the abhorrence of state power in rational planning and social amelioration as evident in the traditional British form of conservatism represented by Michael Oakeshott, among others.[2] In short, Japan's version of state conservatism is a form of conservatism that rejects pluralism and liberalism in society and politics, and fundamentally relies on the normative role of the state as the monopolistic source of values and knowledge.

It would not be difficult to see here that law served as a tool of the bureaucrats to achieve their objectives instead of having the bureaucrats play mere agents of the law in the Weberian sense. Further, as argued by Maruyama Masao, it is an essential feature of the Japanese state that it continues to reject the "technical, neutral character" of the modern European model of governance, and relies on the substantive values rooted in the Confucian "rule of virtue" tradition that the state supposedly embodied.[3] Indeed, as Ishida Takeshi pointed out, the moralization

[1] I have previously discussed the concept of state conservatism in Koichi Nakano, *Sengo Nihon no Kokka Hoshushugi: Naimu/Jichi Kanryō no Kiseki* [Postwar State Conservatism: The Career Trajectory of the Bureaucrats of the Ministry of Interior] (Tokyo: Iwanami Shoten, 2013).

[2] Michael Oakeshott, *Rationalism in Politics and Other Essays* (London: Methuen, 1962).

[3] Maruyama Masao, "Chōkokkashugi no ronri to shinri" [Logic and Psyche of Ultra-Nationalism], in *Gendai Seiji no Shisō to Kōdō* [Thoughts and Actions of Contemporary Politics] (Tokyo: Miraisha, 1964), 12; Maruyama Masao, *Maruyama Masao Kōgiroku*

of the Japanese state with traditional values was made possible as the term "state" is translated as "*kokka*" (drawing on the existing Chinese word) that combined the Chinese characters of "country" with "family." Thus, the modern Japanese state is actually a conservative state grounded on Confucian moral values.

This puts the modern Japanese state in contrast to Western states, including even France, a country that is known for a strong statist tradition. To the extent that the modern French Republic positively embodies moral values, they are made up of universalistic values as basic human rights, liberty, and equality. On the other hand, in the normative projections of the prewar Japanese state, the "national morality" ("*kokumin dōtoku*") that the state school system inculcated in the minds of the nationals were based on the imperial system and the analogy of the state as a large family with the emperor as the national patriarch. The teachings of the Imperial Rescript on Education preached loyalty to the emperor and filial piety as one and the same thing, and patriotism and devotion to the state as central duties of being an imperial subject.

13.2   Persistence of Bureaucratic Authoritarian Legality in the Postwar Japan

The defeat of the Japanese Empire in World War II, and the US occupation and democratization reforms that followed ushered in a new era of constitutionalism. In spite of the fact that the right in power continued to resent and contest the new 1947 Constitution of Japan,[4] particularly its pacifist Article 9 as a US imposition, it had to admit and accept that constitutional due process had to be observed for the country to readopt a "self-made" constitution. It is an understatement to note that as compared to the prewar cleavage in constitutional politics that pitted the advocates of constitutionalism against their opponents ("*rikken*" vs. "*hirikken*"), the fault lines in the postwar period lay between those who sought to defend and those who sought to revise the Constitution ("*goken*" vs. "*kaiken*").

As much as the postwar regime change was a break from the past, it is of utmost importance to note that considerable continuity existed in terms of Japan's state conservatism and its legal system. In addition to

---

Daiyonsatsu Nihon Shisōshi 1964 [Maruyama Masao Lectures Vol. 4 History of Japanese Thoughts 1964] (Tokyo: Tokyo Daigaku Shuppankai, 1998), 123.

[4] Prime Minister of Japan and His Cabinet, "Constitution of Japan, effective May 3, 1947," japan.kantei.go.jp/constitution_and_government_of_japan/constitution_e.html

legal continuity itself, there was also continuity among the legal professionals. Indeed, the US occupation left the judiciary from the militarist
period largely intact. In fact, in comparison with the other two branches
of government, the judicial branch was the least affected by the purge.
A study revealed that the Japanese judges who collaborated with the
militarists in the puppet government of Manchukuo came home free,
without taking any responsibility whatsoever for their roles in Japanese
aggression and colonial rule, and assumed top posts in the postwar courts
back in Japan.[5] The Japanese courts continued to be very timid and
unwilling to challenge the executive branch overall even in the postwar
period. When the de facto remilitarization of Japan began with the sign-
ing of the US–Japan Security Treaty[6] and the setting up of the Self-
Defense Force in spite of the pacifist Article 9 of the Constitution, the
courts simply acquiesced in the decisions of the government.

   One crucial and symbolic figure is Ishida Kazuto, who as the Chief
Justice of the Supreme Court between 1969 and 1973, led what was
tantamount to the red purge of the judges. Upon retirement from the
Supreme Court, Ishida started to be openly involved in activities to
sustain and boost the position of Yasukuni Shrine, by advocating its
renationalization as well as the official visits by the emperor and the
prime minister. He not only served as the head of various lobby groups
with revisionist, right-wing causes, including a predecessor of "Japan
Conference" (Nippon Kaigi), the most influential of such groups today,
but also played a critical role in selecting the new head priest of Yasukuni
Shrine who pushed through the highly controversial enshrinement of
Class-A War Criminals in 1978.[7] Even as recently as 2001–15, Miyoshi
Tōru, another former chief justice of the Supreme Court, served as the
chair of Nippon Kaigi and revealed a continuous, but otherwise hidden,
affinity between the judicial establishment and revisionist causes in
Japan. Miyoshi built his career as a judge in the postwar, but had attended
the Naval Academy as a youth during the wartime. This political

---

[5] Ueda Seikichi, *Shihōkan no Sensō Sekinin: Manshū Taiken to Sengo Shihō* [War
Responsibility of Judicial Bureaucrats: Manchu Experience and Postwar Justice] (Tokyo:
Kadensha, 1997).

[6] Ministry of Foreign Affairs of Japan, "Treaty of Mutual Cooperation and Security between
Japan and the United States of America, signed January 19, 1960," www.mofa.go.jp
/region/n-america/us/q&a/ref/1.html

[7] Mainichi Shinbun "Yasukuni" Shuzaihan, *Yasukuni Sengo Hishi: A-kyu Senpan wo Gōshi
shita Otoko* [Secret History of Yasukuni: The Man Who Enshrined the Class-A War
Criminals] (Tokyo: Mainichi Shinbunsha, 2007).

conservatism arguably offered a solid political foundation for judicial conservatism.

While the judicial branch had turned out to be a blind spot where the US occupation failed to push through in its democratization efforts, much more significant efforts were pursued in the executive branch with the foremost example of the Ministry of Interior (*Naimushō*), which was abolished by the Supreme Commander of the Allied Powers (SCAP) at the end of 1947. The Ministry of Interior boasted a wide scope of control comprising the Police Affairs Bureau (including the notorious secret police, the Special Higher Police) and the Local Affairs Bureau which controlled the local governments. These agencies under the Ministry of Interior were also placed in charge of health, welfare, labor, and public works policies, in addition to religious matters relating to state Shintoism. It was precisely because that the Ministry of Interior was regarded by the SCAP as a bastion of authoritarian legality that it was disbanded alongside the army and the navy.

In reality, breaking the iron hold of bureaucratic authoritarian legality was much harder than the SCAP had realized. For instance, as the US occupation sought to transform the haughty and domineering "emperor's servants" ("*Tennō no kanri*") into public servants of a democracy when it established a new "Personnel Authority" agency housed in the very premises that the former Ministry of Interior used to occupy. Other than the first president who hailed from an academic background and retired in 1961, the next four presidents until 1990 all originally hailed from the Ministry of Interior, including those who were purged before Japan regained its independence in 1952 (Table 13.1).[8]

Another SCAP invention that aimed at the thorough reform of the Japanese bureaucracy was the creation of the Administrative Management Agency, but it similarly met with bureaucratic resistance. As soon as the US occupation ended, bureaucrats from the Ministry of Interior who had served in the colonial governments of Kwantung and Taiwan, the Ministry of Colonial Affairs, and the Manchurian Railways during wartime, continued to occupy positions of power in the Administrative Management Agency. It was only in 1983 that the first bureaucrat without ties to the prewar Ministry of Interior ascended to the top post.[9]

[8] Nakano, *Sengo Nihon no Kokka Hoshushugi: Naimu/Jichi Kanryō no Kiseki* [Postwar State Conservatism: The Career Trajectory of the Bureaucrats of the Ministry of Interior] 10–12.
[9] Ibid., 12.

Table 13.1 *Presidents of personnel authority (1948–90)*

Name [Term]	Background	Previous posts held
Asai Kiyoshi [1948–61]	Keio University	Chair, Ad Hoc Personnel Commission
Irie Seiichirō [1961–2]	Interior	Local Affairs Bureau Chief
Satō Tatsuo [1962–74]	Interior	Director General, Cabinet Legislation Bureau
Fujii Sadao [1974–84]	Interior	Director General, Fire Management Agency
Utsumi Hitoshi [1984–90]	Interior	Vice Minister, Defense Agency

The bureaucrats from the Ministry of Interior also took control of the administrative head position (vice director) in the Prime Minister's Office for twenty years since its inception in 1958. Particularly well represented here are those with police backgrounds, including the former head of the Special Higher Police of the Tokyo Metropolitan Police Agency between April and October 1945, who made a comeback to officialdom when he was de-purged at the end of the US occupation with a stint as the first chief of staff of the brand-new Air Self-Defense Force.[10]

The Cabinet Legislation Bureau also played a unique role in entrenching authoritarian legality in postwar Japan. One of its functions was to provide government with the official interpretation of the Constitution and the laws in Japan. The SCAP took the view that the prewar Cabinet Legislation Bureau was under the control of the Ministry of Interior and thus proceeded to abolish it in 1948. Its functions were transferred to the Ministry of Justice. The Legislation Bureau was, however, revived in 1952 as part of the prime minister's cabinet when the occupation ended.[11]

The Cabinet Legislation Bureau does not hire new recruits to the bureaucracy; instead, mid-career bureaucrats from other ministries are transferred to it. In the prewar period, the directors general of the Cabinet Legislation Bureau came from diverse ministerial backgrounds that included the Ministry of Interior, the ministries of Agriculture and Commerce, Post, Finance, and even the Navy. At times, the directors general were placed in the top role by way of transfer from other

[10] Ibid., 12–13.
[11] Ibid., 21–4.

ministries without going through the promotion process within the Cabinet Legislation Bureau. Occasionally, the post was filled by politicians from the House of Representatives, with backgrounds in the bureaucracy or in the legal professions. In other words, it was a post that was filled by political appointees.

Interestingly, and perhaps in order to make up for the democratization reforms of the occupation, the appointment to the director general post of the Cabinet Legislation Bureau is depoliticized and bureaucratized in the postwar era so that decisions to do with the constitutionality and legality of bills do not fall in the hands of democratically elected representatives of the people. The unwritten rules of postwar state bureaucracy are: (1) the directors general would first serve as the deputy director general and as department chief in the Cabinet Legislation Bureau before being appointed to the top post; and (2) only bureaucrats who were originally from the Ministry of Interior (later reorganized as the Ministry of Local Autonomy), the Ministry of Finance, the Ministry of Commerce and Industry (later renamed as the Ministry of International Trade and Industry), and the Ministry of Justice would be appointed to serve as the director general.

The list of the directors general of the Cabinet Legislation Bureau in Table 13.2 also reveals the fact that the service term used to be much longer in the early postwar period and coincided with the political term of individual prime minister and his cabinets. A change of patterns took place in the mid-1970s, when the term of the directors general became shorter and were delinked from the prime minister's terms. This shows that further bureaucratization of the personnel management of the Cabinet Legislation Bureau took place over time. When Abe Shinzō returned to power in December 2012, he soon proceeded to break these conventions, including the two unwritten rules mentioned above. We shall discuss these matters in more details later in the chapter.

For now, let us take a look at another key position which demonstrates the persistent nature of bureaucratic authoritarian legality in the postwar period. This is the post of the Deputy Chief Cabinet Secretary, which is commonly regarded today as the top bureaucratic position of the government, comparable to the post of Cabinet Secretary in the United Kingdom (UK).[12] In spite of its importance, it was only in September 1945 that the position was created. In the prewar period, the Chief Cabinet Secretary position was often filled by a member of the bureaucracy. However, this

---

[12] Ibid., 25–34.

KOICHI NAKANO

Table 13.2 *Directors general of the Cabinet Legislation Bureau (1952–2019)*

Name [Term]	Cabinet	Background
Satō Tatsuo [1952–54]	Katayama, Ashida, and Yoshida	Interior
Hayashi Shūzō [1954–64]	Hatoyama, Ishibashi, Kishi, and Ikeda	Finance
Takatsuji Masami [1964–72]	Satō	Interior
Yoshikuni Ichirō [1972–6]	Tanaka and Miki	Commerce and Industry
Sanada Hideo [1976–9]	Miki, Fukuda, and Ōhira	Judge (Justice)
Tsunoda Reijirō [1979–83]	Ōhira, Suzuki, and Nakasone	Interior
Mogushi Shun [1983–6]	Nakasone	Finance
Mimura Osamu [1986–9]	Nakasone, Takeshita, and Uno	Prosecutor (Justice)
Kudō Atsuo [1989–92]	Kaifu and Miyazawa	Trade and Industry
Ōide Takao [1992–6]	Miyazawa, Hosokawa, Hata, and Murayama	Local Autonomy
Ōmori Masasuke [1996–9]	Hashimoto and Obuchi	Judge (Justice)
Tsuno Osamu [1999–2002]	Obuchi, Mori, and Koizumi	Finance
Akiyama Osamu [2002–4]	Koizumi	Trade and Industry
Sakata Masahiro [2004–6]	Koizumi	Finance
Miyazaki Reiichi [2006–10]	Abe, Fukuda, Asō, and Hatoyama	Prosecutor (Justice)
Kajita Shinichiro [2010–11]	Hatoayama, Kan, and Noda	Local Autonomy
Yamamoto Tsuneyuki [2011–13]	Noda and Abe 2nd	Trade and Industry
Komatsu Ichirō [2013–14]	Abe 2nd	Foreign
Yokohata Yūsuke [2014–]	Abe 2nd	Prosecutor (Justice)

post was turned exclusively into a political position to be occupied by a member of the parliament in 1947 and went on to became one of the most important cabinet positions. Subsequently, the post of the Deputy Chief Cabinet Secretary was set up to be filled by a senior bureaucrat. The law was further amended to make it possible for the prime minister to appoint up to two Deputy Chief Cabinet Secretaries.

By the 1960s, the convention emerged that one of the two Deputy Chief Cabinet Secretaries would be an elected politician in charge of political affairs, and the other would be a bureaucrat in charge of administrative affairs. Since 1998, the law permits the appointment of up to three Deputy Chief Cabinet Secretaries, and the current convention is to appoint one politician each from the Houses of Representatives and Councilors respectively, and the remaining position is to be filled by a bureaucrat. The political Deputy Chief Cabinet Secretaries are often junior, up-and-coming politicians.

The administrative Deputy Chief Cabinet Secretary is in charge of coordinating the policies of all the ministries and agencies and he chairs regular meetings with the top bureaucrat from each ministry. Thus, the administrative Deputy Chief Cabinet Secretary is regarded as the highest-ranking bureaucrat of the land, although it bears emphasizing that there is no legal basis to treat his position any differently from the other Deputy Chief Cabinet Secretaries who are conventionally appointed from among the politicians. Table 13.3 lists the Deputy Chief Cabinet Secretaries who are commonly regarded as being in charge of administrative affairs, either because they were from the bureaucracy or because they did not hold any seat in the parliament, but as noted above, the convention of dividing responsibilities between political affairs and administrative affairs was not firmly established until the 1960s, and up to the mid-1970s, even administrative Deputy Chief Cabinet Secretaries continued to be highly "politicized" appointments. After all, Japan's perennial ruling party during the Cold War, the Liberal Democratic Party (LDP), was to a significant degree little more than the political branch of the state bureaucracy in the early postwar period.

What seems obvious from Table 13.3 is that up to the end of the 1950s, the administrative Deputy Cabinet Secretary position was used as a launch pad for a bureaucrat to join politics as many of these secretaries would go on to stand for election to enter the parliament. The other way in which the highly politicized nature of the post is apparent is the frequency with which bureaucrats with a police background occupied the position. This is because the police bureaucrats have access to sensitive police intelligence, and could potentially wield influence over police investigations in election law violations against political rivals and opponents or instigate police crackdowns on labor disputes or student protests, for instance. Indeed, the whole decade of the 1960s saw two police bureaucrats, Hosoya Kiichi and Ishioka Makoto, who served as Special Higher Police bureaucrats in the prewar period, holding the post of

Table 13.3 *Administrative Deputy Chief Cabinet Secretaries (1946–2019)*

Name [Term]	Cabinet	Background	Previous posts held	Subsequent entry to politics[1]
Sutō Hideo [1946–7]	Yoshida	Agriculture	Director General, Prices Agency	Elected
Sone Eki [1947–8]	Katayama	Foreign	Kyoto Office Chief, Reconstruction Authority	Elected
Fukushima Shintarō [1948]	Ashida	Foreign	Osaka Liaison Coordination Office Chief	
Arita Kiichi [1948]	Ashida	Post	Maritime Transport Agency Chief	Elected
Hashimoto Ryūgo [1948]	Yoshida	Finance	Economic Stabilization Board	Elected
Kōri Yūichi [1948–50]	Yoshida	Interior	Local Affairs Bureau Chief	Elected
Sugano Yoshimaru [1949–53]	Yoshida	Railways	Staff Bureau Chief, JNR	Defeated
Inoue Seiichi [1950–1]	Yoshida	Interior	Deputy Governor, Kyoto Prefecture	Elected
Kennoki Toshihiro [1951–2]	Yoshida	Education	Vice Minister	Elected
Eguchi Mitoru [1952–4]	Yoshida	Interior	VM, Labor Ministry Deputy Chief, Police Reserve	
Tanaka Fuwazō [1953–4]	Yoshida	Railways	General Affairs Bureau Chief	Defeated
Taniguchi Yutaka [1954]	Yoshida	Interior	Deputy DG, National Police Agency	
Tanaka Eiichi [1955–7]	Hatoyama, Ishibashi, Kishi	Interior	Super-Intendant, Tokyo Metropolitan Police Agency	Elected
Okazaki Eijō [1957–8]	Kishi	Interior	Public Safety, Police Bureau	Incumbent
Suzuki Shunichi [1958–9]	Kishi	Interior	VM, Local Affairs Agency	Local
Ogasa Kōshō [1959–60]	Kishi	Commerce	Enterprises Agency Chief	Elected

Hosoya Kiichi [1960–4]	Ikeda	Interior	Kagawa Prefectural Police Chief	
Ishioka Makoto [1964–70]	Ikeda and Satō	Interior	Cabinet Intelligence Office Chief	
Koike Kinichi [1970–2]	Satō	Interior	Cabinet Secretariat Chief Councilor	
Gotōda Masaharu [1972–3]	Tanaka	Interior	DG, National Police Agency	Elected
Kawashima Hiromori [1973–6]	Tanaka and Miki	Interior	Cabinet Intelligence Office Chief	
Umemoto Yoshimasa [1976]	Miki	Health	Vice Minister	
Dōshō Kunihiko [1976–8]	Fukuda	Labor	Vice Minister	
Okina Kyūjirō [1978–82]	Ōhira and Suzuki	Health	Vice Minister	
Fujimori Shōichi [1982–7]	Nakasone	Health	VM, Environment Agency	
Ishihara Nobuo [1987–95]	Takeshita, Uno, Kaifu, Miyazawa, Hosokawa, Hata, and Murayama	Local Autonomy	Vice Minister	Local Defeated
Furukawa Teijirō [1995–2003]	Murayama, Hashimoto, Obuchi, Mori, and Koizumi	Health	Vice Minister	
Futahashi Masahiro [2003–6]	Koizumi	Local Autonomy	Vice Minister	
Matoba Junzō [2006–7]	Abe 1st	Finance	Cabinet Domestic Policy Office Chief	
Futahashi Masahiro [2007–8]	Fukuda	Local Autonomy	Vice Minister, National Land Agency	
Uruma Iwao [2008–9]	Asō	Police	Vice Minister	

Table 13.3 (*cont.*)

Name [Term]	Cabinet	Background	Previous posts held	Subsequent entry to politics[1]
Takino Kinya [2009–11]	Hatoyama and Kan	Local Autonomy	VM, Ministry of Internal Affairs and Communications	
Taketoshi Makoto [2011–12]	Noda	Construction	VM, Ministry of Land, Infrastructure, Transport, and Tourism	
Sugita Kazuhiro [2012–]	Abe 2nd	Police	Cabinet Crisis Management Office Chief Cabinet Intelligence Office Chief	

[1] "Elected" means subsequent election to national politics, while "Defeated" means failure to get elected. "Incumbent" means that the former bureaucrat was already elected to national parliament when appointed to the post. "Local" means a successful contest for a local elected office, whereas "Local Defeated" means a failure to get elected to a local executive position. The space is left blank when the person did not seek an elected office.

administrative Deputy Chief Cabinet Secretary. It was only from the mid-1970s that the post became somewhat less overtly political, and the turnover less frequent.

By then, the unwritten convention was firmly established that the administrative Deputy Chief Cabinet Secretary was to be chosen from among the former administrative vice ministers of a successor ministry of the Ministry of Interior, which had long since been abolished. As the police bureaucrats were shunned as being overly political since the Lockheed Scandal shook the LDP, in reality this meant that for thirty years between 1976 and 2006, top bureaucrats from either the Health and Welfare Ministry or the Local Autonomy Ministry monopolized the administrative Deputy Chief Cabinet Secretary position.

Thus, in spite of the significant democratization reforms, including most notably the adoption of the pacifist Constitution, bureaucratic control of politics and legality persisted after some adaptation to the democratization effort in the postwar period. "The politicians reign and the bureaucrats rule" Chalmers Johnson famously observed in his seminal study of the developmental state in Japan.[13] Johnson further observed that "The politicians provide the space for bureaucrats to rule, and they legitimate and ratify the decisions taken by bureaucrats. The bureaucrats in turn formulate developmental policies, draft and administer the laws needed to implement the policies, and make midcourse adjustments as problems arise."[14] The extensive continuity of top-government prewar personnel, including those with roots in the most authoritarian branches of the empire, in the postwar state shows that the prewar bureaucratic authoritarian legal traditions persisted well beyond the sphere of developmental industrial policy.

13.3 Neoliberal Transformation of Politics Since the Late 1980s

The prolonged life of bureaucratic authoritarian legality in Japan came to face serious challenges from around the last decade of the Cold War. This change of tide, needless to say, was part of a global change that was taking place at the time – the neoliberal turn of conservatism in the UK and the US, respectively led by Margaret Thatcher and Ronald Reagan; the

---

[13] Chalmers Johnson, *MITI and the Japanese Miracle: The Growth of Industrial Policy, 1925–1975* (Stanford: Stanford University Press, 1982), 154.
[14] Ibid.

"reform and opening-up" policies introduced by Deng Xiaoping; the rise of the democratization movements in South Korea; and Mikhail Gorbachev's perestroika and glasnost policy changes in the USSR. Freedom was in the air, and in Japan too, popular aspiration for choice and change was having an impact on politics.

Administrative reform, including privatization, deregulation, and decentralization, was supposed to replace the high-handed a priori administrative control of everything by the government bureaucrats with enhanced individual freedoms which would only be subject to a posteriori legal check. Similarly, the establishment of a more competitive, two-party system, through the introduction of a majoritarian electoral system, the central element of the political reform, was argued to bring about regular alternation in power on the basis of policy-based (as opposed to personality-based) electoral campaigning, which in turn would result in the creation of a responsible and accountable government based on stronger prime ministerial leadership as well as ministerial leadership over bureaucratic power.[15] With power centralized around the party leadership, party discipline would prevail over factional struggles, and would thus put an end to money politics, as it was argued.

In reality, it was not until 2009 that a clear alternation of power took place. As a matter of fact, the LDP's iron grip on power was loosening by the late 1980s and it fell from power for the first time in 1993, albeit briefly. A new era of fluid, coalition politics began. Thus, the stabilization and depoliticization of the post of the administrative Deputy Chief Cabinet Secretary mentioned above, and particularly the very long terms served by Ishihara Nobuo and Furukawa Teijirō, who served nearly sixteen years put together from the late 1980s to the early 2000s, should precisely be understood in this context. This was a period which seemed as if that the changing party politics was going to take precedence over the deep-rooted bureaucratic traditions, with the elite bureaucrats retreating to a more limited, technical role of advising and assisting their political masters. In retrospect, this was something of an "Indian summer" of liberalism in Japan, when the emergence of competitive party politics brought about a better balance between the roles and power of the politicians and those of the bureaucrats. This also opened up new possibilities for liberal-democratic legality to be explored.

[15] See, for instance, Ichiro Ozawa, *Blueprint for a New Japan: The Rethinking of a Nation* (Tokyo: Kodansha International, 1994).

An important part of the neoliberal reform agenda at the time had to do with the notion of "small government," that is, making cuts in public expenditure and eliminating wasteful spending in particular. This was not all, however. Changes in political dynamics especially from the mid-1990s saw political representatives advocating for enhanced "democratic control of government" to challenge bureaucratic authoritarian legality. This challenge to bureaucratic authoritarian legality took place under the framework of coalitional politics where there would be real policy changes from the elected office holders.[16]

The furtherance of democratic accountability of the government represented a novel conceptualization of administrative reform that was unlikely to be promoted by a governing party. It was placed on the political discourse as a new policy goal of administrative reform for the first time when the LDP fell from power after thirty-eight years of uninterrupted rule.

There are, in fact, two aspects to the goal of "democratic control of government." One, which may be termed the liberal approach, is the idea that the government should be kept in check by the other branches of the state such as the legislature, judiciary, local governments, or civil society.[17] Given the long reign of the LDP, it is not difficult to see why it was not inclined to seriously adopt such a liberal approach to impose checks on itself. In fact, even in countries where alternation of political parties in government takes place, there will be calls to reinforce the legislature's power to keep the executive in check, or to devolve power closer to the people at the local level. Frequently, it would be the opposition party that advocates such an approach, but once it forms the government, there would be a rapid decline of enthusiasm for the checks and balances to restrain their own power in policy implementation.[18]

The other, which manifests the neoliberal facet of "democratically accountable government," regards not the democratic control of the executive from the outside as key; rather, it is about the control of the career-bureaucrats by democratically elected representatives of the people (i.e. the ministers), and their political aides.[19] However, the issue lies in whether the ministers really have the power to make important decisions, and whether

---

[16] See also Koichi Nakano, "The Politics of Administrative Reform in Japan, 1993–1998: Toward a More Accountable Government?" *Asian Survey* 38(3) (1998): 291.

[17] Ibid., 299.

[18] See Koichi Nakano, *Party Politics and Decentralization in Japan: When the Opposition Governs* (London: Routledge, 2010).

[19] See, for instance, Ozawa, *Blueprint for a New Japan*.

there is a sufficient number of political appointees (e.g. the junior ministers and advisers) to assist them in doing so. Even on this front, the LDP under the condition of one-party dominance (and as a party that started off as the political branch of the bureaucracy) did not make any policy initiative that would impinge on elite bureaucrats' powers.

According to this neoliberal view of democratic control, elections are operated by analogy with the political marketplace where electors make their choice by selecting their preferred party to govern.[20] Once the political party forms the government, the party could make swift implementation of policies that exert democratic control on any required reorganization through the centralized authority of the prime minister (or the party leaders).

As we have already seen in some detail, decades of one-party rule by the LDP did not lead to a sharp separation of functions between the LDP and the bureaucracy, but, instead, the bureaucracy continued to play a significant role in government. Thus, with regard to "tribe" politicians ("*zoku*" politicians) who gained certain expertise in specific policy areas (in part thanks to LDP's long hold over power), rather than behaving like democratic representatives of the people seeking to hold the bureaucracy to account, they essentially "work with bureaucrats in the bureaucrats' system," as Leonard Schoppa observed in his study of the education "*zoku*."[21] Indeed, this is why Inoguchi and Iwai point out in their seminal work on the "*zoku*" phenomenon that the advent of "*zoku*" politicians, as discussed below, has not fundamentally modified "bureaucracy-led" governance in Japan.[22]

As Japan's perennial governing party since its foundation in 1955, the LDP had always relied on the bureaucracy to govern and to stay in power. While their relationship was by no means tension-free, the LDP was generally more interested in staying in power and in enjoying the fruits of power, than in confronting the bureaucracy with any coherent policy program of its own. This symbiotic relationship demonstrated that the bureaucrats would help the LDP to survive politically, while the LDP

---

[20] A classic exposition of this view can be found in Joseph Schumpeter, *Capitalism, Socialism and Democracy* (London: George Allen & Unwin, 1976) ch. 22. For a contemporary application of this paradigm to an analysis of Japanese politics, see J. Mark Ramseyer and Frances McCall Rosenbluth, *Japan's Political Marketplace* (Cambridge, MA: Harvard University Press, 1993).

[21] Leonard Schoppa, "Zoku Power and LDP Power: A Case Study of the Zoku Role in Education Policy," *Journal of Japanese Studies* 17(1) (1991): 104.

[22] Inoguchi Takashi and Iwai Tomoaki, *"Zoku Giin" no Kenkyū* [A Study of "Tribe Politicians"] (Tokyo: Nihon Keizai Shinbunsha, 1987), 33 and 104.

would help the bureaucrats to hold power. The LDP's *raison-d'être* was to be in power; it was much less important what it did in power.

Indeed, the LDP was a broad church, earning itself the nickname of a "super catch-all" party. While broadly conservative, its members ranged from liberal conservatives to revisionist right-wingers who never came to terms with the war defeat. Lacking a coherent ideological backbone, even its electoral platforms were usually crafted with extensive help from the bureaucrats. The LDP's institutional coherence had also remained rather weak. Factions and *"zoku"* politicians embodied the fragmented and decentralized structure of the party. The party president, who was usually also the prime minister, was at best only one of the party's bosses. Party structure was virtually nonexistent at the constituency level, and each politician relied on his/her personal support groups for electoral campaigning, where personality and pork-barrel politics featured more prominently than policy proposals.

Since political party contestation until the 1990s did not present any realistic prospect of alternation in power, the LDP was able to stay in power without having to forge any real coalition with other political parties. If political control of the bureaucracy was commonly reinforced by the need for political parties to fulfill their electoral promises, even in the face of potential bureaucratic resistance, such pressure did not really exist for the LDP in the past. Thus, once again, one-party dominance went a long way in explaining the persistence of bureaucracy's continued control of government and the LDP's lack of interest in expanding political appointments prior to 1993.

The end of LDP's one-party dominance in 1993 began a new era of delicate coalitional politics and intense electoral competition. The changes in party politics made potential coalition partners and electoral rivals out of members of non-LDP parties, some of which were newly founded by former opposition party members as well as former LDP members. With varying degrees of enthusiasm and emphasis, these non-LDP parties pushed for the policy of "democratic control of government" as a way to reform the administration. Examples of such reform advocates were New Party Sakigake and Ozawa Ichirō's New Frontier Party, which later joined forces under the banner of the Democratic Party of Japan (DPJ).

While it may be said that some of these advocates really believed in the need to further democratize the Japanese government because of ideological reasons or because of their long experience in the wilderness, it also made partisan sense to do so in the context of post-1993 politics.

Even though the LDP was no longer the majority on its own, it remained by far the biggest party whether in opposition or later again in power from June 1994. At the same time, the non-LDP parties needed clear identities of their own either because they threw away their long-held ideology (i.e. socialism) or because their leaders used to belong to the LDP. In the face of the formidable LDP and the sharpening of political polarization, the advocacy of democratic government reform allowed the non-LDP parties to differentiate themselves as the true voice of the people. The LDP was later to react to this challenge in its own way, but, for some time, the non-LDP parties were able to define for themselves with this new policy goal for administrative reform.

In general, it may be said that Sakigake emphasized the liberal approach to the issue of "democratic control of the government," while the New Frontier Party took on the neoliberal approach. The DPJ which was formed originally in 1996 through the merger of some core members of Sakigake and the centrists from the Socialist Party, initially carried over the liberal approach from Sakigake, but gradually shifted toward the neoliberal stance. Over time, the liberal approach to "democratic control of government" more or less disappeared from the policy debate, particularly since the DPJ merger with Ozawa's Liberal Party established the neoliberal consensus as a way to confront bureaucratic control.

Nevertheless, the challenge to bureaucratic authoritarian legality, induced by the liberal approach to democratic control, lasted until the late 1990s. For instance, there was an attempt in the 1990s to set up an organization in the parliament to supervise the government.[23] In December 1996, the DPJ submitted its 1996 Administration Supervision Authority (the Japanese GAO) Bill (1996 Administration Bill) to the parliament as a private member's bill. The bill stipulated the establishment of a supervisory organ in the parliament, with full powers to assess and supervise the bureaucracy. Consisting of three commissioners, appointed by the Speakers of both Houses from outside the bureaucracy, the supervisory organ was to investigate, report, demand submission of government papers and witnesses (accompanied by the power to demand punishment for non-cooperating officials) at the request of parliamentary committees and members of the parliament. The supervisory organ was to receive the administrative support of eight hundred officials transferred from the General Affairs Agency, whose Administrative Inspection Bureau was to

---

[23] The cases referred to here were treated more fully in Nakano, "Politics of Administrative Reform," 302.

be abolished simultaneously. The LDP, however, made it clear immediately that it opposed to the abolition of the Administrative Inspection Bureau, and the bill was scrapped in spring 1997.

The LDP then made a proposal in summer 1997 to reorganize the existing Audit Standing Committee in the House of Representatives into an Audit and Administration Supervision Standing Committee. This plan has been put to effect from January 1998 (coupled with a new Administration Supervision Committee in the House of Councilors), but as was widely expected, in view of the lack of supervisory power of committees in the past, the new committee turned out to be nothing more than window dressing.

Limited progress was also made in the area of government information disclosure. Legal provisions for disclosure of administrative information have been commonplace not only among developed countries, but also for many local authorities within Japan. The government deliberative council published its final report in December 1996,[24] recognizing the basic principle of disclosure, while also allowing six areas in which non-disclosure was permitted and leaving some crucial details to be determined by government and ministerial ordinances. Sakigake insisted on the enactment of the 1997 Disclosure of Government Information Bill (1997 Disclosure Bill) in the first half of 1997, but the Hashimoto's LDP government limited the scope of the bill to the disclosure of special corporations' financial statements. Hashimoto promised the submission of the 1997 Disclosure Bill to the Diet by March 1998, but in the meantime left the drafting of the bill to the bureaucrats, who were clearly determined to make it less inconvenient for themselves. Although the bill was eventually submitted for Diet deliberation on March 27, 1998, it was carried over for several Diet sessions, and after a few compromise deals, including the LDP's concession to opposition parties' demand that the law was to be revised four years after its implementation, it was finally enacted in May 1999 and took effect two years later in April 2001.

Prior to the implementation of the law, the Mori government appointed the members of the "third-party" board in charge of adjudicating disputes when citizens contested a ministry's refusal to disclose certain information. As it turned out, no fewer than four of the nine board members were former bureaucrats, and all the three full-time

---

[24] Administration Reform Commission (Gyōsei Kaikaku Iinkai), "Report on the Establishment of Government Information Legislation" (Jōhō Kōkai Hōsei no Kakuritsu ni kansusu Iken).

members were ex-bureaucrats. Despite the fact that the law stipulates that
all information should be disclosed in principle (in other words, nondisclosure should only happen in exceptional cases), an *Asahi* newspaper
survey two months after the implementation of the law found that the
disclosure rate was at an averaged 62 percent.[25]

Last but not least, one can also point to the enactment of the non-profit
organization law as an important step in the attempted transition toward
a more vibrant liberal-democratic system. The absence of a non-profit
organization law, and the resulting lack of legal status and tax breaks for
most non-profit organizations (NPOs) have long been blamed for the
relative weakness of Japan's non-profit sector. The existing system of
"public-interest corporations" ("*kōeki hōjin*"), based on the 1896 Civil
Code, provided legal status and tax breaks to bureaucracy-friendly NPOs
only. The supervisory ministry would judge whether the objectives of the
NPO served the "public interest." As a result, many public-interest
corporations were forced to accept "*amakudari*" bureaucrats (retired
bureaucrats getting cushy positions, in a practice known as "descent
from heaven"), or were even founded on a ministry's behest.

The active participation of civic groups in the rescue operation of the
Hanshin earthquake provided an impetus to the cause of NPO support.
Sakigake began its discussion on an NPO bill in January 1995, with
a three-party project team in action from the following month. The
legislative process was derailed when the LDP came up with a draft of
its own (which was subsequently enacted in 1998), stipulating that in
order to receive legal recognition, an NPO should make the promotion of
the public interest its objective and must not have any political agenda.

13.4   The Emergence of Corporatist Authoritarian Legality

The neoliberal impetus opened up some significant possibilities for the
advancement of liberal-democratic governance in the 1990s, but with the
acceleration of the two-party trajectory in the party system since 1998
when Ozawa disbanded the New Frontier Party, and the DPJ became the
main alternative to the LDP, the neoliberal approach to "democratic
control of government" emerged as the new consensus against bureaucratic control, where the final check and balance was predicated on the

---

[25] *Asahi Shinbun*, "Jōhō Kōkai no Kaijiritsu, Heikin 62% Gaimushō, Kimitsuhi no
Shito Subete Fukaiji" [Average 62% Disclosure Rate and Nondisclosure of All Ministry
of Foreign Affairs Secret Fund Expenses] June 6, 2001, 3.

existence and viability of an equally powerful political alternative. It was in December 2012, when the DPJ government collapsed and the LDP consolidated its dominant position in alliance with Komeito that the fatal weakness of the new political system, which was less dependent on a priori bureaucratic control, and thus more fluid and potentially less stable.

The fact of the matter is that the majoritarian political institutions, including the first-past-the-post electoral system, which the neoliberal reforms transplanted from Britain to Japan, did not bring about the same political consequences. First, the adoption was only partial – when the winner-takes-all rule was imported, the Japanese failed to have it accompanied by the complementary and crucial understanding of what those who lost the elections were supposed to do. There was a profound lack of understanding of the legitimate role of opposition in a majoritarian democracy. Second, as the transplantation was done in a foreign soil, where there had already existed a firmly rooted (albeit temporarily shaken) one-party dominance of the ruling LDP, rather than a two-bloc system (as in the case of Italy), any electoral reform was not able to achieve its principal goal of regular alternation of power between two major parties.

What resulted from these developments was a heavily distorted understanding and practice of majoritarian democracy that was basically boiled down to the "government of the day" facing no institutionalized check, critics, or opposition to speak of . The illiberal, statist, conservative traditions of the Japanese establishment, which had been somewhat contained and moderated by the postwar democratic institutions and practices, were by then to a significant degree undermined by the neoliberal administrative and political reforms. Consequently, corporatist authoritarian legality emerged as the government structure was expected to model upon a corporation, with power and authority to be concentrated on the CEO – that is, the prime minister – but crucially, without the discipline of market competition once the DPJ collapsed and the LDP no longer faced any rival in the party system.

The goal of "democratically accountable government" initially contained two different strands: the liberal strand that was more focused on the civil society controlling the state, while the neoliberal approach placed stronger emphasis on strengthening the democratically elected political leaders vis-à-vis the unelected bureaucrats. Put differently, enhanced democratic control at some point in the mid-1990s was reduced to the notion of enhanced political leadership – concentrating more and more power around the party leaders, and ultimately in the hands of the prime minister.

If we take another look at Table 13.3, we can see that the right-wing LDP Prime Ministers Abe and Asō broke with the newly formed tradition of the appointment of depoliticized administrative Deputy Chief Cabinet Secretary, as Abe (in his first term) appointed a personal friend from the Ministry of Finance from his cabinet, while Asō and Abe (later in his second term) appointed police bureaucrats. However, it was the DPJ government between 2009 and 2012 that sought to significantly weaken the power and role of the administrative Deputy Chief Cabinet Secretary, for instance, by abolishing the meeting of the administrative vice ministers in order to enhance the leadership of the prime minister and his ministers against what they regarded as bureaucratic usurpers.

Similarly, it was Abe in his current government that broke with the postwar tradition of a depoliticized Cabinet Legislation Bureau (Table 13.2), meddling with its personnel routine by effectively sacking Yamamoto and appointing the former diplomat Komatsu with the sole purpose of forcing through a new government interpretation of the Constitution that would enable him to lift the decades-long ban on the exercise of the right of collective self-defense. Komatsu passed away in office prematurely, but the damage was done, as his successor continued in the footsteps of his immediate predecessor and kowtowed to the authoritarian neglect of constitutionalism of the prime minister of the day.

However, it was none other than Ozawa Ichirō, the longtime leader of the opposition and the mastermind behind the DPJ's short-lived term in power, who first propagated the neoliberal view that it was undemocratic to let the bureaucratic Cabinet Legislation Bureau have the final say on the government's position on the constitutionality of the bills and laws, and who argued that, through a change of the interpretation of the same text of the postwar constitution, the Self-Defense Force troops might be able to take part in overseas missions under the auspices of the United Nations, if not under a US-led exercise of collective self-defense. Moreover, on the basis of such views about the enhanced leadership of the politicians, the DPJ government banned the Cabinet Legislation Bureau Chief from answering questions in the parliament as the ultimate authority on the constitutionality and legality of bills and policies, and instead designated certain ministers (the Chief Cabinet Secretary in most cases) to be responsible for explaining the government's position.

The neoliberal approach to enhanced "democratic control of government" made certain sense so long as the vastly reinforced power of the government of the day, and of its central political executive in particular, was kept in check by vibrant party competition that provided choices, and thus a means to replace the government with another, to the voters. When Japan's two-party system became defunct with the collapse of the DPJ government and the LDP's return to power in December 2012, however, another era of one-party dominance and monopoly of power was ushered in. By then, Prime Minister Abe and his inner circle dominated not only the opposition, but also the bureaucrats, and the resulting absence of check and balance led to the severe undermining of the principles of rule of law and constitutionalism.

On July 1, 2014, the Cabinet made the decision to reinterpret the Constitution in order to enable the government to exercise "limited" collective self-defense. All this time, the text of Article 9 of the Constitution remains unchanged since May 1947:

> Article 9. Aspiring sincerely to an international peace based on justice and order, the Japanese people forever renounce war as a sovereign right of the nation and the threat or use of force as means of settling international disputes.
>
> In order to accomplish the aim of the preceding paragraph, land, sea, and air forces, as well as other war potential, will never be maintained. The right of belligerency of the state will not be recognized.

Up to July 1, 2014, successive governments had taken the view that the Constitution permitted only the exercise of individual self-defense: (1) when there is an imminent and illegitimate act of aggression against Japan; (2) when there is no appropriate means to deal with such aggression other than by resorting to the right of self-defense; and (3) when the use of armed force is confined to the minimum necessary level.

While the recognition of the right of individual self-defense was initially controversial (and remains so to a degree today), it has since become widely accepted that Article 9 still functions as a powerful check on the government as well as on the Self-Defense Forces. This was also precisely why some advocated the revision of Article 9 to make Japan a "normal" country.

With the lifting of the ban on collective self-defense, the Japanese government has changed the conditions for the use of force as follows: (1) when an armed attack against Japan has occurred, or when an armed attack against a foreign country that is in a close relationship with Japan occurs and as a result threatens Japan's survival and poses a clear danger to fundamentally overturn people's right to life, liberty, and pursuit of happiness; (2) when there is no other appropriate means available to repel the attack and ensure Japan's survival and protect its people; and (3) when the use of armed force is confined to the minimum necessary level.

The fundamental problem with this new interpretation of Article 9 is that it now no longer seems to ban anything other than a war of aggression, and even though there is the "limitation" that the country's survival and a clear danger to its people is needed to be recognized when exercising the right of collective self-defense, it would be for the government of the day to make that judgment.

The contempt for the principle of constitutionalism that Abe showed as he arbitrarily lifted the constitutional ban on collective self-defense through the government's reinterpretation of the same text of the Constitution was met with strong public contestation and was reported worldwide, but it was hardly the only example of the corporatist authoritarian legality that was instituted by the Abe government. Earlier in December 2013, Abe forced through the illiberal 2013 Designated Secrets Law,[26] and in June 2017 the equally controversial Conspiracy Law.[27] In each case, it is the potentially limitless discretion granted on the government of the day that raised the biggest concerns. The designation of special secrets is not subject to any meaningful check and review by actors outside of the government. The conditions that constitute a conspiracy to commit a crime that is yet to be committed are largely left to the police to determine and decide.

At least there was some semblance of the rule of law in the period of bureaucratic authoritarian legality – as Abe and his clique increasingly personalized state power and its institutions, the rule of man came to become the "new normal" in the age of corporatist authoritarian legality. The Moritomo and Kake scandals,[28] and the cover-up scandal that

---

[26] Usaki Masahiro, "What Japan's Designated State Secrets Law Targets, "*Asia-Pacific Journal* 21(1) (2014): 12.

[27] Richard Lloyd Parry, "UN Condemns Japan's Conspiracy Law," *The Times*, May 24, 2017.

[28] Moritomo Gakuen, a school operator backed by Prime Minister Abe's wife, was found to have received a discount of more than 85 percent when purchasing land from the Ministry of Finance. It was later revealed that more than 300 passages from a dozen public documents had been doctored by the bureaucrats to eliminate inconsistencies with the government's responses to opposition questions in the parliament. Kake Gakuen, another school corporation operated by a close personal friend of the prime minister, benefited from exceptional favors to win a state bid to open a veterinary school, similarly raising suspicions of cronyism and subsequent cover-ups.

followed, attest to the extent to which cronyism, tampering of public documents, and lying to parliament have become commonplace and go unpunished in Abe's Japan.[29]

13.5   Civil Society Resistance to Authoritarian Legality

Before ending this chapter, let us take a brief overview of the civil society resistance to the rise of corporatist authoritarian legality in the recent years. The first sign of renewed civic activism appeared in the form of a students' group called SASPL (Students Against Secret Protection Law) that was established right after the passage of the Designated Secrets Law in December 2013. They organized demonstrations, and sought to raise public awareness of the problems of the new law. This group of students subsequently formed SEALDs (Students Emergency Action for Liberal Democracy-s) on Constitution Day (May 3, 2015), as the Abe government pushed the security legislation in the ordinary session of the parliament that summer.

On the side of the scholars, a group that consists mainly of constitutional law scholars and political scientists established the Save Constitutional Democracy group (Rikken Demokurashī no Kai) in April 2014 in opposition to the government's move to reinterpret Article 9 to enable the exercise of collective self-defense. This group was co-headed by the late Professor Okudaira Yasuhiro (succeeded by Professor Higuchi Yōichi) and Professor Yamaguchi Jirō, and included such other renowned constitutional law experts as Professors Hasebe Yasuo, Ishikawa Kenji, Kobayashi Setsu, and Mizushima Asaho, among others. Another group of scholars was launched in June 2015, the Association of Scholars Opposed to the Security-related Bills (known in Japan as Association of Scholars (Gakusha no Kai)) that drew an even larger number of scholars from various disciplines. The Association of Scholars was founded by Professor Satō Manabu, a renowned scholar of education, and a long list of top scholars in Japan, including Professor Hirowatari Seigo, a law scholar and former President of the Science Council of Japan. The Association of Scholars joined SEALDs in the protest in front of the parliament through the summer of 2015.

---

[29] Koichi Nakano, "In Japan, Too, Outrageous Is the New Normal," *New York Times*, June 11, 2018, www.nytimes.com/2018/06/11/opinion/shinzo-abe-japan-scandal-land.html

Mothers Against War (Mama no Kai) was also established in July 2015
by Ms. Saigō Minako who was a doctorate candidate from the University
of Kyoto. The movement soon spread very quickly as anyone (not just
mothers) who embraced the group's slogan "We shall not let anyone's
child be killed" and who opposed the security legislation could form their
own Mama no Kai.

These new groups joined the "old-school" movement called Sōgakari
Kōdō Jikkō Iinkai (All Out Action Committee, or Sōgakari for short),
which brought together mostly the older, baby-boom generation to the
protests. Even though the core members of Sōgakari are seasoned veter-
ans of protest politics, the Committee was a creation of a groundbreaking
agreement between three different strands of pacifist groups in
December 2014: an alliance of non-partisan pacifist groups, a peace
movement led by the trade unions that supported the DPJ, and another
that brought together various movements and unions that are close to the
Japan Communist Party (JCP).

Once the security bills that lifted the constitutional ban on the exercise
of collective self-defense were rammed through the parliament in
September 2015, representatives of these five civic groups – SEALDs,
Save Constitutional Democracy, Association of Scholars, Mothers
Against War, and Sōgakari – came together to form the Civil Alliance
for Peace and Constitutionalism (Shimin Rengō for short) to pursue the
abolition of security legislation and to rescind the cabinet's decision of
July 1, 2014 to interpret Article 9 of the Constitution that lifted the ban on
collective self-defense.

The efforts to overcome the division in the opposition camp have been
met with considerable difficulties. However, while the LDP continues to
dominate the party system, a more energetic main opposition party,
called the Constitutional Democratic Party of Japan, is now in parliament, and in spite of Abe's professed desire to revise the Constitution,
including Article 9, he has so far been unable to make headway in
instigating a national referendum.

13.6 Conclusion

This chapter has examined the long tradition of bureaucratic authoritarian legality that constituted a central pillar of the state conservative
governance of the modernization process in Japan. The postwar US
occupation reforms pushed through significant democratization of politics and legality, but authoritarian legality persisted as the bureaucrats

adapted themselves successfully to the new conditions in the Cold War under the one-party dominance of the LDP. Key segments of state power were, in fact, bureaucratized in the postwar era and became off-limits for the elected politicians. These depoliticized parts of the state served as pockets in which bureaucratic authoritarian legality survived alongside democratic institutions and practices.

In the final phase of the Cold War, the spread of the neoliberal norms worldwide presented fresh challenges to the persistence of bureaucratic control as party politics entered a new stage of fluctuation. This culminated in the brief moment of triumph from the mid-to-late 1990s when liberal-democratic legality showed considerable promise of advancement. This was not to last for long, as the introduction of the first-past-the-post majoritarian electoral system from 1996 brought about the emergence of a new consensus over a neoliberal approach to "democratic control of government," which undermined bureaucratic dominance while paradoxically compromising the principle of bureaucratic neutrality.

In the neoliberal views and discourses, a priori bureaucratic control was to be replaced by a posteriori political check and balance. For that mechanism to work, parties and government had to be remodeled after the corporate structure, and, consequently, power and responsibility was to be concentrated in the CEO – the prime minister. Similar to deregulation aimed at maximizing corporate freedom, constitutional and legal constraints were increasingly challenged in order to "free" central executive power.

This neoliberal model of the electoral marketplace may possibly be argued to work as long as check and balance is secured through a viable and competitive two-party system, but with the demise of the DPJ government in December 2012, which in turn brought about the collapse of the political opposition in the face of an almighty LDP government of the right-wing Abe Shinzō, Japan entered a new era of corporatist authoritarian legality. The ongoing crisis of constitutionalism and the rule of law in Japan need to be understood in the context of the shifting modes of authoritarian legality that this chapter sought to explicate. It is also precisely because of the failure of representation through the party system that direct protests from the legal professionals, scholars, students, workers, and citizens from all walks of life have regained strength in recent years. Whether the prospect for liberal-democratic legality can be revived depends on their efforts to instill new energy into the divided and weakened opposition.

14

Authoritarian Legality after Authoritarianism

Legal Governance of Parties and Elections before and after Democratic Transition in South Korea

ERIK MOBRAND

14.1 Introduction

The Republic of Korea (ROK) was designed as a Cold War democracy. It started as an electoral regime with formal commitments to democratic values, but institutions made to protect the country from Pyongyang had massive ramifications for domestic political struggle. From 1948 to the democratic transition of 1987, the political system shifted between democratic and authoritarian regimes. A legal framework for governing party and electoral politics emerged from these regimes. Even as successive regimes built and retained extraconstitutional and extralegal measures for dealing with political opponents, this legal framework existed alongside formal elections.

"Authoritarian law can develop characteristics of its own independent of regime type," as Hualing Fu and Michael Dowdle argue in this volume.[1] The conceptual separation of authoritarian legality from the type of regime is useful. This separation offers a means of identifying similarities and differences within authoritarian regimes, which may vary in the extent to which law is a force for retaining or exerting state power. It also makes it possible to locate illiberal streaks in otherwise democratic regimes. This perspective is especially helpful for reflecting on political change in South Korea. The country has had several regimes that might be labeled "authoritarian." From

This work was supported by the Research Resettlement Fund for new faculty at Seoul National University. I would also like to thank the editors and fellow contributors for helping me to improve the chapter.
[1] Chapter 2.

the standpoint of regime type, these governments might all be labeled as nondemocratic. Attention to the use of law vis-à-vis noninstitutionalized governing instruments can help draw more precise distinctions among these regimes. Furthermore, the liberation of the concept of authoritarian legality from authoritarianism as a regime raises the possibility that South Korea's democratic transition might not have erased earlier authoritarian uses of law. Authoritarian legality might, therefore, have staying power. This possibility, which points to tensions within democracy, is the subject of this chapter.

The focus of this chapter is the legal framework governing party and electoral politics. This framework comprises the laws that are directly relevant to political parties and elections. It includes rights and restrictions related to formation of parties, conditions for disbanding parties, stipulations concerning party organization and activities, monitoring of elections, campaign finance, and other aspects of electoral campaigning. South Korea possesses a sprawling legal framework related to parties and elections. This framework includes one of the world's first laws about political parties, a powerful and influential election commission, and detailed laws regulating a campaigning politician's every action. In this chapter, I largely exclude discussion of the electoral system because it has received sufficient treatment elsewhere, with a great deal of current scholarship conceiving of parties and party systems as responses to the incentives of an electoral system.

Here, I examine the various tools that have been used to govern the political sphere from the country's establishment to the present. Why were such laws developed, and how did they matter? What was their fate after the democratic transition of 1987? These questions point to broader themes related to authoritarian legality. Can an authoritarian regime make a commitment to rules governing electoral and party politics? Why would it make such a commitment? And why would it revoke one? What happens to that legal framework after a democratic transition? I trace the construction of the legal framework and weigh the significance of this framework against other tools used for governing the political sphere in different time periods. My main theme is the striking continuity in the legal framework guiding party and electoral politics. In particular, I point to the way legal innovations that reached their final form in 1963 under Park Chung Hee became the basis for the governance of post-1987 democracy. Given the illiberal purpose of the framework, this continuity stands in sharp contrast to the liberalism that pervades many portions of contemporary South Korea.

14.2 Governance of Party and Electoral Politics over Time

In examining the South Korean example, there are immediate ambiguities. First, which periods in the country's history should be labeled as authoritarian? From its inception, the state has claimed to be a democracy. Elections were held. The period from 1972 to 1987 was, however, clearly a dictatorship because there were no meaningful elections. The period from 1963 to 1972 was once treated as democratic with the shift in 1972 interpreted as an instance of democratic breakdown.[2] Today, political scientists might instead label the regime of 1963–72 an "electoral authoritarian" one. Second, how can the extent of the government's commitment to the Constitution of the Republic of Korea be assessed? South Korea's governments have possessed a variety of mechanisms for regulating political space. These include constitutional articles, bodies of law related specifically to parties, legal measures that sit in tension with the Constitution, and the extralegal use of force.

An approach suggested here is to consider the various devices used to govern electoral and party politics in distinct periods of time. Three categories of devices are most relevant in South Korea. The first comprises the Constitution and laws governing the political space. This is the core territory of authoritarian legality. The second comprises measures that supersede the Constitution, in particular the National Security Law. While these measures are formulated on a legal basis, they also form what Fu and Dowdle refer to as "zones of exception."[3] Instead of applying constitutional laws, the regime can declare that a case involves a threat to national security and use other means to resolve the case. The third is extralegal repression, through police, military, or nonstate agents of intimidation. This category has little to do with law. For any given period, a particular combination of these governing instruments can be identified. By identifying these combinations for multiple periods, I shall document how the governance of electoral and party politics has shifted over time. Doing so should offer a guide to the shifts relevant to the questions of authoritarian legality. By placing contemporary South Korea in this framework, it is possible to make an assessment of any legacies of authoritarian legality as well. In keeping with the themes stressed in this volume, especially the contributions by Fu and Dowdle, and Jacques

---

[2] Sungjoo Han, *The Failure of Democracy in Korea* (Berkeley and Los Angeles: University of California Press, 1974); Baeg Im Hyug, "The Rise of Bureaucratic Authoritarianism in South Korea," *World Politics* 39(2) (1987).
[3] See Chapter 2 in this volume.

deLisle, this approach allows authoritarian legality to be distinguished from authoritarianism as a regime type. This conceptual distinction frees analysis from relying on regime-type labels, and also raises the possibility of finding authoritarian legality in democratic contexts.

This framework also points to a way of thinking about the reasons for a regime to commit to the legal regulation of political space. If the legal instruments prove to be sufficiently effective for this purpose, then other forms of regulation may be rendered unnecessary. There could be reasons related to building legitimacy that would encourage leaders to take this route. However, if these legal instruments threaten state power, or if there are other reasons which make legitimacy through elections less significant, then a regime may revoke this commitment.

14.2.1   A Violent Electoral Regime: 1948–1958

The Republic of Korea was established in 1948 as an electoral regime. In the three preceding years of rule by a US military government, state-building and the construction of the electoral sphere had influenced each other. The Americans preferred groups with anticommunist credentials as such groups contributed both to building state institutions and to fighting popular forces. By 1948, two main political cliques dominated politics and government: a rightist group centered on Syngman Rhee, who had lived in the United States during the colonial period, and a rightist group centered on individuals who had been in Korea before 1945.[4] The founding of the Republic as the southern portion of the peninsula meant the exclusion of left-leaning groups from politics. The elections of May 1948 were held without the participation of communist and other left-wing parties.[5]

The Constitution, drafted by delegates selected in the May election, outlined a system with an elected assembly, which in turn elected the president. There were few rules on party or electoral politics. Election campaign laws were not detailed. One important rule, though, was inherited from the US military government. In early 1946, the authorities

---

[4] On this interplay between party politics and the projection of state power, see Pak Ch'an-p'yo, *Han'guk ŭi kukka hyŏngsŏng kwa minjujuŭi: Naengjŏn chayujuŭi wa posujŏk minjujuŭi ŭi kiwŏn* [State Formation and Democracy in Korea: Cold War Liberalism and the Origins of Conservative Democracy] (Seoul: Humanit'asŭ, 2007).

[5] On politics in these crucial few post-1945 years, see Bruce Cumings, *The Origins of the Korean War, Vol. 1: Liberation and the Emergence of Separate Regimes, 1945–1947* (Princeton, NJ: Princeton University Press, 1981).

had introduced a requirement that any political party must register as such and provide detailed information on members, financing, and relations with other parties. The purpose of this law was to ensure that all communist-sympathizing groups could be identified or deterred from operating legally. Under the 1948 Constitution, this law remained in force.

Within a few months of the ROK's establishment, the new government, led by Syngman Rhee, passed the National Security Law. In the name of stamping out domestic allies of Pyongyang, the law allowed the state to use extrajudicial measures to detain and punish those with communist sympathies. This law was useful for keeping forces associated with workers or farmers out of electoral politics.

Syngman Rhee revised the Constitution in 1952 to make the presidency directly elected. He sought and retained office over the course of the 1950s. Along the way, he established the country's first mass mobilizing party, the Liberal Party. In this period, electoral politics was highly chaotic. Rhee liked elections as they could be cited to boost his democratic credentials. Yet, he liked them because he had all the tools for winning them. He could use his control over state resources in order to fund his political party. His Liberal Party was also increasingly drawn to using both state coercion and nonstate violence to harass the opposition and generate support at election time. Instruments like the National Security Law added another layer of protection by ensuring popular forces were demobilized.[6] This period is characterized by a formal constitutional order, buttressed by regular elections, but also a leadership that through its actions had demonstrated hardly any commitment to the legalistic governance of party and electoral politics.

14.2.2   Creation of a New Order: 1958–1963

The violent nature of the First Republic (1948–60) reached its peak in the late 1950s and in 1960. Rhee turned increasingly to illegal means of winning votes. He ordered banks to give funding to his Liberal Party. He put close allies in charge of ensuring that a range of administrative organs would support him and his party in elections. The police, for example, were given funds for helping to secure the correct electoral

[6] Son Pong-suk, "Yi Paksa wa chayudang ŭi tokchu" [Dr. Rhee and the Liberal Party's Dominance], in *Han'guk ŭi chŏngdang, che-1 p'yŏn: 8.15 esŏ chayudang punggoe kkaji* [Korea's Political Parties, Vol. 1: From August 15 to the Liberal Party's Collapse], ed. Han'guk ilbosa (Seoul: Han'guk ilbosa, 1987).

outcome. The Liberal Party manipulated all stages of the electoral process, from candidate registers to voting and monitoring to the vote count. Rhee's regime demonstrated no respect for electoral procedures. In early 1960, leaked Liberal Party plans for rigging the upcoming presidential and vice-presidential election prompted mass protests. The regime's violent response led to further outrage and finally to the demise of the First Republic.[7]

This period was one of transition. Between 1958 and 1963, a new set of institutions for governing party and electoral politics was developed. This period also saw four different regimes in South Korea. Excessive electoral manipulation combined with police violence directed at demonstrators led to the First Republic's downfall in April 1960. The opposition Democrats gained power under a revised constitution in 1960. Less than a year into that government, a bloodless military coup put a junta into office. In 1963, the military officers, led by Park Chung Hee, restored civilian rule. The institutions that would be in place from 1963 involved reforms instituted by each of the first three of these governments.

The first institution was a set of campaign rules written into the Lower House (minŭiwŏn) Election Law of 1958. In the 1956 presidential election, the sudden death of the opposition candidate weeks before the election led the Democrats to accept the Progressive Party candidate Cho Pong-am as their nominee. Cho hailed from outside the main elite groups but was nonetheless able to win over 30 percent of the vote. Cho's relative success made the ruling Liberal Party nervous and it made the opposition Democrats equally concerned that their status as the main party out of office could be under threat from a third party. This shared anxiety led the National Assembly in 1958 to pass a revision to the election law. The revision represented a new approach to regulating electoral campaigns. The law banned all sorts of opportunities for contact between candidates and voters, including door-to-door visits, and imposed limits on the numbers of rallies and speeches. Such rules were justified in the name of preventing "overheated" elections. Excessive competition, it was claimed, created opportunities for politicians to accept bribes or coerce voters. The real purpose of the reform, however – which was not lost on commentators at the time – was to prevent third parties from gaining opportunities to campaign. The leading third party was Cho's Progressive Party. Sure enough, in the 1958 National Assembly

---

[7] Son Pong-suk, "Yi Paksa."

election, third-party candidates fared much more poorly than in 1954.[8]
A two-party system was coming into being.

The Rhee regime, though, was unsatisfied to use only laws to marginalize competitors. In 1958, the administration claimed Cho was
a communist sympathizer, and he and his several party members were
detained under the National Security Law. Cho was executed in 1959 and
Rhee banned the Progressive Party.

The Progressive Party episode provided the impetus to the second
institution, the party dissolution system. After the collapse of Rhee's
government in 1960, legislators set about stipulating the conditions
under which the executive can order a party to be banned. The fates of
Cho and the Progressive Party made the Democrats afraid that, under
a future regime, they could find themselves in Cho's position. They
realized that the Constitution failed to provide a legitimate way for the
executive to ban a party. This recognition is interesting. Legislators might
have concluded that stronger protections on parties were necessary.
Instead, perhaps because they liked the idea of threatening third parties,
they formalized a system for dissolving parties. An article was added to
the Constitution that would allow the president to dissolve a party that
threatens the political order, which would require support from a newly
devised Constitutional Court. The design was meant to serve as a check
and balance and was adapted to the local context from an interesting mix
of foreign institutions. The reformers looked to West Germany for
a model of "militant democracy,"[9] though of course there was no threat
from a fascist party or a prior ruling group. They looked to liberal models
for the check provided by a constitutional court.[10] In the end, the

---

[8] Sŏ Pok-kyŏng, "Chehanjŏk kyŏngjaeng ŭi chedohwa: 1958-yŏn sŏn'gŏpŏp ch'eje" [The
Institutionalization of Limited Competition: The System of the Lower House (minŭiwŏn)
Election Law of 1958], *Sŏn'gŏ yŏn'gu* [Electoral Studies] 3(1) (2013).

[9] Karl Loewenstein, "Militant Democracy and Fundamental Rights, I," *American Political
Science Review* 31(3) (1937). A discussion related to South Korea is set out in Han Su-ung,
"Chŏngdang ŭi kaenyŏm kwa chŏngdang tŭngnok chedo ŭi hŏnpŏpjŏk munjejŏm:
Hŏnjae 2006.3.30 2004 hŏnma 246 kyŏljŏng e taehan p'allye p'yŏngsŏk ŭl chungsim
ŭro" [The Concept of a Political Party and Constitutional Problems with the Party
Registration System: A Commentary on the Decision in Case hŏnjae 2006.3.30
2004 hŏnma 246], *Chŏsŭt'isŏ* [Justice] 104 (2008).

[10] For more on the party registration cancellation system, see Yi Chong-su, "Chŏngdangje
minjujuŭi ŭi hyŏnanmunje ŭi kŏmt'o: Hyŏnhaeng chŏngdang tŭngnok chedo mit
chŏngdang tŭngnok ch'wiso chedo wa chŏngch'i chagŭm chedo rŭl chungsim ŭro" [An
Investigation into the Pending Issues of Party Democracy: The Current Party Registration
System, the Party Registration Cancelation System, and the Political Finance System],
Hŏnbŏphak yŏn'gu [Constitutional Studies] 13(2) (2007).

Constitutional Court was not established before the coup of May 1961. The subsequent regime, thus, inherited the party dissolution system, though it could not be invoked until the Constitutional Court was set up decades later.

The remaining institutions were established in 1962–3 as the post-coup regime prepared for the transfer to civilian government. The junta's priority was to design institutions that would allow the party it was forming to gain power through elections. The previous institutions were kept, including the stringent laws on campaigning and the party dissolution law. The military leaders designed a new Political Parties Act, which was one of the first independent laws anywhere that specifically targeted political parties.[11] West Germany's, introduced in 1967, is often understood as the first but South Korea's actually preceded it. The Political Parties Act set out the scope for all aspects of party organization and activity. It required parties to be national organizations with head-quarters in Seoul and stipulated the organizational structure of parties. It also set out terms for revoking their registration.[12]

The final institution was the Central Election Management Commission (CEMC). In 1960, the existing election commission had been elevated to a constitutional body. Park then overhauled the body and changed its name. The renamed CEMC was rolled out in 1963 along with the Political Parties Act. It was designed to enforce the strict campaign laws that had been inherited from the First Republic. The central themes of the CEMC stressed the need for orderly elections and the importance of preventing politicians from having excessive contact with citizens. The wild electio-neering of the late 1950s buttressed the regime's claim that such concerns deserved priority. In this vision of democracy, values such as "participation," "contestation," or "competition" had little place.

By the time civilian rule was restored in 1963, a set of legal institutions for governing party and electoral politics was in place. The considera-tions driving this commitment were multiple. First, there had been a consensus among the political elites on the need to regulate political space. This consensus was seen in the Lower House (minŭiwŏn) Election Law of 1958 and in the party dissolution system introduced in

---

[11] For an overview of laws governing political parties around the world, see Kenneth Janda, *Political Parties and Democracy in Theoretical and Practical Perspectives: Adopting Party Law* (Washington, DC: National Democratic Institute for International Affairs, 2005).

[12] See Sŏ Pok-kyŏng, "Han'guk chŏngch'i kyŏlsa chehan ch'eje ŭi yŏksajŏk kiwŏn" [The Historical Origins of Korea's System of Limits on Political Assembly], *Tonghyang kwa chŏnmang* [Trends and Prospects] 90 (2014).

1960. Second, the electoral manipulation under the First Republic allowed the Park government to justify more easily the types of constraints that it introduced to the political system. Third, the regime was under pressure from the United States to reintroduce elected government[13] and needed a way to do so in a politically expedient manner. The institutions which were completed by 1963, thus, advantaged Park and his allies in view of forthcoming elections.

14.2.3   A Regulated Electoral Regime: 1963–1972

In the period from the restoration of civilian rule in 1963 to the suspension of direct presidential elections in 1972, South Korea held three sets of presidential and legislative elections. Park Chung Hee and his Democratic Republican Party remained in power throughout this period. Electoral politics was nonetheless lively and even competitive. The opposition consolidated its base in cities, while the ruling party developed support in rural areas. Control over rice procurement prices and the use of the agricultural cooperative system helped Park to build electoral support in the countryside.[14]

The chaos surrounding the elections of the late 1950s also declined precipitously. While the Liberal Party had resorted to hiring local toughs to harass voters, the Park regime largely refrained from doing so. In post-1963 South Korea, the Liberal Party's measures would have seemed crude or unsophisticated. Instances of gang members roughing up opposition party workers did emerge, but they appear to have been a less regular feature of politics. The regime had more institutional means of managing elections. Regime critics still faced the threat of coercion from the intelligence services and under the National Security Law. Anticommunism provided the basis for preventing any political organization of labor, as well for ensuring that any union activities were done on state or business terms.[15]

There was also a kind of ideological commitment to a vision of democracy in this period. The First Republic's downfall had created an

---

[13] Gregg Brazinsky, *Nation Building in South Korea: Koreans, Americans, and the Making of a Democracy* (Chapel Hill, NC: University of North Carolina Press, 2007), ch. 5.

[14] Young Jo Lee, "The Countryside," in Byung-kook Kim and Ezra F. Vogel (eds.), *The Park Chung Hee Era: The Transformation of South Korea* (Cambridge, MA: Harvard University Press, 2011).

[15] Jang Jip Choi, *Labor and the Authoritarian State: Labor Unions in South Korean Manufacturing Industries, 1961–1980* (Seoul: Korea University Press, 1989).

opportunity for Park. Electoral manipulation had brought the regime down. The movement that formed against Rhee became known as the "April Revolution," and today it is considered the foundation of South Korea's struggle for democracy. A wide range of civil society groups continue to hold the April Revolution up as a pivotal moment in the nation's progress. Park, though, was able to claim the mantle of the April Revolution.[16] He presented his coup of 1961 as a continuation of the April Revolution. The junta, critical of the ineptness of the prior regime, immediately brought Rhee's cronies to justice. Trials were held for Rhee's key allies and for agents of the Liberal Party's violence, with five leading figures executed within seven months of the coup.[17] Such measures showed that Park and his Democratic Republican Party were serious about fighting Rhee-style cronyism. Park highlighted the electoral manipulations of Rhee's regime in order to champion a notion of democracy that made political competition or participation secondary. Real democracy, Park insisted, focused on a government that served the people. He promised a nationalist democracy in which strengthening the nation through economic growth would indicate that the people's interests were being served.[18] Having elections that inspire citizen participation would instead be a peripheral concern. South Korea between 1963 and 1972 was, therefore, hardly liberal. However, rules governing parties and elections were essential to the political system and retaining elections was a necessity for both international and domestic reasons, with the Park regime remaining committed to the operation of an electoral system.

14.2.4 A Nonelectoral Interlude: 1972–1987

In 1972, Park brought the period of rule by elected politicians to an end. He revised the Constitution to make himself president for life by eliminating direct presidential elections. Under the new "*Yusin*" regime, legislative elections became uncompetitive and control by the ruling party became guaranteed. Multiple factors drove this move, but international geopolitical circumstances were the most relevant. As the war in Vietnam looked grimmer for the United States, its allies in Asia became

---

[16] Park Chung Hee, *The Country, the Revolution and I*, trans. Leon Sinder (Seoul: Hollym Corporations, 1963), 19–20.

[17] Erik Mobrand, "The Street Leaders of Seoul and the Foundations of the South Korean Political Order," *Modern Asian Studies* 50(2) (2016).

[18] Park Chung Hee, *To Build a Nation* (Washington, DC: Acropolis Books, 1971).

nervous that their patron would abandon them. Under these conditions, Park was able to claim that the country needed stronger leadership. In the Philippines, Marcos – even without a security situation akin to the Korean peninsula's – had thrown out the Constitution. Observing that Marcos did not face repercussions from the United States, Park might have been emboldened to make his move just three weeks later.[19]

Domestic political considerations also contributed to the shift to the "*Yusin*" regime. In 1969, Park had revised the Constitution to remove the president's term limits, which would have meant the end of his presidency. In the next election in 1971, the challenger Kim Dae Jung came uncomfortably close to Park's vote count. In the wake of that election, Park and his allies lost faith in the capacity of the legal framework for elections to keep his position secure. Kim's showing had raised the prospect that the institutions devised for making elections conducive for the regime's perpetuation were no longer sufficient. This factor behind the 1972 "*Yusin*" reform, thus, suggests a reason why authoritarian leaders may revoke a previous commitment to constitutionalism.

After 1972, legislative elections continued. Parties not affiliated with the regime had no chance to win, as the electoral system offered an unassailable advantage (through the distribution of at-large seats) to the regime's allies. However, opposition parties were allowed to organize. This meant that both elections and legislative politics gave opposition forces opportunities to speak and be heard by the public. Urban districts continued to support the opposition parties. In the National Assembly, opposition lawmakers regularly gave speeches criticizing the regime. These speeches had no impact on legislation, but reporting on them in the press meant that citizens could listen in on conflictual politics.[20] Further, the National Security Law and the intelligence services continued to be used widely in politics. The most notorious attack on a regime opponent was the kidnap of opposition figure Kim Dae Jung. He was taken from a hotel room in Tokyo to a boat from where he would presumably have been cast overboard had it not been for US interference at the last moment.

The assassination of Park Chung Hee in October 1979 set in motion a protracted coup leading to the Fifth Republic under General Chun Doo

---

[19] On the Park-Marcos comparison, see Paul D. Hutchcroft, "Reflections on a Reverse Image: South Korea under Park Chung Hee and the Philippines under Ferdinand Marcos," in Kim and Vogel (eds.), *Park Chung Hee Era*.

[20] Choi, *Labor and the Authoritarian State*, 220.

Hwan. The same basic institutions remained in place with the presidency remaining indirectly elected. While the leaders of the Fifth Republic tinkered with the electoral and party laws, much of the legal structure persisted. As in the preceding period, these rules were far less important than the effects of an indirectly elected presidency and unfair advantage to the ruling party in National Assembly elections. In fact, so iron-clad was Chun's hold on office that some rules governing elections were liberalized, such as allowing independent candidates to run for office. Repression of dissent, however, continued and both Kim Dae Jung and Kim Young Sam were banned from political activities for much of the period.

14.2.5   After Democratic Transition: 1987–Present

The central piece of the democratic transition was a swiftly nego-tiated constitutional reform. This reform was promised by President-in-waiting Roh Tae Woo in June 1987 in response to pressure on the streets. The reform restored direct presidential elections. A revision to the electoral system meant that opposition parties gained some chance of winning control of the National Assembly. The institu-tional basis to the "*Yusin*" regime and the Fifth Republic was, thus, removed.

Persecution through legal and extralegal means also declined precipi-tously. The political rights of the most prominent dissidents were restored immediately in 1987. Politicians and their campaigns were no longer subject to state-sponsored violence. Indeed, the civility of electoral politics was remarkable. There was nothing like a return to the use of "political gangsters" to harass regime opponents. In the first elections, rabble-rousers – presumably hired by the regime – turned up at rallies and caused disturbances. More seriously, thugs disrupted the establish-ment of a unified opposition party in spring 1987. The episode, however, came to nothing, as the intervention had no impact on the opposition's campaigning. The civility of electoral politics almost immediately after the constitutional reform in 1987 distinguishes the post-1987 period from the First Republic of the 1950s.

State intervention in electoral politics also declined in specific ways. The military was progressively phased out of politics in the early and mid-1990s. While figures with military backgrounds had taken many seats in the National Assembly in the 1980s, by the mid-1990s such figures had nearly disappeared from party and electoral politics. The intelligence agency presumably intervened less in political affairs.[21] Making an accurate assessment on this issue is difficult, however. State intervention did not completely disappear. Indeed, investigations after the 2012 presidential elections uncovered evidence that the intelligence agency had paid people to make negative comments about Park Geun-hye's rivals in online forums.[22] The National Security Law also remained in force. In 1991, the National Assembly passed an amendment that limited the scope of its use,[23] but no other revisions to the law have been made. Attempts to abandon the law have also failed. While not used as indiscriminately as in the past, the National Security Law continues to be used to detain and penalize individuals and groups accused of having North Korean sympathies.[24]

What is most remarkable, though, is that the laws and institutions governing elections and parties underwent little change during or after the 1987 constitutional reform. The legal architecture of the post-1963 institutions had persisted during the 1972 to 1987 period. In that decade and a half, though, this system mattered little. The elimination of direct presidential elections and a skewed electoral system for the legislature, together with state-sponsored violence against opposition, ensured that the regime was safe from electoral and party politics. In 1987, the constitutional reform rolled back those repressive features of the "*Yusin*" regime and the Fifth Republic, but the institutions governing elections remained fully intact. Each of the core parts of the institutional framework either experienced limited change or features that restricted party and electoral politics were enhanced.

The election commission also stayed in place. Instead of being reformed, the mandate of the CEMC only expanded. In 1989, as the first by-election was under way, the CEMC warned all of the major

---

[21] Accounts of the rollback of the state's coercive forces can be found in Robert E. Bedeski, *The Transformation of South Korea: Reform and Reconstitution in the Sixth Republic under Roh Tae Woo, 1987–1992* (New York: Routledge, 1994) and in Carl J. Saxer, *From Transition to Power Alternation: Democracy in South Korea, 1987–1997* (New York: Routledge, 2002).

[22] Han Sang-jin, "Wŏn Se-hun kukchŏngwŏn, ch'ongnisil min'ganin sach'al kwanyŏ" [About Wŏn Se-hun's National Intelligence Agency Spying on People with the Prime Minister's Office], *Sindonga* 646 (2013).

[23] Pak Wŏn-sun, *Kukka poan pŏp yŏn'gu I, II, III* [Research on the National Security Law, Vols. I, II, and III] (Seoul: Yŏksa pip'yŏngsa, 2004).

[24] On the use of the National Security Law after democratization, see Stephan Haggard and Jong-sung You, "Freedom of Expression in South Korea," *Journal of Contemporary Asia* 45(1) (2015): 167.

political parties of "excessive heat" during the campaign period.[25] Headed by former prosecutor and later two-time conservative presidential candidate Yi Hoe-ch'ang, the commission claimed it needed more resources for monitoring elections. From 1989, the budget and organizational resources of the CEMC expanded tremendously. Most of its energies were directed toward monitoring activities. It coordinated with police and prosecution offices to launch campaign-style crackdowns on illicit election campaigning before each election. The CEMC's purpose in promoting civic education expanded as well. The CEMC now design material for school children to learn about democracy and elections. The commission has not reimagined democracy for the post-1987 period. In 2013, the organization celebrated its fiftieth anniversary with no apparent sense of the political tension in pinpointing the advent of Park's electoral regime as the institution's defining moment.[26] Its official history gives almost no mention to 1987 and democratization in this period. Astonishingly, the two-page preface to the official history of the CEMC published in 1994 does not contain the word "democracy," but refers four times to "fair elections" ("*kongmyŏng sŏn'gŏ*").[27]

The Political Parties Act also stayed in place.[28] The first amendment came in 1989, which made no substantial changes to the substantive content of the legislation. Over time, lawmakers added more restrictions to party organizing and activities. The party law also persisted. With respect to the election laws, the restrictions on campaigning remained the same after the transition.[29] As with the Political Parties Act, restrictions on political activities only increased. Where revisions were made, they were often done in the name of fighting corruption as was the case in the establishment of the post-1963 institutions.

---

[25] Chungang sŏn'gŏ kwalli wiwŏnhoe, *Taehan min'guk sŏn'gŏsa* [History of Elections in the Republic of Korea], vol. 5 (Kwach'ŏn: Chungang sŏn'gŏ kwalli wiwŏnhoe, 2009), 145–6.

[26] Chungang sŏn'gŏ kwalli wiwŏnhoe, *Sŏn'gŏ kwalli wiwŏnhoe 50-yŏn sa: 1963–2013* [Fifty Years of the Election Management Commission: 1963–2013] (Kwach'ŏn: Chungang sŏn'gŏ kwalli wiwŏnhoe, 2013).

[27] Chungang sŏn'gŏ kwalli wiwŏnhoe, *Sŏn'gŏ kwalli wiwŏnhoe sa, 1963–1993* [History of the Election Management Commission: 1963–1993] (Seoul: Chungang sŏn'gŏ kwalli wiwŏnhoe, 1994), preface.

[28] Sŏ Pok-kyŏng, "Pak Chŏng-hŭi chŏngdang pŏp ŭl p'yegihara" [Abolish the Park Chung Hee Political Parties Act], *Han'gyŏrye* 1011 (2014), h21.hani.co.kr/arti/politics/politics_general/37045.html

[29] Erik Mobrand, "The Politics of Regulating Elections in South Korea: The Persistence of Restrictive Campaign Laws," *Pacific Affairs* 88(4) (2015).

14.3   A Case Study: Conditions for Revocation
of Party Registration

More specific insight into how the democratic transition in 1987 altered legal governance of party and electoral politics can be gleaned from studying the laws relating to the conditions for revocation of party registration. These laws represent a good point of entry because they relate directly to the ability of groups unaffiliated with the regime to form organizations that can contest elections. The purpose behind these laws in different periods can be studied and compared, which can reveal further insight into the post-1987 reforms.

There are two relevant sets of laws. One, as discussed above, is the article in the Constitution that gives the president the right – with the Constitutional Court's approval – to disband a political party. While it remained as a threat on the books, the law was never used. In 1987 and in the following years, neither the government nor the National Assembly moved to challenge the law. In 2013, President Park Geun-hye invoked the article for the first time. The use was directed at the United Progressive Party (UPP), a labor party that had won thirteen seats in the 2012 assembly elections. As prosecutors had discovered a decade-old note composed by the party's leader pledging socialist revolution, this figure, Yi Sŏk-ki, was arrested under the National Security Law and expelled from the National Assembly. Park then revoked the party's registration and in 2014, the Constitutional Court in an 8:1 decision approved the move.[30] The UPP lost all its seats in the assembly. The episode reflects the significance of these legal continuities from the early 1960s. It also points to the continuing political basis in bipartisan support for laws that marginalize labor as a political force.

The other law on party dissolution is found in the Political Parties Act.[31] Article 38 of the original 1962 Political Parties Act had provided that parties could have their registration revoked if they fail to follow the regulations on the number of party branches and the minimum number of members per branch, with the exception that revocation would be

---

[30] The text of the decision is available online at www.ccourt.go.kr: "T'onghap Chinbodang haesan" (Dissolution of the United Progressive Party), case 2013 hŏnda 1, p'allyejip 26–2 ha, 1, December 19, 2014.

[31] A thoughtful discussion of this law is in Song Sŏk-yun, "Chŏngdang haesan simp'an ŭi silch'ejŏk yogŏn: Chŏngdang haesan simp'an chedo ŭi chwap'yo wa kwallyŏn hayŏ" [The Actual Conditions for Ruling That a Political Party Should Be Dissolved: Guidelines for the System of Ruling on the Dissolution of Political Parties], *Sŏul taehakkyo pŏphak* [Seoul National University Legal Studies] 51(1) (2010).

postponed if such infringement occurs only three months before or after a National Assembly election. In 1980, the article was amended to add two further grounds for the revocation of registration: (1) the failure to nominate candidates in National Assembly elections; or (2) the failure to either win a seat or obtain 2 percent of the votes. This revision also made it easier to form smaller parties: each party needed to have branches in only one-quarter (instead of one-third) of districts and only thirty members per branch (down from fifty). In 1989, after the democratic transition, the legislature revised the Political Parties Act to remove the grounds for revocation with respect to the failure to nominate candidates in National Assembly elections. The minimum requirement for the number of branches was reduced to one-fifth of districts, with the requirement of thirty members per branch unchanged. A second democratic-era reform in 1993 put the number at one-tenth, with the rest of the conditions remaining the same.

The next revision came in 2000. In the late 1990s, there was a flurry of adjustments to these laws. One change was made to Article 38 of the Political Parties Act. The 1980 provision on the dissolution of parties that do not run in National Assembly elections was restored, though with different wording: under the amended wording, if a party failed to run for a National Assembly race or local election for four years, it would lose its registration. In 2004, a revision to the law abolished the branch party, which implied changes to the grounds for dissolution. The required regional presence of a party was set at five provincial party chapters, each with 1,000 members. A full revision of the Act a year later changed the article's number to 44 but the content remained the same. In sum, post-transition governments in South Korea have largely maintained the framework for the dissolution of political parties established by the junta in 1962.[32]

The Constitutional Court has had opportunities to review this article. There have been a number of challenges to the Political Parties Act brought before the Constitutional Court. Several cases related to the conditions under which a party can have its registration revoked. What is most vexing to small parties that run afoul of these rules is that a separate article in the Political Parties Act dictates that disbanded parties are prohibited from using the same name again. Several parties have, thus, found themselves in a situation in which

---

[32] The text of the various versions of the Political Parties Act is available from the State Legal Information Center, website, www.law.go.kr

they have failed to win enough votes and thereby lost their registration, but are unable to continue to build up a base under a new party name. In most cases, the affected parties have claimed that the restrictions under the relevant articles of the Political Parties Act violate the Constitution's preservation of the right to political expression and assembly.[33]

Of the fourteen Constitutional Court cases related to the Political Parties Act, in only one has the Court ruled that a portion of the Act is unconstitutional. This case relates to the conditions with respect to the revocation of party registration. The case was brought by three minor parties, namely a labor party, an environmental party, and a youth party, each of which had performed poorly in the 2012 National Assembly election. Under Article 44, they had their registrations revoked. As a consequence, following Article 41, they could not use their respective names again in future elections. The Court decided that Article 44, Clause 1, Paragraph 3, which contained the requirement that parties win at least 2 percent of the vote, was unconstitutional. A reason given for the decision was that performance in National Assembly elections may not indicate a party is small. A party may do very well in a presidential election or local elections, but not do well in National Assembly elections. Another reason for the judgment was based partly on the context in which the paragraph was introduced. The paragraph was introduced in November 1980, when South Korea was in the throes of the protracted military coup following Park Chung Hee's demise, which rendered the revision suspicious. The Court noted that the record from the time and from later revisions to the Political Parties Act gave no indication of the legislative intent behind the revision. Therefore, it decided that the law infringed the right to establish parties under Article 8 of the Constitution. The Court also added that registration can be revoked for small parties, but only in cases when they threaten social order, public interest, or national security.[34] The Court has, thus, signaled a willingness to question laws made during the 1972–87 period but not those that had been enacted by 1963.

---

[33] On the ways party law has mediated political representation, see Erik Mobrand, "Limited Pluralism in a Liberal Democracy: Party Law and Political Incorporation in South Korea," *Journal of Contemporary Asia* 48(4) (2018).

[34] *Chŏngdang pŏp 44 cho 3 hang 1 ho tŭng wihŏn hwagin* [Decision Confirming That Article 44, Clause 3, Paragraph 1 of the Political Parties Act Is Unconstitutional], 2012 hŏn'ga 19 (Constitutional Court, 2014).

A few aspects of the reform of the Political Parties Act are note-worthy. First, it was never overhauled after the democratic transition and adjustments were only made incrementally. In fact, the 1989 and 1993 amendments only continued the direction of previous revisions by changing the minimum number of branches and members that parties were required to maintain. This type of change shows more continuity than drastic change. Second, revisions tended to roll back the 1980 law to conform with the 1963 version. The 1989 revision to eliminate a condition was such an instance, with the 2014 Constitutional Court's decision being another. At the same time, a revision in 2000 reintroduced the logic of the 1980 revision. Third, there is no indication that legislators ever considered over-hauling this system. This point indicates a continuing consensus among the political elite on this issue.

South Korea experienced a sharp transformation in 1987. In the subsequent decade, liberal politicians with dissident credentials came to power. This transformation is universally described as a democratic transition both by scholars and by all mainstream political actors in Seoul. Yet, liberal lawmakers never sat down to rethink how electoral and party politics should be governed in this new system. Many had made great sacrifices in opposing the country's dictators but by then, they simply accepted the legal framework established by Park Chung Hee. While there have been numerous opportunities to abandon or redesign this framework, legislators have tinkered endlessly with the laws without proposing substantial reforms. Continuity is seen outside the legislature as well. The Constitutional Court has not suggested that interpretations of law should be different in the context of a post-1987 democracy. The civil servants and former legal officers who run the election commission – even those with the power to propose amend-ments – have also not challenged the basis of the authoritarian laws governing politics. As the political scientist Sŏ Pok-kyŏng commented on this odd situation: "The first thing that politicians who say they will put down their privileges should do is abolish the 'Park Chung Hee Political Parties Act' system, which uses law to enforce the parties' oligopolistic system."[35] If 1987 was such a crucial turning point, it is peculiar that politicians, judges and bureaucrats have not attempted to overturn party and electoral laws that were created explicitly to demo-bilize popular political forces.

---

[35] Sŏ Pok-kyŏng, "Pak Chŏng-hŭi chŏngdang pŏp."

14.4   Legacies of Authoritarian Legality in Party and Electoral Politics: a Comparative Discussion

South Korea's democratic transition can be compared with others in the region in order to better understand the legacies of authoritarian legality. Two examples are Taiwan and Indonesia. Both Taiwan and Indonesia had founding constitutions that had persistent symbolic value, but for decades those constitutions had little meaning in the actual governance of electoral or party politics. In these cases, democratic transitions involved the construction or reconstruction of the constitutional order.

In Taiwan, as Weitseng Chen observes in this volume, leaders only turned to law once political liberalization started and not before.[36] The ruling Kuomintang (KMT) was hardly constrained by the Republic of China (ROC) Constitution.[37] Instead of following or revising the Sun Yat-Sen-inspired document, garrison command ruled the island from 1948. Temporary provisions for the reach of government authority were established to justify counterinsurgency measures. There were no elections for national government posts. The Leninist party, with cells in many social organizations, aspired to exert full control over society. Presidents Chiang Kai-shek and later Chiang Ching-kuo did not permit new political parties to form.[38] The appearance of organized opposition in the 1950s and 1960s was met with coercion from the state. In 1950, the KMT introduced local elections, which the Japanese had first put in place in the 1930s. The goal of these elections was to shore up legitimacy with the local population. KMT-nominated candidates were encouraged to have local ties, as such links would help the KMT build support among ordinary Taiwanese.[39]

---

[36] Chapter 12.

[37] Constitution of the Republic of China (Taiwan), effective December 25, 1947, https://english.president.gov.tw/Page/93

[38] English-language accounts of Taiwan politics in this period frequently note that the formation of new political parties was banned under martial law or the temporary provisions. However, no document explicitly prohibited the establishment of a new party. As the legal scholar Wu Tzung-Mou from Academia Sinica points out, the government could prevent parties from forming by neglecting their registration application, but Chiang Kai-shek's regime did not create a legal basis for prohibiting new parties. See Taiwan Institute of Legal History, "Ni suo bu zhidao de dangjin" [The Party Ban You Did Not Know About], June 5, 2015, legalhistorytw.blogspot.dk/2015/06/blog-post.html

[39] Yun-han Chu, *Crafting Democracy in Taiwan* (Taipei: Institute for National Policy Research, 1992), 27–9; Shelley Rigger, *Politics in Taiwan: Voting for Democracy* (New York: Routledge, 1999).

This structure in Taiwan meant that as the country liberalized, there were few institutions for governing electoral and party politics that could be retained. New parties would have to be permitted and new offices would have to be opened for election. The election commission was established in 1980 during the early days of political opening. Campaign laws, to the extent they were restrictive, had never been taken seriously because not much had been at stake in elections.[40] There was no law restricting party organization or activities, because other tools had been used to ensure that no formal opposition parties formed. The Civil Associations Act, which bears similarities to a party law, was rewritten thoroughly in 1989.[41] Enacted after the regime had already committed to a great deal of liberalization, the revised law focuses on protecting political parties rather than limiting them. Indeed, precisely because opposition parties had been banned, Taiwan has seen greater sensitivity to the problem of preserving rights to organize and oppose the regime. South Korea, partly because of its longer history of open opposition, did not develop institutions reflecting this same sensitivity.

In Indonesia, most governments since independence have agreed on the sanctity of the 1945 Constitution.[42] Both Sukarno and Suharto embraced the preamble's notion of "*Pancasila*" – the five key principles – as a foundation of the nation. Into the 1950s, as the new state emerged as a core member of the nonaligned movement, democracy was less closely identified with anticommunism as in Taiwan or South Korea. However, from 1957, Sukarno shifted his position, moving toward "guided democracy." This move meant limiting political space considerably.[43] With the rise of Suharto in 1965, political space tightened further. He adapted the Golkar functional group into a ruling party. To keep up appearances, he allowed two other parties – but no others – to exist. Elections had little meaning during his New Order. The Constitution, though, remained unchanged, and Suharto could claim he continued to respect "*Pancasila*."

---

[40] Hung-mao Tien, *The Great Transition: Political and Social Change in the Republic of China* (Stanford, CA: Hoover Institution Press, 1989), 177–9.

[41] The full text of the law, originally promulgated on February 10, 1942, is available on the Ministry of Justice webpage: Civil Associations Act, adopted June 15, 2011, law .moj.gov.tw/LawClass/LawAll.aspx?PCode=D0050091

[42] Constitution of the Republic of Indonesia of 1945, adopted August 18, 1945, www .unesco.org/education/edurights/media/docs/b1ba8608010ce0c48966911957392ea8c da405d8.pdf

[43] Adrian Vickers, *A History of Modern Indonesia* (Cambridge, UK: Cambridge University Press, 2005), ch. 5.

Indonesia under authoritarian rule did not adopt an institutionalized legal infrastructure governing electoral politics.

With Suharto's downfall in 1998 after the Asian financial crisis, Indonesia set about building a new constitutional order. The process was long, and negotiations were complicated. The Constitution and other key documents were revised multiple times between 1999 and 2002.[44] New rules for governing the political sphere were also designed. A new political party law was promulgated with the aim of protecting multiparty democracy while also ensuring that parties aggregated interests on a national scale so as to mitigate fragmentation of the archipelago.[45] While there are many legacies of the New Order in Indonesia's political economy,[46] there are fewer in the governance of elections and parties.[47]

Neither Taiwan before the 1980s nor Indonesia before the 1990s had periods during which elaborate legal instruments for governing elections and parties were institutionalized. South Korea did, and powerful forces associated these instruments with "democracy." This "democracy" was infused with a strong authoritarian legality streak. In all three countries, the founding constitutions had important liberal elements and these constitutions were also interrupted. South Korea's rulers in the 1950s and 1960s, though, maintained an electoral regime and therefore needed to develop tools for ensuring that elections were secure. In Taiwan and Indonesia, the rulers did not face the same issue. As a result, South Korea was in a different situation from Taiwan or Indonesia at the time of democratic transition. South Korea had gone further in making authoritarian legal commitments in the electoral domain. When South Korea experienced a democratic transition, the laws from the earlier period were simply retained as the foundation for the new order. Relative to this pattern of building on previous regimes, Taiwan's democratic transformation involved a deeper shift in how the state would rule formal politics. This comparison helps explain the particular conditions that led to the persistence of South Korea's legal framework. An implication may be that

[44] Donald L. Horowitz, *Constitutional Change and Democracy in Indonesia* (Cambridge, UK: Cambridge University Press, 2013), ch. 3.

[45] Ibid., ch. 6.

[46] Edward Aspinall, "The Triumph of Capital? Class Politics and Indonesian Democratization," *Journal of Contemporary Asia* 43(2) (2013).

[47] On shifts in the party system after Suharto, see Leo Suryadinata, "The Decline of the Hegemonic Party System in Indonesia: Golkar after the Fall of Soeharto," *Contemporary Southeast Asia* 29(2) (2007); Marcus Mietzner, *Money, Power, and Ideology: Political Parties in Post-Authoritarian Indonesia* (Honolulu: Asian Studies Association of Australia in association with University of Hawai'i Press, 2013).

institutionalized limits on the political sphere can, in the long run, be more harmful to the construction of open politics.

14.5 Conclusion

The South Korean example sheds light on the conditions under which a regime would make or revoke a commitment to the rule of law. The role of the United States in Cold War geopolitics was crucial both in forcing the military junta to embrace elections in 1962–3 and for giving Park Chung Hee an opportunity to close the electoral system in 1972. Domestic political concerns also mattered, as seen in Park's capitalization of the April Revolution's democracy movement. Commitments to authoritarian law may certainly occur under other conditions, but South Korea's experience serves as a reminder of the ways US support for the Cold War national security state could shape the turn to, or away from, law.

In this chapter, I have noted the historical origins of democratic South Korea's legal framework for governing party and electoral politics. In the 1960s, the commitment to a set of legal institutions, albeit unfair ones, characterized the regime's governance of political space. In both the 1950s and the 1970s, rulers relied comparatively less on legal institutions and more on coercion and zones of exception than in the intervening decade. With the democratic transition, the unsystematic nature of governance declined and, overall, law became more important. Much of that law, however, was designed to undermine collective representation of popular political forces. Authoritarian legality in this sphere did not disappear with the democratic transition.

In reaching this conclusion, care should be given to the point, central to this volume, that "authoritarian legality" refers not just to any laws established under authoritarian regimes but specifically to an approach to ruling that relies on the commitment to a set of laws that enhance state or regime interests against individual rights and collective, nonstate rights. Such caution is important because South Korea has known multiple kinds of nondemocratic orders. In suggesting that authoritarian legality has persisted into the democratic era, attention should be drawn to the legal institutions that were most significant in the 1963–72 period. I do not wish to imply that governance of electoral politics in contemporary South Korea is simply undemocratic, which could be taken to mean it is similar to what occurred between 1972 and 1987. It is rather the earlier effort to systematize a legal framework for limiting political representation that gives today's laws their authoritarian character.

Authoritarian legality might characterize other portions of political rule in South Korea today. The argument presented here feeds into ongoing discussions about the uses of law in dealing with dissent, especially under the administrations of Lee Myung Bak (2008–13) and Park Geun Hye (2013–17). An example of such use is the rise of defamation suits to deal with criticism of the government.[48] This trend reflects a common authoritarian legal strategy, observed in this volume by Jacques deLisle,[49] of treating political cases as "normal" cases in order to punish or deter dissent in accordance with the law as a means to carry out persecution. Attempts to silence or discredit criticism led to suggestions that South Korea was sliding toward "illiberal democracy"[50] or that the country was turning into a "post-democracy,"[51] in which basic individual freedoms exist but popular influence on government is sidelined. Reflection on the sources and character of laws governing political space adds to the growing picture of the tensions in South Korea's democracy.

[48] Jong-sung You, "The Cheonan Incident and the Declining Freedom of Expression in South Korea," *Asian Perspective* 39(2) (2015); Stephan Haggard and Jong-sung You, "Freedom of Expression in South Korea," *Journal of Contemporary Asia* 45(1) (2015); Jae-Jung Suh, "Korea's Democracy after the Cheonan Incident: The Military, the State, and Civil Society under the Division System," *Asian Perspective* 39(2) (2015).

[49] Chapter 1.

[50] Yu Chong-sŏng [Jong-sung You], "Han'guk minjujuŭi wa p'yohyŏn ŭi chayu: 'chayu minjujuŭi' ŭi wigi" [Korean Democracy and Freedom of Expression: A Crisis of "Liberal Democracy"], *Tonghyang kwa chŏnmang* [Trends and Prospects] 90 (2014).

[51] Jamie Doucette and Se-Woong Koo, "Pursuing Post-Democratization: The Resilience of Politics by Public Security in Contemporary South Korea," *Journal of Contemporary Asia* 46(2) (2016).

INDEX

Lightning Source UK Ltd.
Milton Keynes UK
UKHW022216221022
410945UK00023B/416